Preparing for the
ACT
English & Reading

Dr. Robert D. Postman

AMSCO

AMSCO SCHOOL PUBLICATIONS, INC.

315 Hudson Street, New York, N.Y. 10013

Robert Postman is a college professor and a test-preparation expert.
He is the author of over 30 books, which have sold millions of copies
and are found in schools and in bookstores throughout the country.

Reviewers

Warren Jones
    Educational Consultant
    State of Illinois

Mary Mitchell
    English Department
    Weber High School, Chicago

Please visit our Web site at:
www.amscopub.com

Composition: Sierra Graphics, Inc.

When ordering this book, please specify:
either **R 321 W** *or* PREPARING FOR THE ACT: ENGLISH & READING

ISBN 1-56765-128-3

Printed in the United States of America

2 3 4 5 6 7 8 9   08 07 06 05

PREFACE

Preparing for the ACT: English & Reading shows you how to get your highest possible score on the English, Reading, and Writing sections of the ACT. The result of a three-year effort, the book includes a thorough subject review with extensive practice and effective test-taking strategies. This book will help you win admission to the college of your choice, and once there, to get the most out of college that you can. It is a once-in-a-lifetime opportunity. I wish you well as you prepare to continue your education.

My special regard goes to my wife Liz, who has been a constant source of support. I could not have completed this project without her. My children Chad, Blaire, and Ryan have been an inspiration as I have worked on this and other books over the years.

I am grateful to the teachers who reviewed the manuscript. I am also indebted to two doctoral students who contributed significantly to the development of this book: Lisa Preston, who received her undergraduate degree from Washington and Lee University and is finishing her doctoral work in English at George Washington University; and Jennifer Roberts, who completed her undergraduate work at Union College and is completing her doctoral work in English at the Catholic University of America.

The ACT Writing Test was first field tested in Montana, and I am grateful to Dr. Jan Clinard, the Director of Academic Initiatives for the Montana Commissioner of Higher Education, who organized that field test. Dr. Clinard's office sponsors a Web site called Webwriters (*http://webwriters.msugf.edu/*), which is designed to help students with the ACT Writing Test. I am also grateful to Mr. Jonathan Moore and Ms. Robyn Wingo, holistic scorers trained for the ACT field test, who contributed scored essays to this book.

My enduring gratitude goes to Auditi Chakravarty, the Director of Language Arts at Amsco, and to Emily Vail, who edited this edition. Many of the special touches in this book are due to their impressive knowledge of English and to their attention to detail.

Special thanks go to those at ACT who were very helpful as I worked on this manuscript. It was wonderful to speak with people who are truly interested in the students who take their test.

Robert D. Postman

CONTENTS

Section I

Overview and Introduction

CHAPTER 1

PREPARING FOR THE ACT

The ACT Assessment

The ACT Assessment is a college admissions test. Colleges use ACT scores to help determine which students will be admitted as freshmen or as transfer students. The ACT consists of four separate multiple-choice tests: English, Reading, Mathematics, and Science Reasoning.

Each test has a different number of items. The composite score is an average of the four reported scores. ACT score reports show the composite score, the score for each test, and subscores for groups of items that show achievement in particular areas.

You'll find more detailed information about these tests, scores, test preparation and test-taking strategies, subject reviews, and practice tests starting in the next chapter. This book will lead you through the preparation you need to get your absolute best ACT score.

Comparison of the ACT and the SAT

There are two national college-admissions tests, the ACT from the American College Testing Program and the SAT from the College Board and the Educational Testing Service. Let me explain why you should take the ACT whether or not you take the SAT. The ACT focuses more on achievement and is related to the high school curriculum. ACT test makers are very clear about the material covered on the test and about the number of test items devoted to each area. If those at the ACT say there will be six grammar and usage items, that's exactly how many there will be. Since items on the ACT are related to the curriculum, you *can* effectively prepare for this test.

All the items on an ACT Assessment count toward your final score. On the SAT, one of the sections is experimental and does not count.

ACT score reporting and other policies are people-friendly. The ACT reports your scores quickly, which gives you plenty of time to decide about retaking the test. You can even decide which ACT scores will be reported to colleges, even after you have seen the scores.

The SAT penalizes you for incorrect answers. There is no incorrect answer penalty on the ACT, and you can guess whenever you can't determine the correct answer.

About as many students take the ACT as take the SAT. Every college accepts ACT scores, and over 60 percent of students attending college in recent years have taken the ACT. Many colleges use subscores of the ACT as achievement scores and placement scores. So if you take the ACT, you may not have to take the SAT II Achievement Tests.

Registering for the ACT

You should register in advance for the ACT. ACT registration packets should be available in your high school. If you can't find a registration packet, ask your guidance counselor, advisor, or teacher. You can also contact the ACT for a registration packet:

ACT Registration Department
P.O. Box 414
Iowa City, IA 52243-0414

(319) 337-1270
(Monday–Friday, 8:00 A.M.–8:00 P.M. Central Time)

You can also call this number to check on a late or delayed admission ticket, or to change your test date or test center. I have called the ACT offices dozens of times while I worked on this book. Everyone I talked to was extremely helpful and pleasant. They want to help you, and you should feel very comfortable about calling.

The ACT has its own Web site (**www.act.org**). This page has complete information about the ACT, including registration information, test dates, and test sites. You can also register, and e-mail the ACT through links on this page. This page will be updated regularly. If you're on-line, drop in to see what additional features or services have been added.

Regular ACT administrations occur on a Saturday in October, December, February, April, and June. Check the registration packets for test dates and registration deadlines. Registration ends about a month before the test date. Late registration, for an additional fee, ends about 15 days before the test date.

When and Where to Take the ACT

You have to make three important registration decisions: (1) where to take the test, (2) in which school year to take the test, and (3) when during the school year to take the test.

You should take the ACT as close to home as possible. The test may even be given in your high school. The ACT is not given at every site on every test date. Check the registration packet to be sure the test is given at one of your preferred sites on the date you will take the test.

You should first take the ACT in your junior year. You can always take the test again in your senior year. Besides, application deadlines for many colleges and scholarship programs require you to take the ACT as a junior. Take the test toward the end of your junior year. I recommend the April test date. Since the ACT is closely tied to course content, junior-year classes will probably help. If you are taking the test in your senior year, take it early so the test scores are available to colleges.

Special Scoring Dates. You can receive a copy of the test items, your scored answer sheet, and the correct answers if you take the test in December, April, or June. If you are taking the test in New York State, this service is available only for the October test date. This scoring information can be a valuable diagnostic tool. I discuss using this scoring service as a part of the testing strategy later in this section. You can request this service on the registration form or you can apply for this service when you receive your test scores in the mail. The test items, answers, and your answer sheet will be mailed to you eight to twelve weeks after the test date.

Forms of Identification

You must bring an acceptable form of identification to the test center. If you don't have an acceptable ID, you probably won't be able to take the test. Acceptable forms of identification include an up-to-date official photo ID or a picture from a school yearbook showing your first and last name. Unacceptable forms of identification include unofficial photo ID, learner's permit or license without a photograph, a birth certificate, or a social security card. If you are not sure whether or not you have an acceptable ID, the ACT has a special number for you to call, the ACT ID Requirements Office, at (319) 337-1510.

Standby Registration

You may be able to register as standby at an ACT test center. Needless to say, you should do everything you can to avoid standby registration. There is a good chance that there will be no room for you.

Show up at a center on test day with a valid ID, a checkbook, a credit card, and some hope. All those registered at that center are seated first. If there's room, those registered at other centers are seated next. If there's still room, you can fill out an application on the spot and take the test. There is an extra fee for this service.

Alternate Testing Arrangements

The ACT provides a wide variety of alternate testing arrangements. These arrangements can involve special test dates, special testing for those with a disability, or special accommodations for a disability on regular test dates.

Special Test Dates. Special test dates are arranged through the ACT Universal Testing Office. You can call or write them at the number and address below if you think you need or qualify for a special test date.

> ACT Universal Testing
> P.O. Box 4028
> Iowa City, IA 52243-4028
> (319) 337-1332

Sunday Testing. If your religious beliefs prevent you from taking a Saturday test, you may take the ACT on the following Sunday. A limited number of sites in each state offer Sunday testing. If you live within 50 miles of one of those sites, you must take a Sunday test there. Fill out a regular registration form. If you live further than 50 miles from a Sunday test site, write or call ACT Universal Testing at the address or number on the previous page.

Homebound, Hospitalized, Incarcerated. If you are in one of these categories you may qualify for a special test date. Do not fill out a registration form. Contact ACT Universal Testing for information.

Active Military Service. If you are on active military service, you may qualify for a special test date. Do not complete a registration form. Check with your base education office about testing on the base or contact ACT Universal Testing.

Testing Outside the 50 States. You may be able to take the ACT outside the 50 United States. Do not complete a registration form. Contact ACT Universal Testing for information.

Disabled and Needing More Than Five Hours or Needing Nonprint Test Materials. If you have a diagnosed disability and you need more than five hours to take the test or you need Braille or nonprint test materials, you may qualify for special testing. If you qualify, the test will be administered on a special test date. Learning-disabled students must have been professionally evaluated during the past three years, or have a current IEP or Section 504 Plan on file. You or your counselor should contact ACT Universal Testing for a copy of the "Request for ACT Assessment Special Testing."

Special Accommodations for a Disability on Regular Test Dates. Apply for a special accommodation if you can complete the test in five hours or less using regular print or large-type materials. Special accommodations at the test center can be arranged through the ACT Test Administration Office.

> ACT Test Administration
> P.O. Box 4028
> Iowa City, IA 52243-4028
> (319) 337-1270

Contact the ACT Test Administration Office for information about the types of accommodations that are available. Fill out a registration form and attach a note explaining your disability and the type of accommodation you need.

Scoring

The maximum reported score for each test is 36, although each test has a different number of items. The composite score is an average of the four reported scores. The maximum composite score is 36. ACT score reports show the composite score, the score for each test, and subscores for groups of items that show achievement in particular areas. Many colleges use these subscores for placement.

Score Reporting. Those at the ACT treat your scores as though they were your property. That means you decide who sees your scores, which scores they see, and when they see them. I discuss this score-reporting policy as a part of the overall testing strategy later in this section.

Colleges use ACT scores in different ways. Some colleges will just take your highest composite score. Some colleges may use the highest score you earned on each individual test. But suppose you received a composite score of 23 for one administration, and 27 on another administration. It is often better for a college admissions office to see only the higher score.

Automatic Reporting. Your ACT scores are automatically sent to you. Copies are also sent to the high school and high school counselor you list on the registration form. If you do *not* want scores sent to the high school, do not list a high school code on your ACT registration form.

Scores are also automatically sent to state and regional scholarship programs. If you do *not* want scores reported to these agencies, write in the week following the test to ACT Reporting Services, P.O. Box 168, Iowa City, IA 52243-0168, or call (319) 337-1313.

Score Recipients Listed on the Registration Form. Your ACT scores are sent free of charge to up to six colleges and scholarship programs you list on the registration form. There is an extra charge for additional choices. You have the following options:

1. Do not list the colleges for which you think a particular score is needed or required. Wait four weeks for ACT to report the scores to you. Then decide whether and where to send the scores. I prefer this option, particularly if you know that a college may require a minimum score for admission. No sense confusing the admissions office of a college with a lower score than you are capable of.

2. List all the colleges to which scores should be sent. If you think you did poorly on the test, you can ask the ACT to cancel some or all of your college choices. Your answer sheet will still be scored. Call by noon on the Thursday following the test date to (319) 337-1270 and tell the person there which colleges should not be sent scores. Be careful. You may not have an accurate view of your performance on the test. But if you ask the ACT office not to send the scores, and it turns out that you like them, you can have them sent out at a later date.

3. Cancel your scores. You must make this request at the test center. There is not much reason for doing this unless you have to leave the test early because you are sick or for some other reason.

Additional Score Reports (ASRs). You can always request the ACT to send out a score report for any of your test dates. There is a fee for each ASR, which includes the scores for just that one test date. For an additional fee you can have your report processed in one day and usually delivered the next day.

ASRs can be requested by mail or by phone. The phone service entails a fee in addition to the ASR fee. Call (319) 337-1313. You must use a credit card for this service. A single report sent to one college could cost a total of $25 or more. However, it is worth the expense if you need to get a score report to a college within a day or two.

ACT Realities

You take the ACT because it is required for college admissions or because it will help you get admitted to a college of your choice.

Tests can be unfair. A lucky guesser may occasionally do better on a multiple-choice test than someone who knows the material. Someone who knows the answers may get a lower score because he or she mismarks the answer sheet. Students who are sick the day of the test may do more poorly than they would have otherwise.

Some students may get a higher score than they have any right to expect. Other students may get a lower score than they need and deserve to receive. Students who know strategies for taking multiple-choice tests will often do better than students who don't know these strategies. You've got to make the best of it and get your highest score. This book will show you how.

It's Just People. The ACT is designed and written by people who have their own personal strengths and weaknesses. They are not perfect, and neither is the test they create.

Consultants throughout the country make recommendations to the ACT test designers about the content that should be included on the test. These recommendations are based on the consultants' knowledge of the subject matter and on the topics currently taught in American high schools.

The final list of topics is sent to test writers who actually prepare the test items. The test writers may be full-time employees of the ACT, or they may be freelance writers from all over the country. The writers submit the items to the ACT, where the items are reviewed and edited. Then each item is reviewed further and tried out. The items that pass this review process are used on an ACT. Each item is used only once in its original form, but some items are revised and used in other ACTs.

CHAPTER 2

THE ACT

The ACT consists of four separate tests: English, Mathematics, Reading, and Science Reasoning. The tests are always given in that order and they must be taken together. You have 2 hours and 55 minutes to answer the items on these tests. On the typical test day you will check in at about 7:30 A.M., begin the tests at 8:00 A.M., and leave around 12:15 P.M.

This book provides you with a complete subject and strategy review and four ACT English practice tests, four ACT Reading practice tests, and four ACT Writing practice tests. An overview of the English, Reading, and Writing Tests is given below. A brief description of the Mathematics and Science Reasoning Tests follows.

English Test Overview

The English Test consists of 75 multiple-choice items. Each item is based on one of the five prose passages. Each item has four answer choices, and most have NO CHANGE as one of the answer choices. You have 45 minutes to complete the test.

The test measures English skills in two broad areas, Usage/Mechanics and Rhetorical Skills. The number of test items in each of these broad areas is shown below. Following that is a list of the topics tested in each area and examples of ACT test items.

ACT English: 45 minutes—75 items

Area	Number of Items
Usage/Mechanics	**40**
Punctuation	10
Grammar and Usage	12
Sentence Structure	18
Rhetorical Skills	**35**
Strategy	12
Organization	11
Style	12

Scores Reported: Usage/Mechanics
Rhetorical Skills
Total Number Correct

Usage/Mechanics (40 Items)

The topics tested by the ten punctuation items are:

Commas	Periods
Colons and semicolons	Question marks
Parentheses	Exclamation points
Apostrophe	

The 12 grammar and usage items cover:

Nouns	Subject-verb agreement
Use of appropriate pronouns	Parallel form
Verb formation	Adjectives and adverbs
Verb tense	Comparatives and superlatives
Tense shift	Idioms

The 18 sentence-structure items cover:

Run-on sentences	Misplaced modifiers
Comma splices	Shifts in construction
Sentence fragments	

This book contains a thorough review of each of these topics.

Sample Usage/Mechanics Test Items. A paragraph from a typical passage is shown below, followed by examples of the three different types of usage/mechanics items.

 **Example**

Directions: Look at the item with the same number as the underlined portion of the passage. Pick the best replacement for the underlined portion. If the current portion is best, then choose NO CHANGE.

Why did the world heap such fame and glory upon

Amelia Earhart? There <u>was</u> at least two reasons.
                    1

Sentence Structure

1. **A.** NO CHANGE
   B. were
   C. has been
   D. will be

Grammar and Usage

<u>A year earlier</u>, in 1927, Charles Lindbergh had made
    2

the first daring solo flight across the Atlantic Ocean.

2. **F.** NO CHANGE
   G. OMIT underlined phrase.
   H. A year sooner
   J. A year faster

Punctuation

Taking off from <u>New York City. He had</u> landed in
                        3

Paris, France. The public went wild over this

handsome young American pilot. "Lindy" became

the greatest hero of his time.

3. **A.** NO CHANGE
   B. New York City? He had
   C. New York City he had
   D. New York City, he had

Rhetorical Skills

The topics tested in each Rhetorical Skills area are shown below. Just look these over to familiarize yourself with the test. The book contains a thorough review of each of these topics.

Strategy. All 12 strategy items are one of these three types:

1. Choose appropriate transitional, opening, and closing statements and sentences.
2. Choose a sentence most appropriate to the passage's intended readers or to the author's purpose.
3. Evaluate the impact of adding, deleting, and revising supporting material and details in the passage.

Organization. The 11 Organization items ask you about the best order or placement of sentences or paragraphs. There are two primary types of organization items:

1. Place a new sentence in a paragraph or in a passage.
2. Reorder the sentences in a paragraph or the paragraphs in a passage.

Style. The 12 style items are about how well the passage communicates. There are a number of different types of style items:

1. Identify wordy or redundant sentences and clichés.
2. Choose the correct word or words.
3. Choose wording which ensures that pronouns clearly refer to their antecedents.
4. Choose wording which maintains the level of style and tone of a passage.
5. Choose wording which maintains the effectiveness of the sentence.

Sample Rhetorical-Skills Test Items. Portions of a typical passage are shown on the next page, with an example of each of the three different types of rhetorical-skills items.

 **Example**

Directions: Look at the item with the same number as the underlined portion of the passage. Pick the best replacement for the underlined portion. If the current portion is best, then choose NO CHANGE.

Strategy

It was a beautiful warm fall day. <u>In spite of this</u>, the
                                              1
walkers wore shorts and short-sleeve shirts.

1. **A.** NO CHANGE
   B. Therefore
   C. Nevertheless
   D. But

Organization

[1] Some clouds are caused by convection. [2] If you've ever been at the beach, you may have seen puffy clouds early in the day. [3] As the day wore on, these puffy clouds may have grown into convective rain clouds. [4] Later in the afternoon there may have been a rain shower or a thunderstorm.

2. The author wants to add this sentence:

   These convective rain clouds are called cumulonimbus clouds.

   The sentence should be added to the paragraph after sentence:
   F. 1.
   G. 2.
   H. 3.
   J. 4.

Style

Speaking of the weather, have you ever been outside during sleet <u>(rain which freezes as it falls to earth)</u>?
                                                                           3

3. **A.** NO CHANGE
   B. (freezes as it falls to earth)
   C. (rain)
   D. OMIT the underlined portion.

Reading Test Overview

The ACT Reading Test consists of 40 multiple-choice items based on one of four passages. Each item has four answer choices. You have 35 minutes to complete the test. The passages are in four broad areas shown below along with the number of test items in each of these areas.

ACT Reading: 35 minutes—40 items

AREA	NUMBER OF ITEMS
Prose Fiction	10
Humanities	10
Social Studies	10
Natural Sciences	10

Scores Reported: Total Number Correct
  Arts Literature (prose and humanities)
  Social Studies (social studies and natural sciences)

 **_Example_**   **Reading Test Items.** A portion of a reading passage and several sample reading test items are shown below.

HUMANITIES: Adapted from *Psychology,* by Green and Sanford, © 1995 by Amsco School Publications.

Sometimes the competing demands of the id and superego trap the hardworking ego into a no-win position. Imagine you've just backed dad's car into a neighbor's expensive new car. The id tells
5   you to just leave, while the superego tells you it would be wrong to run away.

Both drives are too strong to be ignored. Caught in such a bind the ego often chooses a response that disguises or compromises the id's socially unacceptable
10   desires. In this case the ego might choose to stay with the damaged car, thus obeying the law. To reduce the anxiety level, the ego may also choose to distort reality by rationalizing the accident by "saying" that it was a choice between hitting the car or hitting a small child
15   who ran out behind the car. Freud made one of his most enduring contributions to psychology when he identified a number of these ego-protecting behaviors. Known as *defense mechanisms,* their use is thought to be largely unconscious. Even though you may in time
20   become expert at spotting their use by others, you're unlikely to be aware of the degree to which you depend on one or more of the following defense mechanisms.

Repression protects you from disturbing memories, forbidden desires, or painful feelings by
25   burying such material in the unconscious. Repressed feelings remain "alive," however, capable of influencing behavior without the person's awareness. For example, say that a girl named Rachel was attacked by a large watchdog when she was seven,
30   but she escaped serious injury. Part of Rachel wants to like dogs, but whenever she gets close to one, the old repressed fear takes over.

Similarly, repressed material can affect normal physical drives such as hunger or sex. Doctors also
35   know that repression can lead to physical ailments. Anna O., one of Freud's earliest patients, was an extreme example of someone who experienced a *psychosomatic illness.* Even today, some medical experts estimate that up to 40 percent of the patients a
40   physician sees each day may be suffering from illnesses with origins that are psychological, not physical.

21. Psychological defense mechanisms can be thought of as:

   A. reflecting reality.
   B. mostly unconscious.
   C. psychosomatic illness.
   D. protecting the id.

22. Which of the following phrases best describes the defense mechanism of repression?

   F. A defense mechanism which affects a person's awareness
   G. A defense mechanism responsible for up to 40 percent of visits to physicians
   H. A defense mechanism which makes it impossible to remember something
   J. A defense mechanism which might lead to overeating

23. According to this passage, repressed feelings result from:

   A. attacks by animals.
   B. a need for protection.
   C. psychosomatic illnesses.
   D. inability to open up.

Writing Test Overview

The optional ACT Writing Test gives you thirty minutes to write a persuasive essay in response to a prompt. The test gives the topic for your essay and asks you to convince someone or some group of your position on the topic. For example, you may write an essay about whether or not a school should have a dress code.

Two readers evaluate your essay holistically, and assign a score from 1 to 6. Holistic scoring means a reader's evaluation is based on his or her informed impression of your writing. The readers do not go into detailed analysis. If the readers' scores differ by more than 1 point, a third reader evaluates the essay.

Here is an example of a Writing Prompt.

PROMPT

Some parents asked the Town Council to impose a curfew requiring students under the age of 18 to be off the streets by 10:00 P.M. to reduce disciplinary problems and to help ensure children's safety. Other parents do not agree with a curfew. They believe that imposing a curfew will not necessarily ensure students' safety and it should be up to parents to decide what time their children should be off the streets. In your opinion, should the Town Council impose a curfew for students under the age of 18?

Take a position on the issue outlined in the prompt. Choose one of the two points of view given in the prompt, or you may present your own point of view on this issue. Be sure to support your position with specific reasons and details.

Mathematics and Science Reasoning Tests Overview

This section gives a brief overview of these tests. Get a copy of Amsco's *Preparing for the ACT: Mathematics and Science Reasoning* for a thorough description with sample tests and explained answers.

Mathematics Test

The sixty-minute Mathematics Test consists of 60 multiple-choice items, each with five answer choices. The Mathematics Test measures mathematical skills in six areas.

Pre-Algebra (14 items), Elementary Algebra (10 items), Intermediate Algebra (9 items), Coordinate Geometry (9 items), Plane Geometry (14 Items), Trigonometry (4 items)

Science Reasoning Test

The thirty-five-minute Science Reasoning Test consists of 40 multiple-choice items, each with four answer choices. The test focuses on your ability to read, understand, and interpret written material about biology, physical sciences, chemistry, and physics in three broad areas.

Data Representation (15 items), Research Summaries (18 items), Conflicting Viewpoints (7 items)

CHAPTER 3

TEST STRATEGIES

Test-Preparation Strategies

Use these strategies and the ACT Review Checklist on the following pages as you prepare to take the ACT. They take you right up to test day.

- **Start early.**

  If you are going to take the test in April or June, start preparing in September. Do some work each week rather than cramming just before the test.

- **Eliminate stress.**

  Stress reduces your effectiveness. Moderate exercise is the best way to reduce stress. Try to find some time each day to walk, run, jog, swim, or play a team sport. Remember to exercise within your limits.

- **Be realistic.**

  You are not going to answer all the items correctly. The composite score is the total score for the entire test, and the highest ACT composite score is 36. The national average ACT composite score has been just below 21.

  About 56 percent correct on the entire test will likely earn you an above-average score. The percent correct on each test shown below would earn a composite ACT score of about 21.

English	60 percent correct
Mathematics	45 percent correct
Reading	55 percent correct
Science Reasoning	60 percent correct

  Other combinations of test scores could also earn an above-average composite score. You can always take the ACT over again.

ACT REVIEW CHECKLIST

Complete the following steps in the order shown to take the test in April of your junior year. Follow these steps but adjust the time line to take the test on other dates. You will be following the same steps for the Mathematics and Science Reasoning Tests.

September

☐ Review this chapter.

☐ Complete the English Topic Inventory on pages 25–27.

☐ Start work on the English section (page 33).

October

☐ Continue work on the English section.

November

☐ Complete work on the English section.

☐ Take the Diagnostic English ACT on page 149 under test conditions.

☐ Use the Diagnostic Study Chart and review problem areas noted on the Diagnostic English ACT.

December

☐ Start work on the Writing section (page 385).

☐ Take the Diagnostic ACT Writing Test (page 390).

☐ Review the essay with your teacher.

☐ Start work on the Reading section (page 177).

January

☐ Begin "How to Write the ACT Essay" on page 397.

☐ Continue work on the Reading section.

February

☐ Complete work on the Reading section.

☐ Complete work on "How to Write the ACT Essay."

☐ Take the Diagnostic Reading ACT on page 236 under test conditions.

☐ Review problem areas noted on the Diagnostic Reading ACT.

March

☐ Review problem areas noted on the Diagnostic English, Reading, and Writing Tests.

☐ Review the test-taking strategies on pages 21–22 and the writing strategies on pages 399–402.

☐ Register for the April ACT. List only the colleges you want the scores sent to immediately after your test is scored. I recommend not listing colleges if you know that a particular minimum score is required for admission.

The Saturday seven weeks before the test

☐ Take Model English ACT I, Model Reading ACT I, and ACT Developmental Writing Test I under simulated test conditions.

☐ Score the tests. Review the answer explanations.

☐ Review the essay with your teacher.

☐ Rewrite your essay.

Six weeks to go

☐ Review the problem areas noted on the Model ACTs and on the Writing Tests.

The Saturday five weeks before the test

☐ Take Model English and Reading ACT II and ACT Writing Test II under simulated test conditions.

☐ Score the tests.

☐ Review the essay with your teacher.

Four weeks to go

☐ Review the problem areas noted on the Model ACTs.

☐ Review the test-taking strategies on pages 21–22 and the writing strategies on pages 399–402.

April

Saturday two weeks before the April test date (This Saturday may come in March.)

☐ Take Model English and Reading ACT III and ACT Writing Test III under simulated test conditions.

☐ Score the tests.

☐ Review the essay with your teacher.

Two weeks to go

☐ Review the problem areas from the Model ACTs and the Writing Tests. Refer back to the review sections. Get up at the same time every day that you will on the morning of the test. Work for a half hour each morning on items from one of the Model ACTs and write a paragraph or two.

Test Week

You may continue your review through Thursday, if you want.

☐ Monday
  Make sure you have your registration ticket.
  Make sure you know where the test is given.
  Make sure you have valid forms of identification. If you are not sure whether or not you have a valid form of ID, call the ID Requirements Office at (319) 337-1510. They will help you.

☐ Tuesday

Visit the test site, if you haven't done it already.

☐ Wednesday

Set aside some sharpened No. 2 pencils, a digital watch or clock, a good eraser, and the calculator you will use for the Mathematics Test.

☐ Thursday

Complete any forms you have to bring to the test.

☐ Friday

Relax. Your review is over.

Get together any snacks or food for test breaks.

Get a good night's sleep.

☐ Saturday — TEST DAY

Dress in comfortable clothes.

Eat the same kind of breakfast you've eaten every morning. Don't overeat!

Get together things to bring to the test including: registration ticket, identification forms, pencils, eraser, calculator, and snacks or food.

Get to the test check-in site about 7:30 A.M.

You're there and you're ready.

Follow the test-taking strategies on pages 21–22 and the writing strategies on pages 399–402.

AFTER THE TEST

May

☐ You will receive your scores about four weeks after the test. Discuss the scores with your guidance counselor, advisor, or teacher. You need YES or NO answers to these two questions:

1. Should ACT send these scores to colleges I did not list on my registration form?

   NO — wait until next time.

   YES — arrange to have Additional Score Reports (ASRs) sent to those colleges. If there is no rush, write to the ACT requesting that an ASR be sent out. If you want a score sent out immediately, call the ACT at (319) 337-1313 for expedited service.

2. Should I take the test again?

   Lots of people take the ACT several times. If you have a bad day test day or you are sick, you might not do your best. You may just feel that you can improve your score through further review. You should consider taking the ACT again if you believe you could improve your score enough to make a difference in college admissions.

   NO — you're finished with this book.

YES — decide if you want to take the test again in June or the following October. A June test date gives you limited opportunity for further review, but the test scores can reach colleges by September. An October test date gives you time to get your scored answer sheet along with the test questions and correct answers, but test scores won't reach colleges before the following November.

June Test Date. You have about a month to prepare. Be sure to register for the test. Go back to "Four weeks to go" on the ACT Review Checklist (page 18) and follow the checklist from there.

October Test Date. Order the test questions and answers and your answer sheet from ACT. You will receive a copy of the test items, your scored answer sheet, and the correct answers. The booklet *Using Your ACT Test Scores* that arrived with your test scores has an order form for these services.

June or early July

The scoring information will arrive.

☐ Compare your answer sheet to the correct answers to make sure the sheet was marked correctly. Look also for any patterns that indicate that you may have mismarked your answer sheet.

☐ Check the answers and note the types of problems that you had difficulty with.

September

☐ Register for the October ACT.

☐ Show the questions, correct answers, and your answers to teachers or others who can explain the types of errors you made. Use the review sections of this book, and help from teachers, to review problem areas on the test.

Four weeks to go

☐ Retake the actual ACT that was returned to you under simulated test conditions.

☐ Mark the test and review any remaining problem areas.

☐ Review the test-taking strategies.

Two weeks to go

☐ Go back to "Two weeks to go" on the ACT Review Checklist (page 18) and follow the checklist from there.

Test-Taking Strategies

There is nothing better than knowing the subject matter for the ACT. But these test-taking strategies can help you get a better score.

- **Relax.**

    Get a comfortable seat. Don't sit near anyone or anything that will distract you. If you don't like where you are sitting, move or ask for another seat. You have a right to favorable test conditions.

- **You're going to make mistakes.**

    You are going to make mistakes on this test. The people who wrote the test expect you to make them. Remember the average score for the ACT is about 55 percent correct.

- **All that matters is which circle you fill in.**

    A machine will score the English and Reading sections of your test. The machine detects whether or not the correct place on the answer sheet is filled in. Concentrate on filling in the correct circle. The machine can't tell what you are thinking.

- **You can know the answer to an item but be marked wrong.**

    If you get the right answer but fill in the wrong circle, the machine will mark it wrong.

- **Save the hard items for last.**

    You're not supposed to get all the items correct, and some of them will be too difficult for you. Work through the items and answer the easy ones. Pass the other ones by. Do these items the second time through. If an item seems really hard, draw a circle around the item number in the test booklet. Save these items to the very end.

- **They try to trick you.**

    Test writers often include distracters. Distracters are traps — incorrect answers that look like correct answers. It might be an answer you're likely to get if you're doing something wrong. It might be a correct answer to a different item. It might just be an answer that catches your eye. Watch out for these trick answers.

- **Watch out for *except, not,* or *least.***

    ACT items can contain these words. The answer to these items is the choice that does not fit in with the others.

- **Still don't have the answer? Eliminate and guess.**

  If you can't figure out the correct answer, eliminate the answers you're sure are incorrect. Cross them off in the test booklet. **Guess** the answer from those remaining choices.

  NEVER leave any item blank. Unlike the usual classroom test, there is no penalty for guessing on the ACT.

- **Do your work in the test booklet.**

  The test booklet is not scored. You can write anything in it you want. Use it for scrap paper and to mark up diagrams and tables in the booklet. You may want to do calculations, underline important words, or draw a figure. Do your work for an item near that item in the test booklet. You can also do work on the cover or wherever else suits you.

- **Write the letter for the answer choice in your test booklet.**

  Going back and forth from the test booklet to the answer sheet is difficult and can result in a mismarked answer sheet. Use this approach to help avoid mismarking the answer sheet:

  Write the letter for the answer choice big next to the item number in the test booklet. See the example below. When you have written the answer choice letters for each two-page spread, transfer the answer choices to the answer sheet.

☞ Example

Why did the world heap such fame and glory upon

Amelia Earhart? There <u>was</u> at least two reasons.
        1

B

1. **A.** NO CHANGE
   B. were
   C. has been
   D. will be

<u>A year earlier</u>, in 1927, Charles Lindbergh had
    2
made the first daring solo flight across the Atlantic

F

2. **F.** NO CHANGE
   G. Omit underlined phrase
   H. A year sooner
   J. A year faster

Ocean. Taking off from <u>New York City. He had</u>
            3
landed in Paris, France. The public went wild over

this handsome young American pilot. "Lindy" became

the greatest hero of his time.

D

3. **A.** NO CHANGE
   B. New York City? He
   C. New York City he had
   D. New York City, he had

Chapter 4

ENGLISH TOPIC INVENTORY

Introduction

The ACT English Test consists of five passages with 13 to 17 questions about each passage, for a total of 75 questions. Each question refers to an underlined portion in the passage. You have 45 minutes to complete this test. That gives you about 30 seconds for each item.

The ACT tests specific English skills. This section is organized to help you review and practice these skills as a part of the overall preparation steps on pages 16–20.

First take the English Topic Inventory below. Following the test you'll see the correct answers and a study chart which will point you to the English skills you need to study. Chapters 4, 5, 6, and 7 review the English skills tested on the ACT.

At the end of the section, strategies for taking the English ACT are discussed. Then you have a chance to practice your English skills and test-taking strategies on a Diagnostic English ACT. The Diagnostic English ACT is just like the real thing. However, it is specially designed to detect and direct you to the English skills you should review further.

There are three model ACT English Tests in Section IV of this book. Take these under simulated test conditions according to the schedule on pages 17–20.

Begin with the English Topic Inventory. You'll find out what you need to study, and you'll begin to think about English.

Topic Inventory

Each numbered item contains a single error or no error at all. Correct each error. There may be more than one way to correct an error. Circle the number of each item that does not contain an error. Don't guess. If you are not sure, put a question mark (?) next to the item.

 **Examples**

           had
  A. The lake ~~was~~ been stocked with fish earlier in the year.

  (B.) The lake is about two miles deep at the deepest point.

1. We decided to go fishing, but it turned out that no one had a fishing pole. *Correct*

2. I was just preparing to roller-skate, ~~but~~ I had to go inside to eat dinner. *but*

3. The teams were ready, the stands were full, the weather was beautiful. *and*

4. The first goal was scored on a penalty kick, ~~As~~ the time for the half ran out. *as*

5. To be good enough to play professional soccer, ~~That~~ was one of his great desires.

6. When I was younger I had a dog named Dirk, ~~a dog~~ who swam across the lake.

7. I used to drive Dirk, to the lake. *(who was lame,)*

8. While at the lake one day, it was sunny and windy. *correct*

9. The wind was blowing; ~~who~~ had to hold Dirk so he would not be blown overboard. *I*

10. Where all the ~~mouse~~ had gone was a mystery. *mice*

11. The pot was too small for eight ~~potatos~~. *potatoes*

12. John's favorite saying is, "The sky's the limit." *correct*

13. Who~~m~~ has the keys to the stockroom?

14. Somebody took their textbook home by mistake. *correct*

15. The three boys took the lawn mower to get it fixed. *correct*

16. The warm water feels. *adj.*

17. The lonely stargazer dreams. *correct*

18. The band is playing my favorite song. *correct*

19. The interesting performance ~~begun~~ just as I arrived. *began*

20. I arrived just in time to see that the singer ~~is~~ standing on the stage. *was*

21. The crowd was restless as they ~~wait~~ for the second act to begin. *waited*

22. Erin and Ryan ~~decides~~ to move west. *decided*

23. The contestant with the most points ~~win~~ the game. *wins*

24. Why ~~are~~ everyone running? *is*

25. Into the purple splendor of the fall foliage ~~walks~~ the alert hikers. *walked*

26. Hikers often find their packs are too heavy and they have tight shoes. *correct*

27. The lead hiker said she would rather walk than ~~go by car~~. *side* ~~~~

28. Matt walked very ~~slow~~ *slowly* to school.

29. Harry and Kitty decorated their house really well. *correct*

30. David played golf badly. *correct*

31. Danny was the ~~less~~ *least* concerned of his four brothers and sisters.

32. Julie was the ~~more~~ *most* concerned of her four sisters.

33. Tim concluded that he differed from his parents' point of view. *correct*

34. Ralph was occupied with his pets. *correct*

35. Well, that certainly was an interesting experience.

36. I wiped Dirk off with a towel, before he got out of the boat. *correct*

37. Either Dirk was going to be dry, or he was not getting back in my car. *correct*

38. I was ready to go, but Dirk was still sniffing around the water.

39. You should keep these things in the trunk of your car; jack, spare tire, and flares.

40. Some scientists use sidereal, (star) time.

41. It's very likely that I will play softball this weekend. *correct*

42. The men's softball league is having a tournament. *correct*

43. The question is, "Will it rain this weekend"?

(Answers to the Topic Inventory, with explanations, appear on the following pages.)

Topic Inventory Answers Explained

Compare your answers to the correct answers shown below. If your answer is incorrect, or you were not sure of the answer, circle the number for that item. Then turn to the Study Chart on page 32. Check the box for a study topic if you circled any of the items for that topic. Carefully review each topic you check.

1. We decided to go fishing, but it turned out no one had a fishing pole.
   [This sentence is correct.]

   but
2. I was just preparing to roller-skate, ∧ I had to go inside to eat dinner.
   [Add a conjunction that suggests a contrast after the comma to separate these two main clauses.]

   ;   **; and**
3. The teams were ready ∧ the stands were full ∧ the weather was beautiful.
   [Use a semicolon or a comma (followed by a conjunction) to separate independent clauses.]

   as
4. The first goal was scored on a penalty kick. ~~As~~ the time for the half ran out.
   [The second "sentence" is a sentence fragment — a phrase.]

   , that
5. To be good enough to play professional soccer. ~~That~~ was one of his great desires.
   [The first "sentence" is a sentence fragment — a dependent clause. Use a comma (or a dash) to separate the dependent clause from the independent clause. Or, delete the comma and "that," so the prepositional phrase is the subject of the sentence.]

6. When I was younger I had a dog named Dirk, a dog who swam across the lake.
   [This sentence is correct.]

   , who was lame,
7. I used to drive Dirk ∧ to the lake.
   [The modifier "who was lame" is misplaced. Move it nearer to the word it modifies.]

   I was
8. While ∧ at the lake one day, it was sunny and windy.
   [Insert words such as "I was" so that the words being modified by "at the lake" are in the sentence.]

9. The wind was blowing; ~~who~~ had to hold Dirk so he would not be blown overboard.
   [Replace "who" with the word which tells who had to hold Dirk. The pronoun "I" is one possible solution.]

mice

10. Where all the ~~mouse~~ had gone was a mystery.
    [Use the plural form.]

potatoes

11. The pot was too small for eight ~~potatos.~~
    [Use the correct spelling for the plural form.]

12. John's favorite saying is, "The sky's the limit."
    [This sentence is correct.]

Who

13. ~~Whom~~ has the keys to the stockroom?
    [Use the subjective form of the pronoun.]

her or his

14. Somebody took ~~their~~ textbook home by mistake.
    [Use the singular form to agree with the singular subject "Somebody."]

15. The three boys took the lawn mower to get it fixed.
    [This sentence is correct.]

16. The warm water feels **nice (soothing,** etc.).
    [The verb "feels" is a linking verb which must be linked to a word that describes the subject.]

17. The lonely stargazer dreams.
    [This sentence is correct.]

18. The band is playing my favorite song.
    [This sentence is correct.]

had begun *or* **began**

19. The interesting performance ~~begun~~ just as I arrived.
    [Use the past participle or the past tense.]

was

20. I arrived just in time to see that the singer ~~is~~ standing on the stage.
    [This is a tense shift. Use the past tense in the subordinate clause.]

waited

21. The crowd was restless as they ~~wait~~ for the second act to begin.
    [This is also a tense shift. Use the past tense in the subordinate clause.]

decide *or* **decided**

22. Erin and Ryan ~~decides~~ to move west.
    [Use the plural form of the verb to agree with the plural subject "Erin and Ryan." The past tense is also acceptable, depending on meaning.]

wins

23. The contestant with the most points ~~win~~ the game.
    [Use the singular form of the verb to agree with the singular subject "contestant."]

is

24. Why ~~are~~ everyone running?
    [Use the singular form of the verb to agree with the singular subject "everyone."]

walk *or* **walked**

25. Into the purple splendor of the fall foliage ~~walks~~ the alert hikers.
    [Use the plural form of the verb to agree with the plural subject "hikers."]

their shoes are too tight

26. Hikers often find their packs are too heavy and ~~they have tight shoes~~.
    [Rewrite the sentence to maintain a parallel form.]

ride

27. The lead hiker said she would rather walk than ~~go by car~~.
    [Rewrite the sentence to maintain a parallel form.]

slowly

28. Matt walked very ~~slow~~ to school.
    [Use the adverb "slowly" and not the adjective "slow."]

29. Harry and Kitty decorated their house really well.
    [This sentence is correct.]

30. David played golf badly.
    [This sentence is correct.]

least

31. Danny was the ~~less~~ concerned of his four brothers and sisters.
    [Use the superlative form "least" in place of the comparative form "less."]

most

32. Julie was the ~~more~~ concerned of her four sisters.
    [Use the superlative form "most concerned" in place of the comparative form "more concerned."]

with

33. Tim concluded that he differed ~~from~~ his parents' point of view.
    [Use the idiom "differ with" in this context.]

by
34. Ralph was occupied ~~with~~ his pets.
    [Use the idiom "occupied by" in this context.]

         ,
35. Well ∧ that certainly was an interesting experience.
    [Set off the introductory phrase with a comma.]

towel before
36. I wiped Dirk off with a ~~towel, before~~ he got out of the boat.
    [Eliminate the comma. The phrase is not introductory.]

37. Either Dirk was going to be dry, or he was not getting back in my car.
    [This sentence is correct.]

       go, but
38. I was ready to ~~go; but~~ Dirk was still sniffing around the water.
    [Replace the semicolon before the conjunction with a comma.]

                         car: jack,
39. You should keep these things in the trunk of your ~~car; jack,~~ spare tire, and flares.
    [Replace the semicolon with a colon.]

           (star)
40. Some scientists use sidereal~~, star,~~ time.
    [Use parentheses to set off this parenthetical word.]

It's
41. ~~Its~~ very likely that I will play softball this weekend.
    [Use an apostrophe in the contraction for "It is."]

   men's
42. The ~~mens'~~ softball league is having a tournament.
    [Use the plural possessive form.]

                        ?"
43. The question is, "Will it rain this weekend~~"?~~
    [Put the question mark inside the quotation mark.]

Study Chart

STUDY TOPIC	QUESTION NUMBERS	PAGES TO STUDY
Sentence Structure		
☑ Sentences (Everyone should review this section.)		33–35
☐ Run-on sentences and comma splices	1, 2, 3	35–38
☐ Sentence fragments	4, 5, 6	38–43
☐ Misplaced modifiers and shifts in construction	7, 8, 9	43–47
Grammar and Usage		
☐ Nouns	10, 11, 12	55–57
☐ Pronouns	13, 14, 15	57–62
☐ Verbs	16, 17	62–65
☐ Verb tense	18, 19	65–70
☐ Tense shift	20, 21	70–74
☐ Subject-verb agreement	22, 23, 24, 25	74–77
☐ Parallel form	26, 27	77–81
☐ Adjectives and adverbs	28, 29, 30	81–85
☐ Comparative and superlative adjectives and adverbs	31, 32	85–87
☐ Idioms	33, 34	87–89
Punctuation		
☐ Commas	35, 36, 37	105–109
☐ Semicolons and colons	38, 39	109–111
☐ Parentheses	40	111–112
☐ Apostrophe	41, 42	113–114
☐ Periods, question marks, exclamation points, and quotation marks	43	114–117
Rhetorical Skills		
☑ Strategy	Everyone should	126–129
☑ Organization	review these	132–134
☑ Style	sections.	137–139

Chapter 5
SENTENCE STRUCTURE

There are 18 sentence-structure questions on the ACT.

Sentences

A sentence is a group of words with a subject and a predicate. Sentences begin with a capitalized word and usually end with a period, a question mark, or an exclamation point. Good sentences convey a complete thought. Good sentences make sense.

A sentence can be a statement or a question. The **subject** of the sentence usually tells what the sentence is about. The **predicate** of a sentence tells about the subject or tells what the subject is doing. Here are some examples of sentences showing the subject and predicate.

SUBJECT	PREDICATE
The large, red <u>dog</u>	ran quickly down the path.
ACT <u>scores</u>	can be improved through study and practice.
<u>Ed</u>	is the English editor for this book.
<u>He</u>	preferred warm weather.

Clauses and Phrases

A **phrase** is part of a sentence which does not contain its own subject and predicate.

A **clause** is part of a sentence which contains its own subject and predicate. An **independent (main) clause** makes sense on its own. A **dependent (subordinate) clause** does not make sense on its own.

 **Examples**

<u>After school</u>, <u>Larry studied this ACT book and took the practice tests.</u>
    Phrase   **Independent clause**

<u>After he finished studying</u>, <u>Larry went to baseball practice.</u>
    Dependent clause   **Independent clause**

<u>Larry felt a lot better</u> <u>after he studied for the test.</u>
    Independent clause   **Dependent clause**

Modifiers

Modifiers develop sentences. Modifiers may be either words, phrases, or clauses. Modifiers can come either before or after the words they modify.

Basic sentence: The sun rose.

Word modifier: The <u>warm</u> sun rose.
                 [The word "warm" modifies the word "sun."]

Word modifier: The <u>warm</u> sun rose <u>slowly</u>.
                 [The word "slowly" modifies the word "rose."]

Phrase modifier: The warm sun rose slowly <u>from the east</u>.
                 [The phrase "from the east" modifies the word "rose."]

Clause modifier: The warm sun, <u>which cast its rays on the river</u>, rose slowly from the east.
                 [The clause "which cast its rays on the river" modifies the word "sun."]

Notice how these modifiers help build the basic sentence into a more complete and descriptive sentence.

PRACTICE

Underline and identify the phrases and clauses in each sentence below (P = phrase, IC = independent clause, DC = dependent clause).

 **Example**

> <u>Before the ballgame,</u> <u>Rob went home to study.</u>
>   **P**   **IC**

1. The car screeched to a stop near the intersection.

2. Mark went to the store and then he went to the movies.

3. Until she is able to drive, Lisa cannot buy a car.

4. The ACT exam will be easier after you finish the practice tests.

5. Lisa bought a dog.

6. When he gets his new boat, Matt will take everyone water-skiing.

7. After school, John works at the grocery store.

8. Laura will move to Oregon but not until she graduates from college.

9. If it rains, the picnic will be canceled.

10. It is hot.

Identify the modifiers in the following sentences.

 **Example**

> The ballpark, <u>across the river,</u> will open <u>next</u> year.
> **modifies** *ballpark*　　**modifies** *year*

11. Mary came to work in a bright red car.

12. Mark has a shiny new bike.

13. The hiker, who has a red backpack, climbs the mountain carefully.

14. Jane ran quickly.

15. The old man walked slowly down the hall.

(Answers on page 48)

Run-on Sentences and Comma Splices

Run-on Sentence

A run-on sentence consists of two or more independent clauses with no punctuation or connector between them. Run-on sentences must be corrected.

Run-on:　We headed off to the game during the rain the rain stopped before we got there.

Corrected:　We headed off to the game during the rain. **T**he rain stopped before we got there.
　　　[Change the run-on sentence into two separate sentences.]
　　　　or
We headed off to the game during the rain, **but** the rain stopped before we got there.
　　　[Use a comma and the connector "but" between the clauses.]
　　　　or
We headed off to the game during the rain; the rain stopped before we got there.
　　　[Use a semicolon between the clauses.]

Comma Splice

A comma splice is like a run-on sentence, except that a comma separates the two clauses. Comma splices must be corrected.

Comma splice:　The computer is an invaluable tool, it links together millions of people.

Corrected: The computer is an invaluable tool **because** it links together millions of people.
>   [Insert the connecting word "because" to replace the comma.]

>   *or*

The computer is an invaluable tool**;** it links together millions of people.
>   [Replace the comma with a semicolon.]

>   *or*

The computer is an invaluable tool**.** It links together millions of people.
>   [Make two separate sentences.]

 MODEL ACT **PROBLEMS**

These Model ACT Problems show how this topic might be tested on the real ACT. The answers and explanations immediately follow the problems. Try the problems and then review the answers and the explanations.

Mark and Laura rode their bikes into <u>town, they stopped at</u>
1

1. **A.** NO CHANGE
   B. town they stopped at
   C. town. They stopped at
   D. town they stopped. At

the ice-cream store for a cone. <u>Then they rode to the</u>
2

<u>zoo; they</u> did not go inside.
2

2. **F.** NO CHANGE
   G. Then they rode to the zoo they
   H. Then, they rode to the zoo they
   J. Then they rode to the zoo, they

**ANSWERS**

1. The sentence is a comma splice. To correct it, separate the two independent clauses with either a period, a semicolon, or a connector word. Choice B is a run-on sentence. In choice D, the words "At the ice-cream store for a cone" are not a sentence.

   C is the correct choice.

2. The sentence is correct as it is because the semicolon separates the two independent clauses. Choice G is a run-on sentence. The sentence in choice H is also a run-on because the two independent clauses are not separated. Choice J is a comma splice.

   F is the correct choice.

Correct the run-on sentences and comma splices. Some sentences are correct.

1. I like to use my computer when I have to write a paper.

2. The scorekeepers at the game use a computer they use it to keep track of statistics.

3. When the computer stops working, I call the Computer Doctor.

4. The referee blew the whistle, the game came to a halt.

5. Running through the rain, the player sprinted toward the clubhouse.

6. The clubhouse door would not open the player was soaking wet.

7. It will be a long time before I go to a game on a rainy day.

8. My clothes are drenched, water is dripping out of my shoes.

9. I put the wet clothes in the dryer right away, although I was concerned they might shrink.

10. The rain stopped the sun came out.

11. The player dried off, the game resumed.

12. The score was tied the team's best player was at bat.

13. After they won the game, the players went out for pizza.

14. I like pizza with pepperoni and sausage Rob hates mushrooms on his pizza.

15. In the fall I'll go to college, but this summer I'm working at a pizza place.

(Answers on pages 48–49)

ACT-TYPE PROBLEMS

Look at the item that matches the number of the underlined part. Pick the best replacement for the underlined part. If the underlined part is the best, then select NO CHANGE.

There are lots of animals <u>at the zoo I like</u> to go there on
1

1. A. NO CHANGE
   B. at the zoo, I like
   C. at the zoo; I like
   D. at the zoo? I like

the weekends. I really <u>like the monkeys, they're so</u>
2
much like people. Sometimes I make faces

2. F. NO CHANGE
   G. the monkeys. They're so
   H. the monkeys. Their so
   J. the monkeys they're so

<u>at them, sometimes they make</u> faces at me. After the
3

3. A. NO CHANGE
   B. at them sometimes they make
   C. at them sometimes, they make
   D. at them. Sometimes they make

monkey house, I often go to see the pandas. They are
4

very rare it is interesting to watch them.
5

Andrew and Talia went to the ballgame, they bought
6

hot dogs. Before the game started. The players were
7

signing autographs. Talia got her program signed by

the pitcher Andrew caught a foul ball. It was a
8

great night! They both had a good time. After
9

the game, Andrew and Talia watched the highlights
10
on television.

(Answers on page 50)

4. **F.** NO CHANGE
   G. monkey house. I often go
   H. monkey house; I often go
   J. monkey house! I often go

5. **A.** NO CHANGE
   B. very rare, it is interesting
   C. very rare. It is interesting
   D. very rare it is. Interesting

6. **F.** NO CHANGE
   G. the ballgame they bought
   H. the ballgame, and they bought
   J. the ballgame they. Bought

7. **A.** NO CHANGE
   B. game started? The players
   C. game started; the players
   D. game started, the players

8. **F.** NO CHANGE
   G. the pitcher. Andrew caught
   H. the pitcher, Andrew, caught
   J. the pitcher, Andrew caught

9. **A.** NO CHANGE
   B. great night they both
   C. great night, they both
   D. great night until they both

10. **F.** NO CHANGE
    G. the game. Andrew and
    H. the game; Andrew and
    J. the game Andrew and

Sentence Fragments

A sentence must contain a subject and a predicate. A sentence must make sense on its own. A sentence fragment is a part of a sentence that is written as though it were a sentence. Some sentence fragments may appear to be acceptable sentences. The ACT asks you to identify and correct sentence fragments.

Sentence-fragment errors as shown below appear frequently on the ACT.

The Sentence Fragment Is a Dependent Clause

A dependent clause does not stand on its own. A single word may change an independent clause to a dependent clause. Be particularly alert for clauses beginning with words such as *although, as, because, despite, what, when.*

A dependent clause usually leaves you feeling up in the air, as though you were waiting for the other shoe to drop.

Independent clause: Ann went to the football game.
[This clause is a sentence. It has a subject and a predicate, and it stands on its own.]

Dependent clause: As Ann went to the football game.
[This clause is a sentence fragment. It does not stand on its own. We are left wondering what happened as Ann went to the football game.]

Fragment: The football game continued. <u>While the band played in the background.</u>
[The underlined portion is a sentence fragment. It has a subject and a predicate, but it does not stand on its own.]

Corrected: The football game continued**, while** the band played in the background.
[Make one sentence with a comma separating the clauses.]

or

The football game continued. **The** band played in the background.
[Remove the word "while" to change the sentence fragment to a sentence.]

The Sentence Fragment Is a Verbal Phrase

A verbal phrase begins with words such as *to jump, to sleep, jumping, sleeping, jumped,* and *slept.* This phrase cannot be made into a sentence by just dropping a word or two. Look at these examples:

Fragment: I have one goal for this month. <u>To score well on the ACT.</u>
[The underlined verbal phrase is a fragment. There is no subject.]

Corrected: I have one goal for this month**,** to score well on the ACT.
[Make one sentence with a comma separating the phrase from the clause.]

Fragment: Liz made a big mistake this weekend. <u>Sleeping on the beach.</u>
[The underlined verbal phrase is a fragment.]

Corrected: Liz made a big mistake this weekend. **She fell asleep** on the beach.
[Rewrite the fragment to form a sentence.]

The Sentence Fragment Is an Appositive

An appositive is a group of nouns, or words that describe a noun, which are not sentences. Look at these examples:

Fragment: I like to go shopping no matter where it is. <u>Malls, department stores, grocery stores, convenience stores.</u>
  [The underlined appositive is a fragment.]
Corrected: I like to go shopping no matter where it is—malls, department stores, grocery stores, convenience stores.
  [Make one sentence with a comma (or a dash) separating the phrase from the clause.]

Fragment: My favorite gift was a small statue. <u>A figure who stood cheerily, unflinching, through the best and worst of times.</u>
  [The underlined appositive is a fragment.]
Corrected: My favorite gift was a small statue, a figure who stood cheerily, unflinching, through the best and worst of times.
  [Make one sentence with a comma separating the phrase from the clause.]

The Sentence Fragment Is Missing Sentence Part(s)

Many fragments are just lacking sentence parts. Remember, at first glance a fragment may appear to be a sentence.

Fragment: When I was young I had a favorite form of transportation. <u>A bus that traveled to the beach.</u>
  [The underlined portion is a fragment. There is no predicate.]
Corrected: When I was young I had a favorite form of transportation, a bus that traveled to the beach.
  [Make one sentence with a comma separating the phrase from the clause.]

Fragment: There were some great rides at the amusement park. <u>Was open from 9:00 A.M. to 11:00 P.M.</u>
  [The underlined portion is a fragment. There is no subject.]
Corrected: There were some great rides at the amusement park, **which** was open from 9:00 A.M. to 11:00 P.M.
  [Make one sentence with a comma and a connecting word separating the clause from the phrase.]

MODEL ACT PROBLEMS

These Model ACT Problems show how this topic might be tested on the real ACT. The answers and explanations immediately follow the problems. Try the problems and then review the answers and the explanations.

Before going to <u>the party. Kate bought</u> a new dress.
₁

1. **A.** NO CHANGE
    B. the party, Kate bought
    C. the party; Kate bought
    D. the party! Kate bought

It was a new <u>spring dress. One with red</u> polka dots.
₂

2. **F.** NO CHANGE
    G. spring dress; One with red
    H. spring dress one with red
    J. spring dress, one with red

When <u>she arrived, everyone was</u> already dancing and
₃

3. **A.** NO CHANGE
    B. she arrived. Everyone was
    C. she arrived; Everyone was
    D. she arrived? Everyone was

having fun. Someone bumped <u>into her. Spilling punch</u>
₄
on her new dress.

4. **F.** NO CHANGE
    G. into her, spilling punch
    H. into her; spilling punch
    J. into her! spilling punch

 **ANSWERS**

1. The dependent clause "Before going to the party" is a sentence fragment. It cannot stand on its own, but leaves the reader wondering what happened before the party.

    B is the correct choice.

2. "One with red polka dots" is an appositive fragment. It describes the dress, but has no subject or verb of its own. It is corrected by making the two sentences one sentence, separated by a comma.

    J is the correct choice.

3. This sentence is correct. "When she arrived" cannot stand on its own as a sentence.

    A is the correct choice.

4. "Spilling punch on her new dress" is a verbal phrase, not a sentence.

    G is the correct choice.

Correct the sentence fragments. Some items are correct.

1. I was running to my house. Suddenly, a breeze blew up from the east.

2. The wind reminded me of something. An assignment on weather I had to complete.

3. Cars, trucks, and motorcycles. They whizzed by on the highway.

4. As I was standing by the side of the road. I saw horse-drawn carriages in the distance.

5. They looked like ghosts from the past. Buckboards, carriages, and stagecoaches went by.

6. This was my idea of fun. To ski by moonlight.

7. I saw skiers silhouetted against the spotlights. Like silent movie stars on a modern stage.

8. I gazed silently at the setting sun. Like a flaming meteor, it glowed against the distant horizon.

9. To be at the beach right now. That is my fondest desire.

10. The waves were breaking softly on the beach. The seabirds were skimming along the waves.

11. I like fresh garden vegetables in the summer. Tomatoes, peppers, and carrots.

12. After a long day in the sun. I like to go swimming in the lake.

13. Water-skiing in the evening, that is my favorite summer activity.

14. Standing on the roof, I saw the people down below. Like tiny ants in a maze.

15. As I watched them, I dreamed I was a giant.

(Answers on pages 51–52)

ACT-TYPE PROBLEMS

Look at the item that matches the number of the underlined part. Pick the best replacement for the underlined part. If the underlined part is the best, then select NO CHANGE.

Growing up <u>in Idaho. I was used</u> to life in a small town.
 1

1. **A.** NO CHANGE
   B. in Idaho, I was used
   C. in Idaho! I was used
   D. in Idaho; I was used

Traffic jams, crime, and <u>deadlines. These</u> things did not
 2

2. **F.** NO CHANGE
   G. deadlines; these
   H. deadlines, these
   J. deadlines these

concern me. After <u>college, however. I moved</u> to Seattle.
 3

3. **A.** NO CHANGE
   B. college. However, I moved
   C. college, however? I moved
   D. college, however, I moved

While I had to deal with the <u>problems. I also learned</u>
4

good things about city life. In a <u>large city, new</u>
5
things can be experienced every day. Trying

<u>new restaurants. That's one</u> good thing. Chinese,
6

Thai, Ethiopian <u>and Mexican, these are all new foods</u>
7
I've learned to like. I also enjoy meeting all kinds

<u>of people. They each</u> have something different to
8

contribute. While living in the city has <u>its bad</u>
9
<u>points. The good ones</u> can outweigh them.
9

For <u>me, however, I will</u> eventually return to
10
small-town life.

(Answers on page 52)

4. F. NO CHANGE
   G. problems; I also learned
   H. problems I also learned
   J. problems, I also learned

5. A. NO CHANGE
   B. large city. New
   C. large city; new
   D. large city new

6. F. NO CHANGE
   G. new restaurants? That's one
   H. new restaurants, that's one
   J. new restaurants; that's one

7. A. NO CHANGE
   B. and Mexican. These are all new foods
   C. and Mexican? These are all new foods
   D. and Mexican: these are all new foods

8. F. NO CHANGE
   G. of people, they each
   H. of people they each
   J. of people they. Each

9. A. NO CHANGE
   B. its bad points, the good ones
   C. its bad points; the good ones
   D. its bad points the good ones

10. F. NO CHANGE
    G. me, however. I will
    H. me, however; I will
    J. me. However, I will

Misplaced Modifiers and Shifts in Construction

Adjectives, adverbs, and groups of words serving as modifiers should clearly refer to the word they modify. The ACT items for misplaced modifiers and construction shifts test the same material with slightly different question types. **Be sure the placement of the modifier makes sense.** To correct such errors, move the modifier closer to the word it modifies.

Misplaced: The truck drove through the tunnel and it was large.
                [We cannot be sure whether the adjective "large" modifies "truck" or "tunnel."]

Corrected: The large truck drove through the tunnel.
                or
              The truck drove through the large tunnel.

Misplaced: The driver brought a delivery to the store in a red container.
                [The modifier is "in a red container." It doesn't make sense for the store to be in a red container. These words must modify "delivery," so move them close to "delivery."]

Corrected: The driver brought a delivery in a red container to the store.

Misplaced: The driver shifted the van into first gear and firmly drove out of the parking lot.
                [This example is a little trickier. The phrase "firmly drove" seems to place the modifier near the word it modifies. But does it make sense to firmly drive a van? No. But it does make sense to shift gears firmly. The modifier "firmly" is misplaced.]

Corrected: The driver shifted the van firmly into first gear and drove out of the parking lot.

Be sure the word being modified is in the sentence. To correct such errors, include the word being modified in the sentence.

Misplaced: While on vacation in Iowa, a tornado alert was issued.
                [The modifier is "While on vacation in Iowa." But the word it modifies is not in the sentence, and the sentence looks silly.]

Corrected: While **we** were on vacation in Iowa, a tornado alert was issued.
                or
              There was a tornado alert while **we** were on vacation in Iowa.
                [Any pronoun or noun could be added to the sentence.]

Misplaced: The wind was howling, which had to take cover under a highway overpass.
                [The word "which" makes no sense here. Replace it with the word that tells what or who "had to take cover under a highway overpass."]

Corrected: The wind was howling**, and we** had to take cover under a highway overpass.
                [Replace "which" with "we." Remember to include ", and" because the second part of the sentence changes from a phrase to a clause.]

MODEL ACT PROBLEMS

These Model ACT Problems show how this topic might be tested on the real ACT. The answers and explanations immediately follow the problems. Try the problems and then review the answers and the explanations.

The brakes were <u>faulty, which</u> had to go into the shop.
            1

1. **A.** NO CHANGE
   B. faulty which
   C. faulty, and the car
   D. faulty, the car

The boy <u>dropped his ball off the building which bounced.</u>
              2

2. **F.** NO CHANGE.
   G. The boy, which bounced, dropped his ball off the building.
   H. The boy which bounced dropped his ball off the building.
   J. The boy dropped his ball, which bounced, off the building.

 **ANSWERS**

1. In this sentence, "which" modifies the word "car." One would not send just the brakes into the shop, so the sentence must be changed. Choice B is incorrect because it does not change the sentence; it just drops the comma. Choice D is incorrect because changing "which" to "the car" makes the second part of the sentence a clause, not a phrase. Without a connector word, such as *and* in choice C, the sentence becomes a comma splice.

   C is the correct choice.

2. The phrase "which bounced" modifies the noun "ball." Choice F is not correct because we cannot be sure which noun "bounced" modifies — boy, ball, or building. Choice G is incorrect because "bounced" incorrectly modifies "boy" (a boy *who* bounces, not *which* bounces). Choice H is incorrect for the same reason.

   J is the correct choice.

PRACTICE ▷

Correct the misplaced modifiers. Some sentences are correct.

1. I went to school to take the ACT in my mother's car.

2. The room was empty; who had to go to another room.

3. I was on the way to my house, which was about a mile away.

4. John drove a van into the night that had no lights.

5. Ron was driving to school in a car with dirty windows.

6. It started to rain when on the way to the beach.

7. A road alert when an accident caused hazardous conditions was issued.

8. Lisa completed her assignment and brought it to school with careful attention to detail.

9. Which car should I take to the store?

10. Leon turned his head and his eyes looked slowly into the store window.

11. Matt bought a bowl for his fish which was broken.

12. Ann has a room that is full of toys.

13. While still at school a blizzard started.

14. The boy with two pieces missing has a jigsaw puzzle.

15. Mark rode his bike down the path which has no pedals.

(*Answers on page 53*)

ACT-TYPE PROBLEMS

Look at the item that matches the number of the underlined part. Pick the best replacement for the underlined part. If the underlined part is the best, then select NO CHANGE.

Sue looked out over the sea who was scared.
 1

1. A. NO CHANGE
   B. Sue looked out over the sea who was scared.
   C. Sue, who was scared, looked out over the sea.
   D. Sue looked out, who was scared, over the sea.

A foghorn had sounded when on the way home.
 2

2. F. NO CHANGE
   G. foghorn had sounded when on the way home.
   H. foghorn, when on the way home had sounded.
   J. foghorn had sounded when she was on the way home.

She knew the boat was missing with the green paint.
 3

3. A. NO CHANGE
   B. knew the green paint was missing with the boat.
   C. knew the boat with the green paint was missing.
   D. knew with the green paint the boat was missing.

Sue knew her brother often used the boat, which was
 4

missing an oar.
 4

4. F. NO CHANGE
   G. knew her brother, which was missing an oar, often used the boat.
   H. which was missing an oar, knew her brother often used the boat.
   J. knew, which was missing an oar, her brother often used the boat.

A radio announcement as the storm rose issued a
<u>5</u>

<u>warning to all boats.</u>
5

Just then, <u>a sharp knock sounded at her door.</u>
6

Sue <u>peered through the peephole at the figure outside</u>
7

<u>with one eye.</u>
7

<u>A man in a raincoat stood outside.</u>
8

In <u>a flash of lightning, she saw it was John, her brother.</u>
9

<u>Sue opened the door and let her brother in with a cry of</u>
10

<u>delight.</u>
10

(Answers on page 54)

5. **A.** NO CHANGE
   B. A radio announcement issued a warning as the storm rose to all boats.
   C. As the storm rose, a radio announcement issued a warning to all boats.
   D. A radio announcement issued as the storm rose a warning to all boats.

6. **F.** NO CHANGE
   G. then, sounded at her door a sharp knock.
   H. then, her door a sharp knock sounded.
   J. then, a sounded at her door sharp knock.

7. **A.** NO CHANGE
   B. peered, with one eye, through the peephole at the figure outside.
   C. peered through the peephole with one eye at the figure outside.
   D. through the peephole peered at the figure with one eye outside.

8. **F.** NO CHANGE
   G. A man stood outside in a raincoat.
   H. A man stood in a raincoat outside.
   J. In a raincoat a man stood outside.

9. **A.** NO CHANGE
   B. a flash of lightning her brother she saw it was John.
   C. she saw it was John in a flash of lightning, her brother.
   D. she saw it was John, her brother in a flash of lightning.

10. **F.** NO CHANGE
    G. With a cry of delight, Sue opened the door and let her brother in.
    H. Sue opened the door with a cry of delight and let her brother in.
    J. Sue opened the door and let with a cry of delight her brother in.

1. The car screeched to a stop near the intersection.
       IC   P

2. Mark went to the store and then he went to the movies.
       IC   IC

3. Until she is able to drive, Lisa cannot buy a car.
       DC   IC

4. The ACT exam will be easier after you finish the practice tests.
       IC   DC

5. Lisa bought a dog.
       IC

6. When he gets his new boat, Matt will take everyone water-skiing.
       DC   IC

7. After school, John works at the grocery store.
       P   IC

8. Laura will move to Oregon but not until she graduates from college.
       IC   DC

9. If it rains, the picnic will be canceled.
       DC   IC

10. It is hot.
        IC

11. Mary came to work in a bright red car
        modifies / modifies
        red / car

12. Mark has a shiny new bike.
        modify *bike*

13. The hiker, who has a red backpack, climbs the mountain carefully.
        modifies *hiker*   **modifies** *climbs*

14. Jane ran quickly.
        modifies *ran*

15. The old man walked slowly down the hall.
        modifies *man*   **modifies** *walked*

1. I like to use my computer when I have to write a paper.
   [No comma splice or run-on errors.]

2. The scorekeepers at the game use a computer; they use it to keep track of statistics.
   [You could also have created two sentences, or put a comma and a conjunction between the clauses.]

3. When the computer stops working, I call the Computer Doctor.
   [No comma splice or run-on errors.]

4. The referee blew the whistle; the game came to a halt.
   [You could also have created two sentences, or put a comma and a conjunction between the clauses.]

5. Running through the rain, the player sprinted toward the clubhouse.
   [No comma splice or run-on errors.]

6. The clubhouse door would not open; the player was soaking wet.
   [You could also have created two sentences, or put a comma and a conjunction between the clauses.]

7. It will be a long time before I go to a game on a rainy day.
   [No comma splice or run-on errors.]

8. My clothes are drenched; water is dripping out of my shoes.
   [You could also have created two sentences, or put a comma and a conjunction between the clauses.]

9. I put the wet clothes in the drier right away, although I was concerned they might shrink.
   [No comma splice or run-on errors.]

10. The rain stopped; the sun came out.
    [You could also have created two sentences, or put a comma and a conjunction between the clauses.]

11. The player dried off, **and** the game resumed.
    or
    The player dried off. **The** game resumed.
    or
    The player dried off; the game resumed.

12. The score was tied; the team's best player was at bat.
    or
    The game was tied. **The** team's best player was at bat.
    or
    The game was tied, **but** the team's best player was at bat.

13. This sentence is correct.

14. I like pizza with pepperoni and sausage; Rob hates mushrooms on his pizza.
    or
    I like pizza with pepperoni and sausage, **but** Rob hates mushrooms on his pizza.
    or
    I like pizza with pepperoni and sausage. Rob hates mushrooms on his pizza.

15. This sentence is correct.

1. There are two independent clauses—both able to stand on their own. Therefore, they must either be separated by a semicolon, a comma and a conjunction, or a conjunction, or be made into two sentences. This correct choice separates them with a semicolon.

   C is the correct choice.

2. There are two independent clauses—both able to stand on their own. Therefore, they must either be separated by a semicolon or a comma and a conjunction, or be made into two sentences. Both choice G and choice H separate them into two sentences. The correct form for *they are* is *they're,* found in choice G.

   G is the correct choice.

3. There are two independent clauses—both able to stand on their own. Therefore, they must either be separated by a semicolon or a comma and a conjunction, or be made into two sentences. This correct choice separates them into two sentences.

   D is the correct choice.

4. No change is needed. The phrase "After the monkey house" is not an independent clause, so it should be separated by a comma.

   F is the correct choice.

5. The first independent clause, "They are very rare," must be separated from the second by a period—making two sentences.

   C is the correct choice.

6. There are two independent clauses—both able to stand on their own. Therefore, they must either be separated by a semicolon or a comma and a conjunction, or be made into two sentences. This correct choice separates them with a conjunction.

   H is the correct choice.

7. "Before the game started" is an introductory phrase, not an independent clause. Therefore, it is separated from the rest of the sentence by a comma.

   D is the correct choice.

8. Both parts of the original sentence are independent clauses.

   G is the correct choice.

9. No change is needed. The sentences are both complete and independent.

   A is the correct choice.

10. No change is needed. "After the game" is a phrase and should be separated by a comma as shown in the paragraph.

    F is the correct choice.

The first line of each answer shows the original practice sentence.

1. I was running to my house. Suddenly, a breeze blew up from the east.
   [No sentence-fragment errors.]

2. The wind reminded me of something. An assignment on weather I had to complete.

   The wind reminded me of something, **an** assignment on weather I had to complete.

   or

   The wind reminded me of **an assignment** on weather I had to complete.

3. Cars, trucks, and motorcycles. They whizzed by on the highway.
   Cars, trucks, and motorcycles whizzed by on the highway.

4. As I was standing by the side of the road. I saw horse-drawn carriages in the distance.

   I was standing by the side of the road. I saw horse-drawn carriages in the distance.

   or

   As I was standing by the side of the road, I saw horse-drawn carriages in the distance.

5. They looked like ghosts from the past. Buckboards, carriages, and stagecoaches went by.
   [No sentence-fragment errors.]

6. That was my idea of fun. To ski by moonlight.
   To ski by moonlight, that was my idea of fun.

7. I saw skiers silhouetted against the spotlights. Like silent movie stars on a modern stage.
   I saw skiers silhouetted against the spotlights, like silent movie stars on a modern stage.

8. I gazed silently at the setting sun. Like a flaming meteor, it glowed against the distant horizon.
   [No sentence-fragment errors.]

9. To be at the beach right now. That is my fondest desire.
   To be at the beach right now is my fondest desire.

10. The waves were breaking softly on the beach. The seabirds were skimming along the waves.
    [No sentence-fragment errors.]

11. I like fresh garden vegetables in the summer. Tomatoes, peppers, and carrots.
    I like fresh garden vegetables in the summer—tomatoes, peppers, and carrots.

12. After a long day in the sun. I like to go swimming in the lake.
    After a long day in the sun, I like to go swimming in the lake.

13. Water-skiing in the evening, that is my favorite summer activity.
    Water-skiing in the evening is my favorite summer activity.

14. Standing on the roof, I saw the people down below. Like tiny ants in a maze.
    Standing on the roof, I saw the people down below, like tiny ants in a maze.

15. As I watched them, I dreamed I was a giant.
    [No sentence-fragment errors.]

✔ANSWERS *(pages 42–43)*

   1: **B.** "Growing up in Idaho" is a sentence fragment.

   2: **H.** The fragment "Traffic jams, crime, and deadlines" needs to be made part of the sentence, but must be separated from the rest of the sentence by a comma.

   3: **D.** The fragment must be connected to the sentence.

   4: **J.** The fragment needs to be made part of the sentence, but must be separated by a comma.

   5: **A.** No change is needed.

   6: **H.** The fragment "Trying new restaurants" needs to be made part of the sentence, but must be separated from the rest of the sentence by a comma.

   7: **A.** No change is needed. The introductory phrase is separated from the rest of the sentence by a comma.

   8: **F.** No change is needed Both sentences are complete.

   9: **B.** The fragment "While living in the city has its bad points" needs to be made part of the sentence, but must be separated from the rest of the sentence by a comma.

  10: **F.** No change is needed.

The first line of each answer shows the original practice sentence.

1. I went to school to take the ACT in my mother's car.
   I went to school in my mother's car to take the ACT.

2. The room was empty; who had to go to another room.
   The room was empty; **someone** had to go to another room.

3. I was on the way to my house, which was about a mile away.
   [No modifier errors.]

4. John drove a van into the night that had no lights.
   John drove a van that had no lights into the night.

5. Ron was driving to school in a car with dirty windows.
   [No modifier errors.]

6. It started to rain when on the way to the beach.
   It started to rain when **we were** on the way to the beach.
   [There are other possible substitutions for "we were."]

7. A road alert when an accident caused hazardous conditions was issued.
   A road alert was issued when an accident caused hazardous conditions.

8. Lisa completed her assignment and brought it to school with careful attention to detail.
   Lisa completed her assignment with careful attention to detail and brought it to school.

9. Which car should I take to the store?
   [No modifier errors.]

10. Leon turned his head, and his eyes looked slowly into the store window.
    Leon slowly turned his head, and his eyes looked into the store window.

11. Matt bought a bowl for his fish which was broken.
    Matt bought a bowl, which was broken, for his fish.

12. Ann has a room that is full of toys.
    [No modifier errors.]

13. While still at school a blizzard started.
    While **we were** still at school, a blizzard started.

14. The boy with two pieces missing has a jigsaw puzzle.
    The boy has a jigsaw puzzle with two pieces missing.

15. Mark rode his bike down the path which has no pedals.
    Mark rode his bike, which has no pedals, down the path.

1: C. Sue is the one who was scared, not the sea.

2: J. She was on the way home, not the foghorn.

3: C. The boat has green paint; the boat and the green paint are not two missing items.

4: F. No change is needed.

5: C. The announcement issued the warning.

6: F. No change is needed.

7: B. Sue is peering with one eye. Neither the peephole nor the figure has one eye.

8: F. No change is needed.

9: A. No change is needed.

10: G. Sue is crying with delight.

Chapter 6

GRAMMAR AND USAGE

There are 12 grammar and usage questions on the ACT.

Nouns

Nouns may name a person, place, thing, attribute, or idea. There is a noun to name everything you can think of. The subject of a sentence can contain nouns such as "dog," "scores," and "Ed."

Singular and Plural Nouns

Singular nouns name one thing. Plural nouns name more than one thing. Follow these rules for changing singular nouns to plural nouns.

Add *s* to most singular nouns.

SINGULAR	PLURAL
student	students
computer	computers
monkey	monkeys
CD	CDs
television	televisions

Drop the *y* and add *ies* when the singular noun ends in *y* preceded by a consonant.

SINGULAR	PLURAL
mystery	mysteries
sky	skies
fly	flies

Add *es* to singular nouns ending in *s, sh, ch, x,* or *z.*

SINGULAR	PLURAL
glass	glasses
match	matches
lash	lashes
fox	foxes
waltz	waltzes

Some plurals are special cases. The plural may have a different form than the singular. The plural may be the same as the singular.

SINGULAR	PLURAL
mouse	mice
zero	zeroes *or* zeros
foot	feet
child	children
cactus	cacti
sheep	sheep
thief	thieves

 ## MODEL ACT PROBLEM

This Model ACT Problem shows how this topic might be tested on the real ACT. The answer and explanation immediately follow the problem. Try the problem and then review the answer and the explanation.

There were <u>a dozen boxs</u> in the truck.
        1

1. **A.** NO CHANGE
  B. a dozen box
  C. a dozen boxes
  D. a dozen of boxes

✔ **ANSWER**

1. Any word that ends in *x*, such as box or fox, has *es* added to it to make it plural. Since there are a dozen in the truck, the word must be plural.

   C is the correct choice.

 ## PRACTICE

Write the plural of each singular noun.

1. tree _____
2. echo _____
3. leaf _____
4. cry _____
5. church _____

6. lady _____
7. hippopotamus _____
8. deer _____
9. tooth _____
10. calf _____

11. goose _____
12. game _____
13. boy _____
14. couch _____
15. party _____

(*Answers on page 92*)

ACT-TYPE PROBLEMS

Look at the item that matches the number of the underlined part. Pick the best replacement for the underlined part. If the underlined part is the best, then select NO CHANGE.

All the <u>house</u> were decorated for the holidays. The
1

trees had colored lights, and there was a wreath on

each front <u>door</u>.
2

1. **A.** NO CHANGE
   B. hice
   C. houses
   D. houseses

2. **F.** NO CHANGE
   G. doors
   H. doorses
   J. doores

(*Answers on page 92*)

Pronouns

Pronouns take the place of nouns. Pronouns include the words *I, we, she, him, them, my, their, whose.* Look at these examples:

Liz drove <u>her</u> car to school. <u>She</u> parked <u>it</u> near the front door.

The pronouns "her" and "she" refer to the noun "Liz." "Liz" is the antecedent of the pronouns "her" and "she." The pronoun "it" refers to the noun "car." "Car" is the antecedent of the pronoun "it."

Clear Reference

A pronoun must clearly refer to its antecedent. Look at these examples:

Unclear reference: Andy wanted Nathan to use his car.
　　　　　　　　　　[The pronoun "his" does not clearly refer to a
　　　　　　　　　　particular noun.]
Clear reference: 　Andy wanted Nathan to use his own car.
　　　　　　　　　　　　or
　　　　　　　　　　Andy wanted Nathan to use Andy's car.

Unclear reference: Ann got them and handed them over to Julia.
　　　　　　　　　　[The antecedent for the pronoun "them" is not stated.]
Clear reference: 　Ann got the keys and handed them over to Julia.

Case

Pronouns can be in the subjective, objective, or possessive case. Look at these examples.

Subjective pronouns are used as the subject of a sentence or a clause, or to refer to the subject:

> **Who** is supposed to take the garbage out today?
> Liz announced it was **she.**
> [The pronoun "she" refers to the subject "Liz."]

Objective pronouns are the object of a verb or preposition:

> Inga decided to help **her.**
> I don't know if I should help **them.**

Possessive pronouns show possession:

> It seemed to me that Inga and Liz could do **their** work.
> I decided not to run the risk of spraining **my** back.

Number

A pronoun may be singular or plural. Here is a list of singular and plural pronouns in each case:

Singular			**Plural**		
SUBJECTIVE	OBJECTIVE	POSSESSIVE	SUBJECTIVE	OBJECTIVE	POSSESSIVE
I	me	my, mine	we	us	our, ours
he	him	his	you	you	your, yours
it	it	its	they	them	their, theirs
she	her	hers	who	whom	whose
you	you	your, yours			
who	whom	whose			

Indefinite pronouns, shown below, are always singular.

anyone	neither	everyone
each	anybody	no one
either	everybody	somebody

Gender

A singular pronoun referring to a third person may be masculine, feminine, or neuter. All other pronouns, including plural pronouns, are neuter.

 **Examples**

The man got ready to leave for **his** vacation.
> [The pronoun is masculine because it refers to the noun "man."]

Mrs. James was driving **her** car.
> [The pronoun is feminine because it refers to the noun phrase "Mrs. James."]

Every dog has **its** day.
> [The pronoun is neuter because animals are referred to as neuter unless the sex is known.]

I'm up to **my** old tricks.
> [The pronoun is neuter—first-person pronouns are neuter.]

The two boys ran until **they** got to the school.
> [The pronoun is neuter because all plural pronouns are neuter.]

Agreement

Each pronoun must agree in number (singular or plural) and gender (male, female, or neuter for the third-person singular) with the noun, noun phrase, or pronoun it refers to. Look at these examples:

Nonagreement in number: Joan and her sister ran to catch the plane, but she was too late.
> [The singular "she" does not agree with the plural "Joan and her sister."]

Agreement: Joan and her sister ran to catch the plane, but they were too late.

Nonagreement in number: Everyone went home to get their raincoats.
> [The plural "their" does not agree with the singular "everyone." Recall that indefinite pronouns such as "each" and "everyone" are singular.]

Agreement: Everyone went home to get her or his raincoat.

Nonagreement in gender: The girls took their car to get her brakes fixed.
> [The feminine "her" does not agree with the noun "car."]

Agreement: The girls took their car to get its brakes fixed.

Nonagreement in gender: The man on the platform waited for the woman to get off the train, which he had been on for three hours.
> [The masculine "he" does not agree with "woman."]

Agreement: The man on the platform waited for the woman to get off the train, which she had been on for three hours.

These Model ACT Problems show how this topic might be tested on the real ACT. The answers and explanations immediately follow the problems. Try the problems and then review the answers and the explanations.

<u>It</u> was broken and wouldn't start. Mark took his car
1

1. **A.** NO CHANGE
   B. They
   C. He
   D. The car

to the shop and discovered <u>their</u> battery was dead. The
2

2. **F.** NO CHANGE
   G. her
   H. its
   J. your

mechanic replaced Mark's battery, and <u>he</u> was happy.
3

3. **A.** NO CHANGE
   B. Mark
   C. it
   D. they

ANSWERS

1. "It" has no referent in the sentence. Therefore, it needs to be replaced with the noun "car."

   D is the correct choice.

2. The pronoun refers to the car, which is singular, and neuter.

   H is the correct choice.

3. Replace the pronoun with the noun "Mark". The referent "he" is vague and could also refer to the mechanic. The pronoun "it" would indicate that the car is happy, not Mark. The pronoun "they" is plural, not singular. Both the mechanic and Mark could be happy, but the verb "was" is singular.

   B is the correct choice.

PRACTICE

Correct the pronoun errors in these sentences:

1. Lisa and Jenn wanted to take her car.

2. Lisa went to get them.

3. Each car handles differently, depending on how it is pressed.

4. Paul's dog chased their tail.

5. The storms destroyed every house she hit.

Correct the case and number errors in these sentences. Some sentences do not have errors.

6. Whom was the coach of the team?

7. The javelins were kept in the case.

8. After the meeting everyone are going to Jan's house.

9. Send the winning times to we.

10. Them are a great relay team.

11. Did you ever meet him parents?

12. Whom lives closer to the stadium than you do?

13. Do your feet hurt after you finish the decathlon?

Correct the agreement errors in these sentences. Some sentences do not have errors.

14. The player waited for their turn at bat.

15. Either of the teams can win if they are consistent.

16. The bat was cracked near his handle.

17. She checked each bat for her cracks.

18. I am responsible; the responsibility is ours.

19. As the players got off the team bus, he called out to them.

20. The dogs ran out onto the field, and the players tried to chase it off.

21. He paid for children to get into the game because that's the kind of person he is.

22. The girls waited for the band to pass before she continued across the field.

23. Whoever of the six players hit the most home runs, they win the contest.

24. Her time was the best at the track meet.

25. Her was the best runner at the track meet.

(Answers on pages 92–94)

ACT-TYPE PROBLEMS

Look at the item that matches the number of the underlined part. Pick the best replacement for the underlined part. If the underlined part is the best, then select NO CHANGE.

One day, the circus came to town, and <u>he</u> set up
                                       1
a big tent at the fairgrounds. Many performers set up

equipment so <u>they</u> could practice their acts. Each person
             2

1. A. NO CHANGE
   B. it
   C. she
   D. the manager

2. F. NO CHANGE
   G. he or she
   H. it
   J. their

wanted to be sure <u>their</u> act was perfect for the big night.

3

Before the circus started, Mary and Sharon went to see

<u>her</u> favorite animal, the tiger. The girls also bet on

4

which one of the them would see the most clowns; <u>they</u>

5

would win an ice cream cone.

(Answers on page 94)

3. **A.** NO CHANGE
   B. his or her
   C. its
   D. your

4. **F.** NO CHANGE
   G. his
   H. its
   J. their

5. **A.** NO CHANGE
   B. their
   C. she
   D. it

Verbs

Every predicate contains a verb. The main verb is underlined in each predicate below.

SUBJECT	PREDICATE
The large, red dog	<u>ran</u> quickly down the path.
ACT scores	can <u>be</u> improved through study and practice.
Ed	<u>was</u> the English editor for this book.
He	<u>preferred</u> warm weather.

Verbs are the heart of a sentence. The main verb provides the action in a sentence, or the main verb links the subject to a word or words that describe the subject. So there are two types of main verbs — action verbs and linking verbs.

Action Verbs and Linking Verbs

The ACT will never ask you to identify a verb as an action verb or a linking verb. But it is very important to be able to spot these verbs in the passage.

Action verbs describe an action. That is, an action verb tells what the subject is doing. Look at these examples:

The dog <u>ran</u>.
The student <u>studies</u> every night.
The actress <u>strode</u> upon the stage.

Linking verbs connect the subject to its complement. That is, a linking verb links the subject to a word that describes the subject. The most common linking verbs include "am," "are," "is," "was," and "were." Verbs that may be linking verbs include "appear," "feel," "grow," "look," "smell," and "taste."

The dog <u>is</u> running.

The student <u>is</u> studying.

Christina <u>appears</u> tired.

I <u>feel</u> great.

Some words can be either action verbs or linking verbs, depending on the context.

ACTION	**LINKING**
The vine <u>grew</u> up the building.	He <u>grew</u> tired of the extra work.
<u>Smell</u> the burning leaves in the fall air.	The pies <u>smell</u> wonderful.

Singular Verbs and Plural Verbs

Most singular third-person verbs end in *s*. Most plural verbs do not. Look at these examples:

SINGULAR	**PLURAL**
runs	run
says	say
helps	help
thinks	think
passes	pass

Some singular verbs have special plural forms:

SINGULAR	**PLURAL**
am, is	are
was	were

 # MODEL ACT PROBLEM

This Model ACT Problem shows how this topic might be tested on the real ACT. The answer and explanation immediately follow the problem. Try the problem and then review the answer and the explanation.

The track star <u>run</u> very fast.
      1

1. **A.** NO CHANGE
   B. are running
   C. runs
   D. do run

*ANSWER*

1. The verb must be singular to agree with the noun "star." Notice that "runs" is a traditional third-person singular verb which ends in *s*.

   C is the correct choice.

Underline the main verb. Write A for action or L for linking, S for singular or P for plural.

Example

> The passenger <u>seems</u> tired.
>   L   S

1. Planes fly every day to my hometown.

2. The seats on some planes are very narrow.

3. Other planes carry only cargo.

4. Hear the roar of the jet engines.

5. Planes taxi very carefully near the passenger terminal.

6. I'll steer you to the waiting room.

7. The pilots steer north after takeoff.

8. Occasionally a plane is held at the gate for a passenger.

9. Hold onto the armrests during landing.

10. The air traffic controller in the tower radioed the pilot to hold fast.

11. The plane circled above the airport.

12. The passengers were waiting for the all-clear bell.

13. Upon arrival, the plane pulled up to the terminal at Gate B.

14. Passengers, please exit the jetway to your right.

15. The flight is over now.

(*Answers on pages 94–95*)

ACT-TYPE PROBLEMS

Look at the item that matches the number of the underlined part. Pick the best replacement for the underlined part. If the underlined part is the best, then select NO CHANGE.

The <u>concert tomorrow seem like</u> a good time.
        1

1. **A.** NO CHANGE
   B. concert tomorrow seems like
   C. concert tomorrow were seeming like
   D. concert tomorrow are seeming like

<u>Kevin and I plans to pick</u> you up at five. The
        2

2. **F.** NO CHANGE
   G. Kevin and I is planning to pick
   H. Kevin and I plan to pick
   J. Kevin and I was planning to pick

concert start at eight. First, <u>we are going out</u> to
   3   **4**

dinner. Then, <u>Al and Maureen is joining</u> us.
                     5

3. A. NO CHANGE
   B. concert are starting at
   C. concert starts at
   D. concert were starting at

4. F. NO CHANGE
   G. we goes out
   H. we is going out
   J. we was going out

5. A. NO CHANGE
   B. Al and Maureen was joining
   C. Al and Maureen joins
   D. Al and Maureen are joining

(Answers on page 95)

(Answers on page 95)

Verb Tense

The tense of a verb tells what time — past, present, or future — the verb refers to. The following explanations contain some special names for verbs, such as present participle, third-person singular, and past participle. The ACT will never test you on the names for verbs, but rather on whether or not you use verbs correctly.

Present Tense

Use the present tense of a verb to refer to something that is occurring now, that is generally true, or always occurs.

> <u>Drop</u> the car keys.
> The wind <u>is blowing</u> leaves against the windshield.
> Those trees <u>lose</u> their leaves in the fall.
> She <u>speaks</u> very loudly.

The present tense is the basic form of the verb. Present tense verbs include *is, are, run, sing, stand,* etc.

Third-Person Singular. The third-person singular is formed by adding *s* to the first-person form. Some third-person singular verbs have a special spelling.

Present Participle. The present participle also expresses present action. To form the present participle, add *-ing* to the present tense. Some present participles have special spelling. The present participle is always preceded by a helper verb such as *are, am, be,* and *is.*

Present Tense

FIRST- AND SECOND-PERSON AND PLURAL	THIRD-PERSON SINGULAR	PRESENT PARTICIPLE
stand	stands	standing
fix	fixes	fixing
save	saves	saving
run	runs	running

 **Examples**

Present:	You <u>stand</u> still.
Third-person singular:	Joan <u>stands</u> still
Present participle:	He <u>is standing</u> still.

Present:	You <u>fix</u> the tire.
Third-person singular:	She <u>fixes</u> the tire.
Present participle:	You <u>are fixing</u> the tire.

Present:	I <u>save</u> money when I use discount coupons.
Third-person singular:	Bob <u>saves</u> money when he uses discount coupons.
Present participle:	I <u>am saving</u> money when using discount coupons.

Present:	<u>Run</u> three laps around the track.
Third-person singular:	Aaron <u>runs</u> three laps around the track.
Present participle:	I <u>am running</u> three laps around the track.

Past Tense

Use the past tense of a verb to refer to something that has occurred in the past.

> You <u>dropped</u> the car keys.
> The wind <u>blew</u> leaves against the windshield.
> The trees <u>lost</u> their leaves in the fall.
> She <u>spoke</u> very loudly.

To form the past tense of <u>regular</u> verbs, add *d, t,* or *ed.* The past tenses of <u>irregular</u> verbs often have special forms.

Past Participle. You can use the past participle to express past action. For regular verbs, the past participle is the past tense form preceded by helper verbs such as *had, has,* and *have.* For irregular verbs, the past participle is the special past participle form preceded by helper verbs such as *had, has,* and *have.* A common error is to use the past participle form of an irregular verb without a helper verb ("We spoken to the dean").

Regular Verbs

PRESENT TENSE	PAST TENSE	PAST PARTICIPLE
face	faced	(had, has, have) faced
pose	posed	(had, has, have) posed
mean	meant	(had, has, have) meant
hoist	hoisted	(had, has, have) hoisted
rent	rented	(had, has, have) rented
drop	dropped	(had, has, have) dropped

Irregular Verbs

PRESENT TENSE	PAST TENSE	PAST PARTICIPLE
do	did	(had, has, have) done
know	knew	(had, has, have) known
speak	spoke	(had, has, have) spoken
fall	fell	(had, has, have) fallen
grow	grew	(had, has, have) grown

An extensive list of the principal parts of irregular verbs follows these examples.

Examples

Present: I <u>rent</u> the apartment for the summer.
Past: I <u>rented</u> the apartment for the summer.
Past participle: I <u>have rented</u> the apartment for the summer.

Present: I <u>do</u> my best in class.
Past: I <u>did</u> my best in class.
Past participle: I <u>have done</u> my best in class.
  [*Incorrect:* I <u>done</u> my best in class.]

Present: Alicia <u>knows</u> how to get downtown.
Past: Alicia <u>knew</u> how to get downtown.
Past participle: Alicia <u>had known</u> how to get downtown.
  [*Incorrect:* Alicia <u>known</u> how to get downtown.]

Here is a list of the present, past, and past participle forms of some irregular verbs. Remember! The past participle of a verb <u>must</u> be preceded by one of these helping verbs: *had, has,* or *have.*

Irregular Verbs

PRESENT TENSE	PAST TENSE	PAST PARTICIPLE (preceded by "had," "has," or "have")	PRESENT TENSE	PAST TENSE	PAST PARTICIPLE (preceded by "had," "has," or "have")
am, is, are	was, were	been	grow	grew	grown
become	became	become	know	knew	known
begin	began	begun	lay	laid	laid
blow	blew	blown	lie	lay	lain
break	broke	broken	raise	raised	raised
bring	brought	brought	ride	rode	ridden
catch	caught	caught	run	ran	run
choose	chose	chosen	see	saw	seen
come	came	come	speak	spoke	spoken
do	did	done	swim	swam	swum
drink	drank	drunk	take	took	taken
drive	drove	driven	teach	taught	taught
eat	ate	eaten	tear	tore	torn
fall	fell	fallen	throw	threw	thrown
freeze	froze	frozen	wear	wore	worn
give	gave	given	write	wrote	written
go	went	gone			

Future Tense

Use the future tense to refer to something that will occur in the future. To form the future tense, use the words *shall* or *will* before the present tense form of the verb.

> You <u>will drop</u> the car keys.
> The wind <u>will blow</u> leaves against the windshield.
> The trees <u>shall lose</u> their leaves in the fall.
> She <u>will speak</u> very loudly.

These Model ACT Problems show how this topic might be tested on the real ACT. The answers and explanations immediately follow the problems. Try the problems and then review the answers and the explanations.

Long ago, people <u>are believing</u> elves roamed the
                 1

1. **A.** NO CHANGE
   B. believe
   C. will believe
   D. believed

earth. However, today, most people <u>did not see</u> them.
                            2

2. **F.** NO CHANGE
   G. do not see
   H. will not see
   J. had not seen

But who knows? Maybe in the future we <u>will learn</u> to
                            3
believe again.

3. **A.** NO CHANGE
   B. learn
   C. are learning
   D. learned

 **ANSWERS**

1. The sentence starts "Long ago," setting the time and tense as past. Choices A and B are present tense; answer C is future tense.

   D is the correct choice.

2. The sentence is talking about today, now, which is present tense. Choice H is in future tense; choices F and J are in the past tense.

   G is the correct choice.

3. Choices B and C are present tense; choice D is past tense.

   A is the correct choice.

PRACTICE

Correct the tense errors. Some sentences are correct.

1. Eddie is sitting in a chair under a big tree.

2. Dawn begun to understand the reason why she needed to take the ACT.

3. Did you ran around the track yesterday?

4. I shall spoken to my mother about this year's vacation.

5. The dog swam across the pond every day.

6. Harry had driven two hours to reach the bookstore.

7. Fixing cars is not my idea of fun.

8. I will drive to the lake yesterday.

9. Tim thrown the ball out on the field for the players to use.

10. Joann will lost her bag if she leaves it in the store.

11. The cat was soaked if it stays out in the rain.

12. Tomorrow we will go to the beach.

13. I ride my bike to the park next week.

14. The dog will go to obedience school last year.

15. Lisa and Maddy drove to the zoo yesterday.

(Answers on pages 95–96)

ACT-TYPE PROBLEMS

Look at the item that matches the number of the underlined part. Pick the best replacement for the underlined part. If the underlined part is the best, then select NO CHANGE.

Last week, the mayor <u>decided</u> to close the park in
                    1

order to build a new office building. The people

1. **A.** NO CHANGE
   B. decides
   C. will decide
   D. decide

<u>will be</u> very upset when they heard about it. The people
2

2. **F.** NO CHANGE
   G. are
   H. was
   J. were

<u>meet</u> yesterday to discuss their options. Right now, they
3

3. **A.** NO CHANGE
   B. met
   C. will meet
   D. meets

<u>are talking</u> to the mayor about moving the mall to a
4

4. **F.** NO CHANGE
   G. talked
   H. will talk
   J. had talked

nearby vacant lot. If he won't agree, they <u>formed</u> a
                                  5

picket line in front of his office tomorrow.

5. **A.** NO CHANGE
   B. form
   C. will form
   D. had formed

(Answers on page 96)

Tense Shift

Verbs in a sentence should reflect time sequence. If events represented by the verbs occurred at the same time, the verbs should have the same tense. Look at these examples:

Correct: The rain <u>splattered</u> on the windshield as I <u>drove</u> to the store.
                   past   **past**

Correct: As I <u>dig</u> the hole I <u>throw</u> the dirt up onto a pile.
           present   **present**

Correct: I <u>will get</u> to the airport any way I can and then I <u>will board</u> the plane.
           future   **future**

Some tense shifts are acceptable. Mixing tenses is acceptable when the verbs represent events that happened at different times. Look at these examples:

Correct: Jean <u>will march</u> in the parade tomorrow so she <u>is</u> practicing now.
           future   **present**

> [Jean is practicing now (present tense) for something that will happen tomorrow (future tense).]

Correct: Ben <u>is</u> fixing the vase he <u>broke</u> last week.
           present   **past**

> [Ben is fixing something now (present tense) that broke last week (past tense).]

Correct: I <u>will always</u> love dogs because of the years I <u>spent</u> with my dog Nougat.
           future   **past**

> [Something will occur (future tense) because of something that has already happened (past tense).]

Avoid faulty tense shifts. A faulty shift between present tense and past tense is a common error. Look at these examples:

Incorrect: She <u>ran</u> home and <u>eat</u> dinner.
             past   **present**
> [It seems that this sentence describes something that happened in the past.]

Correct: She <u>ran</u> home and <u>ate</u> dinner.

Incorrect: Dave <u>saves</u> money for the game, and he <u>saved</u> money for souvenirs.
             present   **past**

> [These events both happened at the same time. It may be in the present, or it may be in the past.]

Correct: Dave <u>saves</u> money for the game, and he <u>saves</u> money for souvenirs.

           or

Dave <u>saved</u> money for the game, and he <u>saved</u> money for souvenirs.

Incorrect: Just as Pam <u>was</u> putting away her book bag, her dog <u>runs</u> past her.
                         past   **present**

> [These events both happened at the same time. It may be in the present, or it may be in the past.]

Correct: Just as Pam <u>was</u> putting away her book bag, her dog <u>ran</u> past her.

   or

   Just as Pam <u>is</u> putting away her book bag, her dog <u>runs</u> past her.

 # MODEL ⒶⒸⓉ PROBLEMS ─────────

These Model ACT Problems show how this topic might be tested on the real ACT. The answers and explanations immediately follow the problems. Try the problems and then review the answers and the explanations.

Last year, Will <u>did extra jobs and saves</u> the money.
    1

Now, <u>he is buying a car and planned</u> a trip. Since he
     2

<u>made enough money last year, he will take</u> his brother
     3
with him when he goes.

1. **A.** NO CHANGE
   B. did extra jobs and saving
   C. did extra jobs and saved
   D. does extra jobs and will save

2. **F.** NO CHANGE
   G. he is buying a car and planning
   H. he bought a car and planning
   J. he bought a car and will plan

3. **A.** NO CHANGE
   B. makes enough money last year, he will take
   C. made enough money last year, he had taken
   D. will make enough money last year, he will take

✔**ANSWERS**

1. Both things, working and saving, happened "last year," so the verb should be in the past tense.

   C is the correct choice.

2. Both of these events are happening *now.* Therefore, both should be in the present tense.

   G is the correct choice.

3. No change is necessary. An event that happened in the past, saving money, is allowing him to take his brother with him in the future, on the trip. Therefore, "made enough money" is past tense, and "he will take" is future tense.

   A is the correct choice.

**PRACTICE** ────────────────

Correct the tense shifts. Some sentences are correct.

1. I liked to make money, so I play the stock market.

2. Michael wanted to be a great basketball player, so he practices every day.

3. Ava runs ten miles a day because she will run in a marathon next month.

4. Stephen will load his car because he left for a long trip.

5. Art raised his hand because he wants to answer the question.

6. It was amazing to see that the dog barked as he jumps over the couch.

7. Kit-cat rolls over and then purred very softly.

8. Jim headed out the door as he calls out a good-bye to his friends.

9. I already went to the store, but I am going there again.

10. The guard lowers the drawbridge as the knight rode up to the gate.

11. At the carnival, Susie rode the Ferris wheel, and Bill is playing arcade games.

12. Tomorrow I will start football practice, and my sister was starting soccer practice.

13. I broke my leg two weeks ago, and the cast will come off next month.

14. Judy ran out into the street after her ball, and the car stops quickly.

15. After school I will go to band practice, and then I will stop at the store on my way home.

(Answers on pages 96–98)

ACT-TYPE PROBLEMS

Look at the item that matches the number of the underlined part. Pick the best replacement for the underlined part. If the underlined part is the best, then select NO CHANGE.

Last week, I begin to prepare for the first day of
     1

1. **A.** NO CHANGE
   B. Last week, I will begin to
   C. Last week, I began to
   D. Last week, I am beginning to

school. To begin, I will go shopping for school clothes.
     2

2. **F.** NO CHANGE
   G. To begin, I went shopping
   H. To begin, I am going shopping
   J. To begin, I will shop

Then, a couple of days ago, I bought my notebooks and
     3

3. **A.** NO CHANGE
   B. days ago, I will buy my
   C. days ago, I buy my
   D. days ago, I am buying my

folders. Right now, I will be picking out my outfit for
     4

4. **F.** NO CHANGE
   G. Right now, I am picking
   H. Right now, I picked
   J. Right now, I was picking

the first day. Tomorrow morning, I was getting up at six
     5
and caught the bus at seven.
     5

5. **A.** NO CHANGE
   B. Tomorrow morning, I was getting up at six and will catch the bus
   C. Tomorrow morning, I will get up at six and caught the bus
   D. Tomorrow morning, I will get up at six and will catch the bus

(Answers on page 98)

Subject-Verb Agreement

You have already read about singular and plural nouns, pronouns, and verbs. All this leads up to subject-verb agreement, a topic frequently tested on the ACT.

The subject and verb of a sentence must agree in number. Singular subjects take singular verbs. Plural subjects take plural verbs.

Examples

Singular: Lisa wants to go to the library after school.
Plural: Lisa and Terri want to go to the library after school.

Singular: The practice test helps me prepare for the ACT.
Plural: The practice tests help me prepare for the ACT.

Singular: The club meets every Saturday afternoon.
Plural: The club members meet every Saturday afternoon.

Some examples of incorrect and corrected subject-verb agreement are given below:

Incorrect: Chad want to get to the soccer game on time.
Corrected: Chad wants to get to the soccer game on time
          [The singular noun "Chad" takes the singular verb "wants."]

Incorrect: The players wants to do their best in the game.
Corrected: The players want to do their best in the game.
          [The plural noun "players" takes the plural verb "want."]

Incorrect: Bob and Liz referees the game.
Corrected: Bob and Liz referee the game.
          [The plural subject "Bob and Liz" takes the plural verb "referee."]

Incorrect: Everyone are at the door.
Corrected: Everyone is at the door.
          [The singular subject "Everyone" takes the singular verb "is." Indefinite pronouns such as "everyone" and "someone" are always singular.]

Locate the Subject and Verb

The subject and verb may come anywhere in a sentence. Say the subject and verb to yourself. If it sounds right, it probably is right.

 **Examples**

Find the subject and verb.

The ACT Practice Test, which Liz took on Saturday, prepared her for the actual test.

The verb is "prepared." But what is the subject?
"Saturday" comes just before "prepared." Say "Saturday prepared her." That's not right. Saturday did not prepare her for the actual test. Try "Practice Test." Say "Practice Test prepared her." That's correct. The Practice Test prepared her for the actual test. "Practice Test" is the subject.

The person with the highest test scores wins an award.

Say "test score wins an award." That's not correct. Test scores don't win awards. Say "person wins an award." That makes sense. The person wins the award. "Person" is the subject, and "wins" is the verb.

What is your name?

Say "Your name is what?" "Name" is the subject, and "is" is the verb.

Through the looking glass of life gazes the thoughtful mind.

Say "Mind gazes." "Mind" is the subject, and "gazes" is the verb.

 MODEL ACT PROBLEMS

These Model ACT Problems show how this topic might be tested on the real ACT. The answers and explanations immediately follow the problems. Try the problems and then review the answers and the explanations.

Those are the horses Jan <u>are riding</u> this summer at
                                  1

1. **A.** NO CHANGE
  B. is riding
  C. were riding
  D. are ridden

camp. Jan and her friends <u>rides</u> every day.
                               2

2. **F.** NO CHANGE
  G. is riding
  H. ride
  J. was riding

**ANSWERS**

1. The subject of the sentence is not "horses." Say "the horses are riding;" that doesn't make sense. But "Jan is riding the horses" does. Since Jan is singular, the verb must also be singular.

   B is the correct choice.

2. The subject of the sentence, "Jan and her friends," is plural. Therefore, the verb must also be plural.

   H is the correct choice.

PRACTICE

Correct any subject-verb agreement errors. Some sentences may be correct.

1. Everyone, including Renee and Louise, climb the mountain this morning.

2. Who do you think she were?

3. Over the crest of the ridge ride the lone horseman.

4. Robert and Ryan skis as often as they can.

5. The tickets Renee bought gives her a reason for going out on Saturday night.

6. The class arrange a trip to the science center.

7. A pair of sneakers are all that reminds her of her basketball career.

8. The fastest times for the 220-yard and 440-yard runs are posted on the wall.

9. The 23 members of the soccer team practices each day at 4:00 P.M.

10. Each person who climbs the hundred steps mention the beautiful view.

11. James and Karen both like to dance, but they dances to different music.

12. The stable were full of horses waiting for lunch.

13. Everyone on the team were ready to play.

14. Andrew and Marcus were ready to go, but Karen was late.

15. Each person is allowed five minutes to speak.

(*Answers on pages 98–99*)

Look at the item that matches the number of the underlined part. Pick the best replacement for the underlined part. If the underlined part is the best, then select NO CHANGE.

<u>Chuck and Ann is trying</u> to go to Atlanta. While
       1

1. **A.** NO CHANGE
   B. Chuck and Ann are trying
   C. Chuck and Ann was trying
   D. Chuck and Ann has tried

packing, <u>each of them lose something</u> important, such as
         2
car keys and tickets. By the time they get to the airport,

2. **F.** NO CHANGE
   G. each of them are losing something
   H. each of them loses something
   J. each of them losed something

<u>they are running</u>. Just as the gate is closing,
  3

3. **A.** NO CHANGE
   B. they is running
   C. they was running
   D. they has been running

<u>Chuck and Ann both makes the flight</u>. As they are
       4

4. **F.** NO CHANGE
   G. Chuck and Ann both is making the flight
   H. Chuck and Ann both make the flight
   J. Chuck and Ann both make his flight

sitting down, the pilot announces <u>the flight are delayed</u>
                5
<u>an hour</u> due to bad weather.
  5

5. **A.** NO CHANGE
   B. the flight were delayed an hour
   C. the flight are delay an hour
   D. the flight is delayed an hour

(Answers on page 99)

Parallel Form

Parallel form places sentence elements in the same or similar form to emphasize the equal importance of the elements. These sentences are in parallel forms:

> I like <u>to drive</u> my car and <u>to ride</u> my bike.
> I like <u>driving</u> my car and <u>riding</u> my bike.

There are several specific instances when you should use parallel form.

Phrases and Clauses Linked by a Coordinating Conjunction

Use parallel form when phrases or clauses in a sentence are linked by coordinating conjunctions. The coordinating conjunctions include "and," "but," "nor," "or," and "yet." Look at these examples:

Not parallel: Shopping means taking a walk in a mall and finding bargains.
Parallel: Shopping means walking in a mall and finding bargains.

Not parallel:	The teacher always threatens a detention yet does not ever give a detention.
Parallel:	The teacher always threatens a detention yet never gives a detention.

Not parallel:	Have you decided if you are skiing or going skating?
Parallel:	Have you decided if you are going skiing or going skating?

Phrases and Clauses Linked by Conjunctive Pairs

Use parallel form when the phrases and clauses in a sentence are linked by conjunctive pairs. The conjunctive pairs include "either . . . or," "neither . . . nor," and "not only . . . but also."

Not parallel:	Neither local streets nor a trip on the highway seemed the best way to get home.
Parallel:	Neither local streets nor the highway seemed the best way to get home.

Not parallel:	She was not only an A student, but also someone who was very responsible.
Parallel:	She was not only an A student, but also a very responsible person.

Sentence Elements Compared; Parts of a List

Not parallel:	Gail would rather be a waitress in Colorado than to practice law in a big city.
Parallel:	Gail would rather be a waitress in Colorado than a lawyer in a big city.

Not parallel:	The dog preferred to eat the liver snaps than eating the beef snaps.
Parallel:	The dog preferred the liver snaps to the beef snaps.

Not parallel:	The mathematics test included arithmetic, algebra, and the study of geometry.
Parallel:	The mathematics test included arithmetic, algebra, and geometry.

Do **not** use parallel form when one of the clauses or phrases is subordinated. "Subordinated" means that a sentence element is of lesser importance than another sentence element. The absence of parallel form emphasizes that one sentence element is subordinated to another sentence element.

The words "although," "because," "if . . . then," "when," "where," "while," "which," "that," and "who" signal subordinate sentence elements.

Examples

Subordinate:	I need to go to sleep <u>because</u> I stayed up late last night studying.
	[The conjunction "because" signals that "I stayed up late last night studying" is less important than "I need to go to sleep." Notice that these two clauses are not in parallel form.]

Subordinate: I was studying <u>when</u> my favorite show was on television.
[The conjunction "when" subordinates "my favorite show" to "studying."]

Subordinate: My favorite character on the show is the one <u>who</u> drives the bus.
[The pronoun "who" subordinates "one who drives the bus" to "My favorite character."]

MODEL ACT PROBLEMS

These Model ACT Problems show how this topic might be tested on the real ACT. The answers and explanations immediately follow the problems. Try the problems and then review the answers and the explanations.

I like <u>riding horses and to hike</u> in the mountains.
                    1

I enjoy being outdoors <u>not only when it is sunny, but</u>
                                   2

<u>also in the rain or snow.</u> My favorite <u>place to go is</u>
       2   3

the mountains, <u>although I also spend a lot of time</u>
                          3

on the beach.

1. A. NO CHANGE
   B. riding horses and hiking
   C. riding horses and to go on hikes
   D. to ride horses and hiking

2. F. NO CHANGE
   G. not only when it is sunny, but also when raining or snowing
   H. not only when it is sunny, but also when it is rainy or snowy
   J. not only in the sun, but also when it is raining or snowing

3. A. NO CHANGE
   B. place to go is the mountains, although also to spend a lot of time
   C. place is the mountains, although also spending a lot of time
   D. place to go is the mountains, although also spending a lot of time

**ANSWERS**

1. The verbs must be in parallel form—"riding" and "hiking." Choice C is not parallel, because the verbs are "riding" and "to go." Choice D just reverses the order in the original sentence—"to ride" and "hiking" rather than "riding" and "to hike."

B is the correct choice.

2. The phrase "not only...but also" indicate coordinated elements and the need for parallel construction. Therefore, "it is sunny" must be parallel to "it is rainy or snowy." Neither choice G nor H is in parallel form.

H is the correct choice.

3. No change is necessary. The word "although" sets up the second phrase, "I also spend...," as subordinate to the phrase "My favorite place...." Therefore, the phrases do not need to be parallel.

A is the correct choice.

PRACTICE

Correct any parallel-form errors. Some sentences have no errors.

1. I like to dive and to go swimming when I am at the lake.

2. Motorboats, canoes, and sailboats are my favorite forms of water transportation.

3. Neither the weather nor the condition of the roads will delay his trip.

4. Jim was trying to decide whether to be a newsman or someone who reports the weather.

5. Because I expect the evening news to be interesting, I turn off boring reports.

6. The clouds are threatening, yet it seems unlikely that a rainy day will follow.

7. The day was bright; the weather was cold and crisp.

8. Although they were tired, the small band of travelers pressed on into the night.

9. The barn which is old stood bravely against the wind, but the new house collapsed.

10. His rugged appearance hid the more caring side of his personality.

11. On his trip, Mark was biking in Seattle and then to visit relatives in Idaho.

12. Matt's favorite summer activities are jet-skiing, fishing, and to swim.

13. At the grocery store, Chuck bought tomatoes, grapes, and eggs.

14. On rainy afternoons I often read a good book, but on sunny days I play outdoors.

15. Al runs to the store and then he is driving to the beach.

(Answers on page 100)

ACT-TYPE PROBLEMS

Look at the item that matches the number of the underlined part. Pick the best replacement for the underlined part. If the underlined part is the best, then select NO CHANGE.

Debbie works in an office <u>typing letters, answering phones and she files documents.</u> Each morning

1. A. NO CHANGE
   B. typing letters, answering phones and to file documents.
   C. typing letters, answering phones, and filing documents.
   D. typing letters, to answer phones and file documents.

she <u>walks to the corner and takes the bus</u> downtown.

2. F. NO CHANGE
   G. walks to the corner and to take the bus
   H. is walking to the corner and takes the bus
   J. walks to the corner and is taking the bus

80   English

In the evenings, Debbie likes <u>to cook dinner for her</u>
₃

<u>children and walking the dog.</u> <u>Debbie lives a normal</u>
₃   ₄

<u>life, although she is blind</u>. Debbie achieved her
₄

independence through a <u>program that creates, sustains</u>
₅

<u>and is improving job opportunities</u> for people who
₅

are blind.

3. **A** NO CHANGE
   B. to cook dinner for her children and walks the dog.
   C. cooking dinner for her children and to walk the dog.
   D. cooking dinner for her children and walking the dog.

4. **F.** NO CHANGE
   G. Debbie is living a normal life, although she was blind
   H. Debbie lived a normal life, although she is blind
   J. Debbie is living a normal life, although she is blinding

5. **A.** NO CHANGE
   B. program that creates, sustains, and improves job opportunities
   C. program that is creating, sustaining and improves job opportunities
   D. program that is creating, sustains and improves job opportunities

(Answers on page 101)

Adjectives and Adverbs

Adjectives

Adjectives are used to modify nouns and pronouns. Adjectives add detail and describe nouns and pronouns in more detail and more depth. An adjective may modify a noun or pronoun directly, or be linked to the noun or pronoun by a linking verb.

 **Examples**

DIRECT MODIFIER	LINKING VERB
This is a <u>helpful</u> ACT book.	This ACT book <u>is helpful.</u>
Soccer is a <u>popular</u> game.	The game of soccer <u>is popular.</u>
They are <u>beautiful</u> animals.	The animals <u>are beautiful.</u>

Adverbs

Adverbs modify verbs, adjectives, and other adverbs. An adverb may also modify a phrase, a clause, or a sentence. Adverbs are often formed by annexing *-ly* to an adjective. However, not all adverbs end in *-ly* ("long," "fast," etc.), and some adjectives do end in *-ly* ("lively," "friendly," etc.).

Modify verbs:	The hikers stepped <u>carefully.</u>
	The swimmers stepped <u>gingerly.</u>
Modify adjectives:	It was an <u>exceptionally</u> sunny day.
	It was a <u>very</u> dark night.
Modify adverbs:	The diver <u>very</u> quickly used two air tanks.
	The parachutist will jump <u>fairly</u> soon.
Modify phrases:	The driver arrived <u>just</u> in time.
clauses:	The sun set; <u>unfortunately,</u> the rain did not follow.
sentences:	<u>Regrettably,</u> the teacher is absent today.

Common Adjective and Adverb Errors to Avoid

Do not use an adjective in place of an adverb.

Incorrect: John traveled the course slow.
[The adjective "slow" is used instead of the adverb "slowly."]

Corrected: John traveled the course slowly.

Incorrect: Chris walked up the path quick.
[The adjective "quick" is used instead of the adverb "quickly."]

Corrected: Chris walked up the path quickly.

Do not confuse the adjectives "real" and "sure" with the adverbs "really" and "surely."

Incorrect: Erin sang real well.
[The adjective "real" is used instead of the adverb "really."]

Corrected: Erin sang really well.
[The adverb "really" modifies the adjective "well."]

Incorrect: Ryan was sure playing less than his best.
[The adjective "sure" is used instead of the adverb "surely."]

Corrected: Ryan was surely playing less than his best.
[The adverb "surely" modifies the verb "playing."]

Do not confuse the adjectives "bad" and "good" with the adverbs "badly" and "well."

Incorrect: Bob wanted to perform the dance good.
[The adjective "good" is used instead of the adverb "well."]

Corrected: Bob wanted to perform the dance well.

Incorrect: Liz cooked bad.
[The adjective "bad" is used instead of the adverb "badly."]

Corrected: Liz cooked badly.

MODEL ACT PROBLEMS

These Model ACT Problems show how this topic might be tested on the real ACT. The answers and explanations immediately follow the problems. Try the problems and then review the answers and the explanations.

Every morning, Angie <u>wakes up early</u>. She puts on
           1

her robe and <u>slips downstairs quiet</u>. Then Angie
        2

<u>runs outside real quickly</u> to get the paper. Finally, she
    3

goes into the kitchen and searches the paper for a

<u>job she can do good</u>.
 4

1. **A.** NO CHANGE
 B. wakes up real early
 C. wakes up earl
 D. wakes up soon

2. **F.** NO CHANGE
 G. slips downstairs quietly
 H. slips downstairs real quiet
 J. slip downstairs quietly

3. **A.** NO CHANGE
 B. run outside real quickly
 C. runs outside real quick
 D. runs outside really quickly

4. **F.** NO CHANGE
 G. job she can do well
 H. job she can do goodly
 J. job she can do real good

✔ *ANSWERS*

1. No change is necessary. Choice B is incorrect because the modifier "real" should be "really." Choice C would only be correct if "earl" were a capitalized proper noun.
 A is the correct choice.

2. *Quietly* is the adverb, while *quiet* is the adjective. Answer J is incorrect because the plural verb, "slip," does not agree with the singular subject, "she."
 G is the correct choice.

3. Both "real" and "quick" must be in adverb form—"really quickly."
 D is the correct choice.

4. *Well* is the correct adverb form of *good,* and modifies the verb "do."
 G is the correct choice.

PRACTICE

Correct the adjective and adverb errors. Some sentences contain no errors.

1. Now, this is smoothly ice cream.

2. If you want my opinion, that yogurt is real great.

3. I think that Chris behaved very good today.

4. Unfortunate, the opera singer has a sore throat.

5. But the understudy gave a truly exceptional performance.

6. The commentator conveniently forgot what she had said the previous night.

7. Well, that's an extreme easy thing for you to say.

8. That seems like a needless error, particularly since acting more careful would solve the problem.

9. I have my doubts about the company, but they made me a really large salary offer.

10. The motor behaved bad, so the trip did not go good.

11. Ray is a very slowly learner when it comes to computers.

12. The floors of my house creak, so I try to walk soft when I know Mom is sleeping.

13. Martin ran rapidly through the field to catch the quick, blue butterfly.

14. Since Fred was a well speaker, the class did not go as bad as I had feared.

15. The long freight train pulled slowly out of the station.

(Answers on pages 101–102)

ACT-TYPE PROBLEMS

Look at the item that matches the number of the underlined part. Pick the best replacement for the underlined part. If the underlined part is the best, then select NO CHANGE.

Yesterday, our boat <u>was smooth sailing across</u> the
                              1
lake, when the sky darkened. The wind picked up,

1. A. NO CHANGE
   B. was smooth sailingly across
   C. were smoothly sailing
   D. was smoothly sailing

and we <u>thought our boat would surely be capsized</u>.
                    2

2. F. NO CHANGE
   G. thought our boat would sure be capsized
   H. thought our boat will surely be capsized
   J. thought our boat will sure be capsized

<u>Quick turning for home</u>, we tried to outrun the storm.
        3

3. A. NO CHANGE
   B. Quickly turning for home
   C. Quick turningly for home
   D. Quickly turningly for home

Then, <u>just as sudden as it had started</u>, the storm abated.
                4

4. F. NO CHANGE
   G. justly as sudden as it had started
   H. just as sudden as it will started
   J. just as suddenly as it had started

We decided <u>not to test our well luck</u>, however, and
                    5
called it a day.

5. A. NO CHANGE
   B. not to test our goodly luck
   C. to not test our well luck
   D. not to test our good luck

(Answers on page 102)

Comparative and Superlative Adjectives and Adverbs

Adjectives and adverbs can show comparisons. Use the **comparative form** to compare two items. Use the **superlative form** to compare more than two items.

Comparative Form (Two Items)

The ending *-er* and the words "more" and "less" signal the comparative form. The comparative form includes words and phrases such as "warmer," "colder," "safer," "higher," "less industrious," and "more creative."

INCORRECT	CORRECT
Fran is <u>least</u> creative than Liz.	Fran is <u>less</u> creative than Liz.
Alaska is <u>cold</u> than Florida.	Alaska is <u>colder</u> than Florida.
Ben is <u>proudest</u> than Warren.	Ben is <u>prouder</u> than Warren.
Ray is <u>most happy</u> than Jim.	Ray is <u>happier</u> than Jim.
Ann is <u>most</u> capable than Amelia.	Ann is <u>more</u> capable than Amelia.

Superlative Form (More Than Two Items)

If you can't tell how many items there are, use the superlative form. The ending *-est* and the words "most" and "least" signal the superlative form. The superlative form includes words and phrases such as "happiest," "youngest," "oldest," "highest," "least tired," and "most interesting."

INCORRECT	CORRECT
Ann has the <u>more</u> experience of any pilot flying to Europe.	Ann has the <u>most</u> experience of any pilot flying to Europe.
Julia was the <u>younger</u> student to enter the creative writing contest.	Julia was the <u>youngest</u> student to enter the creative writing contest.
Nathan was the <u>more</u> energetic student in kindergarten.	Nathan was the <u>most</u> energetic student in kindergarten.
Andy received the <u>higher</u> score on the law exam.	Andy received the <u>highest</u> score on the law exam.

MODEL ACT PROBLEMS

These Model ACT Problems show how this topic might be tested on the real ACT. The answers and explanations immediately follow the problems. Try the problems and then review the answers and the explanations.

Although <u>Anne is older than Michael</u>, she is
　　　　　　　　　　1

1. A. NO CHANGE
　　B. Anne is oldest than Michael
　　C. Anne is more oldest than Michael
　　D. Anne is more older than Michael

<u>not the older in the class</u>.
　2

2. F. NO CHANGE
　　G. not the more older in the class
　　H. not the oldest in the class
　　J. not the most older in the class

✔ANSWERS

1. Choices B and C use the superlative *oldest* not the comparative *older.* Choice D is redundant; the word *more* is not needed.

   A is the correct choice.

2. The sentence is comparing more than two items—Anne to Michael and to the entire class—so use the superlative. Answers G and J are incorrect because they use the comparative form.

   H is the correct choice.

◀PRACTICE▶

Circle the number of each sentence that correctly shows the comparison. Correct the sentences that do not correctly show the comparison.

1. Chad was the happier player on the soccer team.

2. Members of the winning team were happier than members of the losing team.

3. Pat was the faster player on the baseball team.

4. The cheetah is the fastest predator in Africa.

5. The taller of the five basketball players was on the bench.

6. She took the lightest of the two grocery bags to the car.

7. Lonnie was among the more creative students in the school.

8. Ron is the least able of the two drivers.

9. His shoe size is the smallest in his class.

10. She was the more capable of the two referees.

11. Cardinals are prettiest than blue jays.

12. Rick is the smaller of the two wrestlers who made the finals.

13. Douglas went to the animal shelter and chose the cuter puppy of them all.

14. Tomorrow will be cloudier than today, but sunnier than yesterday.

15. Sometimes I think I'm the luckier person on earth.

(Answers on pages 102–103)

ACT-TYPE PROBLEMS

Look at the item that matches the number of the underlined part. Pick the best replacement for the underlined part. If the underlined part is the best, then select NO CHANGE.

This year's Halloween party was the better ever.
1

1. A. NO CHANGE
   B. party was the best ever
   C. party was the more good ever
   D. party was the most good ever

The costumes were scariest than last year's. I thought the
2

2. F. NO CHANGE
   G. were more scariest than last
   H. were most scary than last
   J. were scarier than last

decorations were the most colorful so far. The food
3

3. A. NO CHANGE
   B. decorations were the more colorful
   C. decorations were the more color
   D. decorations were the colorest

was even most delicious than I hoped. Plus, everyone
4

4. F. NO CHANGE
   G. even deliciousest
   H. even more delicious
   J. even most deliciouser

said my costume this year was better than Sheryl's
5
costume two years ago.

5. A. NO CHANGE
   B. costume this year was best than Sheryl's
   C. costume this year was most best than Sheryl's
   D. costume this year was more gooder than Sheryl's

(Answers on page 103)

Idioms

Idioms do not follow the rules of standard English usage, but idioms effectively convey a complete thought. Incorrect idioms on the ACT usually use the incorrect preposition. On the following page are examples of incorrect and correct idioms.

INCORRECT	CORRECT
angry <u>in</u> him	angry **with** him
detached <u>to</u> my parents	detached **from** my parents
differ <u>from</u> your view	differ **with** your view
differ <u>with</u> your appearance	differ **from** your appearance
in accordance <u>to</u> the rules	in accordance **with** the rules
independent <u>from</u> your effort	independent **of** your effort
just about the same <u>with</u>	just about the same **as**
occupied <u>with</u> my tenant	occupied **by** my tenant
occupied <u>by</u> my stamp collection	occupied **with** my stamp collection
prior <u>from</u> your visit	prior **to** your visit
wait <u>to</u> the airport	wait **at** the airport
wait <u>on</u> the plane	wait **for** the plane

 # MODEL ACT PROBLEM

This Model ACT Problem shows how this topic might be tested on the real ACT. The answer and explanation immediately follow the problem. Try the problem and then review the answer and the explanation.

Someone cut in front of me as <u>I was standing by</u>
                                           1

the line for tickets.
1

1. **A.** NO CHANGE
   B. I was standing at the line
   C. I was standing in line
   D. I was standing to the line

✔ *ANSWER*

1. The correct idiomatic expression is "standing *in* line."
   C is the correct choice.

 # PRACTICE

Correct the idiom errors. Some sentences have no errors.

1. Whatever we accomplished was independent with her work.

2. I could spend endless days occupied with my books.

3. Notice how much the two men differ with each other in their speech patterns.

4. How much longer do you expect me to wait to the airport?

5. That person has just about the same appearance from you.

6. Although I expected to be free this afternoon, my time was occupied from my friend all day.

7. My opinion on that matter differs greatly from yours.

8. Our trip was delayed because we were waiting on Fred, who was late.

9. Carl is often occupied by his experiments.

10. Although she used to depend on him, Karen has broken with Chris.

(Answers on pages 103–104)

ACT-TYPE PROBLEMS

Look at the item that matches the number of the underlined part. Pick the best replacement for the underlined part. If the underlined part is the best, then select NO CHANGE.

<u>Prior from Mark's visit</u> home, we got along well.
1

1. **A.** NO CHANGE
   B. Prior at Mark's visit
   C. Prior to Mark's visit
   D. Prior of Mark's visit

However, he now seems to be <u>very angry with me</u>.
2
I don't know if something happened then, or if the

2. **F.** NO CHANGE
   G. very angry to me
   H. very angry from me
   J. very angry in me

<u>cause is independent from the trip</u> itself.
3

3. **A.** NO CHANGE
   B. cause is independent to the trip
   C. cause is independent at the trip
   D. cause is independent of the trip

(Answers on page 104)

Grammar and Usage Subtest

This Subtest has the type of grammar and usage items found on the ACT. These items make up part of the Usage and Mechanics (UM) subscore on the ACT. If you don't know an answer, eliminate and guess. Circle the number of any guessed answer. Check page 104 for answers and explanations.

INSTRUCTIONS: Each sentence is numbered in the passage that follows. There is a corresponding item for each numbered sentence. Each item offers three suggestions for changing the sentence to conform to standard written English, or to make it understandable or consistent with the rest of the passage. If the numbered sentence is not improved by one of the three suggested changes, mark NO CHANGE.

Choose the best answer for each question based on the passage. Then fill in the appropriate circle on the answer grid.

1 Ⓐ Ⓑ Ⓒ Ⓓ	5 Ⓐ Ⓑ Ⓒ Ⓓ	9 Ⓐ Ⓑ Ⓒ Ⓓ
2 Ⓕ Ⓖ Ⓗ Ⓙ	6 Ⓐ Ⓑ Ⓒ Ⓓ	10 Ⓐ Ⓑ Ⓒ Ⓓ
3 Ⓐ Ⓑ Ⓒ Ⓓ	7 Ⓕ Ⓖ Ⓗ Ⓙ	11 Ⓕ Ⓖ Ⓗ Ⓙ
4 Ⓐ Ⓑ Ⓒ Ⓓ	8 Ⓕ Ⓖ Ⓗ Ⓙ	12 Ⓕ Ⓖ Ⓗ Ⓙ

[1] All of the animal in the zoo are active today.

1. **A.** NO CHANGE
   B. All of the animals in the zoo are active today.
   C. All of the animals in the zoo were active today.
   D. All of the animal in the zoo were active today.

[2] Some are swimming, some are playing, and some

2. **F.** NO CHANGE
   G. Some are swimming, some play, and some climb the rocks in their pens.
   H. Some are swimming, some are playing, and some are climbing the rocks in the pens.
   J. Some swim, some are playing, and some are climbing the rocks in their pens.

climb the rocks in their pens. [3] Karen and Jim always

3. **A.** NO CHANGE
   B. Karen and Jim always stop in the monkey house when she can.
   C. Karen and Jim always stop in the monkey house when they can.
   D. Karen and Jim always stop in the monkey house when you can.

stop in the monkey house when he can. [4] Karen likes

4. **F.** NO CHANGE
   G. Karen likes them more best than the lions.
   H. Karen likes them better than the lions.
   J. Karen likes them most good than the lions.

them best than the lions. [5] Jim thinks the monkeys are

the more human of all the animals. [6] He especially

likes the largely ape in the corner cage. [7] Inside, the

chimps are running quick back and forth. [8] Each one

is waiting for something. [9] Right now, it seems they

are waiting on lunch. [10] The zookeeper should be in
soon and he was bringing food for all the animals.

[11] After they are fed, the animals will relax and rest.

[12] When he is sleeping, the animals are not as
interesting.

(*Answers on page 104*)

5. **A.** NO CHANGE
   B. Jim thinks the monkeys are the more humaner
   of all the animals.
   C. Jim think the monkeys are the most humanest of
   all the animals.
   D. Jim thinks the monkeys are the most human of
   all the animals.

6. **F.** NO CHANGE
   G. He especially likes the large ape in the corner
   cage.
   H. He especially like the largely ape in the corner
   cage.
   J. He especially like the bigger ape in the corner
   cage

7. **A.** NO CHANGE
   B. Inside, the chimps is running quick back and
   forth.
   C. Inside, the chimps is running quickly back and
   forth.
   D. Inside, the chimps are running quickly back and
   forth.

8. **F.** NO CHANGE
   G. Each one were waiting for something.
   H. Each one are waiting for something.
   J. Each one are waiting on something.

9. **A.** NO CHANGE
   B. Right now, it seems they is waiting on lunch.
   C. Right now, it seems they was waiting on lunch.
   D. Right now, it seems they are waiting for lunch.

10. **F.** NO CHANGE
    G. The zookeeper should be in soon and he were
    bringing food for all the animals.
    H. The zookeeper should be in soon and he will
    bring food for all the animals.
    J. The zookeeper should be in soon and he will
    bring food for all the animal.

11. **A.** NO CHANGE
    B. After they is fed, the animals will relax and
    rest.
    C. After their fed, the animals relaxed and rested.
    D. After they is fed, the animals relaxed and
    rested.

12. **F.** NO CHANGE
    G. When they are sleeping, the animals are not as
    interesting.
    H. When he is sleeping, the animals is not as
    interesting.
    J. When they is sleeping, the animals is not as
    interesting.

1. tree	**trees**	9. tooth	**teeth**
2. echo	**echoes**	10. calf	**calves**
3. leaf	**leaves**	11. goose	**geese**
4. cry	**cries**	12. game	**games**
5. church	**churches**	13. boy	**boys**
6. lady	**ladies**	14. couch	**couches**
7. hippopotamus	**hippopotami**	15. party	**parties**
8. deer	**deer**		

✔ ANSWERS (page 57)

1. The word "All" tells us that there is more than one house. Therefore, the word must be plural. Unlike *mouse*, which has the special plural form *mice, house* follows the standard rules for forming plurals. An *s* is added to the end (and a sounded syllable is added when the singular ends with a sibilant).

C is the correct choice.

2. No change is needed. The word "door" should be singular because the sentence refers to each, *one*, door. Therefore, the other three answers, which are variations of plural words, are wrong choices. (The correctly spelled plural is *doors.*)

F is the correct choice.

✔ ANSWERS (pages 60–61)

The first line of each answer shows the original practice sentence.

1. Lisa and Jenn wanted to take her car.
   Lisa and Jenn wanted to take **Jenn's** car.

   or

   Lisa and Jenn wanted to take **their** car.

   or

   Lisa and Jenn wanted to take **Lisa's** car.

2. Lisa went to get them.
   Lisa went to get **the keys.**
   [Other nouns that make sense in this context could be used in place of "the keys."]

3. Each car handles differently, depending on how it is pressed.
   Each car handles differently, depending on how **the gas pedal** is pressed.
   ["Gas pedal" makes the most sense here, but "brake" or "clutch" might also be reasonable.]

4. Paul's dog chased their tail.
   Paul's dog chased **its** tail.
   > [The pronoun referring to "dog" should be singular and neuter.]

5. The storms destroyed every house she hit.
   The storms destroyed every house **they** hit.
   > [The pronoun referring to "storms" should be plural and neuter.]

   Who
6. ~~Whom~~ was the coach of the team?

7. The javelins were kept in the case.
   > [No case or number errors.]

   is
8. After the meeting everyone ~~are~~ going to Jan's house.

   us
9. Send the winning times to ~~we~~.

   They
10. ~~Them~~ are a great relay team.

    his
11. Did you ever meet ~~him~~ parents?

    Who
12. ~~Whom~~ lives closer to the stadium than you do?

13. Do your feet hurt after you finish the decathlon?
    > [No case or number errors.]

14. The player waited for their turn at bat.

    The player waited for **her or his** turn at bat.

    > *or*

    The **players** waited for their **turns** at bat.

    it is
15. Either of the teams can win if ~~they are~~ consistent.

    its
16. The bat was cracked near ~~his~~ handle.

    its
17. She checked each bat for ~~her~~ cracks.

18. I am responsible; the responsibility is ours.

    I am responsible; the responsibility is **mine.**

    > *or*

    We are responsible; the responsibility is ours.

19. As the players got off the team bus, he called out to them.
    > [No agreement errors.]

20. The dogs ran out onto the field, and the players tried to chase it off.

    The **dog** ran out onto the field, and the players tried to chase it off.

    > *or*

    The dogs ran out onto the field, and the players tried to chase **them** off.

21. He paid for children to get into the game because that's the kind of person he is.
   [No agreement errors.]

22. The girls waited for the band to pass before she continued across the field.

    The girls waited for the band to pass before **they** continued across the field.

    or

    The **girl** waited for the band to pass before she continued across the field.

23. Whoever of the six players **hits** the most home runs **wins** the contest.

24. Her time was the best at the track meet.
   [No case or number errors.]

    She
25. ~~Her~~ was the best runner at the track meet.

✔ *ANSWERS (pages 61–62)*

1: D. The manager set up ("he" is vague—no referent in the sentence).

2: F. No change is needed.

3: B. Use "his or her." Each person is singular.

4: J. Use the plural pronoun. The phrase "Mary and Sharon" is plural.

5: C. The words "which one" are singular.

✔ *ANSWERS (page 64)*

1. Planes <u>fly</u> every day to my hometown.
       A P

2. The seats on some planes <u>are</u> very narrow.
             L P

3. Other planes <u>carry</u> only cargo.
       A P

4. <u>Hear</u> the roar of the jet engines.
    A S

5. Planes <u>taxi</u> very carefully near the passenger terminal.
      A P

6. I'll <u>steer</u> you to the waiting room.
      A S

7. The pilots <u>steer</u> north after takeoff.
       A P

8. Occasionally a plane <u>is</u> held at the gate for a passenger.
      L S

9. <u>Hold</u> onto the armrests during landing.
    A S

10. The air traffic controller in the tower <u>radioed</u> the pilot to hold fast.
    A S

11. The plane <u>circled</u> above the airport.
    A S

12. The passengers <u>were</u> waiting for the all-clear bell.
    L P

13. Upon arrival, the plane <u>pulled</u> up to the terminal at Gate B.
    A P

14. Passengers, please <u>exit</u> the jetway to your right.
    A P

15. The flight <u>is</u> over now.
    L S

✔*ANSWERS (pages 64–65)*

1: B. The word "concert" is singular, so the verb must be singular also.

2: H. The subject is plural—"Kevin and I." Therefore, the verb must be plural.

3: C. The reason is the same as item 1.

4: F. No change is necessary.

5: D. The reason is the same as item 2.

✔*ANSWERS (pages 69–70)*

1. Eddie is sitting in a chair under a big tree.
   [No tense error.]

2. Dawn **began** ~~begun~~ to understand the reason why she needed to take the ACT.

3. Did you **run** ~~ran~~ around the track yesterday?

4. I shall **speak** ~~spoken~~ to my mother about this year's vacation.

5. The dog swam across the pond every day.
   [No tense error — but if it is a continuing occurrence:
   The dog **swims** across the pond every day.]

6. Harry had driven two hours to reach the bookstore.
   [No tense errors.]

7. Fixing cars is not my idea of fun.
   [No tense error.]

drove

8. I ~~will drive~~ to the lake yesterday.
   [The word "yesterday" indicates that the verb must be past tense.]

had thrown

9. Tim ~~thrown~~ the ball out on the field for the players to use.

   or

   Tim **threw** the ball out on the field for the players to use.

lose

10. Joann will ~~lost~~ her bag if she leaves it in the store.

will be

11. The cat ~~was~~ soaked if it stays out in the rain.

12. Tomorrow we will go to the beach.
    [No tense error.]

will ride

13. I ~~ride~~ my bike to the park next week.

went

14. The dog ~~will go~~ to obedience school last year.

15. Lisa and Maddy drove to the zoo yesterday.
    [No tense error.]

✔ *ANSWERS (page 70)*

1: A. No change is necessary.

2: J. The verb must be past tense, plural, because it refers to how people felt "when they heard [past tense]" about it.

3: B. The action happened yesterday, so the verb must be past tense.

4: F. The sentence is correct as it is in the present tense.

5: C. The sentence is talking about action tomorrow, so the verb must be future tense.

✔ *ANSWERS (pages 72–73)*

The first line of each answer shows the original practice sentence.

1. I liked to make money, so I play the stock market.
   I **like** to make money, so I play the stock market.

   or

   I liked to make money, so I **played** the stock market.

2. Michael wanted to be a great basketball player, so he practices every day.
   Michael **wants** to be a great basketball player, so he practices every day.

   or

   Michael wanted to be a great basketball player, so he **practiced** every day.

3. Ava runs ten miles a day because she will run in a marathon next month.
   [No tense-shift errors.]

4. Stephen will load his car because he left for a long trip.
   Stephen **loaded** his car because he left for a long trip.

   or

   Stephen will load his car because he **will leave** for a long trip.

5. Art raised his hand because he wants to answer the question.

   Art **raises** his hand because he wants to answer the question.

   or

   Art raised his hand because he **wanted** to answer the question.

6. It **was** amazing to see that the dog barked as he jumps over the couch.

   It is amazing to see that the dog **barks** as he jumps over the couch.

   or

   It was amazing to see that the dog barked as he **jumped** over the couch.

7. Kit-cat rolls over and then purred very softly.

   Kit-cat **rolled** over and then purred very softly.

   or

   Kit-cat rolls over and then **purrs** very softly.

8. Jim headed out the door as he calls out a good-bye to his friends.

   Jim headed out the door as he **called** out a good-bye to his friends.

   or

   Jim **heads** out the door as he calls out a good-bye to his friends.

9. I already went to the store, but I am going there again.
   [No tense-shift errors.]

10. The guard lowers the drawbridge as the knight rode up to the gate.

    The guard **lowered** the drawbridge as the knight rode up to the gate.

    or

    The guard lowers the drawbridge as the knight **rides** up to the gate.

11. At the carnival, Susie rode the Ferris wheel, and Bill is playing arcade games.

    At the carnival, Susie **is riding** the Ferris wheel, and Bill is playing arcade games.

    or

    At the carnival, Susie **rode** the Ferris wheel, and Bill **played** arcade games.

12. Tomorrow I will start football practice, and my sister was starting soccer practice.

Tomorrow I will start football practice, and my sister **will start** soccer practice.

13. I broke my leg two weeks ago, and the cast will come off next month.
[No tense-shift errors.]

14. Judy ran out into the street after her ball, and the car stops quickly.

Judy ran out into the street after her ball, and the car **stopped** quickly.

or

Judy **runs** out into the street after her ball, and the car stops quickly.

15. After school I will go to band practice, and then I will stop at the store on my way home.
[No tense-shift errors.]

 **ANSWERS** *(page 73)*

1: **C.** Since the time frame is set in the past (last week), the verb must be past tense.

2: **G.** Preparations began "last week," so the verb must be past tense.

3: **A.** No change is necessary.

4: **G.** The time is **now,** so the verb must be present tense.

5: **D.** The time is the future (tomorrow), so the verb must be future tense in both cases.

 **ANSWERS** *(page 76)*

climbs
1. Everyone, including Renee and Louise, ~~climb~~ the mountain this morning.

is
2. Who do you think she ~~were~~?

rides
3. Over the crest of the ridge ~~ride~~ the lone horseman.

ski
4. Robert and Ryan ~~skis~~ as often as they can.

give
5. The tickets Renee bought ~~gives~~ her a reason for going out on Saturday night.

arranges
6. The class ~~arrange~~ a trip to the science center.

is
7. A pair of sneakers ~~are~~ all that reminds her of her basketball career.

8. The fastest times for the 220-yard and 440-yard runs are posted on the wall.
    [No agreement error.]

practice
9. The 23 members of the soccer team ~~practices~~ each day at 4:00 P.M.

mentions
10. Each person who climbs the hundred steps ~~mention~~ the beautiful view.

dance
11. James and Karen both like to dance, but they ~~dances~~ to different music.

was
12. The stable ~~were~~ full of horses waiting for lunch.

was
13. Everyone on the team ~~were~~ ready to play.

14. Andrew and Marcus were ready to go, but Karen was late.
    [No agreement error.]

15. Each person is allowed five minutes to speak.
    [No agreement error.]

✔ *ANSWERS (page 77)*

1: **B.** The subject "Chuck and Ann" is plural; therefore, the verb, "are," must also be plural.

2: **H.** The subject "each" is singular, as in *each one,* and so the verb must be singular—"loses."

3: **A.** No change is necessary.

4: **H.** The subject is plural, and so the verb must be plural as well.

5: **D.** The subject, "flight," is singular, so the verb must also be singular.

swim

1. I like to dive and to ~~go swimming~~ when I am at the lake.

2. Motorboats, canoes, and sailboats are my favorite forms of water transportation.
    [No parallel-form errors.]

road conditions

3. Neither the weather nor the ~~condition of the roads~~ will delay his trip.

a weatherman

4. Jim was trying to decide whether to be a newsman or ~~someone who reports the weather~~.

5. Because I expect the evening news to be interesting, I turn off boring reports.
    [No parallel-form errors. The conjunction "Because" signals subordination.]

rain will follow

6. The clouds are threatening, yet it seems unlikely that ~~a rainy day will follow~~.

7. The day was bright; the weather was cold and crisp.
    [No parallel-form errors.]

8. Although they were tired, the small band of travelers pressed on into the night.
    [No parallel-form errors. The conjunction "Although" signals subordination.]

old barn

9. The ~~barn which is old~~ stood bravely against the wind, but the new house collapsed.

10. His rugged appearance hid the more caring side of his personality.
    [No parallel-form errors.]

visiting

11. On his trip, Mark was biking in Seattle and then ~~to visit~~ relatives in Idaho.

swimming

12. Matt's favorite summer activities are jet-skiing, fishing, and ~~to swim~~.

13. At the grocery store, Chuck bought tomatoes, grapes, and eggs.
    [No parallel-form errors.]

14. On rainy afternoons I often read a good book, but on sunny days I play outdoors.
    [No parallel-form errors.]

drives

15. Al runs to the store, and then he ~~is driving~~ to the beach.

1: **C.** Each verb ends in "ing," creating a parallel form.

2: **F.** No change is necessary. The verbs "walks" and "takes" are in parallel form.

3: **D.** Each verb ends in "ing," creating a parallel form.

4: **F.** No change is necessary. The verbs have different tenses in Choices G and H. Choice J makes no sense.

5: **B.** The verbs "creates, sustains, and improves" create a parallel form.

smooth
1. Now, this is ~~smoothly~~ ice cream.

really
2. If you want my opinion, that yogurt is ~~real~~ great.

well
3. I think that Chris behaved very ~~good~~ today.

Unfortunately
4. ~~Unfortunate~~, the opera singer has a sore throat.

5. But the understudy gave a truly exceptional performance.
   [No adjective or adverb errors.]

6. The commentator conveniently forgot what she had said the previous night.
   [No adjective or adverb errors.]

extremely
7. Well, that's an ~~extreme~~ easy thing for you to say.

carefully
8. That seems like a needless error, particularly since acting more ~~careful~~ would solve the problem.

9. I have my doubts about the company, but they made me a really large salary offer.
   [No adjective or adverb errors.]

badly   **well**
10. The motor behaved ~~bad~~, so the trip did not go ~~good~~.

slow
11. Ray is a very ~~slowly~~ learner when it comes to computers.

softly
12. The floors of my house creak, so I try to walk ~~soft~~ when I know Mom is sleeping.

13. Martin ran rapidly through the field to catch the quick, blue butterfly.
    [No adjective or adverb errors.]

                good   **badly**

14. Since Fred was a ~~well~~ speaker, the class did not go as ~~bad~~ as I had feared.

15. The long freight train pulled slowly out of the station.
    [No adjective or adverb errors.]

ANSWERS (page 84)

1: D. The verb "sailing" is modified by the adverb "smoothly." Choice C is incorrect because the verb "were" is plural, not singular.

2: F. No change is necessary.

3: B. The adverb "quickly" modifies the verb "turning."

4: J. "Suddenly" is an adverb form.

5: D. The word *well* is an adverb. *Good* is an adjective which modifies the noun "luck."

ANSWERS (pages 86–87)

                            happiest
1. Chad was the ~~happier~~ player on the soccer team.

2. Members of the winning team were happier than members of the losing team.
   [No comparison error.]

                           fastest
3. Pat was the ~~faster~~ player on the baseball team.

4. The cheetah is the fastest predator in Africa.
   [No comparison error.]

                         tallest
5. The ~~taller~~ of the five basketball players was on the bench.

                         lighter
6. She took the ~~lightest~~ of the two grocery bags to the car.

7. Lonnie was among the more creative students in the school.
   [No comparison error.]

                         less
8. Ron is the ~~least~~ able of the two drivers.

9. His shoe size is the smallest in his class.
   [No comparison error.]

10. She was the more capable of the two referees.
    [No comparison error.]

                         prettier
11. Cardinals are ~~prettiest~~ than blue jays.

12. Rick is the smaller of the two wrestlers who made the finals.
    [No comparison error.]

cutest
13. Douglas went to the animal shelter and chose the ~~cuter~~ puppy of them all.

14. Tomorrow will be cloudier than today, but sunnier than yesterday.
    [No comparison error.]

luckiest
15. Sometimes I think I'm the ~~luckier~~ person on earth.

✔ *ANSWERS (page 87)*

1: B. Use the superlative because this year's party is compared to all other parties.

2: J. Use the comparative because this year's costumes are compared to last year's costumes.

3: A. No change is necessary.

4: H. Use the comparative—the actual is compared to the hoped-for food.

5: A. No change is necessary.

✔ *ANSWERS (pages 88–89)*

of
1. Whatever we accomplished was independent ~~with~~ her work.

2. I could spend endless days occupied with my books.
   [No idiom error.]

from
3. Notice how much the two men differ ~~with~~ each other in their speech patterns.

at
4. How much longer do you expect me to wait ~~to~~ the airport?

as
5. That person has just about the same appearance ~~from~~ you.

6. Although I expected to be free this afternoon, my time was occupied
   by
   ~~from~~ my friend all day.

with
7. My opinion on that matter differs greatly ~~from~~ yours.

for
8. Our trip was delayed because we were waiting ~~on~~ Fred, who was late.

with

9. Carl is often occupied ~~by~~ his experiments.

10. Although she used to depend on him, Karen has broken with Chris.
    [No idiom error.]

✔ *ANSWERS (page 89)*

1: C. The correct idiomatic form is *prior to.*

2: F. No change is necessary.

3: D. The correct idiomatic form is *independent of.*

✔ *ANSWERS (Grammar and Usage Subtest, pages 90–91)*

1: B. *Animals* should be plural, and the verb should be present tense, as in the following sentence.

2: H. The list should contain parallel forms of the verbs.

3: C. The pronoun must be plural to match the subject.

4: H. Karen is comparing two objects, monkeys and lions, so the comparative, not the superlative, should be used.

5: D. The superlative should be used since the monkeys are compared to many other animals.

6: G. The adjective form of *large* should be used.

7: D. The adverb form of *quick* should be used.

8: F. NO CHANGE.

9: D. The present tense should be used, and the correct idiom is *waiting for.*

10: H. *Animals* should be plural, and future tense should be used.

11: A. NO CHANGE.

12: G. A plural pronoun and verb should be used to match the noun, *animals.*

Chapter 7

PUNCTUATION

There are ten punctuation questions on the ACT.

Commas (,)

Use a Comma to Set Off Introductory Clauses or Phrases

Use commas in these examples. The beginning clauses or phrases are introductory.

Incorrect: Before he began preparing for the ACT Ed talked to his advisor.
Correct: Before he began preparing for the ACT, Ed talked to his advisor.

Incorrect: Well I guess there is no way to tell when we can go swimming.
Correct: Well, I guess there is no way to tell when we can go swimming.

Incorrect: It's a mile to the ocean but you have to travel about nine miles to get there.
Correct: It's a mile to the ocean, but you have to travel about nine miles to get there.

Incorrect: To get to the high school make a left on High Street.
Correct: To get to the high school, make a left on High Street.

Incorrect: Bob are you coming over?
Correct: Bob, are you coming over?

A comma is not required after a short introductory prepositional phrase if the meaning is clear:

Correct: In September I'll leave home for college.

Do not use commas in these examples. The beginning clauses or phrases are not introductory.

Incorrect: Ed talked to his advisor, before he began preparing for the ACT.
Correct: Ed talked to his advisor before he began preparing for the ACT.

Incorrect: Make a left on High Street, to get to the high school.
Correct: Make a left on High Street to get to the high school.

Use a Comma Before a Conjunction That Begins a Clause

Conjunctions: and, but, for, or, nor

Conjunctive word pairs: either . . . or, neither . . . nor, not only . . . but also

Clause: Part of a sentence that could be a sentence itself

Use a comma in this example:

Incorrect: I was in school on time but I was late for homeroom.
Correct: I was in school on time, but I was late for homeroom.

Use Commas to Set Off Parenthetical Expressions

A parenthetical expression does not provide essential information, and it interrupts the flow of a sentence.

Use commas in these examples:

Incorrect: My brother who loves to play soccer wants to be a teacher.
Correct: My brother, who loves to play soccer, wants to be a teacher.

Incorrect: Last summer when I turned 16 I spent a month at a lake.
Correct: Last summer, when I turned 16, I spent a month at a lake.

Do not use commas in these examples:

Incorrect: The girls, who play soccer, will miss the last class.
Correct: The girls who play soccer will miss the last class.
    [The words "who play soccer" provide essential information.]

Incorrect: Everyone, who takes the ACT, should read this book.
Correct: Everyone who takes the ACT should read this book.
    [The words "who takes the ACT" provide essential information.]

Use a Comma to Separate Items in a List

Use a comma in these examples:

Incorrect: The plane entered a long slow spiral.
Correct: The plane entered a long, slow spiral.

Incorrect: Pat liked warm soft breezy nights.
Correct: Pat liked warm, soft, breezy nights.

Incorrect: Ed liked his eggs poached his toast buttered and his coffee black.
Correct: Ed liked his eggs poached, his toast buttered, and his coffee black.

Do not use a comma in this example:

Incorrect: Ralph drove to the ACT test site in a bright, red convertible.
Correct: Ralph drove to the ACT test site in a bright red convertible.
    [The word "bright" describes the color red, not the convertible.]

MODEL ACT PROBLEMS

These Model ACT Problems show how this topic might be tested on the real ACT. The answers and explanations immediately follow the problems. Try the problems and then review the answers and the explanations.

Nathan the guitarist with the short hair was late
<u>1</u>

1. A. NO CHANGE
   B. Nathan the guitarist, with the short hair, was
   C. Nathan, the guitarist with the short hair, was
   D. Nathan the guitarist with the short, hair was

for rehearsal. On his way to band practice, he stopped
2

2. F. NO CHANGE
   G. On his way to band practice he stopped
   H. On his way, to band practice he stopped
   J. On his way, to band practice, he stopped

to pick up snacks and then made two wrong turns. We

weren't angry, however, because he brought sodas
3

potato chips and little pizzas with him. After eating,
3

3. A. NO CHANGE
   B. he brought sodas, potato chips, and little pizzas with
   C. he brought sodas potato chips, and little pizzas, with
   D. he brought, sodas potato chips and little pizzas, with

he picked up his steel, blue guitar, and we began
4

jamming.

4. F. NO CHANGE
   G. picked up, his steel blue guitar
   H. picked up his steel-blue guitar
   J. picked up his steel, blue, guitar

**ANSWERS**

1. The phrase "the guitarist with the short hair" is a nonessential, parenthetical phrase. The sentence would make sense without the phrase—"Nathan was late for rehearsal." The parenthetical phrase gives the reader more information about Nathan.

   C is the correct choice.

2. No change is necessary. The phrase "On his way to band practice" is an introductory phrase and must be separated by a comma.

   F is the correct choice.

3. The items in the list must be separated by commas.

   B is the correct choice.

4. The phrase "steel-blue" is an adjective which modifies guitar. The word "steel" describes the shade of blue rather than the guitar itself.

   H is the correct choice.

Fix the sentences that do not correctly use commas. Some sentences have no comma errors.

1. I had a sophomore slump, but I worked hard in my junior year.

2. Every senior, who is a member of the Circle Club, receives an award.

3. After school, the custodian locked us in.

4. College graduation seems a distant, but desirable, goal.

5. Make a left at the next corner but be sure to turn right at the second corner.

6. In the trunk of my car I found a spare tire, some candy wrappers, and sneakers.

7. Either clean up your room or you can't go out.

8. Before leaving for home, I filled up with gas, but the oil was full.

9. Chad, Blaire, and Ryan attended graduation but they left the car home.

10. In senior or junior year of high school the ACT will be given to college applicants.

11. After a day at school I went to the grocery store to buy milk, bread, and cheese.

12. The girl, in the newspaper photo, just got married.

13. You can go to the game, but come home as soon as it ends.

14. The quarterback whose name is Andrew just won a scholarship to college.

15. Once I finish college, I hope to have a job as an engineer even though I don't like math.

(Answers on page 120)

ACT-TYPE PROBLEMS

Look at the item that matches the number of the underlined part. Pick the best replacement for the underlined part. If the underlined part is the best, then select NO CHANGE.

Ed who lives next door was planning a trip. He
        1

1. **A.** NO CHANGE
   B. Ed, who lives next door, was
   C. Ed who lives next door, was
   D. Ed who lives, next, door was

asked us to look after his dog his cat and his plants.
        2

2. **F.** NO CHANGE
   G. look after his dog his cat, and his plants.
   H. look after, his dog his cat and his plants.
   J. look after his dog, his cat, and his plants.

In addition, we were to water his lawn twice a week.
      3

3. **A.** NO CHANGE
   B. In addition we were to water
   C. In addition, we were to water.
   D. In addition we were to water,

At daybreak on Saturday he left for Hawaii, but we
                                              4

were out of town for the day. His sixteen-year-old,
                                   5

niece fed the animals that day.
  5

(*Answers on page 121*)

4. **F.** NO CHANGE
   G. At daybreak on Saturday, he left for Hawaii but
   H. At daybreak on Saturday, he left for Hawaii, but
   J. At daybreak on Saturday he left for Hawaii

5. **A.** NO CHANGE
   B. His sixteen-year-old niece fed
   C. His sixteen-year-old niece, fed
   D. His, sixteen-year-old, niece, fed

Semicolons and Colons

Semicolon (;)

Use a semicolon to connect independent clauses when the independent clauses are not connected by a conjunction.

Incorrect: The students entered the room, the ACT booklets were handed out.
Correct: The students entered the room; the ACT booklets were handed out.

Incorrect: The bird soared the fish swam.
Correct: The bird soared; the fish swam.

Do not use a semicolon in these examples:

Incorrect: Henry finished studying for the ACT; but he still had to take the test.
Correct: Henry finished studying for the ACT, but he still had to take the test.
                [These two clauses are connected by a conjunction.]

Incorrect: Before he went home; Henry returned the Amsco ACT book to the library.
Correct: Before he went home, Henry returned the Amsco ACT book to the library.
                ["Before he went home" is an introductory clause.]

Colon (:)

Place a colon after an independent clause to introduce a list or illustration.

Incorrect: Bring these items to the ACT, an admission ticket, pencils, erasers, and a watch.
Correct: Bring these items to the ACT: an admission ticket, pencils, erasers, and a watch.

Incorrect: There is only one necessary personal trait, perseverance.
Correct: There is only one necessary personal trait: perseverance.

Do not use a colon in these examples:

Incorrect: You should bring: an admission ticket, pencils, erasers, and a watch to the ACT.

Correct: You should bring an admission ticket, pencils, erasers, and a watch to the ACT.

Incorrect: One necessary trait is: perseverance.
Correct: One necessary trait is perseverance.

 ## MODEL ACT PROBLEMS

These Model ACT Problems show how this topic might be tested on the real ACT. The answers and explanations immediately follow the problems. Try the problems and then review the answers and the explanations.

Today I'm going to <u>the beach, school</u> starts
                    1
again tomorrow. At the beach I can do many

<u>different things: swim, play volleyball</u>, jet-ski,
                    2
or just relax.

1. **A**   NO CHANGE
   B.   the beach school
   C.   the beach; school
   D.   the beach: school

2. **F.**   NO CHANGE
   G.   different things, swim, play volleyball
   H.   different things; swim, play volleyball
   J.   different things swim, play volleyball

✔ *ANSWERS*

1. The two independent clauses need to be separated by either a semicolon or a period.

   C is the correct choice.

2. No change is necessary. The first part is an independent clause, followed by a list. A semicolon cannot be used because the list cannot stand on its own as a sentence.

   F is the correct choice.

 ## PRACTICE

Correct any semicolon or colon errors.

1. Put these things in your trunk; a jack, a spare tire, a flare, and a blanket.

2. In your glove compartment put: your registration and your insurance information.

3. There is only one thing on my shopping list; milk.

4. We went to the store; and the parking lot was filled with cars.

5. We fought our way through the crowds, the store was even more crowded than the parking lot.

6. Although tomorrow is Saturday; we have to be at school for a test.

7. You need to know only one thing in life: be happy.

8. There were nearly 200 children at the park, they were all attending the outdoor puppet show.

9. Annie is my dog; she is a black Labrador.

10. Please bring to the picnic: a dessert, a vegetable, and some hot dog rolls.

(Answers on page 121)

ACT-TYPE PROBLEMS

Look at the item that matches the number of the underlined part. Pick the best replacement for the underlined part. If the underlined part is the best, then select NO CHANGE.

Winnie-the-Pooh is my favorite children's book, I
                                      1
like the personalities of the animals. The book is full of
1

great characters; Pooh, Piglet, Tigger, and Eeyore.
                2

Eeyore is my favorite; he's so gloomy and depressed.
           3

However, I also like the philosophy of Pooh; and the
                           4
energy of Tigger. The best thing about the book is this:
4   **5**

it's still great reading when you're an adult.
5

1. **A.** NO CHANGE
   B. children's book I like the
   C. children's book; I like the
   D. children's book: I like the

2. **F.** NO CHANGE
   G. great characters, Pooh, Piglet, Tigger
   H. great characters: Pooh Piglet Tigger
   J. great characters: Pooh, Piglet, Tigger

3. **A.** NO CHANGE
   B. my favorite, he's so gloomy
   C. my favorite he's so gloomy
   D. my favorite: he's so gloomy

4. **F.** NO CHANGE
   G. philosophy of Pooh, and the energy
   H. philosophy of Pooh and the energy
   J. philosophy of Pooh: and the energy

5. **A.** NO CHANGE
   B. book is this; it's still great
   C. book is this it's still great
   D. book is this, it's still great

(Answers on page 122)

Parentheses ( )

Use parentheses to set off explanations or definitions, as in these examples:

Incorrect: The atmosphere on Venus the planet is not habitable is not like the atmosphere here on Earth.

Correct: The atmosphere on Venus (the planet is not habitable) is not like the atmosphere here on Earth.

[The words "the planet is not habitable" explain something about Venus.]

Incorrect: There is a paucity, scarcity, of information about the most
distant parts of the galaxy.

Correct: There is a paucity (scarcity) of information about the most
distant parts of the galaxy.

[The word "scarcity" defines paucity.]

◆▌▌PRACTICE▐▊▷

Correct any parentheses errors. Some sentences have no errors.

1. The three animals (including two cows) grazed in the field.

2. Pluto, Disney created this doglike character, is one of my favorite cartoons.

3. Diction (using the correct word) is often confused with pronunciation.

4. Following a short delay caused by a rain shower, the game began.

5. One Earth year is about 365 days and six hours long.

6. Most working-age people who are blind nearly 74 percent are unemployed.

7. After the game (we walked to the ice-cream store).

8. Most banks now have ATMs (automated teller machines) in many convenient locations.

9. Personification means giving something inanimate (like a tree) human characteristics.

10. I often use coriander a spice made from cilantro in my cooking.

(*Answers on page 122*)

▌ACT-TYPE PROBLEMS

Look at the item that matches the number of the underlined part. Pick the best replacement for the underlined part. If the underlined part is the best, then select NO CHANGE.

Joan lives on <u>Tipperary Hill named for the county</u>
                1

<u>in Ireland in Syracuse</u>. At one intersection, there is an
   1

1. **A.** NO CHANGE
   B. Tipperary Hill, named for the county in Ireland in Syracuse
   C. Tipperary Hill (named for the county in Ireland) in Syracuse
   D. Tipperary Hill named for the county in Ireland (in Syracuse)

<u>upside-down traffic light (the green is on top)</u>.
              2

2. **F.** NO CHANGE
   G. upside-down traffic light the green is on top
   H. upside-down traffic light, the green is on top
   J. upside-down (traffic light) the green is on top

(*Answers on page 123*)

Apostrophe (')

An apostrophe indicates a missing letter or letters in a contraction.

INCORRECT	CORRECT
wont	won't (will not)
dont	don't (do not)
isnt	isn't (is not)
lets	let's (let us)
its	it's (it is)

The spelling "its" is correct for the possessive personal pronoun.

Use an apostrophe and the letter *s* after a singular noun to form the possessive unless the *'s* makes pronunciation too cumbersome.

INCORRECT	CORRECT
Bens father	Ben's father
Carls' cat	Carl's cat
Louis' car	Louis's car
Moses's sister	Moses' sister

Use an apostrophe after a regular plural noun to form the possessive.

INCORRECT	CORRECT
animal's rights	animals' rights
driver's education	drivers' education
colonies's products	colonies' products

Use an apostrophe to form the possessive of indefinite pronouns but *not* personal pronouns.

INCORRECT	CORRECT
everyones' shoes	everyone's shoes
anyones guess	anyone's guess
it's history	its history
her's shoes	her shoes

◀PRACTICE▶

Correct any apostrophe errors. Some sentences may not contain errors.

1. It's true, but it's hard to believe.

2. Her pitching style could never be confused with anothers' pitching style.

3. Would'nt you like to go to a game this afternoon?

4. The women's softball team had a great pitcher.

5. Wes' glove ended up in the coaches' locker room.

6. Do'nt go to Mel's store today.

7. Everyones' tickets for the play were lost.

8. In the forest, all of the trees' branches were covered in ice.

9. The childrens' matinee was canceled today.

10. The car's door was stuck, and it's brakes squeaked.

(Answers on page 123)

ACT-TYPE PROBLEMS

These Model ACT Problems show how this topic might be tested on the real ACT. The answers and explanations immediately follow the problems. Try the problems and then review the answers and the explanations.

<u>Yesterdays' little</u> league game was rained out.
        1

1. **A.** NO CHANGE
   B. Yesterdays little
   C. Yesterday's little
   D. Yesterday little

Instead, each of the ballplayers went to <u>his' or her's</u>
                         2

<u>house</u> to rest.
 2

2. **F.** NO CHANGE
   G. his or her's house
   H. his' or hers' house
   J. his or her house

(Answers on page 123)

Periods, Question Marks, and Exclamation Points

Period (.)

Use the period to end a sentence unless the sentence is a question, a short interjection, or a command.

Examples

I'm not sure what you mean by that.
That was a great play.
Never leave blank the answer choice for an ACT question.
You shouldn't touch a hot stove.

Question Mark (?)

Use a question mark after a direct question.

 **Examples**

> What do you mean by that?
> What time is it?
> "Are you going to the prom?" he asked.

Exclamation Point (!)

Use an exclamation point at the end of a short interjection or a command.

 **Examples**

> Great play!
> Don't touch that!

◀█ PRACTICE █▶

Correct any period, question mark, or exclamation point errors.

1. I was so tired at the end of the day!
2. Fire.
3. Where did you hear that!
4. Duck. The baseball is heading for us.
5. Is this the last practice exercise in this section.
6. Yesterday I had to study for today's math test?
7. What is her name.
8. "Run!" she yelled.
9. Today is supposed to be a beautiful day!
10. Help.

(Answers on page 124)

Look at the item that matches the number of the underlined part. Pick the best replacement for the underlined part. If the underlined part is the best, then select NO CHANGE.

<u>Oops.</u> Tomorrow is the big test. Do you think
1

1. **A.** NO CHANGE
   B. Oops?
   C. Oops,
   D. Oops!

I can <u>pass without studying!</u>
2

2. **F.** NO CHANGE
   G. pass without studying.
   H. pass without studying?
   J. pass without studying;

(Answers on page 124)

Quotation Marks

Place double quotation marks around direct quotations.

Place single quotation marks around quotations within quotations.

Indirect quotations describe what has been said but not the speaker's exact words. Do not place quotation marks around indirect quotations.

Incorrect:	The teacher turned to the class and said Let's talk about quotation marks.
Correct:	The teacher turned to the class and said, "Let's talk about quotation marks." [Enclose direct quotes in quotation marks.]
Incorrect:	"When I think about history," the teacher said, "Lincoln's words "four score and seven years ago" always come to mind."
Correct:	"When I think about history," the teacher said, "Lincoln's words 'four score and seven years ago' always come to mind." [Lincoln's words inside another quote are enclosed with single quotation marks.]
Incorrect:	Lincoln's words about the "obscurity of his address" turned out to be false.
Correct:	Lincoln's words about the obscurity of his address turned out to be false. [Remove the quotation marks from the indirect quote.]

Place periods and commas following a quotation inside the quotation marks.

Place semicolons and colons outside quotation marks.

Place question marks and exclamation points inside quotation marks if they belong to the quotation.

Incorrect:	"I am taking the ACT next month", John said.
Correct:	"I am taking the ACT next month," John said. [Place the following comma within the quotation marks.]

Incorrect: A person who took the test said, "Don't leave any answers blank;" he added "That is one of the most important strategies."

Correct: A person who took the test said, "Don't leave any answers blank"; he added, "That is one of the most important strategies."
[Place the semicolon after the quotation marks.]

Incorrect: Who wrote, "To be, or not to be; that is the question?"

Correct: Who wrote, "To be, or not to be; that is the question"**?**
[The question mark is not part of the quote. Place it outside the quotation marks.]

◀PRACTICE▶

Correct any quotation mark errors. An item may have no errors.

1. "Turn left at the light to get downtown," said the police officer.

2. The instructor told you to "do your work carefully."

3. The student asked the question, "Who started the civil war"?

4. "It's time to go home", said the coach.

5. "I am going to Jenn's house," said Lisa. Then I am going home.

(Answers on page 124)

ACT-TYPE PROBLEMS

Look at the item that matches the number of the underlined part. Pick the best replacement for the underlined part. If the underlined part is the best, then select NO CHANGE.

"I am thinking of going <u>to the movies", said</u> her friend.
                            1

1. **A.** NO CHANGE
   B. to the movies" said,
   C. to the movies," said
   D. to the movies" said

Her friend wondered if they <u>would "have time to go</u>
                                    2

<u>home first".</u>
  2

2. **A.** NO CHANGE
   B. would, "have time to go home first."
   C. would "have time to go home first."
   D. would have time to go home first.

(Answers on page 125)

Punctuation Subtest

This Subtest has the type of punctuation items found on the ACT. These items make up part of the Usage and Mechanics (UM) subscore on the ACT. If you don't know an answer, eliminate and guess. Circle the number of any guessed answer. Check page 125 for answers and explanations.

INSTRUCTIONS: Certain words or phrases in the following passage are underlined and numbered. There is a corresponding item for each underlined portion. Each item offers three suggestions for changing the underlined portion to conform to standard written English, or to make it understandable or consistent with the rest of the passage. If the underlined portion is not improved by one of the three suggested changes, mark NO CHANGE.

Choose the best answer for each question based on the passage. Then fill in the appropriate circle on the answer grid.

```
1 Ⓐ Ⓑ Ⓒ Ⓓ     5 Ⓐ Ⓑ Ⓒ Ⓓ     8 Ⓕ Ⓖ Ⓗ Ⓙ
2 Ⓕ Ⓖ Ⓗ Ⓙ     6 Ⓐ Ⓑ Ⓒ Ⓓ     9 Ⓐ Ⓑ Ⓒ Ⓓ
3 Ⓐ Ⓑ Ⓒ Ⓓ     7 Ⓕ Ⓖ Ⓗ Ⓙ    10 Ⓐ Ⓑ Ⓒ Ⓓ
4 Ⓐ Ⓑ Ⓒ Ⓓ
```

In the following paragraph, choose the answer with correct punctuation for each sentence. Some sentences may be correct.

It was cold dark and rainy as we set off on our
         1
journey. Our plan was to make it to the mountains

by sunrise we would rest there a day before setting out
2

across the plains. We brought with us only: a few
                       3
clothes some money and food for a week. In order to
3

make it to the ship on time; we needed to be at the coast
              4

1. A. NO CHANGE
   B. It was cold, dark, and rainy
   C. It was: cold dark and rainy
   D. It was: cold, dark, and rainy

2. F. NO CHANGE
   G. by sunrise, we would rest there
   H. by sunrise: we would rest there
   J. by sunrise; we would rest there

3. A. NO CHANGE
   B. us only: a few clothes, some money, and food
   C. us only a few clothes some money and food
   D. us only a few clothes, some money, and food

4. F. NO CHANGE
   G. the ship on time: we needed to
   H. the ship on time, we needed to
   J. the ship on time we needed to

by Saturday. <u>Then as we neared the mountains we</u> heard
                            5

something. <u>Boom? A loud</u> echo rolled across the sky.
                    6

<u>"What is that?" we asked</u> each other.
                7

We saw <u>a horse (we could see no rider) galloping</u>
                            8

along the path. The horse <u>slowed it's pace</u> as it drew
                                    9

near. Then, we saw <u>the rider; he was lying low along</u>
                                10
<u>the horses'</u> neck, urging him onward.
    10

(Answers on page 125)

5. **A.** NO CHANGE
   B. Then, as we neared the mountains, we
   C. Then! As we neared the mountains we
   D. Then as we neared the mountains, we

6. **F.** NO CHANGE
   G. Boom. A loud
   H. Boom! A loud
   J. Boom, a loud

7. **A.** NO CHANGE
   B. "What is that" we asked
   C. "What is that!" we asked
   D. "What is that." we asked

8. **F.** NO CHANGE
   G. a horse we could see no rider galloping
   H. a horse we could see no (rider galloping)
   J. a horse, we could see no rider galloping

9. **A.** NO CHANGE
   B. slowed its' pace
   C. slowed its pace
   D. slowed its's pace

10. **F.** NO CHANGE
    G. the rider he was lying low along the horses' neck
    H. the rider, he was lying low along the horse's neck
    J. the rider: he was lying low along the horse's neck

1. I had a sophomore slump, but I worked hard in my junior year.
   [No comma errors.]

             senior who   **Club receives**
2. Every ~~senior, who~~ is a member of the Circle ~~Club, receives~~ an award.
   [Remove the commas.]

             school the
3. After ~~school, the~~ custodian locked us in.
   [Remove the comma.]

4. College graduation seems a distant, but desirable, goal.
   [No comma errors.]

5. Make a left at the next corner, but be sure to turn right at the second corner.
   [Add a comma before the conjunction to separate the two clauses.]

6. In the trunk of my car I found a spare tire, some candy wrappers, and sneakers.
   [No comma errors.]

7. Either clean up your room, or you can't go out.
   [Add a comma.]

8. Before leaving for home, I filled up with gas, but the oil was full.
   [No comma errors.]

9. Chad, Blaire, and Ryan attended graduation, but they left the car home.
   [Add a comma to separate the clauses.]

10. In senior or junior year of high school, the ACT will be given to college applicants.
    [Add a comma to set off the introductory phrase.]

11. After a day at school, I went to the grocery store to buy milk, bread, and cheese.
    [Add a comma to set off the introductory phrase.]

12. The girl in the newspaper photo just got married.
    [Remove the commas—the prepositional phrase identifies the girl.]

13. You can go to the game, but come home as soon as it ends.
    [No comma errors.]

14. The quarterback, whose name is Andrew, just won a scholarship to college.
    [Add commas; most likely only one quarterback could be referred to.]

15. Once I finish college, I hope to have a job as an engineer, even though I don't like math.
    [Add a comma to separate the clauses.]

1: **B.** The phrase "who lives next door" is a nonessential, parenthetical phrase.

2: **J.** These items are a list.

3: **A.** No change is necessary.

4: **H.** Use a comma to set off the introductory clause.

5: **B.** The phrase "sixteen-year-old" is an adjective modifying niece.

✔ ANSWERS (pages 110–111)

trunk:
1. Put these things in your ~~trunk;~~ a jack, a spare tire, a flare, and a blanket.
   [Replace the semicolon with a colon.]

put your
2. In your glove compartment ~~put: your~~ registration and your insurance information.
   [Remove the colon.]

list: milk
3. There is only one thing on my shopping ~~list; milk~~.
   [Replace the comma with a colon.]

store,
4. We went to the ~~store;~~ and the parking lot was filled with cars.
   [Replace the semicolon with a comma.]

crowds;
5. We fought our way through the ~~crowds,~~ the store was even more crowded than the parking lot.
   [Replace the comma with a semicolon.]

6. Although tomorrow is Saturday, we have to be at school for a test.
   [Replace the semicolon with a comma.]

7. You need to know only one thing in life: be happy.
   [No error—colon is correct.]

8. There were nearly 200 children at the park; they were all attending the outdoor puppet show.
   [Replace the comma with a semicolon.]

9. Annie is my dog; she is a black Labrador.
   [No error—semicolon is correct.]

10. Please bring to the picnic a dessert, a vegetable, and some hot dog rolls.
    [Omit the colon.]

1: **C.** Choices A and B are run-on sentences.

2: **J.** Choice H is incorrect because the items in the list are not separated by commas.

3: **A.** No change is necessary.

4: **H.** No punctuation is needed between the two elements of the compound object.

5: **A.** No change is necessary.

              , including two cows,
1. The three animals ~~(including two cows)~~ grazed in the field.
   [Replace the parentheses with commas.]

          (Disney created this doglike character)
2. Pluto~~, Disney created this doglike character,~~ is one of my favorite cartoons.
   [Replace the commas with parentheses.]

3. Diction (using the correct word) is often confused with pronunciation.
   [No parentheses errors.]

4. Following a short delay caused by a rain shower, the game began.
   [No parentheses errors.]

5. One Earth year is about 365 days and six hours long.
   [No parentheses errors.]

6. Most working-age people who are blind (nearly 74 percent) are unemployed.
   [Add parentheses.]

7. After the game /we walked to the ice-cream store/.
   [Omit the parentheses.]

8. Most banks now have ATMs (automated teller machines) in many convenient locations.
   [No parentheses errors.]

9. Personification means giving something inanimate (like a tree) human characteristics.
   [No parentheses errors.]

10. I often use coriander (a spice made from cilantro) in my cooking.
   [Add parentheses.]

1: **C.** In the other choices, it sounds like Ireland is in Syracuse.

2: **F.** No change is necessary.

1. It's true, but it's hard to believe.
   [No apostrophe errors.]

   another's
2. Her pitching style could never be confused with ~~anothers'~~ pitching style.

   Wouldn't
3. ~~Would'nt~~ you like to go to a game this afternoon?

4. The women's softball team had a great pitcher.
   [No apostrophe error.]

   Wes's
5. ~~Wes'~~ glove ended up in the coaches' locker room.

   Don't
6. ~~Do'nt~~ go to Mel's store today.

   Everyone's
7. ~~Everyones'~~ tickets for the play were lost.

8. In the forest, all of the trees' branches were covered in ice.
   [No apostrophe error.]

   children's
9. The ~~childrens'~~ matinee was canceled today.

   its
10. The car's door was stuck, and ~~it's~~ brakes squeaked.
    [The possesive pronoun *its* has no apostrophe.]

1. **C** is the correct choice.

2. **J** is the correct choice.

1. I was so tired at the end of the ~~day!~~ **day.**

2. ~~Fire.~~ **Fire!**

3. Where did you hear ~~that!~~ **that?**

4. ~~Duck.~~ **Duck!** The baseball is heading for us.

5. Is this the last practice exercise in this ~~section.~~ **section?**

6. Yesterday I had to study for today's math ~~test?~~ **test.**

7. What is her ~~name.~~ **name?**

8. "Run!" she yelled.
   [No punctuation error.]

9. Today is supposed to be a beautiful ~~day!~~ **day.**

10. ~~Help.~~ **Help!**

1. **D** is the correct choice. ("Oops" is an interjection.)

2. **H** is the correct choice.

1. "Turn left at the light to get downtown," said the police officer.
   [There are no quotation mark errors.]

2. The instructor told you to do your work carefully.
   [This is an indirect quote. Remove the quotation marks.]

3. The student asked the question, "Who started the civil war?"
   [The question mark goes inside the quotation marks. It is part of the quote.]

4. "It's time to go home," said the coach.
   [The trailing comma always goes inside the quotation marks.]

5. "I am going to Jenn's house," said Lisa. "Then I am going home."
   [The second sentence is a quote.]

1. **C** is the correct choice. Always place the following comma inside the quotation marks.

2. **D** is the correct choice. There is no quote, so do not use quotation marks.

✔*ANSWERS (Punctuation Subtest, pages 118–119)*

1: **B.** The series needs to be separated by commas, but not set off by a colon.

2: **J.** The two independent clauses should be separated by a semicolon.

3: **D.** The series needs to be separated by commas, but not set off by a colon.

4: **H.** The introductory phrase should be separated from the second part of the sentence by a comma.

5: **B.** The phrase "as we neared the mountains" is a nonessential phrase.

6: **H.** "Boom!" is an exclamation.

7: **A.** NO CHANGE.

8: **F.** NO CHANGE.

9: **C.** The possessive form of *its* has no apostrophe.

10: **J.** The first independent clause should be separated from the second by a colon; *horse* is singular, so its possessive form is *horse's*.

Chapter 8

RHETORICAL SKILLS

There are 35 rhetorical-skills questions on the ACT English Test. The questions are partitioned among strategy, organization, and style, as follows:

Strategy.....................12 questions
Organization ....11 questions
Style........................12 questions

Rhetoric items are unique to the ACT. These items are not based on rules of grammar or punctuation. They are often based on your informed sense about what written English should "sound" like, or about the order in which ideas should occur in a paragraph or passage. I will use examples of ACT question types to review the rhetorical skills.

Strategy

The word "strategy" sounds very substantial. You might even get the idea that you have to detect some detailed strategy in a passage. Nothing could be further from the truth. All strategy questions are one of these three types.

1. **Choose appropriate transitional, opening, and closing statements and sentences.**

    This type of strategy question appears most frequently on the ACT. Most often this question type asks you to identify the correct transition between and within sentences. These are the easiest rhetoric questions on the ACT.

    The transition words discussed below are not a guaranteed way to answer transition questions. However, alertness to these categories of words will usually be a big help.

Connector Words

Cause and Effect: These transition words establish a cause-and-effect relationship:
and so   as a result of   because   consequently   hence   therefore   thus

Continuation: Some transitions show that the same theme is continued or explained in more detail:
also   and   by the same token   further   in addition   in other words   that is   then

Difference: These transition words point out differences:

although	but	contrarily	despite	however
as opposed to	in contrast to	not	nevertheless	
to the contrary	unlike			

Example: These transition words signal an explanation:

for example   for instance   that is

Order: These transition words suggest that elements are being ordered:

first   primarily   then   last   before   after

Similarity: These transition words point out similarities:

alike   also   in common   similar to

2. **Choose a sentence most appropriate to the passage's intended readers or to the author's purpose.**

3. **Evaluate the impact of adding, deleting, and revising supporting material and details in the passage.**

One question type asks you to choose a sentence to match the intended reader and the purpose of the passage. The second question type asks you to choose the best explanation of the impact of adding a particular sentence.

Authors write for a particular audience and for a particular purpose. An author might write an article about a particular health care system to inform the general public. Another author might write an article on the same subject, but to persuade professional health care providers that the system was not a good one.

One passage might present a funny story from the Civil War era to entertain the average reader. Another passage about the Civil War for high school students might describe an actual battle. A third Civil War passage written for immigrants to the United States might inform them about the importance of the war in American history.

Complete the following sample strategy items. Then review the answers and learn how to answer these items on the ACT.

MODEL ACT PROBLEMS

These Model ACT Problems show how this topic might be tested on the real ACT. The answers and explanations immediately follow the problems. Try the problems and then review the answers and the explanations.

Transition

It was a beautiful warm fall day. <u>In spite of this,</u>
$\qquad$ 1

the walkers wore shorts and short-sleeve shirts.

<u>And yet</u> for a skier, it may not have been the most
$\quad$ 2

beautiful day.

1. **A.** NO CHANGE
   B. Therefore,
   C. Nevertheless,
   D. But,

2. **F.** NO CHANGE
   G. Therefore
   H. And
   J. Moreover, as a

 **ANSWERS**

1. This is a classic transition item. The first sentence tells us it's a warm day. The second sentence tells us the walkers wore shorts and short-sleeve shirts. The phrase "In spite of this" connects the first sentence to the second, and also implies a contrast. We would expect the second sentence *not* to flow naturally from the first. And yet it does. The phrase "In spite of this" cannot be correct. The correct choice is B, "Therefore." Choices C and D also imply a contrast.

   B is the correct choice.

2. Another transition question. In this case the original wording is correct. This sentence shows a contrast to the previous sentence. Choice F, "NO CHANGE," is correct. Choices G, H, and J imply that there is no contrast between this sentence and the previous sentence.

   F is the correct choice.

Appropriate Use — Revising Material

[1] Understanding bond yields can be difficult. [2] You have to consider both the price of the bond and the interest rate. [3] And when the interest rate on the bond goes up, the price of the bond goes down. [3]

3. Say that the author of this passage wanted to give an example of the statement about a bond's interest rate and price found in sentence 3. Which of the sentences below would best meet the writer's purpose?

   A. This means that interest rate increases can actually lead to a loss.
   B. To determine yields on common stock you usually have to determine only the gain or loss.
   C. Recently the interest rate on a bond went up 0.1 percent, and the price went down $.90.
   D. Risky bonds can have an interest rate as high as 18 percent while safer bonds can have an interest rate as low as 5 percent.

128   English

3. A question number in a box tells you the question is based on the whole paragraph or the entire passage. The item indicates that the author wants to give an *example* of the statement in sentence 3 that the interest rate on a bond going up means the price will come down. Consider each of the answers in turn:

Choice A is not an example. It describes the consequences of a rate increase.

Choice B has nothing to do with bonds.

Choice C is an example. It describes a specific situation in which the interest rate of a bond went up while the price came down.

Choice D gives an example but of the interest rates of risky and safe bonds.

C is the correct choice.

Coin collectors place a significant premium on the quality of a coin. Coins in mint condition command the highest prices, followed by coins which have never been circulated. The value of a coin with even minor defects can drop by as much as 50 percent. If you are a coin collector, be sure to protect your coins. 4

4. The author of this passage is considering including this sentence after the first sentence:

Quality is also important for art collectors.

Should the author add the sentence?

F. Yes, because the sentence emphasizes the importance of quality for collectors.

G. No, because quality is not as important in artwork since a lot of old paintings sell for high prices.

H. Yes, because the sentence presents an interesting contrast between two types of collecting.

J. No, because the sentence interrupts the flow of the passage.

4. The question number is in a box, so you know that the question is based on the whole paragraph. This item asks you to evaluate the wisdom of adding a sentence. You have to indicate whether the answer should be yes or no, and a reason for your choice.

The sentence "Quality is also important for art collectors" doesn't have much to do with coin collecting. Consider each choice in turn:

Choice F gives a plausible argument for including the sentence.

Choice G does not give a plausible argument for not including the sentence.

Choice H does not give a plausible argument for including the sentence.

Choice J gives a plausible argument for not including the sentence.

The choice is between F and J. Choice J is correct because a sentence about art collectors does not belong in this paragraph. The sentence interrupts the flow of the passage.

J is the correct choice.

Strategy Subtest

This Subtest has the same number and type of strategy items found on the ACT. These items make up part of the Rhetorical Skills (RH) subscore on the ACT. If you don't know an answer, eliminate and guess. Circle the number of any guessed answer. Check pages 142–143 for answers and explanations.

INSTRUCTIONS: Certain words or phrases in the following passage are underlined and numbered. There is a corresponding item for each underlined portion. Each item offers three suggestions for changing the underlined portion to conform to standard written English, or to make it understandable or consistent with the rest of the passage. If the underlined portion is not improved by one of the three suggested changes, mark NO CHANGE.

You will also find questions about a section of the passage as a whole. These questions do not refer to an underlined portion of the passage, but rather are identified by a number in a box.

Choose the best answer for each question based on the passage. Then fill in the appropriate circle on the answer grid.

1 Ⓐ Ⓑ Ⓒ Ⓓ	5 Ⓐ Ⓑ Ⓒ Ⓓ	9 Ⓐ Ⓑ Ⓒ Ⓓ
2 Ⓕ Ⓖ Ⓗ Ⓙ	6 Ⓐ Ⓑ Ⓒ Ⓓ	10 Ⓐ Ⓑ Ⓒ Ⓓ
3 Ⓐ Ⓑ Ⓒ Ⓓ	7 Ⓕ Ⓖ Ⓗ Ⓙ	11 Ⓕ Ⓖ Ⓗ Ⓙ
4 Ⓐ Ⓑ Ⓒ Ⓓ	8 Ⓕ Ⓖ Ⓗ Ⓙ	12 Ⓕ Ⓖ Ⓗ Ⓙ

[1]

Doyle's great sleuth, Holmes, was super-rational, <u>and</u> the famous author himself was the world's best-
₁
known advocate of Spiritualism, the belief that human personality survives death and that the living can communicate with the dead. [2]

1. **A.** NO CHANGE
   B. since
   C. that is
   D. but

2. The author deleted the following sentence, which was originally placed after the first sentence.

   Even today, people look to psychics for help and advice from other worlds and past lives.

   Was deleting the sentence a good decision?

   F. No, because it connects the Spiritualism of the past to today's reader.
   G. No, because it elaborates on Spiritualism.
   H. Yes, because the information is not relevant to the point and interrupts the flow of the passage.
   J. Yes, because people then didn't use psychics.

<u>Nevertheless</u>, spiritualism was all the rage around the
3

turn of the century. Séances, rapping, table turning,

automatic writing and other occult methods of

contacting the spirit world attracted thousands. Doyle

was the antithesis of a man who would try

communicating with the dead; <u>and</u> after converting to
4

Spiritualism, he set about trying to convert others. ☐ **5**

[2]

<u>Eventually</u> Doyle's obsession seriously
6

compromised his reputation and strained his friendships,

most notably with the escape artist Harry Houdini, who

had once been a fake medium <u>since</u> whose training in
7

the "artifices of conjuring" led him to approach

Spiritualism with great skepticism. [2] <u>Although</u> the
8

most damaging blow to Doyle's good name resulted

from his outspoken advocacy of the existence of fairies,

---

3. A. NO CHANGE
   B. And yet
   C. Delete *Nevertheless* and correct the
      capitalization.
   D. In spite of this

4. F. NO CHANGE
   G. so
   H. however,
   J. therefore,

5. The author wants to give an example of Doyle's
conversion here. Which sentence or sentences would
best meet his needs?

   A. As the creator of Sherlock Holmes, Doyle relied
upon facts and proof to support his ideas and
theories. However, once he felt he had
accumulated the "proof" of Spiritualism, Doyle
began to share this proof with others.
   B. Although Doyle created Sherlock Holmes, a
man who relied on facts and clues, Doyle
himself did not feel he needed proof of
communication with the dead. Therefore,
throughout his life, Doyle sought to convince
others that his belief was right.
   C. When Doyle created Sherlock Holmes, he
described him as a man who believed in
Spiritualism. Once that belief became outdated,
however, Doyle edited those passages out of his
books.
   D. Doyle used to believe in Spiritualism. Then he
did not, but he convinced others to believe in it.

6. F. NO CHANGE
   G. In spite of this,
   H. Therefore,
   J. However,

7. A. NO CHANGE
   B. and
   C. but
   D. nevertheless

8. F. NO CHANGE
   G. Since
   H. Perhaps
   J. In spite of this

a matter somewhat fancifully retold in the film

Fairytale—A True Story, starring Peter O'Toole as

Doyle, which is scheduled to be released by Paramount

Pictures in October. [9]

[3]

In 1917, two girls from the Yorkshire village of
10
Cottingley made photographs of themselves cavorting

with fairies. Few took the pictures seriously, therefore
11
Doyle did. He wrote a book defending their

authenticity. [12]

9. The author considers adding the following sentence before Sentence 2:

> Houdini's skepticism of Doyle, since he was a friend of Doyle's and a man of renown himself, led to disbelief from other people as well.

Should he?

A. Yes, because it shows that Houdini was a friend of Doyle's.
B. Yes, because it links the disbelief of one person, Houdini, to that of others.
C. No, because the sentence does not logically flow from the sentence before it.
D. No, because Houdini did believe in Doyle's fairy stories.

10. F. NO CHANGE
G. Throughout the year of 1917
H. In the nineteenth century
J. Until 1917

11. A. NO CHANGE
B. as a result
C. hence
D. but

12. The author wishes to add a conclusion to the passage. Which sentence fits best?
F. Today, no one really believes in fairies.
G. Since the girls did not confess their hoax until 1983, Doyle died in 1930, still a believer.
H. In the movie, Peter O'Toole does a great acting job as Doyle.
J. Houdini never believed in fairies.

(Answers on pages 142–143)

Organization

Organization questions ask you about the best order or placement of sentences or paragraphs. There are two primary types of organization questions:

1. Place a new sentence in a paragraph or in a passage.
2. Reorder the sentences in a paragraph or the paragraphs in a passage.

There are no hard-and-fast rules for answering these questions. Read the passage to find which sentence, including the original sentence, makes the most sense. The one that sounds right probably is right.

The main idea should appear in the first sentence of a paragraph. The middle sentences in the paragraph should contain supporting details and explanations. The last sentence might contain a summary. The first paragraph in a passage should set the topic and tone for the entire passage, and the order of the paragraph should make common sense.

When you are asked about adding a passage, consider only the placements suggested in the answer choices. When reordering sentences or paragraphs, consider only the orders shown in the answer choices.

Complete these sample organization items. Then review the answers to learn how to answer them on the ACT.

 MODEL ACT PROBLEMS

These Model ACT Problems show how this topic might be tested on the real ACT. The answers and explanations immediately follow the problems. Try the problems and then review the answers and the explanations.

[1]

[1] Cloud-watching can often tell you what type of front is moving through. [2] For example, a cold front begins with high cirrus clouds. [3] A person can remember this order of clouds with the mnemonic word CANS. [4] Once you have seen the CANS clouds move through, the front has passed, and the air will probably grow colder. [5] Next come altostratus clouds, nimbostratus (low rain clouds), and finally very low stratus clouds.

5. Which of the following arrangements of sentences will make Paragraph 1 most sensible?

A.   NO CHANGE
B.   1, 4, 3, 2, 5
C.   1, 3, 2, 5, 4
D.   3, 2, 4, 5, 1

[2]

[1] Some clouds are caused by convection. [2] If you've ever been at the beach, you may have seen puffy clouds early in the day. [3] As the day wore on, these puffy clouds may have grown into convective rain clouds. [4] Later in the afternoon there may have been a rain shower or a thunderstorm.

6. The author of Paragraph 2 is considering adding this sentence:

(These convective rain clouds are called cumulonimbus clouds.)

The sentence should be added to the paragraph after sentence

F.   1
G.   2
H.   3
J.   4

5. This question asks for the most sensible arrangement of the sentences from among the choices given. Remember that you are asked to pick only from the choices given. There are 120 possible arrangements of the five sentences. So work backward from the answers and be flexible.

It doesn't make sense to begin with Sentence 3, so eliminate choice D.

Sentence 3 is obviously out of place in the passage, so eliminate choice A, "NO CHANGE." The remaining choices begin with Sentence 1. So the question is which sentence should come next — Sentence 3 or Sentence 4?

Sentence 3 should come next.

C is the correct choice.

6. Question 6 asks you to place a new sentence somewhere in Paragraph 2. The sentence is in parentheses, so we know that it is either a definition or an explanation. It is a definition.

The sentence defines cumulonimbus clouds as convective rain clouds. Look for one of these terms in the passage. "Convective rain clouds" appears in Sentence 3. The definition of convective rain clouds should come right after Sentence 3.

H is the correct choice.

Organization Subtest

This Subtest has the same number and type of organization items found on the ACT. These items make up part of the Rhetorical Skills (RH) subscore on the ACT. If you don't know an answer, eliminate and guess. Circle the number of any guessed answer. Check pages 143–144 for answers and explanations.

INSTRUCTIONS: Each paragraph and each sentence is numbered in the passage that follows. There is a corresponding item for each boxed number, offering three suggestions for changing the paragraph to make it understandable or consistent with the rest of the passage. If the numbered sentence is not improved by one of the three suggested changes, mark NO CHANGE.

Choose the best answer for each question based on the passage. Then fill in the appropriate circle on the answer grid.

```
1 Ⓐ Ⓑ Ⓒ Ⓓ       5 Ⓐ Ⓑ Ⓒ Ⓓ       9 Ⓐ Ⓑ Ⓒ Ⓓ
2 Ⓕ Ⓖ Ⓗ Ⓙ       6 Ⓐ Ⓑ Ⓒ Ⓓ      10 Ⓐ Ⓑ Ⓒ Ⓓ
3 Ⓐ Ⓑ Ⓒ Ⓓ       7 Ⓕ Ⓖ Ⓗ Ⓙ      11 Ⓕ Ⓖ Ⓗ Ⓙ
4 Ⓐ Ⓑ Ⓒ Ⓓ       8 Ⓕ Ⓖ Ⓗ Ⓙ
```

[1]

[1] As the curtain of darkness falls over the land, an entire universe is revealed. [2] Of course, understanding what we see is the goal of all of us who spend hours gazing up at a dark sky. [3] Stars pop out of the velvet darkness, and planets gleam, hiding a deeper truth than a simple telescope can reveal. [1] [2]

[2]

[1] It took many years before Christiaan Huygens, the 17th-century Dutch astronomer who discovered Saturn's moon Titan, figured out what he was seeing while observing Saturn. [2] In 1659 he realized that a set of rings surrounded the solar system's second largest planet, a conclusion that had initially escaped Galileo, who first observed the peculiar appendages in 1610. [3] Galileo's later observations indicate that he had some ideas about the rings' true nature, but he never stated them. [3] [4]

1. What is the best order of sentences in Paragraph 1?
   A. NO CHANGE
   B. 1, 3, 2
   C. 3, 1, 2
   D. 2, 3, 1

2. The author wants to add the following sentence to Paragraph 1:

   The sun is setting over the earth, and the night begins.

   Where should it be placed?

   F. After Sentence 2
   G. After Sentence 3
   H. After Sentence 1
   J. Before Sentence 1

3. The best order of sentences for Paragraph 2 is:
   A. NO CHANGE
   B. 1, 3, 2
   C. 2, 1, 3
   D. 3, 1, 2

[3]

[1] Try it on your neighbors this fall. [2] Today, even the smallest telescope is powerful enough to reveal the delicate structure of the rings. [3] On first sight through a telescope, Saturn makes most people gasp with surprise. | 5 | 6 | 7 |

[4]

[1] Saturn swims among the stars of Pisces the Fish, below the line of dim stars that forms the southern fish. [2] A nearly full moon glides half a degree north of Saturn on October 15. [3] For people in central Africa, Saudi Arabia, and much of Asia (including India, China, and Japan), the moon passes in front of Saturn on this night, occulting it from view. [4] By the end of October, Saturn is clear of the eastern horizon by nightfall and the only bright "star" in that area of sky. | 8 | 9 | 10 | 11 |

4. The author wants to add the following sentence to Paragraph 2:

   In fact, Galileo reported to Johannes Kepler that "Saturn consists of three stars in contact with one another."

   It would best fit:

   F. Before Sentence 1
   G. After Sentence 3
   H. After Sentence 2
   J. After Sentence 1

5. The author wants to delete a sentence (or sentences) in Paragraph 3. The best one(s) to delete are
   A. 1
   B. 2 and 3
   C. 3
   D. 1 and 2

6. The author then wants to replace the deleted sentence(s) with this one:

   Although Saturn is 780 million miles away, it is astounding owing to its radiance.

   Where in the passage should it go?

   F. At the beginning of Paragraph 3
   G. At the end of Paragraph 3
   H. In the middle of Paragraph 3
   J. At the end of Paragraph 2

7. The best order for the sentences in Paragraph 3 is:
   A. NO CHANGE
   B. 1, 3, 2
   C. 3, 2, 1
   D. 2, 3, 1

8. The best order for sentences in Paragraph 4 is:
   F. NO CHANGE
   G. 1, 4, 3, 2
   H. 4, 1, 2, 3
   J. 4, 3, 1, 2

9. The author wishes to delete one of the sentences in the paragraph. Which is best?
   A. Sentence 4
   B. Sentence 3
   C. Sentence 2 and change "this night" in Sentence 3 to "October 15"
   D. Sentence 1

10. What is the best order of paragraphs in this passage?
    F. NO CHANGE
    G. 4, 2, 3, 1
    H. 2, 4, 1, 3
    J. 3, 4, 2, 1

11. The author wants to add the following paragraph.

> Despite its great distance, Saturn has been known since ancient times because it glows so brightly. Bright clouds cover every square inch of its huge surface, reflecting 47 percent of the sunlight striking them. This copious amount of reflected sunlight, compared with the mere 12 percent reflectivity of our moon, gives Saturn much of its radiance.

It should be placed:

A. At the beginning of the essay
B. At the end of the essay
C. Between Paragraphs 1 and 2
D. Between Paragraphs 3 and 4

(Answers on pages 143–144)

Style

Style questions are about how well the passage communicates. There are a number of different types of style questions.

1. Correct wordy or redundant sentences and replace clichés.

These questions ask you to identify clear examples of wordiness. Be particularly alert for phrases which repeat the meaning, or lengthy phrases that could be replaced by a single word. Look at these examples:

Wordy: It was an hour after sunset, at night, when the train arrived at the station.
[The phrases "an hour after sunset" and "at night" repeat the same meaning.]

Revised: It was an hour after sunset when the train arrived at the station.

Wordy: The train was late because of the fact that the tracks were blocked.
[The phrase "because of the fact that" can be replaced by a single word.]

Revised: The train was late <u>because</u> the tracks were blocked.

Correct: Venus, the second planet from the sun, may be more like Earth than any other planet.
[The phrase "the second planet from the sun" provides extra information and is not redundant.]

A cliché is a trite expression, usually referring to everyday events, which has been used so often that it is stale or out of date. Clichés, some of which are shown below, should be replaced on the ACT.

beyond the shadow of a doubt	needle in a haystack	stubborn as a mule
dyed in the wool	on a silver platter	strong as an ox
easier said than done	sneaking suspicion	tried-and-true

2. Choose the correct word or words.

The vocabulary section of the reading review on pages 181–183 will help with this question type.

3. Choose wording which ensures that pronouns clearly refer to their antecedents.

Page 57 reviews pronoun-antecedent agreement.

4. Choose wording which maintains the level of style and the tone of a passage.

5. Choose wording which maintains the effectiveness of the sentence.

There are no hard-and-fast rules for answering questions of this type. Read the passage through to find out which of the wordings, including the original wording, sounds right. The one that sounds right probably is right.

MODEL ACT PROBLEMS

These Model ACT Problems show how this topic might be tested on the real ACT. The answers and explanations immediately follow the problems. Try the problems and then review the answers and the explanations.

Speaking of the weather, have you ever been outside during sleet (rain which freezes as it falls to earth)?
7
Sleet and freezing rain are different depending on conditions as it strikes the earth. Hail is
8
formed, created, when water droplets are blown again
9
and again into high altitudes, where the droplets freeze over and over. That is why hail is formed.
10

7. **A.** NO CHANGE
   B. (freezes as it falls to earth)
   C. (rain)
   D. OMIT the underlined portion

8. **F.** NO CHANGE
   G. as they strike
   H. as it struck
   J. as the rain strikes

9. **A.** NO CHANGE
   B. molded,
   C. structured,
   D. OMIT the underlined portion

10. **F.** NO CHANGE
    G. what
    H. how
    J. which

7. Item 7 is a classic redundancy and wordiness question. Notice that choice D is to omit the entire underlined portion. But the words in parentheses are not redundant. These words give a useful definition of sleet.

   A is the correct choice.

8. The underlined portion that corresponds to item 8 contains a pronoun, so be on guard for a pronoun-reference question. The pronoun "it" in the underlined portion does not have an antecedent in the sentence. Find an answer choice which solves this problem.

   Only choice J corrects the error by replacing the pronoun with a noun. Choice G just uses a plural pronoun, and choice H changes the verb to past tense.

   J is the correct choice.

9. Item 9 is another redundancy/wordiness question. And there is a redundancy. The underlined word "created" is just another way of saying "formed." It has to be removed. Choices B and C are also just synonyms for "formed."

   D is the correct choice.

10. Item 10 has to do with word usage. The word "why" doesn't fit here. The sentence before doesn't tell why hail is formed. It tells *how* hail is formed.

    H is the correct choice.

Style Subtest

This Subtest has the same number and type of style items found on the ACT. These items make up part of the Rhetorical Skills (RH) subscore on the ACT. If you don't know an answer, eliminate and guess. Circle the number of any guessed answer. Check pages 144–145 for answers and explanations.

INSTRUCTIONS: Certain words or phrases in the following passage are underlined and numbered. There is a corresponding item for each underlined portion. Each item offers three suggestions for changing the underlined portion to conform to standard written English, or to make it understandable or consistent with the rest of the passage. If the underlined portion is not improved by one of the three suggested changes, mark NO CHANGE.

Choose the best answer for each question based on the passage. Then fill in the appropriate circle on the answer grid.

1 Ⓐ Ⓑ Ⓒ Ⓓ	5 Ⓐ Ⓑ Ⓒ Ⓓ	9 Ⓐ Ⓑ Ⓒ Ⓓ
2 Ⓕ Ⓖ Ⓗ Ⓙ	6 Ⓐ Ⓑ Ⓒ Ⓓ	10 Ⓐ Ⓑ Ⓒ Ⓓ
3 Ⓐ Ⓑ Ⓒ Ⓓ	7 Ⓕ Ⓖ Ⓗ Ⓙ	11 Ⓕ Ⓖ Ⓗ Ⓙ
4 Ⓐ Ⓑ Ⓒ Ⓓ	8 Ⓕ Ⓖ Ⓗ Ⓙ	12 Ⓕ Ⓖ Ⓗ Ⓙ

[1]

The beauty of some words is <u>natural</u>. Consider
                                    1

these, found near the end of aviatrix Beryl Markham's

West With the Night:

[2]

"Like all oceans, the Indian Ocean seems never to

end, and the ships that sail on it are small and slow.

<u>They have</u> no speed, nor any sense of urgency; they do
 2

not cross the water, they live on <u>it until</u> the land comes
                                 3

home."

1. The author wishes to describe some words as unreal or mysterious:
   A. NO CHANGE
   B. pedantic
   C. unearthly
   D. normal

2. F. NO CHANGE
   G. It has
   H. They has
   J. The ships have

3. A. NO CHANGE
   B. the ocean until
   C. them until
   D. that until

[3]

It's a <u>satisfying</u> irony that when a reader goes
4
looking for thrills in the literature of adventure, what he
or she often finds—perhaps next to a description of a
narrow escape—is an otherworldly passage like the one
from Markham's book.

[4]

Authentic adventure, as surely as a sentence of
hanging, can concentrate the mind, <u>pacifying</u>
5

<u>it</u> to deeper truth, higher purpose. When starting any
6
of the adventure books mentioned here, prepare yourself

for the <u>certainty</u> that you'll discover descriptions you
7
never bargained for.

[5]

If you're looking for <u>boring</u> stories of adventure,
8
the literature of the polar regions is a good place to
start. Mankind in small parties has been venturing into
this geography of <u>beautiful desolation</u> for at least a
9

thousand years, and often <u>him</u> on the trip had decided to
10

take notes. <u>How</u> the enduring interest in the polar
11

regions? For openers, there's the literary <u>gawk factor</u>—
12
readers are drawn to accounts of people who have put
themselves at risk, and risk is commonplace in the
Arctic and Antarctic. One misstep there and the cold
can kill you.

(*Answers on pages 144–145*)

4. F. NO CHANGE
   G. unnatural
   (H.) complete
   J. verbal

5. A. NO CHANGE
   B. pleasing
   (C.) provoking
   D. angering

6. (F.) NO CHANGE
   G. the mind
   H. the adventure
   J. them

7. A. NO CHANGE
   (B.) possibility
   C. unlikelihood
   D. remote chance

8. F. NO CHANGE
   G. uninteresting
   H. vapid
   (J.) compelling

9. A. NO CHANGE
   B. ugly chaos
   C. beautiful chaos
   (D.) remote desolation

10. F. NO CHANGE
    (G.) somebody
    H. she
    J. he

11. A. NO CHANGE
    B. What
    C. When
    (D.) Why

12. (F.) NO CHANGE
    G. close-mindedness
    H. staring
    J. ogling

1: D. The fact that Doyle is an advocate of Spiritualism seems to be the opposite of something his super-rational detective, Holmes, would believe. Therefore, the correct linking word is *but* because it implies that the two (Holmes and Doyle) are not the same. The word *since* is incorrect because it states that Doyle's Spiritualism was caused by Holmes's super-rationalism, which is not proved in the paragraphs following. The introduction *that is* means the author is elaborating on a previous point, which is not the case here.

2: H. While the topic of the deleted sentence makes sense with the rest of the paragraph, the time frame does not. The other sentences refer to Doyle's time, while the deleted sentence refers to our time. Therefore, it makes sense to delete the sentence. J cannot be the correct answer, however, because the following sentences show that people at that time *did* believe in psychics and Spiritualism.

3: C. The word *nevertheless* would be used to state that although he believed in séances, others did not. Since the next sentence shows that others also believed in séances, A cannot be the right answer. The words *and yet* and *in spite of this* imply the same meaning as *nevertheless,* so they are incorrect also.

4: H. Using the word *however* completes the thought that although Doyle wasn't the type to believe in Spiritualism, once he did believe, he tried to convert others. The word *and* simply connects the two thoughts, as if they belonged together, which they don't. It doesn't make sense that if he weren't the type he would convert others; therefore, an explanatory word like *however* is needed. The words *so* and *therefore* both imply that he converted others because he was not the type to believe.

5: A. This sentence elaborates on the one before it, showing that he accumulated the "proof" of Spiritualism. Sentence B merely summarizes the paragraph without giving an example. There is nothing in the passage to support the idea that Holmes ever believed in Spiritualism, and the last choice, D, is the opposite of what the passage states.

6: F. Choices G and H imply that the strain on his relationship caused by his obsession was not related to that obsession and his attempt to convert others. Since this is not the case, they can be ruled out. Choice H implies that his conversion attempts caused his obsession to compromise his friendships. This may be partly true, but other factors, like time, seem to be a factor.

7: B. The word *since* does not make sense. The words "but" and "nevertheless" are also incorrect. They imply that knowing mediums to be fake (as he did) would lead him to believe in Spiritualism, rather than be skeptical.

8: H. Using either *although* or *since* as the opening word makes this sentence a fragment. There is no second half to that thought (such as "although the most damaging blow was this, another factor was. . ."). The phrase *in spite of this* implies that his strained friendship with Houdini was not a damaging blow, which it was.

9: B. The sentence flows logically from the sentence before it which already states that Houdini was a friend of Doyle's who did not believe in fairies. Therefore, the only logical answer is that it helps show how his obsession compromised many friendships.

10: F. The two girls made their photographs at a point in time in the year 1917, which is in the twentieth century. They did not make them all throughout the year, nor did they make any up until that year.

11: D. The words *therefore, hence,* and *as a result* imply that Doyle believed the pictures because others didn't and no causal link for this' is explained. The word *but* merely states that although others didn't believe the pictures, Doyle did.

12: G. The paragraph offers no proof that people today don't believe in fairies or that Houdini never believed in fairies. It is also not concerned with reviewing the movie starring Peter O'Toole. Since the passage gives a brief chronological look at Doyle's belief in Spiritualism and fairies, choice G gives the best conclusion to the essay.

✔ ANSWERS *(Organization Subtest, pages 135–137)*

1: B. The third sentence, "Stars pop out. . . ," makes the most sense if it follows the opening sentence. It is a continuation of the description that begins in that sentence. Then the second sentence adds to the idea of the deeper truth mentioned in Sentence 3.

2: J. The additional sentence lists an event that occurs before the current Sentence 1. By placing it first, the sentence "As the curtain of darkness. . ." elaborates on the idea that the sun is setting and night begins.

3: A. These sentences make sense as they are now. The second sentence cannot be first because then the reader would not know who the "he" is that is realizing something in 1659. Also, the sentence about Galileo cannot go before the opening sentence because then it has no reference—his observations that were later than what?

4: H. This sentence needs to fall between the first mention of Galileo and the final sentence about Galileo's later observations. The "in fact" means that this follows an initial statement about Galileo's findings. However, we know the report he gave to Kepler does not mention rings, and therefore it is not one of his "later observations."

5: A. This initial sentence makes no sense in Paragraph 3 as it stands. The word "it" in the first sentence has no reference—what should the reader try on his or her friends? The other two sentences, however, follow directly from the discussion of Saturn's rings in the paragraph above.

6: G. This sentence explains why people gasp in surprise—because it is so far away, yet so astounding. Therefore, it should go after Sentence 3.

7: D. By moving Sentence 1 to the end of the paragraph, the word "it" makes sense. People gasp with surprise if they look at Saturn through a telescope. So try it on your friends; make them look through the telescope at Saturn.

8: F. The paragraph makes the most sense as it is. The first sentence sets up where Saturn is in the sky. Sentences 2 and 4 explain in chronological order what happens to Saturn in October—the moon passes north of it, and by the end of the month it is the only bright star. Sentence 3 elaborates on Sentence 2—giving more information about it.

9: D. Deleting Sentence 1 would not affect the overall message of the paragraph. The other three sentences all describe Saturn's movement in the sky and the movement of other stars or moons in relation to it. Sentence 1 talks about astrology and could, therefore, be deleted.

10: F. The paragraphs make sense as they are. Paragraph 1 describes nightfall and the idea of looking at stars through a telescope. The second explains a specific instance of observation in relation to a telescope—this one about Saturn. Paragraph 3 elaborates on what we know about Saturn today, and the last tells where to look for Saturn in October.

11: D. This paragraph tells us more about Saturn in general and therefore should fall after Paragraph 3, but should be before Paragraph 4 because the last paragraph is much more specific about finding Saturn in the sky.

✔ *ANSWERS (Style Subtest, pages 140–141)*

1: C. The word *unearthly* describes something not of this earth, which is, therefore, often unreal. The word *natural* describes something belonging to nature or this earth, which would be very real. The word *pedantic* characterizes someone who is obsessed with conforming to rules, which something mysterious or unreal would not do. Finally, the word *normal* obviously does not mean *mysterious*.

2: J. The sentence needs to state the subject of speed—the boats. Since the Indian Ocean is the subject of the first sentence, it could be misread as saying the ocean has no speed.

3: B. Again, the referent "it" could be vague if not spelled out as "the ocean," which is what the boats live on.

4: F. Looking for thrills and adventure in a book is ironic because reading is a safe and nonadventurous task. However, the irony is satisfying in that the reader finds that adventure—rather than being unnatural.

5: C. The adventure spurs the mind on to a deeper understanding, or provokes it. *Pleasing* means the same as *pacifying*—this would not urge the mind on, but calm it into apathy. Also, the mind is not *angered* over this higher truth, so D cannot be correct.

6: F. The referent is not vague here; the word "it" clearly refers to "the mind" mentioned in the previous phrase. Therefore, the sentence does not need to be changed.

7: B. It is not proven that every reader will find descriptions that excite him or her. Also, the word "possibility" relates back to the idea that adventure *can* concentrate the mind—not *will* concentrate the mind.

8: J. The author is trying to promote stories of adventure and, therefore, would not refer to them as boring, vapid, or uninteresting. Instead, they are compelling, pushing the reader on to deeper truths.

9: A. The landscape of the polar regions is vast and empty—therefore, the term "chaos" would not work here. Also, *chaos* promotes a negative feeling, which the author is not trying to promote. The answer D won't work because it is redundant—most desolate places are also remote.

10: G. The terms *he, she,* and *him* don't refer to anyone mentioned in the sentence. Therefore, the correct answer must be *somebody.*

11: D. The only question that makes sense here is "Why?," which refers to cause. *What* refers to place; *when* refers to time; *how* refers to the way something is done.

12: F. The words *ogling* and *staring* don't work because they are not adjectives. *Gawk* gives the same impression in a more descriptive and accurate way.

Chapter 9

DIAGNOSTIC ENGLISH ACT

Take this Diagnostic English ACT after you complete the English review. This Diagnostic ACT is just like a real ACT, and it is the first of four English ACTs in this book. But this Diagnostic ACT is different. It is specially designed to help you decide which parts of the English section to review in more detail.

Take the Diagnostic English ACT under simulated test conditions. Allow 45 minutes to answer the 75 test questions. Use a pencil to mark the answer sheet, and answer the questions in the Test 1 (English) section.

Use the Checklist on pages 163–165 to mark the answer sheet. Review the answer explanations on pages 166–175. After you mark the test, complete the Diagnostic Checklist on pages 163–165. The Checklist directs you to the English skills you should review in more detail.

The test scoring chart on page 374 shows you how to convert the number of correct answers to an ACT scale score. The chart on page 377 shows you how to find the Usage/Mechanics and Rhetorical Skills Subscores.

DO NOT leave any answers blank. There is no penalty for guessing on the ACT. Remember that the test is yours. You may mark up, write on, or draw on the test.

When you are ready, note the time and turn to the Diagnostic English ACT. Stop in exactly 45 minutes.

Diagnostic English Checklist

Answer	Check if missed	Review this section	Pages
1. D	✓	Sentence Fragments	38–40
2. G	☐	Verbs; Verb Tense; Subject-Verb Agreement	62–63; 65–68; 74–75
3. A	☐	Strategy	126–127
4. F	☐	Colons and Semicolons	109–110
5. B	✓	Nouns	55–56
6. H	☐	Commas	105–106
7. D	☐	Verbs; Verb Tense; Subject-Verb Agreement	62–63; 65–68; 74–75
8. J	☐	Style	137–138
9. B	☐	Adjectives and Adverbs	81–82
10. H	☐	Sentence Fragments; Commas; Periods, Question Marks, Exclamation Points	38–40; 105–106; 114–115
11. B	✓	Style	137–138
12. G	☐	Organization	132–133
13. D	✓	Pronouns; Style	57–59; 137–138
14. G	☐	Style	137–138
15. C	☐	Organization	132–133
16. G	☐	Verbs; Verb Tense	62–63; 65–68
17. A	☐	Strategy	126–127
18. J	☐	Sentence Fragments; Periods, Question Marks, Exclamation Points	38–40; 114–115
19. D	☐	Comparative and Superlative Adjectives and Adverbs	85
20. H	☐	Run-on Sentences and Commas Splices; Commas; Periods, Question Marks, Exclamation Points	35–36; 105–106; 114–115
21. C	☐	Strategy	126–127
22. J	☐	Strategy	126–127
23. A	☐	Nouns	55–56
24. G	☐	Commas; Periods, Question Marks, Exclamation Points	105–106; 114–115
25. C	☐	Nouns; Apostrophes	55–56; 113
26. G	☐	Parallel Form	77–79
27. D	☐	Quotation Marks	116–117
28. H	✓	Style; Pronouns	57–59; 137–138
29. B	✓	Pronouns; Style	57–59; 137–138
30. J	☐	Organization	132–133
31. D	☐	Sentence Fragments; Commas; Semicolons and Colons	38–40; 105–106; 109–110;
32. H	☐	Style	137–138

Answer	Check if missed	Review this section	Pages
33. B	☐	Pronouns	57–59
34. H	☐	Strategy	126–127
35. D	☐	Style	137–138
36. J	☐	Run-on Sentences and Comma Splices; Commas; Periods, Question Marks, Exclamation Points	35–36; 105–106; 114–115;
37. B	☑	Comparative and Superlative Adjectives and Adverbs	85
38. F	☐	Strategy	126–127
39. D	☑	Strategy	126–127
40. H	☐	Run-on Sentences and Comma Splices; Commas; Semicolons and Colons; Style	35–36; 105–106; 109–110
41. C	☑	Verbs; Verb Tense; Subject-Verb Agreement	62–63; 65–68; 74–75
42. F	☐	Commas; Semicolons and Colons; Periods, Question Marks, Exclamation Points	105–106; 109–110; 114–115
43. B	☐	Style	137–138
44. G	☐	Strategy	126–127
45. A	☐	Strategy	126–127
46. F	☐	Verbs; Strategy; Style	62–63; 126–127; 137–138
47. C	☐	Strategy; Style	126–127; 137–138
48. J	☑	Run-on Sentences and Comma Splices; Commas; Semicolons and Colons; Strategy	35–36; 105–106; 109–110; 126–127
49. B	☐	Strategy	126–127
50. G	☐	Organization	132–133
51. A	☐	Commas; Periods, Question Marks, Exclamation Points	105–106; 114–115
52. J	☐	Strategy	126–127
53. B	☐	Parentheses; Strategy	111–112; 126–127
54. G	☑	Style	137–138
55. D	☐	Periods, Question Marks, Exclamation Points	114–115
56. H	☐	Adjectives and Adverbs	81–82
57. A	☐	Style	137–138
58. J	☐	Organization	132–133
59. D	☐	Style	137–138
60. F	☑	Strategy	126–127
61. C	☐	Verbs; Verb Tense; Subject-Verb Agreement	62–63; 65–68; 74–75
62. F	☐	Periods, Question Marks, Exclamation Points	114–115
63. B	☐	Strategy	126–127
64. J	☐	Organization	132–133
65. C	☐	Sentence Fragments; Commas; Periods, Question Marks, Exclamation Points	38–40; 105–106; 114–115
66. H	☐	Nouns	55–56

Answer	Check if missed	Review this section	Pages
67. C	☐	Sentence Fragments	38–40
68. J	☐	Organization	132–133
69. B	☐	Pronouns	57–59
70. F	☐	Nouns	55–56
71. A	☐	Run-on Sentences; Sentence Fragments	35–36; 38–40
72. H	☐	Sentence Fragments; Commas; Periods, Question Marks, Exclamation Points	38–40; 105–106; 114–115
73. D	☐	Organization	132–133
74. J	☑	Strategy	126–127
75. A	☐	Organization	132–133

Rhetorical Skills

Diagnostic English ACT Answers Explained

PASSAGE I

*ANSWERS*

1: D. "However" indicates a transition to a new, contradictory idea and must be set apart from the sentence by a comma. By using a period, the word "however" stands alone as a sentence fragment. The ellipses would indicate that words have been left out of this sentence, which does not appear to be the case.

2: G. The preceding clause states that Aristotle lived and wrote more than 2,000 years ago. Therefore, we can assume that he is not alive to complain today. Since this sentence discusses events that occurred in the past, the verb must be in the past tense.

3: A. The word that precedes this quotation, "complained," indicates that the following words are Aristotle's actual complaint. Though we do not know if these words were spoken or written, the authors intend to demonstrate that these words are directly attributable (though translated) to Aristotle. Quotation marks can be used to set off titles of shorter works such as essays and short stories, but the verb "complained" shows us that the following phrase is most likely not a title. There is nothing in this passage to indicate that Aristotle was in favor of juvenile delinquency or that the authors want to emphasize Aristotle's idea above any other ideas in the passage.

4: F. A colon is used to introduce a list or series, linking the words before the colon to the words that come after it. For a colon to be used before a list, the introductory phrase must be an independent clause, as it is here. The words "like these" help us look ahead to the list that follows. If a period or exclamation point were to be used instead, the headlines would not be well connected to the introductory idea. If no punctuation is used, the initial sentence becomes a run-on.

5: B. The writers here are trying to make these headlines stand out as they might in a newspaper (where headlines may or may not be all in capitals). Since the authors have written the remainder of the article using both initial capital and lowercase letters, we can assume that they are not concerned that the readers cannot see lowercase letters. We, as readers, have no way of knowing if these are actual headlines or if they are made up. They are simply representative of headlines that demonstrate juvenile delinquency.

6: H. The subject and the verb of a sentence should not be separated by punctuation, unless the verb comes later in a series of verbs, which must be set off by commas. By inserting a comma or a dash, the authors break up the flow of the sentence. By inserting a period, the independent clause is broken into sentence fragments.

7: D. "Disobeyed" is one verb in a series, including the words "violate" and "behave," both of which are in the present tense. In order to maintain parallel construction in this sentence, the present tense form ("disobey") must be used here.

8: J. All of these items endanger the safety of society. However, these are inappropriate comparisons for they all refer to animals, who are incapable of reason, as opposed to humans, who make conscious decisions to act in delinquent ways. Animals would not be considered delinquents. Additionally, while these animals can endanger the safety of society, they cannot be connected to any of the other parts of the definition of delinquent.

9: B. The word "many" refers to a large but indefinite number of specific items (people, dogs, shoes, etc.), while "much" refers to something that is great in quantity but cannot be counted in individual parts. Here, delinquency is an abstract term and cannot be counted, so "much" must be used. No comma is needed to separate this single adjective from the subject it describes.

10: H. A comma connects the initial independent clause with the dependent clause that follows. By placing a period, question mark, or exclamation point here, the dependent clause becomes a sentence fragment.

11: B. Because this is a formal article discussing juvenile delinquency, the most appropriate choice would be "young people." Though "kids" means the same thing, it is inappropriately informal for this article. Since the article is focused on delinquency by minors, the choice "adults" does not fit here.

12: G. Choice G introduces the subject of more serious teenage crime, sets off a list of examples of these types of crimes in dashes, then returns to the sentence to comment on them. The list, which is interesting, is nonessential information because it does not change the meaning of the sentence. To begin or end the sentence with this list places undue emphasis on this nonessential information and detracts from the impact of the sentence. In choice F, the list comes before we know why the author is presenting it; the reader has difficulty following the awkward sentence and determining its meaning.

13: D. Because the opening adverbial clause refers to "they," the subject immediately following this clause should indicate who this "they" is. Clearly, it is the "youthful criminals" committing crimes, not the courts or the adults who want them to get stricter sentences. While option C begins with "youthful criminals," the remainder of the sentence does not fit in with the remainder of the article, for it refers to adults rather than juvenile delinquents.

14: G. Because this passage contains the definition of delinquency and talks about juvenile delinquency in very broad terms, the article seems to be written to explain the concept to someone who has little or no knowledge of the subject. In no way do the authors make any statements or use any language to indicate that society is to blame or that youths should be treated with any special leniency. Though the authors mention the older pranks, there is no indication that these pranks were fun (especially for the person who had to get the cow down).

15: C. The subject of delinquency is introduced and defined in Paragraph 2. Since the other paragraphs expand on the information presented in this paragraph, it should begin the article. Paragraph 1 clearly does not belong up front because the opening sentence, ending with "however," clearly shows that the topic should already have been introduced elsewhere. Paragraphs 3 and 4 provide information about delinquency that could possibly stand on its own, but since a paragraph in this passage defines delinquency, the definition of delinquency must come first.

PASSAGE II

 ANSWERS

16: G. This form of the verb agrees with the plural subject of the sentence, "two reasons." In choices F and H, a plural subject is matched with a singular verb. The use of the future tense in choice J would indicate that these reasons will be created in the future.

17: A. The phrase "a year earlier" places the first sentence in time. Choice B leaves uncertain the time of Earhart's fame and glory. The adverbs "faster" and "sooner" would not logically apply to "In 1927."

18: J. Choices F and G make the dependent clause "Taking off from New York City" a sentence fragment. Choice H does not have the comma necessary to separate this long clause from the independent clause that follows.

19: D. Choice A is a superlative with absolute meaning. Therefore, it does not accept adverbs like "even." Choice C also tries to modify the superlative "best" by adding yet another adverb. Choice B, while grammatically correct, indicates that having a heroine would be negative, which does not fit in with the positive tone of the earlier sentences.

20: H. Choice F is a run-on sentence. Choice G is a comma splice, separating two independent clauses with a comma. Though the sentences are properly separated in choice J, the first sentence does not ask a question; therefore, the appropriate punctuation is a period, not a question mark.

21: C. Choices A, B, and D indicate a cause-and-effect relationship between being "outgoing and friendly" and being "modest and soft-spoken," characteristics that are generally unconnected. Only C indicates that it is unusual for someone to be both outgoing and soft-spoken at the same time.

22: J. Because the choices F, G, and H reiterate the meaning expressed in the word "across," they are unnecessary.

23: A. The title of a longer work, such as a book or a magazine, is always italicized or underlined.

24: G. A comma is needed to separate a subordinate element (the name George Putnam) from the rest of the sentence. Though this element contributes to the meaning of the sentence, it is not essential to its meaning. Choices H and J make the name George Putnam a sentence fragment.

25: C. Because the writer is describing Earhart's desire to fly, the apostrophe is necessary to form the possessive of "wife." Since Earhart is Putnam's only wife, choice B cannot be correct. Choice A is an incorrect spelling, but also indicates a plural for "wife," which does not make sense in the context of this sentence.

26: G. Choice F uses an adverb instead of a noun to describe one of Earhart's traits. Choice H uses an adjective to name this trait. While choice J uses the noun "intelligence," this noun is not followed by the comma necessary when there is a list of three or more nouns.

27: D. Since this final sentence asks a question, it must end with a question mark.

28: H. Since this sentence speaks only of Earhart, the pronoun that refers to her must be singular and feminine.

29: B. Since this sentence expresses a new thought, it should begin a new paragraph. However, the word "While" in responses A and C sets the reader up for a contradiction that does not occur. The word "while" should be omitted, and the new paragraph should begin with "Amelia."

30: J. Though the word "too" can be placed in many locations throughout the sentence, it most logically fits after the statement that "whatever men could do, women could do." When placed at the beginning of the sentence, "too" appears to be a transition word, leading into the sentence. This is inappropriate here because the sentence gives the reason why Amelia wants to fly, rather than another statement parallel to the previous sentence. The same problem occurs when "too" comes after "wanted" — it connects this sentence incorrectly to the previous sentence. Placing "too" after "men" does not make sense within the framework of the sentence.

PASSAGE III

ANSWERS

31: D. Choice A makes the second half of this sentence a fragment. In choice C, the use of a semicolon also breaks the second part of the sentence into a dependent clause or fragment. Since the dependent clause cannot stand alone, a semicolon cannot be used. A colon is also inappropriate, for it is not being used to introduce a list or explanatory material. A comma should be used to set off this parenthetical phrase from the rest of the sentence.

32: H. There is no language in this passage directed toward people of a certain age or sex. The writer does assume that the readers have a general familiarity with terms like "romanticism," but the material would be too general for someone who already knows a great deal about architecture.

33: B. Because this pronoun refers to people ("literary romantics"), rather than things, the pronoun *who* should be used.

34: H. This sentence focuses on Horace Walpole's importance to the Gothic Revival movement. The fact that he is a writer is of secondary importance, so it is mentioned later.

35: D. All of the suggested phrases are too casual for the more formal tone of this essay. Additionally, the information is not necessary to the meaning of the sentence, which already indicates that the style is a combination of neoclassical and Gothic elements.

36: J. This sentence as it stands is a run-on. By adding the comma, the sentence becomes a comma splice. Since the first clause of this sentence does not need greater emphasis, an exclamation point is inappropriate. Therefore, a period should separate the two independent clauses.

37: B. The word "unique" cannot be made into a superlative. Therefore, choices A, C, and D are all incorrect.

38: F. Because the sentence before this discusses the eccentric William Beckford, the following sentence should begin by focusing on him, rather than his central tower or his builder.

39: D. Choices A, B, and C are all redundant because they express the same idea that is simply reflected by the word "remains" in this sentence.

40: H. The words "In time" introduce a new line of thought. Therefore, the author should begin a new paragraph at this point.

41: C. The first clause of this sentence refers to actions of the architects; therefore, the second clause, in order to maintain parallel construction, should also refer to the actions of the architects. As it stands, the sentence shifts focus from the architects to the buildings.

42: F. In this case, the word "British" is an adjective describing the phrase "Houses of Parliament." Therefore, no comma is necessary. No other punctuation should come between the adjective and the words it describes.

43: B. England is on an island, though it is part of Europe. When the author refers to Germany and France, he refers to other European countries that are on the mainland continent of Europe. The reader must infer the meaning of this statement by examining the language of the passage as a whole.

44: G. Though the article mentions the effects of one particular architectural movement in the United States, the focus of the article is on this specific movement in England.

45: A. The author assumes that the reader is familiar with terms such as "romanticism," "Gothic," "gargoyle," etc. A glossary would help the less informed reader to understand what has been written.

PASSAGE IV

ANSWERS

46: F. The infinitive phrase functions here as a noun. The sentence could be reworded as "To discover . . . was disquieting." None of the other verb forms listed can function as subjects of a sentence. Therefore, choice F is the only acceptable answer listed.

47: C. The language in choices A and B is too informal. The word "stuff" is inappropriate in this context for a scientific essay. However, some lead-in to the many functions is necessary, so C is the best choice because it is formal but provides a connection to the list that follows.

48: J. When illustrating material is inserted into the middle of a larger sentence, dashes are used to set this material off from the rest of the sentence. Because a dash is used to begin the list of uses for this product, a dash must also be used to end the list and bring the reader back to the remainder of the sentence.

49: B. Clearly, some phrase must be inserted at this spot for the sentence to be logically and grammatically correct. Choices A and C offer alternatives that are not parallel in construction with the other items being listed here (which are the noun phrases "skin cancer" and "the weakening of the human immune system"). The noun phrase beginning with "the destruction" would follow correctly in this pattern.

50: G. As it stands, it sounds as if the author is questioning the molecules about their behavior. Since they are not living, speaking beings, this is illogical. By using the expression "the materials in question," the author states that he is referring to specific materials that have already been mentioned in this article.

51: A. As it stands, these sentences are both logically and grammatically correct. A question mark cannot be logically substituted for the period because the first sentence is not a question. By substituting a comma or by taking out punctuation altogether, the sentence becomes a run-on.

52: J. The entire essay is written in third-person point of view. Choices F and H unnecessarily introduce the first-person voice of the author into the passage. Choice G does not add any new information to the passage; based on the other information we've already read, we know the author is discussing the effect of these rays on Earth.

53: B. If this information were removed, it would not alter the main focus of the sentence. This information presents an interesting yet relatively unimportant fact. Brand names are neither secret (in fact, one hopes they are widely known!) nor set apart by parentheses in typical circumstances.

54: G. Choice F reflects language that is too casual for the formal, scientific tone of this essay. Choice J is also too casual, but in addition, it makes no sense (the Dupont people did not have any information that would completely destroy the environmentalists' concerns). Choice H is grammatically correct, but it makes no sense in the context of the sentence, because Dupont was disregarding the claims of environmentalists.

55: D. This sentence is not asking a question or making an emphatic statement. Therefore, a simple period will suffice for end punctuation.

56: H. The word "good" is an adjective and therefore used to describe a noun. "Well" generally functions as an adverb; when it does function as an adjective, it is used to describe a state of feeling. In this instance, the word must be an adjective describing the noun "evidence." Evidence generally cannot feel, so the adjective form of "well" would not apply. "Gooder" is an incorrect form.

57: A. The language of the text indicates that the author is frustrated because chemical companies continued to market dangerous materials for profits. Clearly, the author does not believe that Dupont had proof that CFCs were not harmful (they are) or that environmentalists thought that CFCs were actually good for the planet. Since the scientists produced data that showed CFCs were bad, the author is frustrated with everyone who ignored this data, not at the scientists who produced it.

58: J. The end of Paragraph 3 discusses how the depleted ozone layer allows more ultraviolet rays through to Earth. Paragraph 2 discusses the effect of these ultraviolet rays on Earth's life forms. It makes sense that the author would introduce the topic of ultraviolet rays before discussing their effects.

59: D. Most likely, this essay would be too general for an audience of scientists. While new Dupont employees might find this information interesting, it would probably not help their job performance. The vocabulary used by this author, including words such as "invulnerable" and "precipitating," would be too difficult for a child to understand. Additionally, some language of this essay ("photosynthetic microorganisms," for example) would require that the reader have some familiarity with basic scientific terms.

60: F. The final paragraph provided indicates that there is a connection between CFCs and the thinning of the ozone layer. However, without a specific explanation, the reader cannot be confident that there is a connection between them. While the other choices provide information that might be interesting, none of them offers a proper conclusion to this essay.

PASSAGE V

 ANSWERS

61: C. In order for this paragraph to maintain parallel structure, both verbs that refer to one subject must be in the same tense. Here, the word "buy" is in present tense, while the word "owned" is in past tense. Therefore, "owned" must be changed to "own" to fit with the phrase "could buy."

62: F. These sentences are fine as they are written. It would be illogical to put a question mark in place of the period, for the opening sentence is a statement, not a question. By removing the period or by inserting a comma, the two sentences are fused into a run-on sentence.

63: B. In this sentence, "A pioneer of the assembly-line method" refers to Ford, not the other car manufacturers or the cars themselves. Unless the subject to which the modifier refers directly follows the modifying statement, the modifier is misleading.

64: J. The phrase "in turn" is used to lead from the previous sentence into this sentence. In this instance, "in turn" means the same as "therefore" or "as a result." By removing this phrase from the opening of the sentence, the phrase no longer functions as a transition. In the other options listed, the phrase simply distracts the reader from the actual meaning of the sentence.

65: C. By removing the period, these two dependent clauses are joined together to form one independent clause. As they are written, the first and second sentences of this paragraph are both sentence fragments. The first sentence has no verb, while the second sentence has no subject. A question mark presents the same grammatical problem and is further complicated because the first clause is not interrogative. A comma should not be used to separate the subject of a sentence from its initial verb.

66: H. Because the word "cars" is the first item in a list of three nouns, it must be followed by a comma.

67: C. In options A and B, the words do not form a complete sentence; instead, they form a dependent clause that has no verb. While choice D appears to be a complete sentence, the verb presented is illogical within the framework of the sentence. Suburbs are not alive, and therefore, they could not have sprung up. Instead, the idiomatic expression "sprang up" makes logical sense because it comments on the growth that is occurring.

68: J. Sentences 3, 4, and 5 introduce the "Ford Idea." Sentence 2, which tells how this idea was soon accepted by other industries, belongs after the explanation of what this idea stood for. Additionally, the final sentence of the paragraph follows up on the idea expressed in Sentence 2, further reinforcing the need for Sentence 2 to fall between Sentences 5 and 6.

69: B. The proper pronoun for the subject of this sentence is "They," referring to Ford's workers. This is reemphasized later in the sentence when the author refers to "they" again. The use of "He" or "She" would indicate that the author was referring to Ford himself or to one of his workers. Since the article is entirely in the first person, the use of "We" is inappropriate here, unless the author (and possibly the readers) works for Ford.

70: F. The apostrophe here is unnecessary because the author is not referring to anything belonging to the factories; he is referring to the factories themselves. Therefore, the word as it is in the paragraph is correct.

71: A. As they stand, these two sentences are logically and grammatically correct. Both are independent clauses. Substituting a comma for the period creates a run-on sentence. A colon in this space would indicate that the second independent clause defined or directly expanded on the first clause, which is not the case. And while an exclamation point might be grammatically correct, it is not logically correct, for the sentence does not require any special emphasis.

72: H. The name of Ford's son is considered nonessential information (he had no other son) because it does not change the meaning of the sentence. Nonessential information must be set off from the sentence by some form of punctuation. In this case, the author opens the nonessential clause with a comma; therefore, the clause must also be closed with a comma. Placing a period here would break the sentence into two sentence fragments. While dashes can be used to set off nonessential clauses, there is no opening dash to indicate that a closing dash is necessary.

73: D. Because of the word "also" in this sentence, it is clear that this sentence must build upon similar information presented in another sentence. Since the only other sentence presenting this type of information is 4, this sentence must come after 4.

74: J. While the options listed here might provide interesting information, they would not contribute significantly to the general thesis of the article.

75: A. These paragraphs are already in the correct order. The article discusses Ford's achievements chronologically. The first paragraph begins "In 1900." The second paragraph mentions "Beginning in 1908." The third paragraph refers to "1914." The final paragraph, which discusses the actions of the Ford Foundation, refers to actions that have continued to occur through the present day. The logic of the argument flows along with this chronology.

Section III
Reading

The ACT Reading Test consists of four passages, with ten questions about each, for a total of 40 questions. Those at the ACT say these passages represent the types of materials you will read in college. You have 35 minutes to complete the Reading Test. That gives you a little under 9 minutes to complete the items for each passage.

In the plan there are 3 passages 25 questions 20 minutes

Passage Types

Each test has one prose-fiction passage, one social-science passage, one humanities passage, and one natural-science passage.

The *prose-fiction* passage is a short story or a part of a short story or novel. As the stories in these passages unfold, you pick up lots of information about characters — their actions, feelings, and motivations — and about the settings of the stories. Questions based on this passage often ask you to draw inferences about the characters and about why they feel or act as they do.

The *social-science* passage is about history, political science, economics, anthropology, psychology, or sociology. These passages give straightforward information about the subject, often with lots of detail, and may include the author's own opinions and conclusions. Questions based on this passage often ask you about the subject matter, including details about the subject matter, and ask you to identify or infer the author's opinions and conclusions.

The *humanities* passage is about art, music, philosophy, theater, architecture, or dance. These passages are very similar to the social-science passages, with straightforward information about the subject, and may include the author's own opinions and conclusions. Questions based on this passage often ask you questions about the subject matter, including details about the subject matter, and to identify or infer the author's opinions and conclusions.

The *natural-science* passage is about biology, chemistry, physics, or physical sciences. These passages give straightforward, technical information about a subject, often with lots of detail, and often including technical terms and symbols. Questions based on this passage are usually directly related to the subject matter presented and usually do not call for conclusions or inferences.

Spend more time on the easy ones.

Skills Tested

The ACT does *not* test specific reading or logical skills, but rather tests your general ability to answer questions about reading passages. All the items can be answered from the information in the passage. However, you are presented material out of context and asked to respond to test items in a very limited time period. You never do that in real life. This is what makes the reading test difficult.

In other words, the ACT Reading Test measures your ability to take the ACT Reading Test. It does not measure your ability to read and understand text material in regular situations, but standardized reading tests are like that. So just take the test for what it is. This chapter will help you prepare.

Since the Reading Test does not measure specific skills, this chapter does not begin with a diagnostic test. You should review all the sections in this chapter.

At the end of the chapter you will have a chance to practice your reading test-taking ability on a Diagnostic Reading ACT. The Diagnostic Reading ACT is just like the real thing, and your answers to the Diagnostic Reading ACT will help you decide if you need further review of the sections in this chapter. There are three more model ACT Reading Tests in Section IV of this book. Take these under simulated test conditions to help you prepare for the real ACT.

Chapter 10

VOCABULARY AND CONTEXT CLUES

The ACT Reading Test can include questions about vocabulary. But there will be only a question or two at most. There are no particular words that frequently occur on the ACT. Most of the vocabulary in ACT readings is not extremely difficult, and technical terms are usually explained in the reading. But you will come across some unfamiliar words that you may need to know to answer a question or to understand the passage. This section shows you how to figure out word meanings from context clues.

Context Clues

You can often determine the meaning of a word from its context — that is, from the way the word is used in a sentence. And you don't have to know the word's precise meaning. You just have to figure out enough to understand the meaning in the sentence.

Look at this example of an ACT vocabulary question.

> When Stubby entered the bank, he saw five or six queues standing before the tellers' windows. He took his place at the end of the first line. The bank was a busy place.*

1. The word *queues* in the first sentence most nearly means

   F. letters.
   G. lines.
   H. people.
   J. counters.

The second sentence mentions that he, Stubby, took his place at the end of the first *line*. This is the context clue we need. A *queue* must be a *line*.

Determine Meaning From Context Alone

You may be able to determine word meaning from context alone.

 **Examples**

   1. Jim's long nights in Greenland <u>inured</u> him to the cold.

What does the word *inured* mean in the sentence above? The context tells us that Jim's long nights in Greenland had some impact on his reaction to cold. Nights in Greenland are cold. Someone who had spent long nights in Greenland would be accustomed to cold. Rethink the sentence:

Jim's long nights in Greenland <u>accustomed him to (prepared him for, hardened him to)</u> the cold.

---

* Acknowledgments of sources appear on page 453.

2. Weights worn by divers enabled them to explore
the <u>benthic</u> region of the lake.

What does the word *benthic* mean in the sentence above? The context tells us that benthic refers to a particular region of the lake. Weights take divers deeper in the lake. So the benthic region is probably at or near the bottom of the lake. Rethink the sentence:

Weights enabled the divers to explore the region <u>at the bottom</u> of the lake.

3. Bob's very limited budget requires that he take a
<u>parsimonious</u> approach to gift expenditures.

What does the word *parsimonious* mean in the sentence above? The context tells us that it describes an approach to gift expenditures. A very limited budget means very limited expenditures. Parsimonious must mean something like very economical. Rethink the sentence:

Bob's very limited budget requires that he take a <u>very economical</u> approach to gift expenditures.

Determine Meaning From Synonyms

Synonyms may help you determine the meanings of words.

 **Examples**

4. Doug's presentations always seemed very
haphazard, but Lynn's talks were less <u>desultory</u>.

What does the word *desultory* mean in the sentence above? The context tells us it describes Lynn's talks. We can tell from the context that *desultory* and *haphazard* have very similar meanings. Replace the word *desultory* with the synonym *haphazard*. Rethink the sentence:

Doug's presentations always seemed very haphazard, but Lynn's talks were less <u>haphazard</u>.

5. It took years before a complicated <u>piscatory</u>
treaty was signed by representatives of the two countries.
As for me, I just go fishing.

What does the word *piscatory* mean in the sentence above? The context tells us that it describes a treaty. We can tell from the context that *piscatory* and *fishing* have very similar meanings. Replace the word *piscatory* with the synonym *fishing*. Rethink the sentence:

It took years before a complicated <u>fishing</u> treaty was signed by representatives of the two countries. As for me, I just go fishing.

Determine Meaning From Antonyms

Antonyms may help you determine the meanings of words.

 **Examples**

> **6.** I wish I could get someone to tell me the truth. All the stories I hear about Scott's nomination are <u>apocryphal</u>.

What does the word *apocryphal* mean in the sentence above? The context tells us that it describes the stories about Scott's nomination. We can tell from the context that *truth* and *apocryphal* have opposite meanings. Replace *apocryphal* with the opposite of *truthful*. Rethink the sentence:

I wish I could get someone to tell me the truth. All the stories I hear about Scott's nomination are <u>untruthful</u>.

> **7.** The first computers which filled whole buildings are <u>impuissant</u> compared to the powerful desktop computers of today.

What does the word *impuissant* mean in the sentence above? The context tells us that it describes the first computers. We can tell from the context that *impuissant* and *powerful* have opposite meanings. Replace *impuissant* with the opposite of *powerful*. Rethink the sentence:

The first computers which filled whole buildings are <u>not powerful</u> compared to the powerful desktop computers of today.

◀PRACTICE▶

Use context clues. Write the meaning of the underlined word.

1. After a series of arguments, a consultant was hired to develop <u>comity</u> between team members.

   Peace

2. She loved to recall obscure information. In fact, she was a veritable storehouse of <u>recondite</u> facts and figures.

   Random

3. How dare you question my <u>veracity</u>! I'm no liar.

   Truth

4. His first job required long hours of hard work. His current job was just the opposite, a veritable <u>sinecure</u>.

   easy job

5. The drill sergeant was tired of disciplining the <u>refractory</u> recruit.

disciplining

6. It seemed that the jury would find them guilty until a witness gave <u>exculpatory</u> testimony.

exhonorating, nonguilty

7. After years of a <u>peripatetic</u> existence, Joan finally had a chance to settle down.

unsettled, moving around

8. The huge, friendly monster <u>galumphed</u> across the stage.

move clumsily

9. Charitable contributions increase during the holidays when people are in more of an <u>eleemosynary</u> mood.

Charitable, giving

10. At the beginning of his clarinet lessons, Bob's playing was jarring to the ear. But after several years' lessons, his playing had acquired a <u>euphonious</u> sound.

pleasant to the ear

✔ ANSWERS

Word	Meaning	Key
1. **comity**	courtesy, civility	The reason for hiring a consultant after arguments is to establish friendlier, more courteous, relations.
2. **recondite**	obscure	The context reveals that *obscure* and *recondite* have similar meanings.
3. **veracity**	truthfulness	The context reveals that *liar* and *veracity* have opposite meanings.
4. **sinecure**	job with almost no work	The context reveals that *sinecure* and *job required long hours of hard work* have opposite meanings.
5. **refractory**	disobedient	Drill sergeants spend time disciplining disobedient recruits.
6. **exculpatory**	clear from guilt	The context reveals that *exculpatory* and *find them guilty* have opposite meanings.
7. **peripatetic**	moving from place to place	The context reveals that *peripatetic* and *settle down* have opposite meanings.

8. **galumphed**   walked with a
                      heavy tread

The word *galumphed* sounds like a someone or something walking with a heavy sound when the foot hits the floor.

9. **eleemosynary**   charitable

The context reveals that *charitable* and *eleemosynary* have similar meanings.

10. **euphonious**   pleasing to
                      the ear

The context reveals that *euphonious* and *jarring to the ear* have opposite meanings.

Chapter 11

READ EFFICIENTLY

The ACT Reading Test has two important parts — the passages to read and the items to respond to. This section shows you how to read passages efficiently. The next section shows you how to approach the items. Then I'll put the two together and show you the steps for taking the ACT Reading Test.

Efficient reading is effective reading. Efficient reading means picking out the important points in a passage. Efficient readers never read everything in a passage. And on the ACT Reading Test, you should read very efficiently. You are not responsible for knowing about an entire passage. You just have to know enough to answer the questions.

This section shows you how to identify the topic, main idea, and important details in a paragraph. The terms *topic, main idea,* and *details* are not important in themselves. Nor should they be interpreted rigidly. I just use them to show you how to quickly find the answer to a question.

Skim to Find the Topic of Each Paragraph

The first step in reading a passage is to skim to find the topic of each paragraph. The topic of a paragraph tells what the paragraph is about. Once you know the topic, you know where to look for information about that topic. If there is a test item about a particular topic, you don't have to look through the entire passage. You can go directly to the appropriate paragraph.

You usually find the topic of a paragraph in the first or last sentence. So skim the passage by reading the first and last sentence in each paragraph. You can also glance at any highlighted words. But that's it. You want to find the topic in a few seconds. And if you're not sure what the topic is, don't waste time rereading the sentences and *do not* read the whole paragraph. Jot down your best guess.

Examples

1. Plant leaves come in various shapes. Among the most distinctive leaf shapes are the fanlike, tooth-edged foliage of the *Fatsia japonica* and the deeply lobed leaves of the ubiquitous *Philodendron selloum.* But among the most popular of contemporary plants are the *Dracaena margiinata,* whose long sword-shaped leaves are edged with a reddish tinge.

What is this paragraph about? The first sentence mentions plant leaf shapes. The last sentence gives a specific example of a plant and the shape of its leaves.

A good topic: *shapes of plant leaves.* If a test question asked about plant leaf shapes, we would turn first to this paragraph for an answer.

2. Plant leaves come in various shapes, but sometimes a plant is distinguished by the arrangement of its leaves on the stem rather than by their shape. The oval leaflets of the *Brassais actinophylla* radiate out from one point on the stem, whereas the leaves of the *Pleomele reflexa* break out from the center head in a rosettelike effect.

What is the paragraph about? The paragraph in Example 2 seems very similar to the paragraph in Example 1. But the topics are different. The first sentence in Example 2 mentions plant shapes and leaf arrangements, and the last sentence gives a specific example of a leaf arrangement.

A good topic: *leaf arrangements and plants.* If a test question asked about leaf arrangements in plants, you would first look to this paragraph for an answer.

3. When Stubby entered the bank, he saw five or six queues standing before the tellers' windows. He took his place at the end of the first line. The bank was a busy place. Typewriters sputtered, bookkeeping machines hummed and clattered. People hurried in and out of the bank as though it were the last day of their lives. Business people were making weekend deposits; some carried brown paper bags that contained paper money, checks, and rolls of coins. Senior citizens cashed retirement checks, and others cashed personal checks for weekend shopping. An elderly lady limped along, pushing at her side a two-wheeled shopping cart.

This paragraph describes what is going on inside a bank lobby. A good topic: *bank lobby activities.* If a question asked about activities in the bank lobby, you would turn first to this paragraph.

4. There are two temperature scales in common use, the Fahrenheit and Celsius (also called *centigrade*). The Fahrenheit (F) scale is the one commonly used in the United States. On the Fahrenheit scale, water freezes at 32° and boils at 212°. In the metric system, scientists use the Celsius (C) scale or the Kelvin (K) scale. On the Celsius scale, water freezes at 0° and boils at 100°. On the Kelvin scale, water freezes at 273°K and boils at 373°K.

The first sentence mentions temperature scales. A good topic is just that, *temperature scales.* You don't want to concern yourself with all the details in this paragraph now. But if a question asks about temperature scales, you'll head right for this paragraph.

5. The most important concept in all nature is energy. It represents a fundamental entity common to all forms of matter in all parts of the physical world. Closely associated with energy is work. To a layman, work is a word used to describe the expenditure of one's physical or mental energy. In science, work is a quantity that is the product of force times the distance through which the force acts. In other words, work is done when force moves an object. Work and energy are related because energy is the ability to do work.

This first sentence mentions energy. The last sentence mentions *work and energy*. A good topic: *work and energy*. If a test question asked about work and energy, you would turn first to this paragraph for an answer.

A topic is like a signpost. It tells what the paragraph is about. So on the ACT you will write topics next to paragraphs. This will let you quickly find a paragraph.

Work

and

energy

The most important concept in all nature is energy. It represents a fundamental entity common to all forms of matter in all parts of the physical world. Closely associated with energy is work. To a layman, work is a word used to describe the expenditure of one's physical or mental energy. In science, work is a quantity that is the product of force times the distance through which the force acts. In other words, work is done when force moves an object. Work and energy are related because energy is the ability to do work.

PRACTICE

Finding the topic of a paragraph is more an art than a science. And reasonable people can differ about the topic of a particular paragraph. Remember that the topic is a signpost to take you back to a paragraph which contains the answer to a question. Any topic which accomplishes this task is a good topic. (*Answers immediately follow this Practice.*)

Skim each paragraph. Choose one of the listed topics and write it next to the paragraph.

1. When we think about memory on an intuitive level, it often seems as though our memories just fade away with the passage of time. It is as though some physical or chemical trace of an experience decays or degenerates as time progresses. The decay interpretation of memory is an old one and it is perhaps the most widely believed by the general public. But the idea that memories fade with the passage of time has not been supported by experimental research. Somewhat surprisingly, there is no direct evidence to support the decay interpretation. Although the idea is a simple one, it has not led to fruitful experimentation and must, at present, be taken as nothing more than an interesting possibility.

   Memory   Memory loss   Memory decay

   Remembering   Forgetting   Interesting possibilities

2. The task of classifying emotions, once a popular academic pastime, has fallen on hard times. There are just too many shades and variations among emotions to allow clear-cut, satisfactory definitions of them all. Modern psychology therefore limits identifying a few major emotions and classifying most emotions as either pleasant or unpleasant. (If you think about it, there just don't seem to be many neutral emotions.) In addition to

the pleasant-unpleasant distinction, modern psychology also tends to view emotions along a dimension from weak to strong.

Emotions   (Classifying emotions)   Strong emotions

Academics and emotions   Weak to strong emotions

Skim each paragraph. Write the topic next to the paragraph. You can use abbreviations for words if you wish.

3. All over the world, about 2 trillion gallons of freshwater are needed to meet human needs every day. In the United States alone, some 350 billion gallons of freshwater are used daily. If all the water in rainfall — or even a significant portion — could be regained, the supply of water would be adequate to meet our needs. Unfortunately, much of the water in rainfall cannot be recovered — at least not inexpensively. To make matters worse, tremendous quantities of water are being wasted by pollution and by carelessness of humans.

The needs for fresh water

4. Special pricing possibilities are involved when manufacturers introduce a new product. The most popular approach is called skimming. The manufacturer charges a high price during the introductory stage, later reducing it when the product is no longer a novelty and competition enters the market. Companies that adopt a skimming policy try to recover their development costs as quickly as possible through high initial prices. Typical examples of skimming involved the first television sets and penicillin.

Skimming used in companies' sales

5. The distinctions between positive and normative economics are fundamental. For one thing, a normative economic statement implies a desired outcome or state of affairs; a positive economic statement need not. When the President's Council of Economic Advisors predicts a rise in unemployment, it is merely asserting what it thinks will happen. On the other hand, anyone who maintains that the rate of inflation ought to be reduced of necessity must believe that such a reduction would be a good thing.

positive and normative economics

6. Blows to the head are a common cause of brain damage. The symptoms vary widely depending on the severity and the location of the blow. You have probably heard the term "punch drunk" applied to prizefighters. Their speech is slow and slurred, and their physical movements may be awkward. They are showing the cumulative effects of many contusions, or bruises to the brain tissue, caused by the repeated battering they have received in the ring.

effects of brain damage

7. I went to the woods because I wanted to live deliberately, to confront only the essential facts of life, and see if I could not learn what it had to teach, and not, when I came to die, discover that I had not lived. I did not wish to live what was not life, living is so dear, nor did I want to practice resignation, unless it was quite necessary. I wanted to live deep and suck all the marrow out of life, to live so sturdily and Spartan-like as to put to rout all that was not life, to cut a broad swath and shave close, to drive life into a corner, and reduce it to its lowest terms, and, if proved to be mean, why then to get the whole and genuine meanness of it, and publish its meanness to the world; or if it were sublime, to know by experience, and be able to give a true account of my next excursion.

Why I went to the woods

8. An early humanist writer was Francesco Petrarch (1304–1374). He wrote poems called sonnets in Latin and Italian. Many of the sonnets express his love for a woman named Laura. Another well-known humanist was Giovanni Boccaccio (1313–1375). He wrote a book called *The Decameron*. It was created during the time of the terrible Black Death plague in Italy. The stories are told by a group of ten young men and women. They live in an isolated house in the country to escape the plague. The group amuses itself by making fun of many customs of the Middle Ages.

Writings of Italian humanists

9. Economic models are supposed to provide insight into the operation of the real world (in the same way that a laboratory-built prototype of a new model automobile provides information about the operating characteristics of yet-to-be-built production-line cars). But not all models do this. The effectiveness of a specific economic model is related to its predictive value. This is determined by comparing the theoretical predictions of the model with the appropriate empirical evidence. If there is little or no significant difference between theory and fact, the model is considered an accurate representation of reality. If there is a sizable disparity between the real world and the theory, the model must be modified until it gives a better approximation of reality, or scrapped in favor of an entirely new approach. This is the essence of positive economics.

How models are used for predictions

10. Possibly the greatest of all composers, [he] wrote romantic music: sonatas, concertos, an opera, and nine symphonies. His works marked the transition of music from the court and aristocracy to the concert hall and general public. About the *Third (Eroica) Symphony*, it is said that Beethoven tore up the dedication to Napoleon upon hearing that Napoleon had taken the title of emperor. The *Fifth Symphony,* perhaps best known of all symphonies, opens with four notes that Beethoven likened to fate knocking at the door. Beethoven combined orchestra and chorus, which sings Schiller's *Ode to Joy,* as the final movement in the *Ninth (Choral) Symphony*.

Beethoven's musical compositions.

**ANSWERS**

1. *Memory decay* is the best choice for this paragraph. If there was a question about memory decay, you would come to this paragraph to find the answer. *Memory* is too general a topic. The paragraph is not about *Memory loss,* which is a much more severe condition. Neither *Remembering* nor *Forgetting* captures the essence of this paragraph. The term *Interesting possibilities* just happens to occur in the last sentence.

2. *Classifying emotions* is the best choice for this paragraph. If there was a question about classifying emotions, you would be likely to find the answer in this paragraph. *Emotions* is too general. The terms *Strong emotions* and *Weak to strong emotions* refer to ways of classifying emotions.

3. *Freshwater — needs and waste* is a good topic for this paragraph. The first sentence mentions freshwater needs, and the last sentence mentions that tremendous quantities of water are wasted.

4. *Skimming — a pricing policy* is a good topic for this paragraph. The first sentence mentions pricing policies, and the last sentence mentions skimming. These two terms capture the essence of this paragraph.

5. *Pos. vs. norm. eco.* is a good topic for this paragraph. You will often use abbreviations when you write topics next to paragraphs on the actual ACT. The first sentence gives the topic for this paragraph.

6. *Head blows and brain damage* is a good topic for this paragraph. The first sentence gives the topic for the paragraph.

7. *Why I went to the woods* is a good topic for this paragraph. The first sentence states as much and gives many of the reasons.

8. *Humanist writers* is a good topic for this paragraph. The first sentence mentions a single humanist writer, but the word "group" in the last sentence indicates that the paragraph is about the group of humanist writers.

9. *Positive economic models* is a good topic for this paragraph. The first sentence mentions economic models, and the last sentence mentions positive economics.

10. *Beethoven's compositions (works, music)* is a good topic for this paragraph. The first sentence outlines the works of a composer, and the last sentence mentions Beethoven by name. *Beethoven,* alone, would not be a good topic for this paragraph. You would turn to this paragraph to answer a question about his music, but not to answer a question about his private life.

Read a Paragraph for the Main Idea

If you were taking an actual ACT Reading Test, you would first preview each paragraph for a topic. Then you would read the questions one at a time and return to the passage to find the answer. Quite frequently, the answer to a question is related to the main idea of a paragraph. For now, we are going to skip the questions and go directly to a discussion of the main idea.

The main idea of a paragraph is the most important thing the writer has to say about the topic of the paragraph. The answers to many ACT test items are based on the main idea of a paragraph or a passage. Some ACT questions ask directly for the main idea. We have already found the topics for the paragraphs below.

Stated Main Idea

A stated main idea can be found among the words in the paragraph. The sentence containing the main idea is called the topic sentence. The examples below show the main idea and the topic sentence.

Examples

Shapes of

plant leaves

4. <u>Plant leaves come in various shapes</u>. Among the most distinctive leaf shapes are the fanlike, tooth-edged foliage of the *Fatsia japonica* and the deeply lobed leaves of the ubiquitous *Philodendron selloum.* But among the most popular of contemporary plants are the *Dracaena margiinata,* whose long sword-shaped leaves are edged with a reddish tinge.

The topic of this paragraph is shapes of plant leaves. But what does the author have to say about this topic? In this short paragraph the main idea is easy to spot: *Plant leaves come in various shapes.*

This main idea is found in the first sentence. So the first sentence, underlined above, is the topic sentence.

The paragraph contains other details and explanations that are too specific to be the main idea. But you may need to refer to these details and explanations to answer questions.

Leaf

arrang.

and

plants

5. Plant leaves come in various shapes, <u>but sometimes a plant is distinguished by the arrangement of its leaves</u> on the stem rather than by their shape. The oval leaflets of the *Brassais actinophylla* radiate out from one point on the stem, whereas the leaves of the *Pleomele reflexa* break out from the center head in a rosettelike effect.

A good main idea: *plants can sometimes be distinguished by their leaf arrangements.* The examples of plant leaf arrangements in the paragraph are too specific to be the main idea. However, these details may help you answer a question.

Work

and

energy

6. The most important concept in all nature is energy. It represents a fundamental entity common to all forms of matter in all parts of the physical world. Closely associated with energy is work. To a layman, work is a word used to describe the expenditure of one's physical or mental energy. In science, work is a quantity that is the product of force times the distance through which the force acts. In other words, work is done when force moves an object. <u>Work and energy are related</u> because energy is the ability to do work.

A good main idea: *work and energy are related* is found in the last sentence. The details about how and why work and energy are related are too specific to be the main idea. But these details may help you answer a question.

◖PRACTICE▶

Write the topic next to the paragraph. Underline the topic sentence. Write the main idea below each paragraph. (*Answers immediately follow this Practice.*)

1. Final goods are goods and services purchased by all sectors for final consumption, not for additional processing or resale. Intermediate goods are goods and services that undergo additional processing or are resold. Final goods, thus, are the result of the nation's productive effort, while intermediate goods are all the goods and services that will be processed further to make final goods. The distinction between final and intermediate goods is not necessarily the same as that between finished products and raw materials. In the previous example, polyethylene is an intermediate good when it is used by the waterbed manufacturer to make his product for households. If the polyethylene is sold directly to households, it becomes a final good. A product may be either a final good or an intermediate one, depending on who buys it and for what purpose.

Main idea: _____The difference between final and intermediate goods_____

2. Few of us are totally immune from depression, but in most cases our actions and feelings would not warrant the use of the term *depressive neurosis.* Thus, periods of grief and mourning following the death of a loved one are perfectly natural. In fact, a person who does not show some such reaction probably would be seen by others as a cold, uncaring person. However, if depression is quite persistent and is severe enough to interfere with our lives in some important way, a psychiatric label would be in order. Whether our depression is seen as neurotic or psychotic depends on how much it incapacitates us. We will have more to say about depression when we deal with psychotic depression later in this chapter.

Main idea: _____Depression_____

3. To further economic knowledge, economists often develop models consisting of logically constructed theories of economic behavior in which the assumptions and conclusions bear some resemblance to reality. These models begin with assumptions designed to simplify reality by focusing on the essential characteristics of an economic situation. At the same time, however, the assumptions must be sufficiently realistic so the conclusions logically derived from them will be relevant and meaningful. Ideally, a model reduces the analysis of economic activity to manageable proportions, while preserving the significant features of the real-world problem under investigation.

Main idea: _____Economic models_____

4. The composition of a mixture may vary. Thus, different quantities of iron filings and powdered sulfur can form a variety of mixtures. Recall that the composition of a compound does not vary and that the compound is referred to as homogeneous matter. This means that the composition of the compound is the same throughout the compound. On the other hand, the composition of a mixture may not be the same throughout the mixture — it may vary — and the mixture is referred to as *unhomogeneous* matter.

Main idea: _____Composition of mixtures vs. compounds._____

5. In national income accounting, it is assumed that households consume all the products they buy; hence, every commodity purchased by the household sector for the first time is considered a final good. Items bought by households after the original sale are *not* final products. For example, the acquisition of a new car is included in personal consumption expenditures, and in GNP. But the purchase of a used car is not included because the used car was part of the GNP in the year in which it was sold for the first time. To include the value of any subsequent sale as part of the current production would involve multiple counting. (Remember, the function of the GNP is to measure *output*, not sales.)

Main idea: _____Final sales vs. not final sales,_____

6. In the 1860s and 1870s, a completely different style of painting began in France. It was called *Impressionism*. Impressionists wanted to show the effect of light on their subjects. They generally used much brighter colors than the Romanticists and Realists. In creating their scenes of natural views of everyday life, they used small dabs of color side by side. The eye blended the colors and "saw" the objects the artist had painted. Leading Impressionists were Claude Monet (1840–1926), Pierre Renoir (1841–1919), and Edgar Degas (1834–1917).

Main idea: _____Impressionism_____

7. Obsessional thinking cannot be observed directly, but compulsive behavior is public and so it can be observed easily. Compulsive behavior tends to be very stereotyped and ritualistic, so experimenters have tried to find out what produces such behavior in laboratory animals. One way is to give an animal a problem that cannot be solved, for instance one where it gets unpredictable punishment no matter which way it jumps (Maier, 1949). This training does lead to stereotyped behavior, such as always jumping in the same direction.

Main idea: _____What produces compulsive behavior_____

 **ANSWERS**

1. *Topic:* Final vs. intermediate goods

   Main idea: Final goods are bought for final use while intermediate goods are bought for reprocessing or resale.

   The last sentence confirms that the paragraph is about the difference between final and intermediate goods. The main idea is found in the first two sentences.

2. *Topic:* Depression vs. depressive neurosis

   Main idea: Most depressing feelings do not indicate a depressive neurosis.

   The first sentence provides the topic and the main idea.

3. *Topic:* Economic models

   Main idea: Economic models are logically constructed theories in which the assumptions and conclusions bear some resemblance to reality.

   The first and last sentences confirm that the topic is economic models. It might be tempting to choose "economic knowledge" as the topic since the first sentence begins with these words. However, this paragraph is not about economic knowledge.

   The main idea comes directly from the first paragraph.

4. *Topic:* Composition of a mixture

   Main idea: The composition of a mixture may be unhomogeneous (vary throughout the mixture).

   The first and last sentences confirm that this paragraph is about the composition of a mixture. This is a better topic than just "mixture." If a test question asked about the composition of a mixture, you would want to come right to this paragraph, and a topic of "mixture" might not lead you directly here.

   The last sentence of the paragraph provides the main idea. This paragraph contains information about compounds. The homogeneity of compounds is mentioned to help explain the possible unhomogeneity of a mixture.

5. *Topic:* GNP measures output.

   Main idea: The GNP measures output through the value of goods purchased for the first time.

   The first sentence mentions "national income accounting" and "final good," while the last sentence mentions "GNP."

The paragraph makes a series of logical connections leading to the main idea that only the cost of final goods is included in the GNP.

6. *Topic:* Impressionist painting

Main idea: Impressionist painting founded in France in the 1860s and 1870s used dots of color.

The last sentence and the italic type provide the topic. The names of the painters and the comparison with other painting styles are not a part of the main idea.

7. *Topic:* Obsessional thinking vs. compulsive behavior

Main idea: Obsessional thinking cannot be observed directly; compulsive behavior can be observed easily.

The first sentence provides both the topic and the main idea.

Unstated Main Idea

The main idea of a paragraph may not be stated. If the main idea is unstated, there will be no topic sentence. This type of paragraph may contain details related to the topic. The main idea will summarize or bind together these details. Unstated main ideas are found most frequently in prose-fiction passages. The unstated main idea of a prose-fiction passage may be a description of a character or a scene, or it may convey some other aspect of the story.

Look at this example. I said earlier that a good topic for this paragraph was bank lobby activities. But the main idea is unstated.

☞ *Example*

Bank

lobby

activities

7. When Stubby entered the bank, he saw five or six queues standing before the tellers' windows. He took his place at the end of the first line. The bank was a busy place. Typewriters sputtered, bookkeeping machines hummed and clattered. People hurried in and out of the bank as though it were the last day of their lives. Business people were making weekend deposits; some carried brown paper bags that contained paper money, checks, and rolls of coins. Senior citizens cashed retirement checks, and others cashed personal checks for weekend shopping. An elderly lady limped along, pushing at her side a two-wheeled shopping cart.

The paragraph describes lots of things going on inside the bank lobby. And the main idea is that simple: *The bank lobby is a busy place.* That is what the writer is trying to get across. The writer used details to get this idea across instead of just writing that the bank lobby is a busy place.

Write the topic next to the paragraph. Write the main idea below each paragraph.
(*Answers on page 198*)

1. About fifteen miles below Monterey, on the wild coast, the Torres family had their farm, a few sloping acres above the cliff that dropped to the brown reefs and to the hissing white waters of the ocean. Behind the farm the stone mountains stood up against the sky. The farm buildings huddled like clinging aphids on the mountain skirts, crouched low to the ground as though the wind might blow them into the sea. The little shack, the rattling, rotting barn were gray-bitten with sea salt, beaten by the damp wind until they had taken on the color of the granite hills. Two horses, a red cow and a red calf, half a dozen pigs, and a flock of lean, multicolored chickens stocked the place. A little corn was raised on the sterile slope, and it grew short and thick under the wind, and all the cobs formed on landward sides of the stalks.

   Main idea: _____ The Torres family's farm _____

2. We came from the place where the sun is hid at night, over the great plains where the buffalo live, until we reached the big river. There we fought the Alligewi, till the ground was red with their blood. From the banks of the big river to the shores of the salt lake, there was none to meet us. The Maquas followed at a distance. We said the country should be ours from the place where the river runs up no longer on this stream to a river twenty suns' journey toward the summer. The land we had taken like warriors we kept like men. We drove the Maquas into the woods with the bears. They only tasted salt at the licks; they drew no fish from the great lake; we threw them the bones.

   Main idea: _____ A Native American group fighting for land. _____

3. The [boat] pranced and reared and plunged like an animal. As each wave came, and she rose for it, she seemed like a horse making at a fence outrageously high. The manner of her scramble over these walls of water is a mystic thing, and, moreover, at the top of them were ordinarily these problems in white water, the foam racing down from the summit of each wave requiring a new leap and a leap from the air. Then, after scornfully bumping a crest, she would slide and race and splash down a long incline, and arrive bobbing and nodding in front of the next menace.

   Main idea: _____ A boat in water compared to a horse. _____

4. Fertile, level land and a favorable climate encouraged family-size farms, which produced surplus grain (wheat, corn, and oats) for export to the other colonies. Long, navigable rivers, such as the Hudson, Susquehanna, and Delaware, promoted trade with the Indians for furs. First-class harbors, such as New York and Philadelphia, stimulated trade with other colonies, England, and the European continent.

   Main idea: _____ Trade in colonial times. _____

1. *Topic:* Torres family farm

Main idea: The small, dilapidated Torres farm stands in contrast to the majesty of the sea and mountains around it.

The ACT tests your ability to interpret main ideas in fiction passages such as this one.

2. *Topic:* A tribe's journey

Main idea: The tribe traveled over the plains from the great river (Mississippi?) to the sea, and vanquished their enemies.

Understanding this main idea means understanding the clues provided by the Native American speaker. The first line, "We came from a place where the sun is hid at night," gives a further clue about where this tribe may have originated — further north where the sun shines day and night during the summer.

3. *Topic:* Riding in this boat

Main idea: Riding in this boat is like riding a bucking horse.

The first line compares the boat to an animal, and the second sentence mentions a horse. All the details suggest that the boat is like a bucking horse.

4. *Topic:* Trade in the eastern colonies

Main idea: Favorable growing conditions, navigable rivers, good relations with Native Americans, and first-class harbors helped develop trade in the eastern colonies.

The topic for this paragraph is not immediately apparent. On the actual ACT, do not read the entire paragraph as you skim through the passage. And you have to skim through the entire paragraph before you have the topic and the main idea.

Chapter 12
ITEMS AND ANSWER CHOICES

Items

On the actual ACT Reading Test you will read the items after you skim to find the topic for each paragraph. You read each item and the answer choices and then go back to the passage to identify the correct answer choice. In this section you will learn how to crack the different types of items and answer choices on the ACT.

There are four passages on the ACT Reading Test. There are ten test items for each passage, and each item has four answer choices. One of the answer choices is always correct. Every question can be answered from the information in the passage. But the items are written so they can be hard to answer. Some refer directly to the information in a passage. Others ask you to draw a conclusion or ask you to draw an inference based on the passage. Each item consists of an incomplete statement or a question and four answer choices. First I'll discuss the item statements and questions and then the answer choices.

Item Statements and Questions

Each item begins with a statement to complete or a question to answer. Carefully read each item statement or question. It will tell you which topic to look for in the passage.

Look at this example of how the ACT could get at the same information through a sentence-completion item and a question item. The first item begins with a statement ending in the word "because." The colon signals that this is a completion item. The word "because" signals that the correct completion choice will explain why the United States government blocks freedom of the press during wartime.

Statement:

The United States government often blocks the freedom of the press during wartime because:

A. citizens should be concentrating on the war, not on the news.
B. the government is concerned that the news might endanger the war effort.
C. Americans do not have the right to know what goes on in a war.
D. the press cannot accurately report wartime information.

The correct answer choice is B. The statement, together with the correct answer choice, form a sentence which is true.

The following item begins with a question. The word "Why" at the beginning of the question signals that the correct answer choice will explain why the United States government blocks freedom of the press during wartime.

Question:

Why does the United States government often block freedom of the press during wartime?

A. Because citizens should be concentrating on the war, not on the news

B. Because the government is concerned that the news might endanger the war effort

C. Because Americans do not have the right to know what goes on in a war

D. Because the press cannot accurately report wartime information

The correct choice is B, the only appropriate answer to the question.

Answer Choices

Each item has four answer choices. The correct answer choice correctly completes the item statement or answers the item question. The correct answer choice usually restates the writer's words, purpose, or tone. Oh, occasionally you may come across a correct answer choice taken word for word from the passage. But this is very rare.

Incorrect answer choices are written to make you think they are correct. Test writers call these kinds of answer choices "distracters." Distracters introduce doubt and turn your head from the correct answer. Spotting and eliminating these distracters is an important key to scoring well on the ACT Reading Test.

So spotting the answer choice which correctly restates the author's ideas and spotting distracters are two important keys for doing well on the ACT. On the actual ACT, you will first eliminate incorrect answer choices. And there are three times as many incorrect choices as correct choices. Let's review incorrect choices first.

Eliminate Incorrect Answer Choices

The more answer choices you can eliminate, the easier it is to choose the correct answer. Eliminate answer choices you *know* are false.

Listed below are the most common categories of distracters on the ACT. Not every answer choice fits exactly into one of these categories, and there is certainly no reason for remembering these words. But these categories will help you think about and pick out incorrect choices. Watch out for these distracters. They are out to trick you!

The Weasel. A distracter may try to *weasel* in a misstatement of the author's words. This type of distracter distorts the meaning of the passage. Even a slight change in wording or meaning may make the answer choice incorrect. The weasel is the most popular form of distracter.

The Shift. A distracter may try to *shift* your thinking to choose the correct answer to another question. This type of distracter correctly represents the meaning of the passage.

The Enticer. A distracter may try to *entice* you to choose it just because it is very appealing or appears to be universally true.

The Extreme. An incorrect answer choice may include *extreme* words such as "always" and "completely." If you can think of one exception, or if the answer is debatable, then the extreme answer choice is incorrect. Not all extreme answer choices are incorrect.

The Weasel

The *weasel* is a distracter that misrepresents the passage. Some weasels are sly and just change the author's wording or meaning. Other weasels are sneaky and turn the author's words or ideas around. Yet other weasels are tricky and take words out of context from the passage. Weasels pop up so often that I am going to spend a little extra time with them. Look at the following examples of weaseling.

Examples

1. Fertile, level land and a favorable climate encouraged family-size farms, which produced surplus grain (wheat, corn, and oats) for export to the other colonies.

Now look at these examples of how ACT test writers might use the weasel to distract you.

A. Fertile, level land and a favorable climate produced surplus grain.

This statement does not accurately reflect the passage. The words are taken out of context from the passage. It is not mentioned that the climate and land encouraged family-size farms which in turn produced surplus grain.

B. The need in other colonies for grain encouraged the development of family farms.

This statement turns the author's ideas around. The author *does not* say that the need for grain in other colonies encouraged the development of family-size farms. The author *does* say development of family farms created surplus grain for export to the other colonies.

> **C.** The favorable climate meant that every family who lived on the fertile, level land owned a farm.

Just see how this statement weasels around to try to convince you that it is correct. Almost all the words are from the passage. But the statement misrepresents the meaning of the passage.

> **D.** The grain produced on the family-size farms was exported to the other colonies.

This statement is incorrect because the word "surplus" is omitted. A reasonable inference is that surplus grain, not all grain, was exported to other colonies.

Now read this passage. Each sentence is numbered to make it easier to refer to later.

> **2.** (1) Obsessional thinking cannot be observed directly, but compulsive behavior is public and so it can be observed easily. (2) Compulsive behavior tends to be very stereotyped and ritualistic, so experimenters have tried to find out what produces such behavior in laboratory animals. (3) One way is to give an animal a problem that cannot be solved, for instance one where it gets unpredictable punishment no matter which way it jumps. (Maier, 1949) (4) This training does lead to stereotyped behavior, such as always jumping in the same direction.

There are eight statements below about the passage. Each statement could be an answer choice on a regular ACT. Cross off the letters of the statements that do not accurately reflect the passage, as shown for **A**.

> ~~**A.**~~ Obsessional thinking cannot be observed.
> **B.** Compulsive behavior is easily observed, so it is public.
> **C.** Compulsive behavior tends to be performed as a part of a ritual.
> **D.** Experimenters have tried to find out why compulsive behavior appears in laboratory animals.
> **E.** When you give an animal a problem that can't be solved, it jumps.
> **F.** One way to measure compulsive behavior is to give an animal a problem no matter which way it jumps.
> **G.** Training does lead to stereotyped behavior.
> **H.** Laboratory animals always jump in the same direction.

None of the statements accurately reflects the passage. Given below is a brief review of why each statement does not accurately reflect the passage. I have matched the sentences from the passage with the statements for easy comparison.

Explanation of Example 2

> (1) Obsessional thinking cannot be observed directly, but compulsive behavior is public and so it can be observed easily.

> A. Obsessional thinking cannot be observed.

This statement is word for word from the passage. But the statement is incorrect because the word "directly" was left off. There is a gigantic difference in meaning between "cannot be observed" and "cannot be observed directly." In fact, the passage implies that obsessional thinking can be observed indirectly by observing directly compulsive behavior.

> B. Compulsive behavior is easily observed, so it is public.

This statement turns the author's meaning around. The author doesn't say that "easily observed" means "public." Rather the author says that "public" means "easily observed." That's a world of difference.

> (2) Compulsive behavior tends to be very stereotyped and ritualistic, so experimenters have tried to find out what produces such behavior in laboratory animals.

> C. Compulsive behavior tends to be performed as a part of a ritual.

The weasel at work again. A ritual does not have to be underway for compulsive behavior to occur. It says that compulsive behavior is ritualistic, meaning compulsive behavior tends to take the same form time after time.

> D. Experimenters have tried to find out why compulsive behavior appears in laboratory animals.

The word "why" makes this statement false. The experimenters did not try to find out *why* compulsive behavior appears in laboratory animals. They tried to find out *what* causes compulsive behavior in laboratory animals.

> (3) One way is to give an animal a problem that cannot be solved, for instance one where it gets unpredictable punishment no matter which way it jumps. (Maier, 1949)

> E. When you give an animal a problem that can't be solved, it jumps.

Most of the words are from the passage, but this statement does not reflect the passage—at all. The statement just takes words out of context and tries to weasel you into choosing it because the words sound familiar.

7. One way to measure compulsive behavior is to give an animal a problem no matter which way it jumps.

All of these words are from the passage. But this choice takes words out of context and bears no resemblance to the meaning in the passage.

    (4) This training does lead to stereotyped behavior, such as always jumping in the same direction.

5. Training does lead to stereotyped behavior.

The words are taken directly from the passage and the passage does describe training that leads to stereotyped behavior. But the statement above does not specify the type of training. So the statement means that any training would lead to stereotyped behavior. You can't draw that meaning from the passage.

4. Laboratory animals always jump in the same direction.

The passage does not say that laboratory animals always jump in the same direction. It says that one type of stereotyped behavior is always jumping in the same direction. Big difference!

◀ **PRACTICE** ▶

Write two weasel statements and one true statement about the passage above. See if your friends can figure out which statement is true and which statements are the weasels. Be really tricky and cunning. Mix up the order to make it harder to pick out the weasels.

Weasels

1. _One way to measure compulsive behavior is to give an animal a problem no matter which way it jumps_

2. _Training does lead to stereotyped behavior_

True

1. _Obsessional thinking cannot be observed directly_

PRACTICE

Read this passage.

> Final goods are goods and services purchased by all sectors for final consumption, not for additional processing or resale. Intermediate goods are goods and services that undergo additional processing or are resold. Final goods, thus, are the result of the nation's productive effort, while intermediate goods are all the goods and services that will be processed further to make final goods. The distinction between final and intermediate goods is not necessarily the same as that between finished products and raw materials. In the previous example, polyethylene is an intermediate good when it is used by the waterbed manufacturer to make his product for households. If the polyethylene is sold directly to households, it becomes a final good. A product may be either a final good or an intermediate one, depending on who buys it and for what purpose.

Read each item and cross off the letter of each incorrect answer choice. All incorrect choices are weasels. The answer choice not crossed off is the correct choice.

1. According to the passage, it is true that:

    A. a product can be a final good and an intermediate good.
    B. intermediate goods are the raw materials used to make final goods.
   C. intermediate goods are goods purchased by sectors.
   D. intermediate goods undergo additional processing.

2. According to the passage, final goods:

    F. are goods produced nationwide.
    G. consist of goods purchased by all sectors.
   H. are exemplified by polyethylene.
   J. may have been intermediate goods.

 ANSWERS

1. According to the passage, it is true that:

   A. a product can be a final good and an intermediate good.

   You could have arrived at this correct choice by eliminating the incorrect choices.

   B. intermediate goods are the raw materials used to make final goods.

   This choice changes the meaning of the passage. The passage includes the statement "The distinction between final and intermediate goods is not necessarily the same as that between finished products and raw materials."

¢. intermediate goods are goods purchased by sectors.

There is no mention of intermediate goods being purchased by sectors. The reference to sectors and final goods in the first sentence means that final goods may be purchased by consumers, businesses, manufacturers, etc.

∅. intermediate goods undergo additional processing.

This misstates the passage. Intermediate goods may undergo additional processing or be resold.

2. According to the passage, final goods:

∮. are goods produced nationwide.

This choice misstates the passage. Final goods are used to measure the nationwide output, not to measure the goods produced nationwide.

¢. consist of goods purchased by all sectors.

Something important is left out here. Final goods are purchased by all sectors for final consumption.

∦. are exemplified by polyethylene.

Final goods can be exemplified by polyethylene when the polyethylene is purchased for final use.

J. may have been intermediate goods.

You could have arrived at this correct choice by eliminating the incorrect choices.

The Shift

The *shift* is an incorrect answer choice that could be the correct answer choice to another item.

 **Example**

Read this short passage.

> Fertile, level land and a favorable climate encouraged family-size farms, which produced surplus grain (wheat, corn, and oats) for export to the other colonies. Long, navigable rivers, such as the Hudson, Susquehanna, and Delaware, promoted trade with the Indians for furs. First-class harbors, such as New York and Philadelphia, stimulated trade with other colonies, England, and the European continent.

Read the item below. Cross off the incorrect responses. The choice remaining is the correct choice.

1. According to the passage, the factor which helped promote trade with the Indians was:

   A. fertile, level land and favorable climates.
   B. family-size farms which produced surplus grain.
   C. long, navigable rivers.
   D. first-class harbors.

All of the incorrect answer choices are examples of the shift. Look at the explanations below.

1. According to the passage, the factor which helped promote trade with the Indians was:

   A. fertile, level land and favorable climates.

This choice is incorrect, but it is the correct answer to a question about which factors led to the development of family-size farms.

   B. family-size farms which produced surplus grain.

This choice is incorrect, but it is the correct answer to a question about what produced grain for export to the colonies.

   C. long, navigable rivers.

You could have arrived at this correct choice by eliminating the incorrect choices.

   D. first-class harbors.

This choice is incorrect, but it is the correct answer to a question about which factors stimulated trade with the other colonies, England, and the European continent.

The Enticer and the Extreme

The *enticer* is an incorrect answer choice which entices with incorrect but very appealing wording. The *extreme* is an incorrect answer choice which might be true if it did not include extreme words such as "always," "completely," "perfectly," etc. If an answer choice sounds too nice or too extreme or absolute, it is probably not the correct choice.

 *Example*

Read this passage.

> We came from the place where the sun is hid at night, over the great plains where the buffalo live, until we reached the big river. There we fought the Alligewi, till the ground was red with their blood. From the banks of the big river to the shores of the salt lake, there was none to meet us. The Maquas followed at a distance. We said the country should be ours from the place where the river runs up no longer on this stream to a river twenty suns' journey toward the summer. The land we had taken like warriors we kept like men. We drove the Maquas into the woods with the bears. They only tasted salt at the licks; they drew no fish from the great lake; we threw them the bones.

Read the items below. Cross off the incorrect responses. The choice remaining is the correct choice.

1. According to the passage, the Native American tribe referred to in the passage as "we":

   A. were in harmony with nature and their gods.
   B. fought with more than one other group of Native Americans.
   C. won all their battles.
   D. were steadfast in the face of adversity.

2. When the tribe referred to as "we" reached the banks of the salt lake:

   F. they established an ideal community.
   G. they cared for their sick and wounded.
   H. they had completely vanquished their foes.
   J. they laid claim to the lands to the south.

Explanation

1. According to the passage, the Native American tribe referred to in the passage as "we":

   A̶. were in harmony with nature and their gods.

This choice is incorrect and the classic example of an enticer. The image is appealing, but there is no basis for the statement in the passage. On the actual ACT you may find yourself tempted to choose this type of answer. Resist!

   B. fought with more than one other group of Native Americans.

You could have arrived at this correct choice by eliminating the incorrect choices.

¢. won all their battles.

This choice is incorrect and a classic example of an extreme. The paragraph never says they won all their battles.

ⱷ. were steadfast in the face of adversity.

This sounds so nice and so enticing. You might like to think of the Native American tribe in this way. But there is nothing in the paragraph to support this choice.

2. When the tribe referred to as "we" reached the banks of the salt lake:

ⱷ. they established an ideal community.

This choice is incorrect and is the classic example of an extreme. It is hard to imagine an ideal community under any circumstances. And there is nothing in the passage to confirm this choice.

¢. they cared for their sick and wounded.

This enticing statement is so appealing, so irresistible, and so incorrect. There is nothing in the passage to confirm this statement.

ⱷ. they had completely vanquished their foes.

Incorrect. It seems reasonable to infer that the tribe vanquished their foes. But completely vanquished? Most extreme answer choices such as this one are incorrect, and there is nothing in the passage to confirm this choice.

J. they laid claim to the lands to the south.

You could have arrived at this correct choice by eliminating the incorrect choices.

◖▉PRACTICE▉▶

There are four paragraphs below: one prose fiction, one social science, one humanities, and one natural science. Earlier you found the topic of these paragraphs. There are two items for each paragraph. These items are designed to help you practice eliminating the different types of incorrect answer choices. The pattern of incorrect answer choices may not appear an the actual ACT.

Read each paragraph in turn and read the items for each paragraph. Do not try to find the correct answer. Rather, cross off the incorrect answer choices for each item. Then write *Weasel, Shift, Enticer, Extreme,* or *Correct* in the space provided beneath each answer choice.

(*Answers immediately follow this Practice.*)

Prose Fiction

When Stubby entered the bank, he saw five or six queues standing before the tellers' windows. He took his place at the end of the first line. The bank was a busy place. Typewriters sputtered, bookkeeping
5 machines hummed and clattered. People hurried in and out of the bank as though it were the last day of their lives. Business people were making weekend deposits; some carried brown paper bags that contained paper money, checks, and rolls of coins. Senior
10 citizens cashed retirement checks, and others cashed personal checks for weekend shopping. An elderly lady limped along, pushing at her side a two-wheeled shopping cart.

1. According to the narrator of this story, people in the bank were:

   A. only senior citizens and elderly.
      extreme weasel

   B. content in the bank's friendly atmosphere.
      shift enticer

   C. coming and going.
      correct

   D. humming and clattering.
      weasel shift

2. One purpose of this paragraph is to suggest that Stubby's visit to the bank was set in a time period:

   F. when the bank was always busy.
      shift extreme

   G. of economic prosperity.
      shift

   H. when people thought it was the last day of their lives.
      weasel

   J. a number of decades ago.
      correct

Social Science

When we think about memory on an intuitive level, it often seems as though our memories just fade away with the passage of time. It is as though some physical or chemical trace of an experience decays or
5 degenerates as time progresses. The decay interpretation of memory is an old one and it is perhaps the most widely believed by the general public. But the idea that memories fade with the passage of time has not been supported by experimental research. Some-
10 what surprisingly, there is no direct evidence to support the decay interpretation. Although the idea is a simple one, it has not led to fruitful experimentation and must, at present, be taken as nothing more than an interesting possibility.

1. According to the passage, the decay interpretation of memory:

   A. is a wonderful interpretation which helps the general public.
      shift enticer

   B. is the ideal interpretation of memory.
      extreme weasel

   C. has a physical or chemical basis.
      weasel

   D. is fairly well accepted by the public.
      correct enticer

2. The author mentions physical and chemical traces as an example:

   F. of the cause of memory decay.
      shift

   G. to indicate that the decay interpretation of memory loss has not led to fruitful experimentation.
      weasel correct

   H. to prove that memory loss is a harmonious and natural part of aging.
      enticer shift

   J. of what memory decay seems like.
      correct weasel

Humanities

In the 1860s and 1870s, a completely different style of painting began in France. It was called *Impressionism*. Impressionists wanted to show the effect of light on their subjects. They generally used
5 much brighter colors than the Romanticists and Realists. In creating their scenes of natural views of everyday life, they used small dabs of color side by side. The eye blended the colors and "saw" the objects the artist had painted. Leading Impressionists
10 were Claude Monet (1840–1926), Pierre Renoir (1841–1919), and Edgar Degas (1834–1917).

1. According to the passage, Impressionist painters:

   A. used bright colors.

weasel

   B. showed the effect of light on their subjects.

correct

   C. created beautiful paintings which captured the soul of their subjects.

shift enticer

   D. used small dabs of paint side by side.

shift enticer

2. What does the author mean in line 8 when he writes "The eye blended the colors . . . "?

   F. The artist blended the colors by just looking at them before applying the paint.

weasel

   G. Impressionism was an entirely different style of painting.

enticer

   H. A person looking at the painting blended the colored dots.

correct

   J. Claude Monet, Pierre Renoir, and Edgar Degas

shift

Natural Science

The most important concept in all nature is energy. It represents a fundamental entity common to all forms of matter in all parts of the physical world. Closely associated with energy is work. To a layman,
5 work is a word used to describe the expenditure of one's physical or mental energy. In science, work is a quantity that is the product of force times the distance through which the force acts. In other words, work is done when force moves an object. Work and energy
10 are related because energy is the ability to do work.

1. According to the passage, the scientific concept of work can be described as:

   A. the force it takes to move an object.

weasel

   B. the expenditure of one's physical or mental energy.

enticer

   C. a quantity.

correct

   D. a universal concept which resonates throughout nature.

shift

2. It can reasonably be inferred from the passage that:

   F. energy is created as the result of work.

weasel enticer

   G. the amount of energy depends on the force and the distance.

weasel

   H. scientific and colloquial definitions are often different.

correct

   J. the concept of energy is the most interesting in nature.

shift

Prose Fiction

1. A̶. **The Weasel.** This choice picks out people who were in the bank and then tries to weasel in the word "only." The people in the bank were *not* just senior citizens and elderly people.

   B̶. **The Enticer.** The image of people content in a friendly atmosphere is very enticing, but there is nothing in the paragraph that confirms this statement.

   C. **Correct.** You could arrive at this correct answer choice by just eliminating the incorrect answer choices.

   D̶. **The Shift.** This choice is the correct answer to a question about how bookkeeping machines sounded.

2. F̶. **The Extreme.** The word "always" always makes us suspicious. This is an extreme statement. There is nothing in the statement to suggest that the bank is always busy.

   G̶. **The Enticer.** There is nothing in the paragraph to support this enticing, positive statement.

   H̶. **The Weasel.** This statement takes the phrase "last day of their lives" out of context.

   J. **Correct.** You could arrive at this correct answer choice by just eliminating the incorrect answer choices.

Social Science

1. A̶. **The Enticer.** There is nothing in the paragraph to support this enticing, positive statement.

   B̶. **The Extreme.** The word "ideal" is another of those words that make us suspicious. There is nothing in the paragraph to suggest that the decay interpretation is the ideal interpretation of memory.

   C̶. **The Weasel.** This choice takes some of the words used to describe the sensation of memory decay and incorrectly applies them here.

   D. **Correct.** You could arrive at this correct answer choice by just eliminating the incorrect answer choices.

2. ~~F~~. **The Weasel.** The cause of memory decay is not stated in this paragraph.

   ~~G~~. **The Shift.** This choice is the correct answer to a question about experimental support for the decay theory.

   ~~H~~. **The Enticer.** There is nothing in the paragraph to support this enticing, positive statement.

   J. **Correct.** You could arrive at this correct answer choice by just eliminating the incorrect answer choices.

Humanities

1. ~~A~~. **The Weasel.** The paragraph does not say Impressionists use bright colors, just that they generally used brighter colors than Romanticists and Realists.

   ~~B~~. **The Shift.** This choice is the correct answer to a question about what Impressionists wanted to do.

   ~~C~~. **The Enticer.** There is nothing in the paragraph to support this enticing, positive statement.

   D. **Correct.** You could arrive at this correct answer choice by just eliminating the incorrect answer choices.

2. ~~F~~. **The Weasel.** The context of the sentence shows that the colors are "eye blended" by someone looking at the artist's work, not by the artist.

   ~~G~~. **The Shift.** This choice is the correct answer to a question about Impressionism in the 1860s and 1870s.

   H. **Correct.** You could arrive at this correct answer choice by just eliminating the incorrect answer choices.

   ~~J~~. **The Shift.** This choice is the correct answer to a question which asked for the names of three leading Impressionists.

Natural Science

1. ~~A.~~ **The Weasel.** This choice turns around the meaning of the passage.

   ~~B.~~ **The Shift.** This choice is the correct answer to a question about the unscientific meaning of work.

   C. **Correct.** You could arrive at this correct answer choice by just eliminating the incorrect answer choices.

   ~~D.~~ **The Enticer.** There is nothing in the paragraph to support this enticing, positive statement.

2. ~~F.~~ **The Weasel.** This choice turns around the meaning of the passage.

   ~~G.~~ **The Weasel.** This choice takes the meaning of work and uses it as the meaning of energy.

   H. **Correct.** You could arrive at this correct answer choice by just eliminating the incorrect answer choices.

   ~~J.~~ **The Weasel.** This choice uses words directly from the paragraph but replaces the word "important" with the word "interesting." This makes the choice incorrect.

Choose the Correct Answer

Choosing the correct answer is not a science. The approach I present here is not infallible. No approach is. But if you follow the steps described below, you will significantly improve your chances of getting the correct answer.

Some Answer Choice Truths

Choose the correct answer choice after you have eliminated the answer choices you're sure are incorrect. You may get lucky and eliminate all three incorrect answer choices. The correct answer will be the only choice remaining. But ACT test writers are sneaky. They write incorrect answer choices that are very hard to eliminate. So you will usually have two, three, or sometimes four choices remaining after you have eliminated the incorrect choices.

Each ACT reading test item includes a correct answer. You don't have to come up with the correct answer, just decide which answer choice is correct. ACT writers don't want to have two correct answer choices. And they certainly don't want to have a passage with no correct answers. So those at the ACT will be sure that there is one and only one correct answer choice.

If you just guess without eliminating incorrect choices, you have a 25 percent chance of guessing the correct answer. If you eliminate two incorrect choices, you have a 50 percent chance of guessing the correct answer. I'm not saying to just guess after you have eliminated incorrect choices, although you will always guess if you're not sure of the correct answer. What I am saying is that the answer is there for the choosing.

What makes the test difficult is that the test writers have hours and hours to make the items hard. You just have a few seconds to decipher their deception. I know that this does not happen in real life. This is the reason you learn the steps for taking the test in Chapter 13. You know how to find the topics, main ideas, and details. That's where the answer will most likely be found. There may be some questions about the entire passage. In that case, the topics will still guide you to the correct answer. But most often the test writers will not just take the correct answer word for word from the passage. The correct answer usually restates the author's words.

With all this in mind, go over the steps for taking the ACT Reading Test. Then you'll have a chance to practice the steps on an ACT-type passage. The answer to each question will be explained. Then it's on to the Diagnostic ACT Reading Test, where you'll have a chance to practice the steps on an entire ACT Reading Test.

Chapter 13

STEPS FOR TAKING THE ACT READING TEST

Choose the Order in Which to Read the Passages

The order of passages on the ACT Reading Test is always the same:

Passage I — Prose Fiction
Passage II — Social Science
Passage III — Humanities
Passage IV — Natural Science

But you don't have to work on the passages in that order. Flip through the test booklet and just glance at each passage. This is also a good way to preview the material.

The general wisdom is to **read the easier passages first.** You may decide the order in advance, or you may base your decision on the apparent difficulty of the passages. But **decide the order quickly.**

Write 1, 2, 3, and 4 next to the passage numbers on the test to show the order. Write the numbers big and circle them. Complete the passages in that order. Just remember to match the passage with the correct section on the answer sheet.

Skim each passage. Write a topic next to each paragraph.

You learned how to skim paragraphs and how to identify and write topics earlier in this section. You're going to do the same thing here. Remember, you don't have a lot of time to do this. Skim the passage quickly and write the best topic you can.

Four Steps for Choosing the Correct Answer Choice

After writing the topic for each paragraph, follow these steps to respond to the items. You have already reviewed all these steps. Now you'll have an opportunity to practice using all of them.

Step 1. Read the item statement or question.

Each item begins with an item statement or a question. Read it carefully to be sure you know exactly what the question is asking.

Step 2. Go to the part of the passage most likely to contain the answer.

The item specifically mentions the part of the passage about 25 percent of the time. The item may identify a particular paragraph by number, or the item may refer to particular lines in the passage. In these cases, you know exactly where to look for the answer.

Most of the time you will rely on the topics you have written. Find the topic or topics most likely to contain the answer to the item and focus on those paragraphs.

Step 3. Read the answer choices and eliminate incorrect answer choices.

You know how to do this. Cross off the letters for the answer choices you're sure are incorrect. This is the most important step for finding the correct answer choice. It's usually easier to spot incorrect choices than to spot correct choices. Your chances of choosing the correct answer go up significantly with each incorrect choice you cross off.

Step 4. Choose the correct answer from the remaining choices.

Look at the answer choices that are not crossed off. Choose the correct answer from among the remaining choices. If you are not sure which of the remaining answers is correct — guess, guess, guess.

Practice ACT Passage

Passages on the ACT look exactly like the one on the following page. Each passage begins with the passage number. The circled 1 next to this passage number indicates that we have "decided" to read this passage first.

Next comes the type of passage. The humanities passage is the third passage on the ACT Reading Test. Then comes the source of the passage and, on some forms of the test, one sentence telling what the passage is about. This introductory information can help prepare you for the material you're about to read.

The passage and items are set in two columns. Lines in the passage are numbered by fives. Immediately after the passage are ten questions. Each question has four answer choices. The items are numbered 21 to 30, as are the items for the humanities passage of every ACT. This passage shows you most of the item types you will find on the actual reading test.

Skim each paragraph and write the topic next to each paragraph. Then use the four-step approach to respond to each item. Mark your answers on the answer grid following the questions. The entire process for reading the passage and answering the questions is discussed immediately following the questions.

HUMANITIES: This passage is adapted from *Psychology* by Carl R. Green and William R. Sanford.

Sometimes the competing demands of the id and superego trap the hardworking ego into a no-win position. Imagine you've just backed dad's car into a neighbor's expensive new car. The id tells you to just
5   leave, while the superego tells you it would be wrong to run away.

Both drives are too strong to be ignored. Caught in such a bind, the ego often chooses a response that disguises or compromises the id's socially unaccept-
10 able desires. In this case, the ego might choose to stay with the damaged car, thus obeying the law. To reduce the anxiety level, the ego may also choose to distort reality by rationalizing the accident by "saying" that it was a choice between hitting the car or hitting a
15 small child who ran out behind the car. Freud made one of his most enduring contributions to psychology when he identified a number of these ego-protecting behaviors. Known as *defense mechanisms,* their use is thought to be largely unconscious. Even though you
20 may in time become expert at spotting their use by others, you're unlikely to be aware of the degree to which you depend on one or more of the following defense mechanisms.

Repression protects you from disturbing memo-
25 ries, forbidden desires, or painful feelings by burying such material in the unconscious. Repressed feelings remain "alive," however, capable of influencing behavior without the person's awareness. For example, say that a girl named Rachel was attacked by a large
30 watchdog when she was seven, but she escaped serious injury. Part of Rachel wants to like dogs, but whenever she gets close to one, the old repressed fear takes over.

Similarly, repressed material can affect normal
35 physical drives such as hunger or sex. Doctors also know that repression can lead to physical ailments. Anna O., one of Freud's earliest patients, was an extreme example of someone who experienced a *psychosomatic illness.* Even today, some medical experts
40 estimate that up to 40 percent of the patients a physician sees each day may be suffering from illnesses with origins that are psychological, not physical.

Since you can't "remember" what you have repressed, it sometimes takes a lengthy period of
45 therapy before the hidden material can be uncovered, and when it is unearthed, you must still accept and deal with what you've repressed. In Rachel's case, that would not have been too difficult; her fear of dogs gives an obvious clue where to look. But repres-
50 sion also acts to conceal drives and feelings that peo-

ple cannot admit having — even to themselves. In such cases, the patient often vigorously resists any attempt to open up the repressed material.

When you can't focus your feelings on the per-
55 son or thing that caused them, you often strike out at a less threatening person or object. Freud called this *displacement.* Usually we displace anger, often on weaker people, animals, or inanimate objects. But people sometimes displace nervousness or fear by
60 chewing gum or picking at their fingernails. Some psychologists have described prejudice as displaced aggression, as when an unemployed worker blames all of his problems on a minority group.

Sublimation is a defense mechanism that turns
65 powerful, frustrated drives into socially useful behavior. Freud believed that civilization could not exist without sublimation, for it allows people to contribute to society while also achieving their own inner peace. In this way, a rock-throwing youngster in trouble with
70 the law might find release from his inner tension on the baseball field. Or a woman who has just ended a love affair might feel better if she puts all her energies into creating beautiful ceramic figures. Sublimation does not always absorb all the energy created by frus-
75 tration, however. The aggressive youngster described above might find success in baseball — but still often lose his temper when an umpire's decision goes against him.

21. Psychological defense mechanisms can be thought of as:

A. reflecting reality.
B. mostly unconscious.
C. psychosomatic illness.
D. protecting the id.

22. Which of the following phrases best describes the defense mechanism of repression?

F. A defense mechanism which affects a person's awareness
G. A defense mechanism responsible for up to 40 percent of visits to physicians
H. A defense mechanism which makes it impossible to remember something
J. A defense mechanism which might lead to overeating

23. According to this passage, repressed feelings result from:

A. attacks by animals.
B. a need for protection.
C. psychosomatic illnesses.
D. inability to open up.

24. The passage notes an inconsistency about a defense mechanism in that, while the defense mechanism may lead to suffering and illness, its:

   F. functioning may enable a person to achieve personal satisfaction.
   G. functioning may lead to the development of psychosomatic illnesses.
   H. cause often can't be remembered.
   J. impact may have the effect of distorting reality.

25. Which of the following best expresses the main idea of paragraph 5 (lines 43 – 53)?

   A. The fear of dogs is a common form of repressed memory.
   B. Repression protects a person from feelings and drives that even he or she cannot accept.
   C. Repression is a particularly difficult defense mechanism to deal with.
   D. A person is unlikely to be aware of how much he or she depends on a defense mechanism.

26. By focusing on the defense mechanism of displacement, this passage best illustrates how:

   F. outcomes of defense mechanisms are reflected in society.
   G. defense mechanisms usually single out weaker individuals.
   H. those employing a defense mechanism are nervous or fearful.
   J. defense mechanisms can be a force for good.

27. Based on this passage, all of the following could be examples of the outcome of a defense mechanism EXCEPT:

   A. a player arguing during a baseball game with a referee's decision that went against him or her.
   B. a child with much-displaced anger who finds an outlet for that anger by playing on a soccer team.
   C. a person developing an illness from repressed thoughts and feelings.
   D. a child being unexpectedly attacked by a watchdog or some other animal when he or she is very young.

28. Based on this passage, repressed thoughts or feelings might result in which of the following symptoms?

   I. Illness without a physical cause
   II. Nervous tics
   III. Fear

   F. II only
   G. I and III only
   H. II and III only
   J. I, II, and III

29. As used in the second paragraph in line 19, the word "unconscious" means:

   A. knocked out or asleep.
   B. in a hypnotic trance.
   C. without thought.
   D. without awareness.

30. You can infer from the passage that Freud's investigations of psychology led him to believe which of the following?

   F. Repression can be the most deadly defense mechanism because it is the hardest to uncover and accept.
   G. Everything about a person can be explained by which defense mechanisms he or she uses and the behaviors resulting from the use of these mechanisms.
   H. His work with defense mechanisms has rid many people of suffering and has enabled them to live happier, more creative lives.
   J. Being able to describe defense mechanisms in concrete terms makes it possible for people to better understand these mechanisms.

21 Ⓐ Ⓑ Ⓒ Ⓓ	25 Ⓐ Ⓑ Ⓒ Ⓓ	28 Ⓐ Ⓑ Ⓒ Ⓓ
22 Ⓕ Ⓖ Ⓗ Ⓙ	26 Ⓐ Ⓑ Ⓒ Ⓓ	29 Ⓐ Ⓑ Ⓒ Ⓓ
23 Ⓐ Ⓑ Ⓒ Ⓓ	27 Ⓕ Ⓖ Ⓗ Ⓙ	30 Ⓕ Ⓖ Ⓗ Ⓙ
24 Ⓐ Ⓑ Ⓒ Ⓓ		

Practice Item Responses Explained

Follow along as I review the steps for reading the passage and for responding to the items.

Skim each passage. Write a topic next to each paragraph.

The first step is to skim the passage and write the topic next to each passage. The topic for each paragraph is given below, along with a brief explanation of how the topic was arrived at. Following this, the passage is reprinted with the topics written next to each paragraph.

Paragraph	Topic	Explanation
1	Id vs. superego	The first sentence contains the words "competing demands of the id and superego."
2	Defense mechanisms	The italicized words and the last sentence are the best clues to this topic.
3	Repression	The first word in the paragraph gives the topic.
4	Repression and illness	The last sentence gives the best clue to this topic.
5	Repression and recovery	The first and last sentences talk about what is required to recover from depression. You may have a better topic.
6	Displacement ⎫	The first sentence in each paragraph clearly identifies
7	Sublimation ⎭	these topics.

Passage With Topics

The passage is shown again below with the topics written in.

Id vs.

superego

Sometimes the competing demands of the id and superego trap the hardworking ego into a no-win position. Imagine you've just backed dad's car into a neighbor's expensive new car. The id tells you to just
5 leave, while the superego tells you it would be wrong to run away.

Defense

mech.

Both drives are too strong to be ignored. Caught in such a bind, the ego often chooses a response that disguises or compromises the id's socially unaccept-
10 able desires. In this case, the ego might choose to stay with the damaged car, thus obeying the law. To reduce the anxiety level, the ego may also choose to distort reality by rationalizing the accident by "saying" that it was a choice between hitting the car or hitting a
15 small child who ran out behind the car. Freud made one of his most enduring contributions to psychology when he identified a number of these ego-protecting behaviors. Known as *defense mechanisms,* their use is thought to be largely unconscious. Even though you
20 may in time become expert at spotting their use by others, you're unlikely to be aware of the degree to which you depend on one or more of the following defense mechanisms.

Repression

Repression protects you from disturbing memories, forbidden desires, or painful feelings by burying such material in the unconscious. Repressed feelings remain "alive," however, capable of influencing behavior without the person's awareness. For example, say that a girl named Rachel was attacked by a large watchdog when she was seven, but she escaped serious injury. Part of Rachel wants to like dogs, but whenever she gets close to one, the old repressed fear takes over.

Rep. &

illness

Similarly, repressed material can affect normal physical drives such as hunger or sex. Doctors also know that repression can lead to physical ailments. Anna O., one of Freud's earliest patients, was an extreme example of someone who experienced a *psychosomatic illness.* Even today, some medical experts estimate that up to 40 percent of the patients a physician sees each day may be suffering from illnesses with origins that are psychological, not physical.

Rep. &

recovery

Since you can't "remember" what you have repressed, it sometimes takes a lengthy period of therapy before the hidden material can be uncovered, and when it is unearthed, you must still accept and deal with what you've repressed. In Rachel's case, that would not have been too difficult; her fear of dogs gives an obvious clue where to look. But repression also acts to conceal drives and feelings that people cannot admit having — even to themselves. In such cases, the patient often vigorously resists any attempt to open up the repressed material.

Displace.

When you can't focus your feelings on the person or thing that caused them, you often strike out at a less threatening person or object. Freud called this *displacement.* Usually we displace anger, often on weaker people, animals, or inanimate objects. But people sometimes displace nervousness or fear by chewing gum or picking at their fingernails. Some psychologists have described prejudice as displaced aggression, as when an unemployed worker blames all of his problems on a minority group.

Sublim.

Sublimation is a defense mechanism that turns powerful, frustrated drives into socially useful behavior. Freud believed that civilization could not exist without sublimation, for it allows people to contribute to society while also achieving their own inner peace. In this way, a rock-throwing youngster in trouble with the law might find release from his inner tension on the baseball field. Or a woman who has just ended a love affair might feel better if she puts all her energies into creating beautiful ceramic figures. Sublimation does not always absorb all the energy created by frustration, however. The aggressive youngster described above might find success in baseball — but still often lose his temper when an umpire's decision goes against him.

Use the Four Steps to Find the Correct Answer Choice for Each Item

The following analysis shows how to use the four steps to find the correct answer choice for each item. Refer to the passage above as you read along.

Item 21

Step 1. Read the item statement or question.

> **21.** Psychological defense mechanisms can be thought of as:

This is a statement to complete. The answer is going to be an acceptable definition or description of defense mechanism.

Step 2. Go to the part of the passage most likely to contain the answer.

The item is about psychological defense mechanisms. That's the topic for paragraph 2. Go there.

Step 3. Read the answer choices, eliminating incorrect answer choices.

Choice **A.** Not correct. The paragraph implies these mechanisms are a defense against reality.

Choice **B.** Maybe.

Choice **C.** Not correct. The passage says that defense mechanisms can cause psychosomatic illnesses — not that they are psychosomatic illnesses.

Choice **D.** Maybe.

Cross off the incorrect answer choices, as shown:

> A̶. reflecting reality.
> **B.** mostly unconscious.
> C̶. psychosomatic illness.
> **D.** protecting the id.

Step 4. Choose the correct answer from the remaining choices.

Choices **B** and **D** remain. Go back to the first paragraph to find the answer. The paragraph says that defense mechanisms are "largely unconscious." Choice **B** restates this with the words "mostly unconscious." There is no support in the paragraph for choice **D**.

B is the correct choice.

Item 22

Step 1. Read the item statement or question.

> **22.** Which of the following phrases best describes the
> defense mechanism of repression?

The correct answer choice for this question will describe repression.

Step 2. Go to the part of the passage most likely to contain the answer.

The third paragraph is about repression and the fourth and fifth paragraphs are related to depression. Go there.

Step 3. Read the answer choices, eliminating incorrect answer choices.

Choice **F.** Maybe.

Choice **G.** Not correct. The fourth paragraph says that up to 40 percent of patient visits are caused by psychological problems in general — not by repression.

Choice **H.** Not correct. The word "impossible" makes this answer incorrect. The passage says that repressed material can be remembered but that it can be difficult.

Choice **J.** Maybe.

Cross off the incorrect answer choices, as shown:

> F. A defense mechanism which affects a person's
>   awareness
> ~~G.~~ A defense mechanism responsible for up to 40 per-
>   cent of visits to physicians
> ~~H.~~ A defense mechanism which makes it impossible to
>   remember something
> J. A defense mechanism which might lead to overeating

Step 4. Choose the correct answer from the remaining choices.

Choices **F** and **J** remain. Go back to the third paragraph. The paragraph says repression can influence behavior without a person being aware.

F is the correct choice.

Item 23

Step 1. Read the item statement or question.

> **23.** According to this passage, repressed feelings result from:

The correct completion choice will give the cause of repressed feelings.

Step 2. Go to the part of the passage most likely to contain the answer.

The answer will be in Paragraphs 3, 4, or 5.

Step 3. Read the answer choices, eliminating incorrect answer choices.

Choice **A.** Not correct. The passage cites one example where an animal attack was repressed. However, it does not cite this as a cause of repressed feelings.

Choice **B.** Maybe.

Choice **C.** Not correct. The passage indicates that repression may cause psychosomatic illness, not the other way around.

Choice **D.** Not correct. Inability to open up is given as a reason why repressed thoughts are difficult to deal with, not as a cause of the thoughts.

Cross off the incorrect answer choices, as shown:

> A̶. attacks by animals.
> **B.** a need for protection.
> C̶. psychosomatic illnesses.
> D̶. inability to open up.

Step 4. Choose the correct answer from the remaining choices.

The only choice remaining is choice **B**, and this choice is confirmed in Paragraph 3, when it says that "Repression protects you from . . . ."

B is the correct choice.

Item 24

Step 1. Read the item statement or question.

24. The passage notes an inconsistency about a defense mechanism in that, while the defense mechanism may lead to suffering and illness, its:

The correct completion choice will name something about defense mechanisms that is inconsistent with suffering and illness. In other words, it will name something "positive" or "good."

Step 2. Go to the part of the passage most likely to contain the answer.

Paragraphs 4 and 5 are about repression illness and recovery. But this item asks about defense mechanisms, so we are probably going to look elsewhere in the passage as well.

Step 3. Read the answer choices, eliminating incorrect answer choices.

Choice **F.** Maybe. This choice fits into the "good" category.

Choice **G.** Not correct. This definitely is not "good."

Choice **H.** Not correct. Not remembering a cause may be "good" or it may be "bad."

Choice **J.** Not correct. This definitely is not "good."

Cross off the incorrect answer choices, as shown:

> **F.** functioning may enable a person to achieve personal satisfaction.
> ~~**G.**~~ functioning may lead to the development of psychosomatic illnesses.
> ~~**H.**~~ cause often can't be remembered.
> ~~**J.**~~ impact may have the effect of distorting reality.

Step 4. Choose the remaining choice as the correct answer.

All but one of the choices were eliminated without knowing if it was correct or incorrect, because they did not fit the "good" category.

F is the correct choice.

Item 25

Step 1. Read the item statement or question.

25. Which of the following best expresses the main idea of paragraph 5 (lines 43 – 53)?

This question asks directly for the main idea. The correct answer choice will best convey the meaning of the passage.

Step 2. Go to the part of the passage most likely to contain the answer.

The item tells us to look at Paragraph 5.

Step 3. Read the answer choices, eliminating incorrect answer choices.

Choice **A.** Not correct. The words "common form" make this choice incorrect.

Choice **B.** Maybe.

Choice **C.** Maybe.

Choice **D.** Maybe.

Cross off the incorrect answer choices, as shown:

> A̶. The fear of dogs is a common form of repressed memory.
> **B.** Repression protects a person from feelings and drives that even he or she cannot accept.
> **C.** Repression is a particularly difficult defense mechanism to deal with.
> **D.** A person is unlikely to be aware of how much he or she depends on a defense mechanism.

Step 4. Choose the correct answer from the remaining choices.

Three answer choices remain. The correct choice will be related to the topic of this paragraph, *Repression and recovery*. Choice **B** is true but incorrect. It is not related to the topic of recovery. Perhaps we could have eliminated this choice earlier, but it had a ring of truth to it, and we needed to go back to the paragraph to be sure.

Choice **C** is true, and it is related to the topic and seems to convey the main thought in the paragraph. Choice **D** is true, and it explains one reason why recovery from depression is so difficult. However, it does not convey the full meaning of the paragraph.

C is the correct choice.

Item 26

Step 1. Read the item statement or question.

> **26.** By focusing on the defense mechanism of displacement, this passage best illustrates how:

The passage gives several illustrations or examples of displacement. The correct answer choice will describe the theme found in one of these illustrations.

Step 2. Go to the part of the passage most likely to contain the answer.

Displacement is the topic of the next-to-last paragraph. Go there.

Step 3. Read the answer choices, eliminating incorrect answer choices.

Choice **F.** Maybe.

Choice **G.** Maybe.

Choice **H.** Maybe.

Choice **J.** Not correct. There is nothing in this paragraph about defense mechanisms being a force for good.

Cross off the incorrect answer choice, as shown:

> F. outcomes of defense mechanisms are reflected in society.
> G. defense mechanisms usually single out weaker individuals.
> H. those employing a defense mechanism are nervous or fearful.
> J. defense mechanisms can be a force for good.

Step 4. Choose the correct answer from the remaining choices.

We couldn't just eliminate choices **F, G,** and **H** because they reflect words and phrases found in the next-to-last paragraph. They have to be examined more carefully.

Choice **F** seems correct. The example of prejudice in the passage is an example of how outcomes of defense mechanisms are reflected in society. Choice **G** incorrectly states the wording in the paragraph. Defense mechanisms don't single out weaker people. Rather, people tend to displace their anger on weaker individuals. Choice **H** also incorrectly states the passage, which says that people sometimes displace nervousness or fear.

F is the correct choice.

Item 27

Step 1. Read the item statement or question.

> 27. Based on this passage, all of the following could be examples of the outcome of a defense mechanism EXCEPT:

The correct answer choice will NOT be an example of the outcome of a defense mechanism.

Step 2. Go to the part of the passage most likely to contain the answer.

Just about the entire passage is involved. Focus on the examples of outcomes of the different defense mechanisms.

Step 3. Read the answer choices, eliminating incorrect answer choices.

The incorrect choices are the effects of defense mechanisms.

Choice **A.** Not correct. This outcome of a defense mechanism is described in the last sentence of the paragraph on sublimation.

Choice **B.** Not correct. This outcome of a defense mechanism is described in the displacement paragraph.

Choice **C.** Not correct. This outcome is described in the paragraph on repression and illness.

Choice **D.** Probably.

Cross off the incorrect answer choices, as shown:

A. a player arguing during a baseball game with a referee's decision that went against him or her.
B. a child with much-displaced anger who finds an outlet for that anger by playing on a soccer team.
C. a person developing an illness from repressed thoughts and feelings.
D. a child being unexpectedly attacked by a watchdog or some other animal when he or she is very young.

Step 4. Choose the correct answer from the remaining choices.

D is the only choice remaining. This choice is a cause of repression, not an outcome.

D is the correct choice.

Item 28

Step 1. Read the item statement or question.

28. Based on this passage, repressed thoughts or feelings might result in which of the following symptoms?

   I. Illness without a physical cause
   II. Nervous tics
   III. Fear

The item gives us three possible symptoms of depression. Some of them or all of them may be correct.

Step 2. Go to the part of the passage most likely to contain the answer.

Consider the symptoms discussed in each of the paragraphs.

Step 3. Read the answer choices, eliminating incorrect answer choices.

We approach this type of I, II, III problem a little differently. First let's decide which of the three is actually a symptom.

I. Illness without a physical cause — Yes. This symptom is discussed in the fourth paragraph.

II. Nervous tics — Yes. The next-to-last paragraph mentions displaced nervousness such as chewing gum or playing with fingernails. A nervous tic could be displaced nervousness as well.

III. Fear — Yes. Rachel's fear of dogs was the key to understanding her defense mechanism.

All are correct.

Step 4. Choose the correct answer from the remaining choices.

Choice **J** shows that all three are correct.

    F.   II only
    G.   I and III only
    H.   II and III only
    J.   I, II, and III

J is the correct choice.

Item 29

Step 1. Read the item statement or question.

    29. As used in the second paragraph in line 19, the word "unconscious" means:

This is a typical ACT word-meaning question. The correct choice will define what the word means in this passage.

Step 2. Go to the part of the passage most likely to contain the answer.

We know to go to line 19.

Step 3. Read the answer choices, eliminating incorrect answer choices.

Choice **A.** Not correct. The context does not refer to being knocked out.

Choice **B.** Not correct. There is nothing in the context about being hypnotized.

Choice **C.** Maybe.

Choice **D.** Maybe.

Cross off the incorrect answer choices, as shown:

> ~~A.~~ knocked out or asleep.
> ~~B.~~ in a hypnotic trance.
> **C.** without thought.
> **D.** without awareness.

Step 4. Choose the correct answer from the remaining choices.

The word "unconscious," in this context, refers to the part of the mind that an individual is unaware of. The phrase "you're unlikely to be aware of" is the clue to the word's meaning.

D is the correct choice.

Item 30

Step 1. Read the item statement or question.

> **30.** You can infer from the passage that Freud's investigations of psychology led him to believe which of the following?

The correct answer choice will be the most reasonable of the four inferences about what Freud believed. The inference must be based on the passage.

Step 2. Go to the part of the passage most likely to contain the answer.

The choices could be from anywhere in the passage.

Step 3. Read the answer choices, eliminating incorrect answer choices.

Choice **F.** Maybe.

Choice **G.** Not true. The word "everything" is a clue that this answer choice is just too inclusive.

Choice **H.** Maybe.

Choice **J.** Maybe.

Cross off the incorrect answer choices, as shown:

F. Repression can be the most deadly defense mechanism because it is the hardest to uncover and accept.
~~G.~~ Everything about a person can be explained by which defense mechanisms he or she uses and the behaviors resulting from the use of these mechanisms.
H. His work with defense mechanisms has rid many people of suffering and has enabled them to live happier, more creative lives.
J. Being able to describe defense mechanisms in concrete terms makes it possible for people to better understand these mechanisms.

Step 4. Choose the correct answer from the remaining choices.

Choice **F** is certainly true. More time is spent discussing repression than any of the other defense mechanisms. So this is a reasonable inference from the passage.

Choice **H** is certainly true. And it is just so friendly. But it is not a belief that Freud would have developed from his investigations of psychology.

Choice **J** may well be true. But there is nothing is this passage to support this choice.

F is the correct choice.

Chapter 14

DIAGNOSTIC READING ACT

You should take this Diagnostic ACT after you have completed the Reading review. This Diagnostic ACT is just like a real ACT, and it is the first of four Reading ACTs in this book. But this Diagnostic ACT is different. It is specially designed to help you decide which parts of the Reading section to review in more detail.

Take the Diagnostic Reading ACT under simulated test conditions. Allow 35 minutes to answer the 40 test questions. Tear out the answer sheet at the back of the book and answer the questions in the Test 3 (Reading) section. Use a pencil to mark the answer sheet.

Use the Diagnostic Reading Checklist on page 245 to mark your answer sheet. Review the answer explanations on pages 246–249. After you have marked the test, complete the Diagnostic Checklist. The Checklist will direct you to the reading skills you should review in more detail.

The test scoring chart on page 376 shows you how to convert the number correct to ACT scale scores. The chart on page 381 shows you how to find the Social Studies/Sciences and Arts/Literature subscores.

DO NOT leave any answers blank. There is no penalty for guessing on the ACT. Remember that the test booklet is yours. You may mark up, write on, or draw on the test.

When you are ready, note the time and turn to the Diagnostic Reading ACT. Stop in exactly 35 minutes.

Diagnostic Reading Checklist

Answer	Check if missed		Answer	Check if missed
1. C	☐		21. D	☐
2. H	☐		22. F	☐
3. A	☐		23. D	☐
4. J	☐		24. H	☐
5. B	☐		25. D	☐
6. G	☐		26. J	☐
7. A	☐		27. A	☐
8. G	☐		28. G	☐
9. B	☐		29. A	☐
10. H	☐		30. G	☐
11. C	☐		31. D	☐
12. J	☐		32. E	☐
13. C	☐		33. C	☐
14. H	☐		34. H	☐
15. B	☐		35. B	☐
16. F	☐		36. J	☐
17. C	☐		37. C	☐
18. J	☐		38. F	☐
19. B	☐		39. B	☐
20. G	☐		40. J	☐

Review the answer explanations on the following pages. Then go back to the items you missed. Apply the four steps on pages 216 and 217 to find out how the steps lead you to the correct answsers.

Diagnostic Reading ACT Answers Explained

ANSWERS

1: C. In the very first sentence of this passage, the author notes that trouble was brewing "not alone for [Buck], but for every tidewater dog . . . ." The implication is that Buck is a tidewater dog.

2: H. The author says (line 6) that men "had found a yellow metal." The men searching for the yellow metal gold needed strong work dogs to assist them.

3: A. According to the passage, Buck is the favored dog on Judge Miller's estate. He is "king" over everyone on the estate, "humans included."

4: J. No threatening, frightening, or otherwise negative words are used to describe Judge Miller's place. Judge Miller's place has a warm climate. The area is "sun-kissed," and the children use a pool to keep cool. There is a lot of land, a "great demesne" covered with orchards and trees. There are stables and servants' quarters.

5: B. As a dog, Buck has no power to rule or to create and enforce laws on Judge Miller's estate. However, the passage implies that because of his favored status and his physical strength, he appeared to have control over everyone.

6: G. The passage describes them as a Japanese pug and a Mexican hairless, two different breeds of dogs. Since they are of different breeds, Buck and these two dogs cannot be related. Since Buck "utterly ignored" (line 52) these two dogs, they are not his best friends. Judge Miller's daughters are Mollie and Alice.

7: A. Much of the imagery in this passage indicates the presence of horses. The author describes the "great stables, where a dozen grooms and boys held forth" (lines 21–22) and the "paddocks" (line 50), which indicate the keeping of horses on the estate.

8: G. The first paragraph indicates that "trouble was brewing . . . for every tidewater dog, strong of muscle and with warm, long hair. . . ." The later description of Buck indicates that he meets with this description and gives the reader a sense of foreboding about Buck's situation.

9: B. The opening paragraph indicates that there will be trouble for Buck; the last two paragraphs confirm this, describing how Buck is removed from his happy and comfortable life.

10: H. The implication is that Manuel commits an act of treachery by selling Buck to get money to pay off his gambling debt.

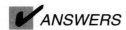

11: C. This passage discusses how the freedom of the press has fluctuated in America. Most often, these fluctuations stem from wartime decisions; however, these wars are not the focus of the passage.

12: J. Since Zenger told the truth in his articles, the jury decided that he should be acquitted. Since there was no U.S. Constitution at this time, he was being protected under British (not American) rule.

13: C. The passage lists each person in the answer, except John Adams, as exerting the rights of freedom of the press. Of those listed, only John Adams is noted for acting against freedom of the press.

14: H. This was the first case in America that supported freedom of the press. There is no information in the passage to indicate that F, G, or J are true.

15: B. According to this passage, there was concern that information could endanger the secrecy of missions, reveal information about troop movements, and otherwise endanger the war effort.

16: F. Because of the wartime situation, John Adams and Congress wanted to stifle any anti-American, pro-French writing. The Alien Acts prevented the immigration of more French to the United States. The Sedition Act simply prevented anyone from speaking out against the government.

17: C. Since the Sedition Act was revoked in 1801, citizens of the United States have had the right to speak out against the American or any other government.

18: J. Though this is a violation of freedom of the press, it is not an act of censorship. By definition, censorship is the deleting or blocking of information that is considered harmful. Choice J is not censorship even though the author is punished.

19: B. The author states (lines 78–79) that freedom of the press is constantly being redefined. The remainder of the passage gives examples which support this statement.

20: G. In describing U.S. censorship, the author notes that many reporters were not censored during World War II because they made sure not to give out information that would endanger the troops (lines 60–62).

 ANSWERS

21: D. The author notes (lines 4–5) that the Renaissance is reflective of Greek sculpture.

22: F. Mona Lisa is the subject of one of Leonardo da Vinci's most famous paintings, not a known painter herself.

23: D. Leonardo da Vinci was a true "Renaissance man." In other words, he was skilled in many areas. The author notes many of Leonardo's achievements in fields other than art.

24: H. The author discusses perspective as the way the human eye distinguishes objects. Masaccio's paintings were advanced because he could make a two-dimensional surface appear to be three-dimensional.

25: D. In this passage, much of the art discussed reflects religious themes.

26: J. According to the author, Raphael was not an innovator. Instead, he adapted the skills he learned from others to paint powerful and beautiful pictures.

27: A. Giotto is known for fresco, Michelangelo for sculpture, and Titian for oil painting. Pastel may have been used, but it is not mentioned in this article.

28: G. Because his paintings were not "three-dimensional," Giotto's figures are described as "stiff" as opposed to Masaccio, whose figures are "creatures of flesh and blood."

29: A. The late fifteenth and early sixteenth centuries witnessed the High Renaissance. These centuries correspond with the late 1400s and early 1500s.

30: G. The author describes the best artists, their works, and their artistic advances. While these other statements may or may not be true, none of these statements reflect the main point of the passage.

31: D. The author indicates (line 9) that, under the rules of the old table, some elements failed to "appear in their proper places." In lines 14–15, the author indicates that in Henry Moseley's table, "every element fell into its proper group."

32: E. Oxygen is a gas, but the author names only helium, krypton, and neon as noble gases.

33: C. The author notes (lines 29–30) that the atomic number indicates the number of protons and electrons in an atom.

34: H. Elements ordered by atomic number, *not by atomic mass,* fall into groups with other elements with similar properties. The English scientist Henry Moseley determined the atomic number of the elements, but the paragraph does not mention that Moseley was working simply to prove he was better than other scientists.

35: B. In the third paragraph, the author defines the revised periodic law: "The properties of the elements are periodic functions of their atomic numbers." The next sentence notes that when "the elements are arranged in order of increasing atomic number, the properties of the elements repeat regularly." You can infer that the table, which reflects the revised periodic law, arranges the elements in order of increasing atomic number. Lines 37–44 also describe the arrangement of the periodic table.

36: J. Whether or not there is a concrete connection between these two concepts, it is not strongly indicated in this passage. Clearly, atomic mass and atomic number are not always the same; if they were, the old periodic table would have worked as well as the revised table. The author notes that, occasionally, elements with higher atomic masses are placed before elements with lower atomic masses.

37: C. The author notes (lines 39–41) that horizontal rows are called periods, while vertical columns are called groups, or families. This is reinforced by the notation on the periodic table, which labels the horizontal rows as "periods."

38: F. Lines 53–54 indicate that both the A and B designations as well as the "representative" and "transition" designations are commonly used by modern scientists. Therefore, both designations are preserved.

39: B. The author notes (lines 72–73) that these rows appear separately to make it "easier to follow the regularities of all the other elements." This statement implies that the rows set aside do not show the regularities of other elements in the table. There is no indication that these elements are any more important or more recently discovered than the other elements in the table.

40: J. The table does not mention color.

Section IV
Model English and Reading Tests

Chapter 15

MODEL ENGLISH AND READING ACT I
With Answers Explained

This Model English and Reading ACT I is just like a real ACT. Take this test after you take the Diagnostic English ACT and the Diagnostic Reading ACT. If you plan to take the optional ACT Writing Test, you should also complete the ACT Developmental Writing Test I on page 403.

Take this model test under simulated test conditions. Allow 45 minutes to answer the 75 English items and 35 minutes to answer the 40 Reading items. Use a pencil to mark the answer sheet, and answer the questions in the Test 1 (English) and Test 3 (Reading) sections.

Use the answer key on page 280 to mark the answer sheet. Review the answer explanations on pages 281–293.

The test scoring charts on pages 374 and 376 show you how to convert the number of correct answers to ACT scale scores. Other charts on pages 378 and 382 show you how to find the Usage/Mechanics and Rhetorical Skills and Social Studies/Sciences and Arts/Literature subscores.

DO NOT leave any answers blank. There is no penalty for guessing on the ACT. Remember that the test is yours. You may mark up, write on, or draw on the test.

When you are ready, note the time and begin.

Model English ACT I

75 Questions—45 Minutes

INSTRUCTIONS: Certain words or phrases in the following five passages are underlined and numbered. There is a corresponding item for each underlined portion. Each item offers three suggestions for changing the underlined portion to conform to standard written English, or to make it more understandable or consistent with the rest of the passage. If the underlined portion is not improved by one of the three suggested changes, mark NO CHANGE. Some items are about the entire passage, and the numbers for these items come at the end of the passage.

Choose the best answer for each question based on the passage. Then fill in the appropriate circle on the answer sheet.

Check pages 280–289 for answers and explanations.

PASSAGE I

It seems that each year we invent new ways to keep

human beings from meeting each other. ☐ 1

Home entertainment is fast becoming the leisure of

choice, as more and more people <u>take</u> advantage
                                      2
of the wide assortment of electronic entertainment

available. Video stores sprout everywhere; videotapes and

DVDs siphon customers from theaters and <u>museums:</u>
                                          3

1. Which of the following options might best explain why the author has opened this article with this one-sentence paragraph?

   A. To emphasize the isolation of sentences, like people, in the modern world.
   B. Because he could not figure out how to elaborate on this idea in greater detail.
   C. In order to highlight and emphasize the thesis of the essay that follows.
   D. To demonstrate his great skill as a writer.

2. **F.** NO CHANGE
   G. have taken
   H. had taken
   J. took

3. **A.** NO CHANGE
   B. museums;
   C. museums,
   D. museums

GO ON TO THE NEXT PAGE.

Model English and Reading ACT I   257

and now <u>video games'</u> attract those who once would
4

have participated in traditional out-of-home sports

such as bowling.

We now have all kinds of food establishments racing

to *deliver* food. Is this the beginning of the
5

end-of-the-restaurant renaissance? Going to a

restaurant involves parking, walking, and sometimes

waiting in line—and even some element of risk from

street crime. Compare this to the <u>no-walking, no-risk,</u>
6

<u>no-parking, no-waiting,</u> no-hassle way of life we have
6

in our own homes when we have our meals delivered.

Even preparing our own food is less of a <u>hassle. With</u>
7

prepackaged meals getting better and better and

microwave ovens making <u>nuking food</u>
8

quick and efficient.

<u>Futurist's</u> call this social phenomenon "cocooning,"
9

where families stay close to the homestead and <u>interact</u>
10

very little with their outside surroundings. Home-shopping

networks, faxed mail, home computers and <u>offices—such</u>
11

things threaten to rip the social fabric by keeping people

---

4. F. NO CHANGE
   G. video game
   H. video games
   J. video game's

5. Which of the following choices best explains why the author chooses to italicize the word "deliver"?

   A. To emphasize that people are having food brought to them so that they won't have to leave their homes
   B. To differentiate between delivery and take-out options
   C. To indicate that food arrives very quickly
   D. To show that food is being mailed to people

6. Which of the following choices represents the most logical order for the underlined phrases?

   F. NO CHANGE
   G. no-parking, no-walking, no-waiting, no-risk
   H. no-waiting, no-risk, no-parking, no-walking
   J. no-risk, no-parking, no-waiting, no-walking

7. A. NO CHANGE
   B. hassle, with
   C. hassle! With
   D. hassle? With

8. F. NO CHANGE
   G. nuking
   H. cooking food
   J. cooking

9. A. NO CHANGE
   B. Futurists'
   C. Futurist
   D. Futurists

10. F. NO CHANGE
   G. interacting
   H. interacts
   J. interacted

11. A. NO CHANGE
   B. offices. Such
   C. offices! such
   D. offices; such

GO ON TO THE NEXT PAGE.

from interacting with each other. In the long run, this

cannot be healthy for our culture. 12

Mingling with other people and exploring our

surroundings should not be abandoned because of

advanced home-entertainment technologies. What we do

in our spare time should not be decided in a combat

between cocooning technology and the lure of their public
13

places. There should be equally time for both.
14

12. Based on the language in this paragraph, which of the
following choices best reflects the author's attitude toward cocooning?

   F. Indifference
   G. Elation
   H. Concern
   J. Shame

13. A. NO CHANGE
   B. their
   C. they're
   D. our

14. F. NO CHANGE
   G. equal
   H. equated
   J. equalest

Question 15 asks about the entire passage.

---

15. Which information would strengthen this article?

   A. An explanation of the cocooning process in cater-
pillars
   B. An explication of the movie *Cocoon*
   C. Examples proving how society is becoming less
interactive
   D. Descriptions of how to use modern technology,
such as fax machines and computers.

PASSAGE II

In the forests of southeastern Canada and the eastern

United States. Indians lived as hunters and farmers.
16

For both activities, they use tools and weapons made
17

16. F. NO CHANGE
   G. States, Indians
   H. States; Indians
   J. States Indians

17. A. NO CHANGE
   B. using
   C. uses
   D. used

GO ON TO THE NEXT PAGE.

of chipped stone, bone, and <u>they were also made of wood</u>.
                                                    18
Not until the arrival of Europeans in the 1500's did the

Indians obtain metal axes and knives.

    [1] One of the largest groups of Indians in the

Eastern Woodlands area <u>was</u> the Iroquois. [2] Five tribes
                        19

formed the Iroquois League of Five <u>Nations Seneca,</u>
                                    20
Cayuga, Mohawk, Onondaga, and Oneida. [3] (The

Tuscaroras later joined the group, making it the League of

Six Nations.) [4] The purpose of the League was to keep

peace among the five tribes <u>who belonged to the Iroquois</u>
                            21

<u>League</u>. [5] The unity and fighting ability of the <u>Iroquois</u>
21   **22**

made them very powerful. ☐**23**

    In their tribal councils, the Iroquois practiced a type

of democracy. <u>Acting as servants of the people, the tribe</u>
                                            24
<u>elected public officials</u>. The government of the League
   24

was in the hands of 50 men called <u>sachems</u>. The leading
                                    25
women of the tribe chose the sachems.

18. **F.** NO CHANGE
    G. the tools were also made of wood
    H. wood
    J. wooden tools

19. **A.** NO CHANGE
    B. were
    C. was,
    D. were,

20. **F.** NO CHANGE
    G. Nations: Seneca
    H. Nations; Seneca
    J. Nations. Seneca

21. **A.** NO CHANGE
    B. who were League of Five Nations members
    C. for the League of Five Nations
    D. OMIT the phrase entirely.

22. **F.** NO CHANGE
    G. Iroquoises
    H. Iroquois'
    J. Iroquoises'

23. For the greatest coherence in this paragraph, where should Sentence 5 be placed?

    A. Where it is now
    B. After Sentence 1
    C. After Sentence 2
    D. At the beginning of the paragraph

24. **F.** NO CHANGE
    G. Acting as servants of the tribe, the people elected public officials
    H. Acting as servants of the people, the public officials represented the tribe members
    J. Acting as servants of the people, the tribe had public officials

25. What information is necessary to clarify the meaning of this passage?

    A. An explanation of the duties of the sachem
    B. A definition of democracy
    C. A list of all the men chosen to be sachem
    D. A detailed explanation of how the women chose the sachem

GO ON TO THE NEXT PAGE.

Anyone could attend meetings of the <u>Council, at</u>
26
these meetings, proposals were either accepted or

<u>trashed.</u> After a great deal of discussion and speechmaking,
27
the sachems would reach a decision about each proposal.

Some historians believe that the men who planned the

government of the United States may have gotten some of

their ideas from the way the League of Five Nations

<u>operated. Women</u> had a great deal of authority among the
28
Iroquois. A woman headed each clan, or group of related

families. The women owned all of the family goods. No

one could inherit anything except from his or her mother.

Young men and women could not choose whom they

would marry. Mothers arranged all marriages.

26. F. NO CHANGE
   G. Council at
   H. Council . . . at
   J. Council. At

27. A. NO CHANGE
   B. they were trashed
   C. rejected
   D. blown off

28. F. NO CHANGE
   G. operated! Women
   H. operated. (begin new paragraph) Women
   J. operated! (begin new paragraph) Women

Questions 29 and 30 ask about the entire passage.

29. Assume that the author's assignment was to write an essay focused on the strength of the Iroquois women. Does he complete this assignment?

   A. Yes, because he spends a paragraph discussing women's roles.
   B. No, because most of the essay focuses on the Iroquois tribe as a whole, not just the function of women.
   C. No, because women cannot be sachems.
   D. Yes, because women were the heads of clans.

30. Based on the language of this essay, which of the following choices best describes the author's intended audience?

   F. Professors of history
   G. Native American women
   H. Senior citizens
   J. People who are unfamiliar with the Iroquois and their traditions

GO ON TO THE NEXT PAGE.

PASSAGE III

> The following paragraphs may or may not be in the
> most sensible order. Each paragraph is numbered,
> and item 45 asks for the sequence of paragraphs
> that will make this passage most sensible.

[1]

Late in 1799, the Department of Aveyron in central

France <u>buzzes</u> with gossip touched off by an unusual
    31

event. Hunters and farmers told of seeing a boy about

14 years old, who lived <u>alone all by himself</u> in the woods
      32

of the region. The reports described the boy as wild and

uncivilized. They said he scavenged for food by digging

roots and bulbs, drank from streams, and <u>runs</u> on all fours.
           33

31. A. NO CHANGE
    B. buzzed
    C. has buzzed
    D. buzzing

32. F. NO CHANGE
    G. alone by himself
    H. alone with himself
    J. alone

33. A. NO CHANGE
    B. is running
    C. ran
    D. had run

[2]

When he was finally captured, the Wild Boy came

under the care of <u>Jean-Marc Itard. A physician</u> at the
       34

National Institute of Deaf-Mutes. Itard believed that he

could civilize the child, but many people disagreed. The

debate touched off by Itard's efforts centered on the

question, "Was Victor (as the boy came to be called)

abandoned because he was an idiot, or was he an idiot

because he was <u>abandoned."</u>
    35

34. F. NO CHANGE
    G. Jean-Marc Itard, a physician
    H. Jean-Marc Itard: a physician
    J. Jean Marc Itard a physician

35. A. NO CHANGE
    B. abandoned.
    C. abandoned?"
    D. abandoned!"

GO ON TO THE NEXT PAGE.

[3]

Jean-Marc Itard, however, had opened new doors for

the education of children. His work with <u>Victor. Rather,</u>
                                              36

inspired Maria Montessori, the <u>famous, Italian educator</u>.
                                         37
Her approach to teaching children, revolutionary when she

opened her first school in the early years of this century,

emphasizes that children should be free to develop their

own capacities for <u>physically and intellectually</u>
                           38
development. Thanks to the Wild Boy of Aveyron,

Montessori children learn carpentry, household tasks, and

other how-to jobs in addition to art, music, and the

traditional subjects.

[4]

Itard stubbornly maintained that Victor could be

helped <u>and refused to be convinced otherwise.</u> After all,
              39
he pointed out, the boy had managed to exist in the

woods, living by his wits, for an unknown length of <u>time!</u>
                                                          40
Victor, he believed, possessed a normal intelligence

stunted by a lack of contact with loving parents and the

social interaction of everyday family life. ☐41☐

36. F. NO CHANGE
G. Victor rather
H. Victor, for example
J. Victor for example

37. A. NO CHANGE
B. famous, Italian, educator
C. famous Italian, educator
D. famous Italian educator

38. F. NO CHANGE
G. physically and intellectual
H. physical and intellectual
J. physical, and intellectual

39. A. NO CHANGE
B. and refuses to be convinced otherwise.
C. and refused to be convinced.
D. OMIT the phrase entirely; end with a period.

40. F. NO CHANGE
G. time?
H. time.
J. time,

41. What, if any, information is needed to clarify the information in this sentence?

A. Definition of normal intelligence
B. Description of Victor's parents
C. Explanation of the social interaction of everyday family life
D. No information is necessary.

GO ON TO THE NEXT PAGE.

Model English and Reading ACT I   263

[5]

Despite Itard's <u>five year</u> training program, Victor did
                  42
not learn to speak more than a few words. He was never

fully comfortable in clothing or sleeping in a bed,

although he would do <u>this</u> to please the people who cared
                        43

for him. Victor died in 1828, still <u>"fearful, half-wild, and</u>
                                         44
<u>unable to learn to speak, despite all the efforts that were</u>
                                         44
<u>made."</u>
44

42. **F.** NO CHANGE
    G. five-year
    H. five years
    J. five-years

43. **A.** NO CHANGE
    B. that
    C. both
    D. OMIT this word.

44. The writer puts this part of the sentence in quotation marks to:

    F. show that this description is directly quoted from a direct source, such as a book.
    G. put emphasis on these phrases.
    H. show that this description is ironic.
    J. highlight his or her own opinion.

Question 45 asks about the entire passage.

---

45. Which of the following sequences of paragraphs make the essay most logical?

    A. NO CHANGE
    B. 1, 5, 2, 4, 3
    C. 2, 1, 3, 4, 5
    D. 1, 2, 4, 5, 3

PASSAGE IV

The following paragraphs may or may not be in the most sensible order. Each paragraph is numbered in brackets. The last item will ask you to choose the sequence of paragraphs that will make the essay the most sensible.

[1]

How is it possible for people today to know about

the distant past, especially in those <u>long</u> centuries before
                                          46

46. **F.** NO CHANGE
    G. one-hundred-year-long
    H. hundred-year-long
    J. longest

GO ON TO THE NEXT PAGE.

the invention of <u>writing the</u> answer has to do with the
47

science of archeology, which uses a variety of <u>different</u>
48
techniques.

47. A. NO CHANGE
  B. writing. The
  C. writing? The
  D. writing, the

48. F. NO CHANGE
  G. different,
  H. various
  J. OMIT the word entirely.

[2]

[1] As for very ancient remains of humans and their

artifacts, scientists <u>are on the ball about</u> the surroundings
49
in which they are found. [2] In general, the lower

something is in an archeological "dig," the older it is.

[3] <u>Therefore,</u> the more crudely something is made, the
50
older it is. [4] If human remains are found together with

the bones of an animal that became extinct 50,000 years

ago, we know that the remains are at least 50,000 years

old. [5] <u>Any once-living thing, plant or animal, gives off</u>
51
<u>certain rays at a known rate for thousands of years after</u>
51
<u>its death.</u> [6] Still another archeological technique is
51
radiocarbon dating. [7] By measuring its rays in a special

machine, archeologists can estimate an <u>objects</u> age.
52

49. A. NO CHANGE
  B. are hip to
  C. pay special attention to
  D. OMIT this phrase.

50. F. NO CHANGE
  G. However
  H. For example
  J. Also

51. To maintain a logical and orderly flow in this paragraph, where should Sentence 5 be located?

  A. Where it is now
  B. After Sentence 1
  C. After Sentence 6
  D. At the beginning of the paragraph

52. F. NO CHANGE
  G. thing's
  H. object
  J. object's

GO ON TO THE NEXT PAGE.

Model English and Reading ACT I 265

[3]

Archeologists, like detectives, make informed guesses from the clues they find. If a "dig" contains a mortar for grinding <u>grain; it</u> is a safe guess that the
53
people probably knew how to farm. If an ancient site yields a bit of amber that could only have come from hundreds of miles away, the inhabitants <u>were</u>
54
probably traders. Burials with many artifacts give a great deal of information. This is especially true with the Egyptians, for Egypt's dry climate has preserved even cloth and wood for thousands of years.

[4]

Of course, with Egypt and most later civilizations archeologists have written symbols to guide <u>them, for</u> a
55
long time, however, no one knew how to read ancient writings. The Greek word for Egyptian writing, hieroglyphics, means "sacred carving"; the Greeks believed that these symbols were magical and could be understood only by Egyptian priests. 56

53. A. NO CHANGE
B. grain, it
C. grain. It
D. grain . . . it

54. F. NO CHANGE
G. was
H. weren't
J. are

55. A. NO CHANGE
B. them for
C. them! For
D. them. For

56. What information, if any, would best support the information provided in this paragraph?

F. No information is necessary.
G. An explanation of how archeologists learned to read ancient writings
H. A detailed description of the complex relationship between the Greek and Egyptian cultures
J. Pictures of hieroglyphic writing

GO ON TO THE NEXT PAGE.

[5]

Thus through a combination of science, scholarship, and chance discovery, we are constantly learning more and more about the creatures — both human and nonhuman, who came before us on this planet.
57

And new and exciting insights into the history of life
58
on earth.
58

57. **A.** NO CHANGE
　　B. nonhuman—
　　C. nonhuman
　　D. nonhuman.

58. **F.** NO CHANGE
　　G. New and exciting insights into the history of life on earth.
　　H. However, this gives new and exciting insights into the history of life on earth.
　　J. This gives new and exciting insights into the history of life on earth.

Questions 59 and 60 ask about the passage as a whole.

59. Which of the following sequences of paragraphs will make the essay most logical?

　　A. NO CHANGE
　　B. 2, 3, 4, 5, 1
　　C. 5, 4, 3, 2, 1
　　D. 2, 1, 3, 4, 5

60. Does this essay answer the question posed by the author in the opening paragraph?

　　F. No, because the author does not discuss "people today."
　　G. No, because the author discusses only Greek and Egyptian civilizations.
　　H. Yes, because the author introduces the subject of archeology and describes how it helps decipher the past.
　　J. Yes, because the author is an archeologist.

GO ON TO THE NEXT PAGE.

PASSAGE V

[1]

After the tornado passed I roamed around and <u>find</u> a
61
broken power line. It banged violently by the Penn

Avenue Curb; it was shooting sparks into the street.

I <u>couldnt</u> bring myself to leave the spot.
62

61. **A.** NO CHANGE
    B. finds
    C. found
    D. founded

62. **F.** NO CHANGE
    G. can't
    H. could'nt
    J. couldn't

[2]

A tornado hit our neighborhood one <u>morning, the</u>
63
tornado broke all the windows in the envelope factory

on Penn Avenue and ripped down mature oaks and maples

on Richard Lane and its side streets — trees about which

everyone would make, <u>in my view</u>, an unconscionable
64
fuss, not least perhaps because they would lie across the

streets for a week.

63. **A.** NO CHANGE
    B. morning the
    C. morning. The
    D. morning? The

64. **F.** NO CHANGE
    G. (place after "perhaps")
    H. (place after "week")
    J. OMIT the phrase entirely.

[3]

The power line was loosing a fireball of sparks that

melted the asphalt <u>from a solid to a liquidy substance</u>.
65

65. **A.** NO CHANGE
    B. from a solid to a liquid
    C. from a liquid to a solid
    D. OMIT the phrase entirely.

It was a thick twisted steel cable <u>usually</u> strung overhead
66
along Penn Avenue; it carried power — 4,500 kilovolts of

<u>it, from</u> Wilkinsburg to major sections of Pittsburgh, to
67
Homewood and Brushton, Shadyside, and Squirrel Hill.

66. **F.** NO CHANGE
    G. (place after "thick")
    H. (place after "It")
    J. (place after "twisted")

67. **A.** NO CHANGE
    B. it—from
    C. it from
    D. it. From

GO ON TO THE NEXT PAGE.

[4]

[1] The live wire's hundred twisted ends spat a thick sheaf of useless yellow sparks that hissed. [2] The sparks were cooking the asphalt gummy; <u>burning a hole.</u>
68

[3] I watched the cable relax and sink <u>into its own pit;</u>
69
I watched the yellow sparks pool and crackle around the cable's torn end and splash out of the pit and over the asphalt in a stream toward the curb and my shoes.

[4] <u>It was melting a pit for itself in the street.</u> [5] My bare
70
shins could feel the heat. [6] I smelled tarry melted asphalt and steel so hot it smoked.

[5]

"If you touch that," my father said, <u>needlessly</u>
71

"<u>your</u> a goner."
72

---

68. **F.** NO CHANGE
G. were burning a hole
H. holes burning through the ground
J. they were burning a hole

69. **A.** NO CHANGE
B. (place after "relax")
C. (place after "cable")
D. (place after "watched")

70. Where does Sentence 4 logically belong in this paragraph?

F. NO CHANGE
G. After Sentence 6
H. Before Sentence 1
J. After Sentence 5

71. **A.** NO CHANGE
B. needlessly,
C. needlessly.
D. needlessly:

72. **F.** NO CHANGE
G. youre
H. you're
J. you

Questions 73 to 75 ask about the entire passage.

---

73. Suppose the author of this passage was assigned to write an article on the effects of tornadoes. Does she fulfill this assignment?

A. Yes, because she tells about the effects of a tornado on her town.
B. Yes, because she presents her own personal experience with tornado damage.
C. No, because the article focuses more on the author's fascination with the live power line than the tornado.
D. No, because the author doesn't talk about the effects of a tornado.

GO ON TO THE NEXT PAGE.

Model English and Reading ACT I 269

74. Is it appropriate that the author of this passage uses "*I*" in this article?

   F. Yes, because she is relating an autobiographical experience from her childhood.

   G. No, because it is never appropriate to use the first-person *I* in an essay.

   H. No, because the essay focuses on the tornado, not her life.

   J. Yes, because the first-person *I* should be used in all essays.

75. Which of the following sequences of paragraphs makes the essay most logical?

   A. NO CHANGE
   B. 2, 1, 3, 4, 5
   C. 1, 3, 4, 5, 2
   D. 5, 4, 3, 2, 1

END OF TEST 1

Model Reading ACT I

Model Reading ACT I

40 Questions — 35 Minutes

INSTRUCTIONS: There are four passages on this test with ten items about each passage. Choose the best answer for each item based on the passage. Then fill in the appropriate circle on the answer sheet.

Check pages 280 and 290–293 for answers and explanations.

PASSAGE I

PROSE FICTION: This passage is from "Her First Ball" by Katherine Mansfield.

HER FIRST BALL

Exactly when the ball began Leila would have found it hard to say. Perhaps her first real partner was the cab. It did not matter that she shared the cab with the Sheridan girls and their brother. She sat back in her
5 own little corner of it, and the bolster on which her hand rested felt like the sleeve of an unknown young man's dress suit; and away they bowled, past waltzing lampposts and houses and fences and trees.

"Have you really never been to a ball before,
10 Leila? But, my child, how too weird—" cried the Sheridan girls.

"Our nearest neighbor was fifteen miles," said Leila softly, gently opening and shutting her fan.

15 Oh, dear, how hard it was to be indifferent like the others! She tried not to smile too much; she tried not to care. But every single thing was so new and exciting . . . Meg's tuberoses, Jose's long loop of amber, Laura's little dark head, pushing above her white fur
20 like a flower through snow. She would remember forever. It even gave her a pang to see her cousin Laurie throw away the wisps of tissue paper he pulled from the fastenings of his new gloves. She would like to have kept those wisps as a keepsake, as a remem-
25 brance. Laurie leaned forward and put his hand on Laura's knee.

"Look here, darling," he said. "The third and the ninth as usual. Twig?"

Oh, how marvelous to have a brother! In her
30 excitement Leila felt that if there had been time, if it hadn't been impossible, she couldn't have helped crying because she was an only child, and no brother had ever said "Twig?" to her; no sister would ever say, as Meg said to Jose that moment, "I've never known your
35 hair go up more successfully than it has tonight!"

But, of course, there was no time. They were at the drill hall already; there were cabs in front of them and cabs behind. The road was bright on either side with moving fanlike lights, and on the pavement happy
40 couples seemed to float through the air; little satin shoes chased each other like birds.

"Hold on to me, Leila; you'll get lost," said Laura.

"Come on, girls, let's make a dash for it," said Laurie.

45 Leila put two fingers on Laura's pink velvet cloak, and they were somehow lifted past the big golden lantern, carried along the passage, and pushed into the little room marked "Ladies." Here the crowd was so great there was hardly space to take off their
50 things; the noise was deafening. Two benches on either side were stacked high with wraps. Two old women in white aprons ran up and down tossing fresh armfuls. And everybody was pressing forward trying to get at the little dressing table and mirror at the far end.

55 A great quivering jet of gas lighted the ladies' room. It couldn't wait; it was dancing already. When

GO ON TO THE NEXT PAGE.

the door opened again and there came a burst of tuning from the drill hall, it leaped almost to the ceiling.

60 Dark girls, fair girls were patting their hair, tying ribbons again, tucking handkerchiefs down the fronts of their bodices, smoothing marble-white gloves. And because they were all laughing it seemed to Leila that they were all lovely.

65 "Aren't there any invisible hairpins?" cried a voice. "How most extraordinary! I can't see a single invisible hairpin."

"Powder my back, there's a darling," cried someone else.

70 "But I must have a needle and cotton. I've torn simply miles and miles of the frill," wailed a third.

Then, "Pass them along, pass them along!" The straw basket of programs was tossed from arm to arm. Darling little pink-and-silver programs, with pink pencils and fluffy tassels. Leila's fingers shook as she took 75 one out of the basket. She wanted to ask someone, "Am I meant to have one too?" but she had just time to read: "Waltz 3. *Two, Two in a Canoe.* Polka 4. *Making the Feathers Fly,*" when Meg cried, "Ready, Leila?" and they pressed their way through the crush in the 80 passage towards the big double doors of the drill hall.

1. The statement "Have you really never been to a ball before, Leila? But, my child, how too weird —" indicates that:
   A. everyone attends balls by a certain age.
   B. all of the Sheridan girls and their friends have been to balls before.
   C. the Sheridan girls do not like Leila and wish that she were not coming with them to the ball.
   D. the ball is an uninteresting event.

2. Leila's relation to the other children in the cab is that:
   F. they are friends from school.
   G. they are her siblings.
   H. they are her cousins.
   J. they are her dates for the ball.

3. The phrase "waltzing lampposts" is significant because:
   A. it shows that the world in which Leila and the Sheridan children are in is magical.
   B. it conveys Leila's sense of excitement and anticipation of dancing at the ball.
   C. it indicates that the cab was moving very quickly.
   D. it reminds Leila of dance lessons.

4. Leila's general mood is:
   F. happy excitement and anticipation.
   G. melancholy sadness.
   H. oscillating between excitement and fear.
   J. great loneliness.

5. The statement "And because they were all laughing it seemed to Leila that they were all lovely" means that:
   A. Leila believes that people who do not laugh are ugly.
   B. Leila is upset because she believes the laughing women around her are more attractive than she is.
   C. Leila believes that all the women around her are laughing at her naiveté.
   D. Leila believes the women's laughter makes them lovely because they are part of the happy excitement of the ball.

6. According to Leila, she has never been to a ball because:
   F. as an only child, she could not go unchaperoned.
   G. her parents disapproved of balls.
   H. she is an orphan and could not get a new dress.
   J. she lives in a rural area where they do not have balls.

7. It gives Leila a "pang to see her cousin Laurie throw away the wisps of tissue paper he pulled from the fastenings of his new gloves" because:
   A. she believes that paper should be recycled.
   B. she cannot afford such nice, new gloves.
   C. she believes that every little thing associated with the ball is special and should be preserved.
   D. she knows that Laurie will need the tissue paper to repack the gloves later.

8. Based on the information in this passage, the Sheridan family is probably:
   F. middle-class.
   G. poor but happy.
   H. miserly and unhappy.
   J. upper-class and fashionable.

9. Leila wonders, "Am I meant to have one too?" when the dance programs are passed out because:
   A. she is at the ball only as a spectator, not to dance.
   B. the programs are expensive, and she cannot afford one.
   C. she finds it hard to believe that she is actually a part of the excitement going on around her.
   D. she doesn't know how to read.

10. Leila's fingers shake as she removes a program from the basket because:
    F. she is excited to be at the ball.
    G. she's afraid she'll be caught stealing.
    H. she wants to make sure she gets a program.
    J. she is terrified of being at the ball.

GO ON TO THE NEXT PAGE.

PASSAGE II

SOCIAL SCIENCE: This passage is from *America Today* by Henry Brun.

THE MULTICULTURAL SOCIETY

Across the United States, the teaching of multiculturalism became an educational priority in the 1990's. Schools were encouraged to teach appreciation
5 for the diversity of American society and to foster respect for the beliefs and practices of all cultures. Students were taught to understand and respect both the similarities and differences among the ethnicities, cultures, and religions in their communities. Instruction in
10 multiculturalism included the study of immigration as a building block of American society. The diversity arising from the growth of America as a "nation of immigrants" has been presented as one of the strengths of American society.

15 However, in a mid-1993 poll conducted by *Newsweek* magazine, 60 percent of those interviewed stated their belief that "immigration was bad for the country." They feared that the nation was losing control of its borders, and they were worried about the
20 long-term prospects for the economy. They were uncomfortable with the fact that so many of the "New Immigrants" have come from Latin America, the Caribbean, and Asia. Some 59 percent stated that immigration had been good for the country in the past.
25 But 66 percent indicated that they did not believe the United States was still a melting pot because newer immigrants maintained their national identities more strongly.

These attitudes have influenced political actions.
30 In August, 1993, Clinton announced his determination to crack down on illegal immigration. The President introduced to Congress a $172.5 million proposal to strengthen the U.S. Border Patrol and reduce visa fraud and false asylum claims.

35 In 1986, Congress attempted to stop illegal immigration with the Immigration Reform and Control Act (IRCA). The IRCA offered amnesty and eventual citizenship to an estimated 3.7 million illegal aliens. It also aimed to shut down the U.S. job market for these
40 people by making it illegal for employers to hire aliens who lacked immigration documents. The IRCA failed. Despite the amnesty, the estimated number of illegal aliens rose to between 2 to 4 million by 1993.

Between 1971 and 1990, 10.5 million legal immi-
45 grants were admitted to the United States. Ninety per-

cent were from Latin America, the Caribbean, and Asia. Many of the new immigrants came as refugees. In addition, an estimated 500,000 illegal aliens entered each year.

50 Since 1970, the United States has accepted 1.5 million Vietnamese, Laotians, Cambodians, Cubans, Russians, and other oppressed nationalities. Most immigrants, however, migrated to the United States seeking greater economic opportunity and a better life.
55 Many Chinese, for example, came from those sections of China where capitalism has begun to develop. Having acquired some business experience, they wished to improve their opportunities by settling in the United States. For similar reasons, immigrants have come
60 from Bangladesh, the Dominican Republic, Mexico, the Philippines, and elsewhere. Rising birth rates and exposure to American TV telecasts have also stimulated immigration. Although many Americans have regarded the new immigrants as poor, uneducated, and
65 unskilled, the majority have proven to be enterprising. Many have begun family businesses. Others have taken jobs that few Americans want.

Some economists have claimed that more immigration will lead to more economic growth and more
70 wealth—and progress for all Americans. However, immigration has led to increased social friction. In some cities, such as Los Angeles, immigrants have flooded the labor market and set off bitter competition for jobs with American citizens.

75 Rising population levels have also been a major concern. In the early 1990's, immigration produced one-third of U.S. population growth. Projections for the future range from a population of about 383 million in 2050 to 436 million in the year 2090. Some envi-
80 ronmentalists have urged an immediate halt to immigration to preserve the ecosystem and the quality of life.

Despite the problems caused by immigration, America will continue to be "a nation of immigrants."
85 As a result, our society will become more multicultural in the 21st century. For some Americans, this will result in increased social stress and economic competition. For others, it will be a continuing source of progress and cultural enrichment.

GO ON TO THE NEXT PAGE.

11. This author would define the study of *multiculturalism* as:

    A. the belief in the existence of many cultures all at the same time.
    B. the beliefs of immigrant culture.
    C. the use of many immigrant cultures.
    D. the appreciation of the similarities and differences of various cultures in American society.

12. America is defined as "a nation of immigrants" because:

    F. of all the illegal immigrants who have crossed the borders.
    G. most Native American tribes live on reservations.
    H. all Americans except those of Native American ancestry come from immigrant ancestry.
    J. immigrants have been allowed into the United States only in the twentieth century.

13. According to this passage, which of the following is NOT a reason that immigrants currently leave their own countries?

    A. Widespread poverty
    B. Desire for new opportunities
    C. To discover uninhabited frontier land
    D. Escape from repressive governments

14. The teaching of multiculturalism has become an educational priority:

    F. to prevent hostilities between different ethnic groups from increasing.
    G. to encourage students to think of others as different.
    H. to show children all the types of immigrants that live in America.
    J. because the education system needed a new subject to teach.

15. The attitudes of the majority of the people who responded to the *Newsweek* survey are:

    A. hostile and threatened by immigration.
    B. happy and excited to have new immigrants come to America.
    C. excited that immigration might stimulate the economy.
    D. indifferent to the issue of immigration altogether.

16. Many Americans are uncomfortable that so many of the new immigrants are from Asia, Latin America, and the Caribbean because:

    F. all the immigrants from these countries are smarter than Americans.
    G. they are generally easily definable as minorities, and therefore "different."
    H. these cultures are especially threatening to Americans.
    J. these people are wealthy and can take over the country.

17. According to the information presented in this passage, legislation attempting to stop illegal immigrants from coming to the United States is:

    A. highly effective.
    B. nonexistent.
    C. extremely controversial.
    D. extremely ineffective.

18. A benefit of immigration could be:

    F. increased social tensions.
    G. an enriched cultural life.
    H. a significant population increase.
    J. increased use of environmental resources.

19. Some environmentalists believe that immigration must be prevented to maintain the U.S. ecosystem because:

    A. immigrants always use more natural resources than their American counterparts do.
    B. the dramatic increase in population in a relatively short time period could put unbearable strain on our resources.
    C. with an increased human population, animals will not survive.
    D. environmentalists are generally in favor of immigration.

20. The statement that best summarizes the author's main point in the final paragraph is:

    F. Increased multiculturalism is inevitable and will produce positive and negative results in the future.
    G. We can stop the influx of immigrants now if we work harder.
    H. Cultural enrichment will definitely outweigh all the negative aspects of increased immigration in the twenty-first century.
    J. Economic competition is always a negative factor in American society.

GO ON TO THE NEXT PAGE.

PASSAGE III

HUMANITIES: This passage is from *Western Civilization* by Gerson Antell and Walter Harris.

A GLORIOUS ERA IN MUSIC

The great change that took place in music around the year 1600 occurred in Florence, where a group of Italian poets and artists met to discuss classical drama.
5 They thought that the actors of ancient Greece and Rome had either sung their roles or spoken them to musical accompaniment. So the Florentines too wanted to write music that would set off words. (In sixteenth-century music, an elaborate style of writing had
10 generally made words secondary and frequently unintelligible.) As a leading spokesman said, "Let the word be the master, not the servant, of the music."

For words to be masters rather than servants, they had to be clearly understood. This led to an emphasis
15 on solos, for both voices and instruments. And of course an emphasis on communication gave the listener new importance too. In a way the spirit of Renaissance individualism expressed in art and literature was now to be expressed in music.

20 Baroque music meant much more than an emphasis on words and on solos. There were new musical forms as well. One was opera, the union of drama and music. One of the very first operas was *Orfeo* by Claudio Monteverdi, first produced in 1607. The composer
25 used an orchestra to create a dramatic mood for the solo voices, which acted out the ancient Greek myth of the poet Orpheus and his beloved wife, Eurydice.

Another musical form of the baroque period was the oratorio, a composition that tells a dramatic story
30 but, unlike opera, does not use stage settings, costumes, or gestures. Most oratorios are based on a religious subject, such as the Exodus from Egypt or events in the life of Christ. Related to the oratorio is the cantata, usually shorter and lacking a dramatic narrative.

35 The baroque period also witnessed the development of many musical instruments as we know them today. The organ came into its full splendor. Other instruments that took their present form included the oboe, bassoon, trumpet, trombone, violin, viola, cello,
40 and double bass.

Baroque music flourished in Italy, and Italian musicians had enormous influence elsewhere in Europe.
Monteverdi, choirmaster of St. Mark's Cathedral in Venice, composed operas (only a few of which sur-
45 vive) and also many religious works and shorter vocal pieces called madrigals. His contemporary Giovanni Gabrieli was the organist at St. Mark's. Gabrieli was a pioneer in developing the concerto. His music was also the first to indicate dynamic markings (degrees of vol-
50 ume) and specify which instruments were to be played when a work was performed.

Elsewhere in Europe the baroque style was modified somewhat according to local needs. In Germany, Heinrich Schütz—a pupil of Gabrieli's and director of
55 music at the court of Dresden—wrote oratorios and other religious compositions for Protestant services. In France, the court of Louis XIV boasted Jean Baptiste Lully (born Lulli in Florence), who wrote ballets and operas for the king's pleasure. In England, James II
60 and William and Mary were patrons of Henry Purcell. He wrote both religious works for Anglican services and dramatic music that included an opera, *Dido and Aeneas*.

The two giants of the baroque period, Johann
65 Sebastian Bach and George Frederick Handel, were born in the same year, 1685. Bach held various posts in German cities, but was thought of primarily as an organist. Few of his works were published during his lifetime, but since the nineteenth century he has been
70 recognized as a musical genius. Bach's works include hundreds of compositions for the organ and clavier (a predecessor of the piano); 300 sacred cantatas; and such monumental religious works as the *B Minor Mass* and the *St. Matthew Passion*.

75 Born in Germany, Handel studied in Italy and settled permanently in England after his patron, the ruler of Hanover, had become King George I. Handel wrote several dozen operas but is best known for his noble and dramatic oratorios, mostly notably the *Messiah*.
80 An anthem Handel wrote for the coronation of George II has been performed at every coronation since.

21. According to this passage, baroque music was born in:

A. Italy.
B. Spain.
C. Germany.
D. England.

GO ON TO THE NEXT PAGE.

22. Which of the following is NOT an important development of baroque music?

F. A greater significance for the words
G. An emphasis on individual singers and instruments
H. The development of the opera
J. The creation of the symphony orchestra

23. Composers found the subject matter for most oratorios in:

A. biblical stories.
B. Shakespearean tales.
C. Greek myth.
D. fairy tales.

24. The opera *Orfeo* most likely had:

F. only one performer.
G. a theme based on a biblical story.
H. more than one composer.
J. stage settings and costumes.

25. As it is used in lines 60 and 76, the word "patron" means:

A. one who hates music.
B. one who financially supports an artist.
C. a music lover.
D. royalty.

26. Which of the following statements is supported by the information in lines 70–74?

F. Bach hated to write operas.
G. Bach and Handel fought constantly.
H. Bach was a prolific and talented composer.
J. Bach wrote music only for the organ.

27. The organ, the double bass, and the trumpet were all instruments which:

A. were ignored during the baroque period.
B. were favored by baroque composers.
C. were substantially different during this period than they are today.
D. were developed into their current forms.

28. The passage implies that:

F. baroque music appealed only to royalty.
G. the popularity of baroque music spread from Italy all over Western Europe.
H. baroque composers all invented new instruments or musical forms.
J. baroque music was performed only in churches and cathedrals.

29. According to the passage, George Frederick Handel's works:

A. were better than those of J. S. Bach.
B. were all lost in the London fire of 1666.
C. are still influential today.
D. were written for his wife.

30. According to this passage, the baroque period began around:

F. 1800.
G. 1600.
H. 1700.
J. 1500.

GO ON TO THE NEXT PAGE.

PASSAGE IV

NATURAL SCIENCE: This passage is from "Is Time Travel Possible?" by Mark Davidson.

Contrary to the old warning that time waits for no one, time slows down when you are on the move. It also slows down more as you move faster, which means astronauts someday may survive so long in
5 space that they would return to an Earth of the distant future. If you could move at the speed of light, 186,282 miles a second, your time would stand still. If you could move faster than light, outpacing your shadow, your time would move backward.

10 Although no form of matter yet discovered moves as fast or faster than light, scientific experiments have confirmed that accelerated motion causes a voyager's time to be stretched. Einstein predicted this in 1905, when he introduced the concept of relative time as part
15 of his Special Theory of Relativity. A search is now under way to confirm the suspected existence of particles of matter that move faster than light and therefore possibly might serve as our passports to the past.

Einstein employed a definition of time, for exper-
20 imental purposes, as that which is measured by a clock. He regarded a clock as anything that measured a uniformly repeating physical process. In accordance with his definition, time and time's relativity are measurable by any sundial, hourglass, metronome, alarm clock, or
25 an atomic clock that can measure a billionth of a second because its "tick" is based on the uniformly repeating wobble of the spinning-top motion of electrons.

With atomic-clock application of Einstein's defi-
30 nition of time, scientists have demonstrated that an ordinary airplane flight is like a brief visit to the Fountain of Youth. In 1972, for example, scientists who took four atomic clocks on an airplane trip around the world discovered that the moving clocks moved slightly
35 slower than atomic clocks which had remained on the ground. If you fly around the world, preferably going eastward to gain the advantage of the added motion of the Earth's rotation, the atomic clocks show that you'll return younger than you would have been if you had
40 stayed home. Frankly, you'll be younger by only 40 billionths of a second. Such an infinitesimal saving of time hardly makes up for all the hours you age while waiting at airports, but *any* saving of time proves that time can be stretched. Moreover, atomic clocks have
45 demonstrated that the stretching of time, or "time dilation," increases with speed.

Here is an example of what you can expect if tomorrow's space-flight technology—employing the energy of thermonuclear fusion, matter-antimatter
50 annihilation, or whatever—enables you to move at ultra-high speeds. Imagine you're an astronaut with a twin who stays home. If you travel back and forth to the nearest star at about half the speed of light, you'll be gone for eighteen Earth years. When you return,
55 your twin will be eighteen years older, but you'll have aged only sixteen years. Your body will be two years younger than your twin's because time aboard the flying spaceship will have moved slower than time on Earth. You will have aged normally, but you will have
60 been in a slower time zone. If your spaceship moves at about 90 percent of light-speed, you'll age only 50 percent as much as your twin. If you whiz along at 99.86 percent of light-speed, you'll age only 5 percent as much. These examples of time-stretching, of course,
65 cannot be tested with any existing spacecraft. Yet, they are based on mathematical projections of relativity science, as confirmed by the atomic-clock experiments.

Speed is not the only factor that slows time;
70 so does gravity. Einstein determined in his General Theory of Relativity (the 1915 sequel to his 1905 Special Theory of Relativity) that the force of an object's gravity "curves" the space in the object's gravitational field. When gravity curves space, Einstein reasoned,
75 gravity also must curve time, because space and time are linked in a space-time continuum. The concept of the space-time continuum, developed by one of Einstein's former professors, simply means that time and space must be considered together because time is a
80 fourth dimension of space.

Numerous atomic-clock experiments have confirmed Einstein's calculation that the closer you are to the Earth's center of gravity, which is the Earth's core, the slower you will age. In one of these experiments,
85 an atomic clock was taken from the National Bureau of Standards in Washington, D.C., near sea level, and moved to mile-high Denver. The results demonstrated that people in Denver age more rapidly by a tiny amount than people in Washington.

90 If you would like gravity's space-time warp to extend your life, get a home at the beach and a job as a deep-sea diver. Avoid living in the mountains or working in a skyscraper. If you're taking airplane trips to slow your aging, make sure you fly fast enough to can-
95 cel out the gravity-reduction effect of being high above the Earth's surface. That advice, like the advice about flying around the world, will enable you to slow your aging by only a few billionths of a second.

GO ON TO THE NEXT PAGE.

Nevertheless, those tiny fractions of a second add
100 up to more proof that time-stretching is a reality. The
proof involving gravity suggests that you could have
an unforgettable rendezvous with a black hole, where
gravity is believed to be so powerful that it imprisons
light. In a black hole—a huge, burned-out star that has
105 collapsed into infinite density and, therefore, infinite
gravity—the object's extreme warp of space-time
would make your time stand still. Granted, a black hole
would be an awfully dark and dreary place to spend
eternity, but think of all the time you'd have to redeco-
110 rate.

31. According to the theories in this article, in order for
time to move backward, an object must move:

A. fast enough to break the time barrier.
B. at 186,282 miles a second.
C. at the speed of light.
D. faster than the speed of light.

32. The results of the atomic-clock experiment show that
time:

F. flies when you're having fun.
G. continues at a normal pace.
H. slows down.
J. speeds up.

33. Which of the following theories was NOT developed
by Einstein?

A. Space-time continuum
B. General Theory of Relativity
C. Special Theory of Relativity
D. None of the above theories were developed by
Einstein.

34. According to the information in this passage, people in
Denver age more rapidly than people in Washington,
D.C., because:

F. people in Washington, D.C., understand Einstein's
theory.
G. the climate is better for people on the East Coast.
H. Washington, D.C., is closer to sea level than Denver.
J. the Rocky Mountains are dangerous for those liv-
ing on them.

35. Time for humans is NOT affected by:

A. gravity.
B. life expectancy.
C. speed of travel.
D. closeness to Earth's center.

36. Which of the following statements best reflects the author's main point in this passage?

F. Black holes are very dangerous.
G. Atomic clocks are unreliable indicators of time.
H. Einstein was the greatest scientist in history.
J. Time can be affected by factors such as speed and
gravity.

37. In its context in line 66, the word "projections" means:

A. visual images on a television screen.
B. predicted outcomes.
C. objects that stick out of the ground.
D. objects that fly.

38. In a place of infinite gravity, time:

F. speeds up dramatically.
G. slows down slightly.
H. reverses completely.
J. stops completely.

39. The author mentions redecorating while living in a
black hole (lines 109–110):

A. because when the sun dies, all humans will live in
a black hole.
B. to demonstrate that the concept of black holes is
ridiculous.
C. to prove that life can exist in a place of infinite
density.
D. to add a playful note to an otherwise serious
scientific discussion.

40. If one 20-year-old woman travels in space at 90 percent
of the speed of light for 10 years and her twin stays on
Earth, the space traveler's age when she returns will be:

F. 30.
G. 35.
H. 25.
J. 20.

END OF TEST 3

Model English ACT I

PASSAGE I	PASSAGE II	PASSAGE III	PASSAGE IV	PASSAGE V
1. C	16. G	31. B	46. F	61. C
2. F	17. D	32. J	47. C	62. J
3. B	18. H	33. C	48. J	63. C
4. H	19. A	34. G	49. C	64. F
5. A	20. G	35. C	50. J	65. D
6. G	21. D	36. H	51. C	66. F
7. B	22. F	37. D	52. J	67. B
8. J	23. A	38. H	53. B	68. J
9. D	24. H	39. D	54. F	69. A
10. F	25. A	40. H	55. D	70. H
11. A	26. J	41. D	56. G	71. B
12. H	27. C	42. G	57. B	72. H
13. D	28. H	43. C	58. J	73. C
14. G	29. B	44. F	59. A	74. F
15. C	30. J	45. D	60. H	75. B

Model Reading ACT I

PASSAGE I	PASSAGE II	PASSAGE III	PASSAGE IV
1. B	11. D	21. A	31. D
2. H	12. H	22. J	32. H
3. B	13. C	23. A	33. A
4. F	14. F	24. J	34. H
5. D	15. A	25. B	35. B
6. J	16. G	26. H	36. J
7. C	17. D	27. D	37. B
8. J	18. G	28. G	38. J
9. C	19. B	29. C	39. D
10. F	20. F	30. G	40. H

ACT I English Answers Explained

PASSAGE I

✔*ANSWERS*

1: C. This sentence presents the thesis of the essay that follows. Clearly, the author is quite capable of elaborating on this idea, for he does just this for the remainder of the passage. However, there is nothing special about this sentence that indicates the author to be a great writer. And finally, the author of this passage gives no indication that this sentence is to have symbolic importance.

2: F. In order for this sentence to maintain proper construction, the verbs in the sentence must be in the same tense. Therefore, the verb "to take" must be in the same tense as the earlier present tense verb "is."

3: B. In order to maintain a structure parallel to the other independent clauses in this sentence, a semicolon must separate the clauses here as it does between "everywhere" and "videotapes."

4: H. The author is referring to more than one video game, so the correct answer must be plural. However, a verb follows the noun "video games," so therefore the word cannot be a possessive.

5: A. In context with the language in the passage, the word "deliver" is emphasized to show that people have the option of remaining at home while someone else brings food directly to their door. There is no discussion of mail, how quickly food is brought to the home, or the take-out option in this paragraph.

6: G. Because this sentence repeats ideas mentioned in the previous sentence, the phrases should logically fall in the same order. Since the previous sentence refers first to parking, then to walking, then waiting, and finally risk, the phrases in this sentence should match this order.

7: B. The second "sentence" here is not a sentence at all. Instead, it is a parenthetical adverbial clause describing why preparing our own food is getting easier. Therefore, it needs to be set apart from the remainder of the sentence by a comma.

8: J. Since microwave use has become common, the slang verb "to nuke" was created to describe this type of cooking. However, this is not formal English; therefore, it is inappropriate for a formal essay. There are no other uses of slang in the essay. While choice H appears to make sense, it is redundant, because the word *cooking* implies that food is being cooked.

9: D. The subject of this sentence is followed directly by a verb. If "futurists" were a possessive, it would be an adjective describing the actual subject of the sentence. Since no noun follows, "futurists" stands alone as the subject. It is also important to note that the verb which follows ("call") is a plural verb; therefore, the subject must be plural as well.

10: F. Since this verb refers back to the subject "families" and it should be parallel with the verb "stay," "interact" must be a plural verb in the present tense.

11: A. A period, semicolon, or exclamation point would all separate a dependent clause from an independent clause, making the first part of this sentence a sentence fragment. A dash functions here to separate the explanation of the elements already mentioned.

12: H. The author doesn't take any personal responsibility for the occurrence of cocooning, so it doesn't make him ashamed of himself. His action of writing on this subject proves that he is not indifferent about this subject. His choice of words indicates that he thinks cocooning is not "healthy" and it will "rip the social fabric"; he clearly indicates that he is very concerned about the future of society.

13: D. Throughout this essay, the author has been speaking in the first person plural, stating "us," "we," and "our." A switch in pronouns here would not only be uncharacteristic of this essay, it would show that the author is not a part of the society he's describing. Since he has already described himself as part of this society, the choice of "our" here is the best, most consistent answer.

14. G. In this case, the word "equal" should be an adjective describing the word time. "Equally" is an adverb, which cannot describe a noun. "Equated" is a verb, which is also an inappropriate choice. There is no such word as "equalest," because "equal" is an absolute adjective which cannot be made into a superlative. Something cannot be more or less equal, otherwise it would no longer *be* equal.

15: C. All of the other choices here provide irrelevant information that would distract the reader rather than inform him or her. Choice C, however, offers information which would clarify the author's argument.

PASSAGE II

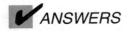**ANSWERS**

16: G. The first "sentence" as it is written is actually a sentence fragment. This fragment is an adverb phrase used to describe where the Indians lived. A long adverb phrase that leads off a sentence is separated from the main, independent clause of the sentence by a comma.

17: D. In the first sentence, the author of this passage discusses the Indians in the past tense. To remain consistent with the author's discussion of an old Indian tribe, this verb should also be in the past tense.

18: H. This sentence lists different materials that Indians used to make tools. However, this sentence does not maintain parallel construction because the third item in the list should be presented in the same manner as the first two. Additionally, all of the options except H repeat ideas that have already been introduced.

19: A. The subject of this sentence is *one.* Therefore, the verb must be singular. No comma should separate the verb from the remainder of the sentence.

20: G. A colon is the appropriate punctuation to set off a list of items from the sentence. By using a period or semicolon, the list of tribes becomes a sentence fragment.

21: D. In this paragraph, the author has already discussed the Iroquois League (League of Five Nations) and the five tribes that have united to form this group. Adding any of the phrases given here would be redundant.

22: F. The word "Iroquois" is both a singular and a plural, like the word "English" or "French." Just as you wouldn't say "the Frenches," you wouldn't say "the Iroquoises." The author demonstrates this in previous mention of this word. In this case, the word is not possessive because "of the Iroquois" is used instead to indicate possession.

23: A. This sentence makes the most sense at the end of the paragraph, where it is already located. The entire paragraph builds ideas which are summed up in this final statement.

24: H. The individuals acting as "servants of the people" are the elected officials, not the tribe. In the other choices given, the opening adverbial clause appears to be describing the tribe rather than the officials.

25: A. The author assumes that the reader of this essay is already familiar with the term "democracy." However, the reader is probably not familiar with the term "sachem" and the way the sachem functioned in the Iroquois governing body. Though an explanation of how the sachem were chosen might be interesting, it is not as helpful as the description of the duties of the sachem. A list of all the men chosen to be sachem would take up a great deal of space and provide no useful information to the reader.

26: J. Choice A presents the reader with a comma splice, a run-on sentence in which the two independent clauses are joined only by a comma. Choice G is a run-on sentence where no punctuation is used to join the two independent clauses. An ellipsis can be used to bridge two sentences, but it would replace missing words—and there don't seem to be any missing words here. Therefore, choice J is most appropriate because it breaks the run-on into two complete sentences.

27: C. The other options present common, slang expressions which have similar meanings to "rejected." However, in the formal context of this passage, especially following the formal word "accepted," the word "rejected" is most appropriate.

28: H. The discussion of women here introduces a new idea; therefore, the author should begin a new paragraph. Because no special emphasis is needed on the sentence ending with "operated," a period is the appropriate punctuation.

29: B. Though the author does mention the powerful roles of women in the Iroquois League, the majority of the article focuses on the League itself and its government. Only one paragraph focuses on the role of women.

30: J. This essay would most likely be too basic for professors of history. While G and H are possible audiences for this essay, the essay is designed to present general information to anyone unfamiliar with this group of people.

PASSAGE III

✔ANSWERS

31: B. Choice B offers the past tense, which is consistent with the discussion of an event in 1799 and the tense of the other verbs in the paragraph. Choices A, C, and D offer verb tenses which are inconsistent with the time frame presented.

32: J. The phrases "by himself," "all by himself," and "with himself" all repeat the meaning of the word "alone." Since these phrases simply repeat the word, rather than modifying it, they are unnecessary.

33: C. In order to maintain parallel construction in this sentence, all of the verbs must maintain the same tense. Since the verbs "scavenged" and "drank" are both past tense, the form of "to run" should be past tense as well ("ran").

34: G. In this case, the comma is necessary to set off Jean-Marc Itard's name from the modifying clause that follows it and provides additional information about him. By using a period, the clause "A physician at the National Institute of Deaf-Mutes" would become a sentence fragment. A colon is inappropriate here because it is not followed by a definition or a list.

35: C. Because the quotation is in the form of a question, the proper punctuation for the end of the sentence is a question mark, followed by closing quotation marks.

36: H. As it stands, the clause "His work with Victor" is a sentence fragment because it has no verb. Furthermore, the word "rather" makes little sense, whereas "for example," set off by commas, connects the first and second sentences of the paragraph.

37: D. Both B and C are incorrect because a comma should not separate the adjective and the word it is describing. Because the adjective "famous" modifies the word clause "Italian educator," the same rule applies. Therefore, no commas are necessary here.

38: H. In choice G, the adverb "physically" is being used in place of the adjective "physical" to describe the noun "development." In choice F, adverb forms are given for both words. In choice J, a comma is not necessary to separate a pair of items.

39. **D.** The clauses "refused to be convinced" or "refused [or refuses] to be convinced otherwise" are unnecessary because the words "stubbornly maintained" in the opening clause imply that Itard would not allow others to influence his opinions.

40: **H.** This is not a question or a statement that would require enough emphasis to need an exclamation point. It is, however, the end of a sentence, so a period rather than a comma is appropriate.

41: **D.** Most readers will not need a definition of choice A or choice C. Choice B would be impossible to discover, since Itard and his peers did not know who Victor's parents were or what they were like. Though it rests on the general assumptions of normal intelligence and everyday family life, the sentence needs no further information.

42: **G.** The words "five-year" form a compound adjective which modifies the words "training program." When a compound adjective precedes the word or phrase it describes, it is hyphenated,

43: **C.** The writer lists two things that Victor was uncomfortable doing. The adjectives "this" and "that" both indicate a single action. An adjective that indicates more than one action is necessary, so "both" is the best option.

44. **F.** Quotation marks should be used for only a few specific purposes: to set off direct quotations, to set off titles of short works, and to set off words that are being used in an unusual manner. This quotation is not a title. Earlier in the paragraph the writer indicates that these words accurately describe Victor's condition. These words must be a direct quotation from a book or another source.

45: **D.** Paragraph 3 sums up how Jean-Marc Itard's work has affected future researchers. When Paragraph 3 is moved to the end of the passage, the other four paragraphs tell an orderly story about the progression of Itard's experiment. (1, 2, 4, 5).

PASSAGE IV

 *ANSWERS*

46. **F.** The author uses the word "long" as an adjective to describe the word "centuries" to emphasize the great length of time that human civilization existed before writing was invented. Choices G and H are simply redundant, reiterating the idea indicated by the word "century." The superlative "longest" makes no sense because no century is any longer than the others.

47: **C.** This sentence begins with the word "How," which should indicate to the reader that, most likely, a question will be asked. Since this first independent clause is asking a question, the proper end punctuation here would be a question mark, not a period. As this sentence stands, it is a run-on. Choice D is a comma splice, which is a run-on where the two independent clauses are connected by a comma.

48: **J.** The word "variety" implies various, meaning different kinds. Therefore, both the words "different" and "various" are redundant. No other word is necessary to convey the idea that there are many different ways that archeologists examine the distant past.

49. **C.** The scientists must devote their time and energy to learning about the surroundings where they find their objects; in other words, they must "pay special attention" to the area. While choices A and B reflect similar concepts, both are slang phrases that are out of place in a formal essay. If this phrase were completely omitted, the sentence would be missing a verb, and therefore would be an incomplete thought.

50: **J.** In this paragraph, the author is listing the different ways an archeologist can determine the age of an item. This is the second item mentioned in the list, so "also" would provide an appropriate transition. "Therefore" implies that there is a connection between this and the preceding sentence, which discussed how deeply an item is buried; there is no logical connection between these statements. "However" implies that the second sentence contradicts the first; this is also not logical. Finally, "for example" indicates that the second sentence provides an example of what was described in the first sentence, when in actuality, it provides another topic of discussion.

51: **C.** This sentence describes the emitting of radiocarbons, and should therefore follow the introduction of the term which occurs in Sentence 6. Any other location in the paragraph would be confusing because it separates two sentences about the same idea.

52: **J.** Because the article "an" precedes this word, we know two things: the word must begin with a vowel (so "thing's" cannot be correct), and it must be singular (so "objects" is incorrect). Additionally, the word in this space must be a possessive because it is describing the age of the object.

53: **B.** Because a long adverbial clause opens this sentence, it must be set apart from the remainder of the sentence by a comma. By using a period or a semicolon, the adverbial clause becomes a sentence fragment. The ellipsis generally indicates that words have been removed from a sentence, though that does not seem to be the case here.

54: **F.** Because this sentence is discussing the habits of people that lived thousands of years ago, the verb must be in the past tense. Preceded by the noun "inhabitants," the verb must also be plural to match the plural subjects. Though "weren't" is grammatically correct in this sentence, it is logically incorrect, for the archeologists are making hypotheses about how these ancient people lived. In the previous sentence, a similar structure is created, noting that if the people did a certain action, then they probably had certain knowledge. Logically, this sentence, which has the same structure, would follow the same pattern.

55: D. This sentence contains two independent clauses that must be broken down into two complete, independent sentences. It is currently a comma splice, a form of a run-on sentence in which the two independent clauses are bound together by only a comma. Choice B is also a run-on sentence. Though choice C is grammatically correct, it adds unnecessary emphasis to the first independent clause.

56: G. The writer of this paragraph states that "no one knew how to read ancient writings." However, this writer has already stated that archeologists can decipher this ancient writing. Since a reader of this article most likely would not know how archeologists broke this ancient written code, an explanation would be necessary for the logical flow of this article. Though pictures of hieroglyphics would be interesting, they would not provide any significant information to the reader. A description of the relationship between the Greeks and the Egyptians would steer the reader away from the central discussion of archeology.

57: B. Here, the author is setting off nonessential information from the remainder of the sentence by using dashes. If the information is preceded and followed by the remainder of the sentence, the nonessential clause must both open and close with a dash, not a comma or a blank space. By using a period here, the clause is fine, but the remainder of this sentence becomes a sentence fragment.

58: J. Choice J offers the only logical and complete sentence to fill this space. Choices F and G are both sentence fragments which are missing subjects and verbs. While choice H is a complete sentence, the word "however" implies that the information that follows will contradict the information given in previous sentences. Since this sentence agrees with, rather than contradicts the previous sentence, choice J is the best answer.

59: A. In an essay that discusses the different techniques of archeology, it's logical to begin the essay by introducing the subject of archeology and its function. All of the other options given here begin by introducing the techniques of archeology before introducing the subject itself.

60: H. The author poses a question in the first sentence of this essay. In the following sentence, the author points out that the answer to this question can be found through the many techniques of archeology. The remainder of this essay fills in the details of these techniques in response to the opening question.

While option J also answers the question affirmatively, the reader has no way of knowing whether or not the author of this passage is an archeologist; therefore, this is not the best possible answer.

Choice F is incorrect because the entire essay is focused on "people today," even if the author does not use these words. It is "people today" who are doing the archeological digs and making hypotheses. Choice G is inappropriate because the author offers a general discussion of archeology, using the Greek and Egyptian cultures as examples. The author does not claim to mention every ancient culture that archeologists have explored.

 *ANSWERS*

61: C. In order to maintain parallel construction in this sentence, both verbs that refer to the sentence's one subject must be in the same tense. Since the initial verb ("roamed") is in the past tense, we must also have the past tense form of *find*, which is "found." While "founded" is an actual past tense verb, it means "to start up" (usually an organization or a business).

62: J. Here, the author is using the contracted form of the words *could not*. Since she is leaving out the *o* in *not*, an apostrophe must take its place. While "can't" is an acceptable contraction, it is inappropriate here because it is in present tense, while the remainder of the paragraph is in past tense.

63: C. As this sentence is currently written, it is actually a form of a run-on sentence known as a comma splice (two independent clauses strung together by a comma). Given the available choices, these independent clauses must be split by a period. Though a question mark would be grammatically correct, it would not be logically correct, for the first independent clause is a direct statement, not a question.

64: F. The author uses this phrase in this place in the sentence to indicate that it is her personal opinion that the fuss about the trees was "unconscionable." If the phrase were placed after "perhaps" or "week," the phrase would seemingly indicate that the "in my view" refers to the trees remaining in the street, which is not a matter of opinion, rather than the nature of the fuss that is being made about them. By removing this phrase entirely, it would appear that the author's opinion is actual fact, which it cannot be.

65: D. This adverbial clause is redundant because it simply repeats the idea that is indicated by the word "melted." Choice C is simply a diversion to throw the reader off, because something cannot melt from a liquid to a solid.

66: F. The author is telling us that this power line, which normally ran along Penn Avenue, had fallen to the ground. The word "usually" refers to the normal location of this line. The other conditions, what it looked like, what it was made out of, are still true; therefore, they cannot be modified with "usually."

67: B. A dash is necessary here to separate the nonessential clause from the remainder of the sentence. Nonessential clauses, those that do not change the meaning of the sentence, can be set off from the rest of the sentence in many different ways. Here, however, the author has opened the nonessential clause with a dash, so the clause must be closed with a dash as well.

68: J. In order to properly use a semicolon, there must be independent clauses on both sides of the punctuation. Semicolons are used to join complete, connected thoughts. Choice J offers the only independent clause; in all the other cases, the words form a dependent clause (sentence fragment).

69: A. This phrase follows the word "sink" because a wire can *sink into* something. The phrase "relax into" is illogical. If the phrase is placed in any location other than directly after "sink," the meaning of the sentence is altered.

70: H. Sentence 4 provides the first mention that the wire was melting a pit into the street. Sentences 2, 3, and 6 all refer to the effects of this melting. Therefore, the information that this pit was being melted must come prior to Sentence 2, which must build upon the information in Sentence 5. Choice H is the only option that allows Sentence 4 to be placed before Sentence 2.

71: B. When you introduce a short quotation with an introductory tag (such as "my father said" or "Jenny claimed"), the introductory tag must be followed by a comma. If the introductory tag were an independent clause or the following quotation were long or formal, a colon would be acceptable, but neither is the case here. Since the two halves of the quotation (indicated by the first quotation's final comma) are part of the same statement, they cannot be separated by a period.

72: H. This quotation is directed toward the author as you. Her father indicates that she is a goner if she touches the power cable. Therefore, the verb "are" must be part of this phrase, indicating that this should be the contraction of the words "you" and "are." Since none of the other options contains the verb, H is the only acceptable choice.

73: C. The author focuses on a live wire that falls on the ground as the result of a tornado, not on the tornado and its general effects on the town. Though she does mention these effects briefly, they are clearly not the focus of this article. She also focuses only on her personal experience with one tornado rather than the general information about the effects of tornadoes that this assignment should contain.

74: F. In this passage the author is directly relating an experience she remembers from her youth. Because this experience is autobiographical, the use of *I* is a logical and appropriate choice.

75: B. In Paragraph 2, the author introduces us to the tornado. She spends the other paragraphs describing the aftermath of this event. Therefore, the paragraph that tells about the tornado hitting should logically come before the paragraphs that describe how the tornado knocked down a high-voltage power line.

ACT I Reading Answers Explained

ANSWERS

1: B. In the social circle of the Sheridan girls, all young women are able to attend balls, though that is not a universal experience for all children. The Sheridan girls clearly believe, however, that all young women should attend balls.

2: H. When she discusses her companions in the cab, she refers to her cousin Laurie. She then notes that Laurie is the brother of Laura, and that Meg and Jose are sisters. They are the Sheridan children, and Leila's cousins.

3: B. The personification of the lampposts is significant, especially since they are waltzing. Since Leila is excited and happy about the possibility of waltzing later in the evening, she imagines that the world is waltzing with her.

4: F. The passage notes that Leila had to "try not to smile too much." Leila could not hide her excitement. Though she contemplates how under other circumstances she might be sad at the lack of a sibling, she does not allow herself to be sad.

5: D. Whether or not these women are actually lovely, Leila sees their happiness and laughter as part of the beauty of the ball. These women are not laughing at her, nor does Leila necessarily believe that these women are more attractive than she is.

6: J. When her cousins question her about not having gone to a ball, Leila claims that it is because she lives in an area where the neighbors live far away from each other. She implies that this distance prevents people from having balls.

7: C. Leila wishes she could keep the tissue paper as a remembrance or a keepsake. She believes that this paper, as much as everything else, is an important part of this momentous occasion in her life. Because the event is so important to her, she wishes she could preserve everything.

8: J. All of the girls seem to be dressed in new, fancy clothes, as is their brother. The indication is that they and all the other ball attendees are of wealthy families with social standing.

9: C. Leila questions her participation in the ball because she cannot believe that something this wonderful can be happening to her. Clearly, she is meant to be a part of the dancing and other activities. There is no indication that these programs cost any money. Since Leila reads the dance program, she must be literate.

10: F. All of the language in the passage leading up to this sentence demonstrates Leila's excitement on being at the ball. As a natural reaction, her hands begin to shake as her fantasy begins to become reality.

 *ANSWERS*

11: D. The author notes that multiculturalism is now widely taught in schools to help students understand and appreciate the various cultures that live together in the United States.

12: H. All of the nation's forefathers (except those of Native Americans) came from other countries, whether it was England, Scotland, Germany, France, or elsewhere. So, in a way, almost all Americans are immigrants.

13: C. When the United States was founded, many immigrants came to this country to expand westward into uncharted territory. However, in the late twentieth century, there is very little (if any) uncharted American land to explore. The other possibilities are all viable reasons for why people come to the United States from other countries.

14: F. As new immigrants continue to come to America, hostilities against groups are on the rise (as demonstrated by the results of the *Newsweek* poll). The best way to prevent this increase in hostility is to teach children to appreciate and respect other cultures so they will grow into respectful adults.

15. A. According to these poll results, the majority of Americans are afraid of the effects that continued immigration will have on their country, despite the fact that the United States was built by immigrants.

16: G. These groups, in particular, might look or behave in ways that prevent them from easily assimilating into the dominant, Caucasian American culture. Because these cultures appear not to blend easily, they are perceived as threatening.

17: D. This passage notes that the Immigration Reform and Control Act (IRCA) failed to stem the tide of illegal immigrants coming to live in the United States. In fact, the number of illegal immigrants entering the country increased by more than two million in less than a decade.

18: G. All of the other choices represent possible effects of immigration, but not positive ones. Of the choices listed, only the idea of an enriched and diverse cultural life offers an interesting and productive possibility for the future of Americans.

19: B. An increase of almost 80 million people in 40 years could affect our food, water, and energy supplies in an extremely negative way.

20: F. In this paragraph, the author points out that "America will continue to be 'a nation of immigrants.'" For some people, this will offer positive opportunities for improvement, while other people will face hardships as a result.

*ANSWERS*

21: A. In the opening paragraph, the author indicates that baroque music began in Florence, an Italian city.

22: J. Baroque music emphasized words (lines 7–8) and solos (lines 14–15), and developed a new musical form, opera (line 22).

23: A. Most oratorios are "based on a religious subject" (lines 31–32). The author then goes on to give examples of the types of stories represented. While some oratorios may have been based on these other choices, the majority was religious in nature.

24: J. The oratorio, "unlike opera, does not use stage settings, costumes, or gestures." Based on this statement (lines 30–31), an opera like *Orfeo* would most likely contain stage settings and costumes.

25: B. While choices C and D may be characteristics of a patron, a patron is generally one who offers financial support to an artist (painters, musicians, etc.) so that the artist can produce.

26: H. The information in this paragraph indicates that Bach wrote hundreds of compositions, including 300 cantatas. The paragraph also expresses that Bach has been recognized as a musical genius. The paragraph clearly states that Bach wrote music for the organ and clavier. Neither F nor G is mentioned.

27: D. In lines 37–40, these instruments are listed as among those that reached their present, familiar form during the baroque period.

28: G. The passage indicates that the baroque movement was founded in Italy, but shows how this style of music spread and was adapted to various cultures.

29: C. There is no information in this passage to support answers A, B, or D. However, the author does mention Handel's most famous oratorio, *Messiah.* The author also notes that his coronation theme is still used.

30: G. The author notes (lines 1–2) that "The great change that took place in music around the year 1600 occurred in Florence." From the context of the rest of the passage, it is clear that this "great change" reflects the onset of the baroque period.

31. **D.** The author notes that if an object can move *faster* than the speed of light (more than 186,282 miles per second), time for that object would move backward (lines 7–9).

32: **H.** The author reports that the scientists discovered that "the moving clocks moved slightly slower than atomic clocks which had remained on the ground" (lines 34–36).

33: **A.** According to lines 77–78, the space-time continuum was developed by one of Einstein's professors. In lines 14–15, the author indicates that Einstein introduced the Special Theory of Relativity, and in lines 70–76, the author discusses Einstein's General Theory of Relativity.

34: **H.** Because Washington, D.C., is closer to sea level and Denver is a mile above sea level, Washington is closer to the Earth's core and therefore has a stronger gravity pull.

35: **B.** Life expectancy is determined by time; it does not control time.

36: **J.** This passage focuses on how time can be sped up, slowed down, or even stopped by the forces of speed and gravity.

37: **B.** When the author describes "mathematical projections," he is discussing the results when certain scientific and mathematical theories are applied to specific occurrences. In this instance, scientists predict a certain occurrence using a mathematical formula.

38: **J.** In lines 104–107, the author claims that in a black hole, a place of infinite gravity, time stands still.

39: **D.** This passage is filled with important scientific information presented so that it will be easy to understand. He provides humor to keep the reader interested and to lighten up an essay filled with abstract theories. The author clearly believes in the existence of black holes, but would not believe that humans could survive in such conditions.

40: **H.** According to the information in lines 60–62, someone traveling at 90 percent of light-speed ages only 50 percent as much as the twin who stays on Earth. In 10 years, the Earthbound twin will be 30 years old, so the other twin will technically only be 25.

Chapter 16

MODEL ENGLISH AND READING ACT II
With Answers Explained

This Model English and Reading ACT II is just like a real ACT. Take this test after you take Model English and Reading ACT I. If you plan to take the optional ACT Writing Test, you should also complete ACT Writing Test II on page 415.

Take this model test under simulated test conditions. Allow 45 minutes to answer the 75 English items and 35 minutes to answer the 40 Reading items. Use a pencil to mark the answer sheet, and answer the questions in the Test 1 (English) and Test 3 (Reading) sections.

Use the answer key on page 320 to mark the answer sheet. Review the answer explanations on pages 321–333.

The test scoring charts on pages 374 and 376 show you how to convert the number correct to ACT scale scores. Other charts on pages 379 and 383 show you how to find the Usage/Mechanics and Rhetorical Skills and Social Studies/Sciences and Arts/Literature subscores.

DO NOT leave any answers blank. There is no penalty for guessing on the ACT. Remember that the test is yours. You may mark up, write on, or draw on the test.

When you are ready, note the time and turn to the page and begin.

ANSWER SHEET

The ACT answer sheet looks something like this one. Use a No. 2 pencil
to completely fill the circle corresponding to the correct answer.
If you erase, erase completely; incomplete erasures may be read as answers.

TEST 1—English

1 Ⓐ Ⓑ Ⓒ Ⓓ	11 Ⓐ Ⓑ Ⓒ Ⓓ	21 Ⓐ Ⓑ Ⓒ Ⓓ	31 Ⓐ Ⓑ Ⓒ Ⓓ	41 Ⓐ Ⓑ Ⓒ Ⓓ	51 Ⓐ Ⓑ Ⓒ Ⓓ	61 Ⓐ Ⓑ Ⓒ Ⓓ	71 Ⓐ Ⓑ Ⓒ Ⓓ
2 Ⓕ Ⓖ Ⓗ Ⓙ	12 Ⓕ Ⓖ Ⓗ Ⓙ	22 Ⓕ Ⓖ Ⓗ Ⓙ	32 Ⓕ Ⓖ Ⓗ Ⓙ	42 Ⓕ Ⓖ Ⓗ Ⓙ	52 Ⓕ Ⓖ Ⓗ Ⓙ	62 Ⓕ Ⓖ Ⓗ Ⓙ	72 Ⓕ Ⓖ Ⓗ Ⓙ
3 Ⓐ Ⓑ Ⓒ Ⓓ	13 Ⓐ Ⓑ Ⓒ Ⓓ	23 Ⓐ Ⓑ Ⓒ Ⓓ	33 Ⓐ Ⓑ Ⓒ Ⓓ	43 Ⓐ Ⓑ Ⓒ Ⓓ	53 Ⓐ Ⓑ Ⓒ Ⓓ	63 Ⓐ Ⓑ Ⓒ Ⓓ	73 Ⓐ Ⓑ Ⓒ Ⓓ
4 Ⓕ Ⓖ Ⓗ Ⓙ	14 Ⓕ Ⓖ Ⓗ Ⓙ	24 Ⓕ Ⓖ Ⓗ Ⓙ	34 Ⓕ Ⓖ Ⓗ Ⓙ	44 Ⓕ Ⓖ Ⓗ Ⓙ	54 Ⓕ Ⓖ Ⓗ Ⓙ	64 Ⓕ Ⓖ Ⓗ Ⓙ	74 Ⓕ Ⓖ Ⓗ Ⓙ
5 Ⓐ Ⓑ Ⓒ Ⓓ	15 Ⓐ Ⓑ Ⓒ Ⓓ	25 Ⓐ Ⓑ Ⓒ Ⓓ	35 Ⓐ Ⓑ Ⓒ Ⓓ	45 Ⓐ Ⓑ Ⓒ Ⓓ	55 Ⓐ Ⓑ Ⓒ Ⓓ	65 Ⓐ Ⓑ Ⓒ Ⓓ	75 Ⓐ Ⓑ Ⓒ Ⓓ
6 Ⓕ Ⓖ Ⓗ Ⓙ	16 Ⓕ Ⓖ Ⓗ Ⓙ	26 Ⓕ Ⓖ Ⓗ Ⓙ	36 Ⓕ Ⓖ Ⓗ Ⓙ	46 Ⓕ Ⓖ Ⓗ Ⓙ	56 Ⓕ Ⓖ Ⓗ Ⓙ	66 Ⓕ Ⓖ Ⓗ Ⓙ	
7 Ⓐ Ⓑ Ⓒ Ⓓ	17 Ⓐ Ⓑ Ⓒ Ⓓ	27 Ⓐ Ⓑ Ⓒ Ⓓ	37 Ⓐ Ⓑ Ⓒ Ⓓ	47 Ⓐ Ⓑ Ⓒ Ⓓ	57 Ⓐ Ⓑ Ⓒ Ⓓ	67 Ⓐ Ⓑ Ⓒ Ⓓ	
8 Ⓕ Ⓖ Ⓗ Ⓙ	18 Ⓕ Ⓖ Ⓗ Ⓙ	28 Ⓕ Ⓖ Ⓗ Ⓙ	38 Ⓕ Ⓖ Ⓗ Ⓙ	48 Ⓕ Ⓖ Ⓗ Ⓙ	58 Ⓕ Ⓖ Ⓗ Ⓙ	68 Ⓕ Ⓖ Ⓗ Ⓙ	
9 Ⓐ Ⓑ Ⓒ Ⓓ	19 Ⓐ Ⓑ Ⓒ Ⓓ	29 Ⓐ Ⓑ Ⓒ Ⓓ	39 Ⓐ Ⓑ Ⓒ Ⓓ	49 Ⓐ Ⓑ Ⓒ Ⓓ	59 Ⓐ Ⓑ Ⓒ Ⓓ	69 Ⓐ Ⓑ Ⓒ Ⓓ	
10 Ⓕ Ⓖ Ⓗ Ⓙ	20 Ⓕ Ⓖ Ⓗ Ⓙ	30 Ⓕ Ⓖ Ⓗ Ⓙ	40 Ⓕ Ⓖ Ⓗ Ⓙ	50 Ⓕ Ⓖ Ⓗ Ⓙ	60 Ⓕ Ⓖ Ⓗ Ⓙ	70 Ⓕ Ⓖ Ⓗ Ⓙ	

TEST 2—Mathematics

1 Ⓐ Ⓑ Ⓒ Ⓓ Ⓔ	9 Ⓐ Ⓑ Ⓒ Ⓓ Ⓔ	17 Ⓐ Ⓑ Ⓒ Ⓓ Ⓔ	25 Ⓐ Ⓑ Ⓒ Ⓓ Ⓔ	33 Ⓐ Ⓑ Ⓒ Ⓓ Ⓔ	41 Ⓐ Ⓑ Ⓒ Ⓓ Ⓔ	49 Ⓐ Ⓑ Ⓒ Ⓓ Ⓔ	57 Ⓐ Ⓑ Ⓒ Ⓓ Ⓔ
2 Ⓕ Ⓖ Ⓗ Ⓙ Ⓚ	10 Ⓕ Ⓖ Ⓗ Ⓙ Ⓚ	18 Ⓕ Ⓖ Ⓗ Ⓙ Ⓚ	26 Ⓕ Ⓖ Ⓗ Ⓙ Ⓚ	34 Ⓕ Ⓖ Ⓗ Ⓙ Ⓚ	42 Ⓕ Ⓖ Ⓗ Ⓙ Ⓚ	50 Ⓕ Ⓖ Ⓗ Ⓙ Ⓚ	58 Ⓕ Ⓖ Ⓗ Ⓙ Ⓚ
3 Ⓐ Ⓑ Ⓒ Ⓓ Ⓔ	11 Ⓐ Ⓑ Ⓒ Ⓓ Ⓔ	19 Ⓐ Ⓑ Ⓒ Ⓓ Ⓔ	27 Ⓐ Ⓑ Ⓒ Ⓓ Ⓔ	35 Ⓐ Ⓑ Ⓒ Ⓓ Ⓔ	43 Ⓐ Ⓑ Ⓒ Ⓓ Ⓔ	51 Ⓐ Ⓑ Ⓒ Ⓓ Ⓔ	59 Ⓐ Ⓑ Ⓒ Ⓓ Ⓔ
4 Ⓕ Ⓖ Ⓗ Ⓙ Ⓚ	12 Ⓕ Ⓖ Ⓗ Ⓙ Ⓚ	20 Ⓕ Ⓖ Ⓗ Ⓙ Ⓚ	28 Ⓕ Ⓖ Ⓗ Ⓙ Ⓚ	36 Ⓕ Ⓖ Ⓗ Ⓙ Ⓚ	44 Ⓕ Ⓖ Ⓗ Ⓙ Ⓚ	52 Ⓕ Ⓖ Ⓗ Ⓙ Ⓚ	60 Ⓕ Ⓖ Ⓗ Ⓙ Ⓚ
5 Ⓐ Ⓑ Ⓒ Ⓓ Ⓔ	13 Ⓐ Ⓑ Ⓒ Ⓓ Ⓔ	21 Ⓐ Ⓑ Ⓒ Ⓓ Ⓔ	29 Ⓐ Ⓑ Ⓒ Ⓓ Ⓔ	37 Ⓐ Ⓑ Ⓒ Ⓓ Ⓔ	45 Ⓐ Ⓑ Ⓒ Ⓓ Ⓔ	53 Ⓐ Ⓑ Ⓒ Ⓓ Ⓔ	
6 Ⓕ Ⓖ Ⓗ Ⓙ Ⓚ	14 Ⓕ Ⓖ Ⓗ Ⓙ Ⓚ	22 Ⓕ Ⓖ Ⓗ Ⓙ Ⓚ	30 Ⓕ Ⓖ Ⓗ Ⓙ Ⓚ	38 Ⓕ Ⓖ Ⓗ Ⓙ Ⓚ	46 Ⓕ Ⓖ Ⓗ Ⓙ Ⓚ	54 Ⓕ Ⓖ Ⓗ Ⓙ Ⓚ	
7 Ⓐ Ⓑ Ⓒ Ⓓ Ⓔ	15 Ⓐ Ⓑ Ⓒ Ⓓ Ⓔ	23 Ⓐ Ⓑ Ⓒ Ⓓ Ⓔ	31 Ⓐ Ⓑ Ⓒ Ⓓ Ⓔ	39 Ⓐ Ⓑ Ⓒ Ⓓ Ⓔ	47 Ⓐ Ⓑ Ⓒ Ⓓ Ⓔ	55 Ⓐ Ⓑ Ⓒ Ⓓ Ⓔ	
8 Ⓕ Ⓖ Ⓗ Ⓙ Ⓚ	16 Ⓕ Ⓖ Ⓗ Ⓙ Ⓚ	24 Ⓕ Ⓖ Ⓗ Ⓙ Ⓚ	32 Ⓕ Ⓖ Ⓗ Ⓙ Ⓚ	40 Ⓕ Ⓖ Ⓗ Ⓙ Ⓚ	48 Ⓕ Ⓖ Ⓗ Ⓙ Ⓚ	56 Ⓕ Ⓖ Ⓗ Ⓙ Ⓚ	

TEST 3—Reading

1 Ⓐ Ⓑ Ⓒ Ⓓ	6 Ⓐ Ⓑ Ⓒ Ⓓ	11 Ⓐ Ⓑ Ⓒ Ⓓ	16 Ⓐ Ⓑ Ⓒ Ⓓ	21 Ⓐ Ⓑ Ⓒ Ⓓ	26 Ⓐ Ⓑ Ⓒ Ⓓ	31 Ⓐ Ⓑ Ⓒ Ⓓ	36 Ⓐ Ⓑ Ⓒ Ⓓ
2 Ⓕ Ⓖ Ⓗ Ⓙ	7 Ⓕ Ⓖ Ⓗ Ⓙ	12 Ⓕ Ⓖ Ⓗ Ⓙ	17 Ⓕ Ⓖ Ⓗ Ⓙ	22 Ⓕ Ⓖ Ⓗ Ⓙ	27 Ⓕ Ⓖ Ⓗ Ⓙ	32 Ⓕ Ⓖ Ⓗ Ⓙ	37 Ⓕ Ⓖ Ⓗ Ⓙ
3 Ⓐ Ⓑ Ⓒ Ⓓ	8 Ⓐ Ⓑ Ⓒ Ⓓ	13 Ⓐ Ⓑ Ⓒ Ⓓ	18 Ⓐ Ⓑ Ⓒ Ⓓ	23 Ⓐ Ⓑ Ⓒ Ⓓ	28 Ⓐ Ⓑ Ⓒ Ⓓ	33 Ⓐ Ⓑ Ⓒ Ⓓ	38 Ⓐ Ⓑ Ⓒ Ⓓ
4 Ⓕ Ⓖ Ⓗ Ⓙ	9 Ⓕ Ⓖ Ⓗ Ⓙ	14 Ⓕ Ⓖ Ⓗ Ⓙ	19 Ⓕ Ⓖ Ⓗ Ⓙ	24 Ⓕ Ⓖ Ⓗ Ⓙ	29 Ⓕ Ⓖ Ⓗ Ⓙ	34 Ⓕ Ⓖ Ⓗ Ⓙ	39 Ⓕ Ⓖ Ⓗ Ⓙ
5 Ⓐ Ⓑ Ⓒ Ⓓ	10 Ⓐ Ⓑ Ⓒ Ⓓ	15 Ⓐ Ⓑ Ⓒ Ⓓ	20 Ⓐ Ⓑ Ⓒ Ⓓ	25 Ⓐ Ⓑ Ⓒ Ⓓ	30 Ⓐ Ⓑ Ⓒ Ⓓ	35 Ⓐ Ⓑ Ⓒ Ⓓ	40 Ⓐ Ⓑ Ⓒ Ⓓ

TEST 4—Science Reasoning

1 Ⓐ Ⓑ Ⓒ Ⓓ	6 Ⓐ Ⓑ Ⓒ Ⓓ	11 Ⓐ Ⓑ Ⓒ Ⓓ	16 Ⓐ Ⓑ Ⓒ Ⓓ	21 Ⓐ Ⓑ Ⓒ Ⓓ	26 Ⓐ Ⓑ Ⓒ Ⓓ	31 Ⓐ Ⓑ Ⓒ Ⓓ	36 Ⓐ Ⓑ Ⓒ Ⓓ
2 Ⓕ Ⓖ Ⓗ Ⓙ	7 Ⓕ Ⓖ Ⓗ Ⓙ	12 Ⓕ Ⓖ Ⓗ Ⓙ	17 Ⓕ Ⓖ Ⓗ Ⓙ	22 Ⓕ Ⓖ Ⓗ Ⓙ	27 Ⓕ Ⓖ Ⓗ Ⓙ	32 Ⓕ Ⓖ Ⓗ Ⓙ	37 Ⓕ Ⓖ Ⓗ Ⓙ
3 Ⓐ Ⓑ Ⓒ Ⓓ	8 Ⓐ Ⓑ Ⓒ Ⓓ	13 Ⓐ Ⓑ Ⓒ Ⓓ	18 Ⓐ Ⓑ Ⓒ Ⓓ	23 Ⓐ Ⓑ Ⓒ Ⓓ	28 Ⓐ Ⓑ Ⓒ Ⓓ	33 Ⓐ Ⓑ Ⓒ Ⓓ	38 Ⓐ Ⓑ Ⓒ Ⓓ
4 Ⓕ Ⓖ Ⓗ Ⓙ	9 Ⓕ Ⓖ Ⓗ Ⓙ	14 Ⓕ Ⓖ Ⓗ Ⓙ	19 Ⓕ Ⓖ Ⓗ Ⓙ	24 Ⓕ Ⓖ Ⓗ Ⓙ	29 Ⓕ Ⓖ Ⓗ Ⓙ	34 Ⓕ Ⓖ Ⓗ Ⓙ	39 Ⓕ Ⓖ Ⓗ Ⓙ
5 Ⓐ Ⓑ Ⓒ Ⓓ	10 Ⓐ Ⓑ Ⓒ Ⓓ	15 Ⓐ Ⓑ Ⓒ Ⓓ	20 Ⓐ Ⓑ Ⓒ Ⓓ	25 Ⓐ Ⓑ Ⓒ Ⓓ	30 Ⓐ Ⓑ Ⓒ Ⓓ	35 Ⓐ Ⓑ Ⓒ Ⓓ	40 Ⓐ Ⓑ Ⓒ Ⓓ

Model English ACT II

75 Questions — 45 Minutes

INSTRUCTIONS: Certain words or phrases in the following five passages are underlined and numbered. There is a corresponding item for each underlined portion. Each item offers three suggestions for changing the underlined portion to conform to standard written English, or to make it more understandable or consistent with the rest of the passage. If the underlined portion is not improved by one of the three suggested changes, mark NO CHANGE. Some items are about the entire passage, and the numbers of these items come at the end of the passage.

Choose the best answer for each question based on the passage. Then fill in the appropriate circle on the answer sheet.

Check pages 320–329 for answers and explanations.

PASSAGE I

The paragraphs in this passage may or may not be in the most appropriate order. The number of each paragraph is found in brackets above the paragraph. The last item for this passage asks for the correct order of paragraphs to make the passage most sensible.

Please read the whole passage before answering Questions 1 and 2.

[1]
<u>It</u> began on October 29, 1929, in the United States.
1
For months, Americans had been on a stock-buying spree.

1. The author of this passage begins with a pronoun rather than the specific name for the event to which she is referring:

   A. because the name of the event is unimportant.
   B. for dramatic effect.
   C. because she is not sure what the event is called.
   D. because she doesn't want the readers to know what she is talking about.

GO ON TO THE NEXT PAGE.

Returns were high, and <u>millions</u> of

2

people dreamed of striking it rich. Suddenly, stock

prices fell and continued to fall rapidly. Panic swept the

nation. People rushed to sell their stocks, often at a

fraction of what they had paid. <u>Millions</u> lost all or

2

most of the money they had invested.

[2]

This was the Crash, and it was followed by something

much <u>worse! The</u> Great Depression. The

3

Crash affected mainly Americans who had invested

in the stock market, but the Depression affected almost

everyone. <u>With less income, employees were</u>

4

<u>laid off by businesses that were cutting production.</u>

4

One out of every four workers <u>were</u> unemployed.

5

Many banks had invested in stocks, and their losses

caused them to <u>lose their shirts.</u> Thus people often

6

lost most of their life's savings in bank failures.

2. Choose the best reason to explain why the writer uses the word "millions" twice in this opening paragraph.

   F. Because she wants to emphasize how many people were affected by this disaster
   G. Because she was careless
   H. To remind people of money
   J. To scare the readers

3. A. NO CHANGE
   B. worse. The
   C. worse: the
   D. worse the

4. F. NO CHANGE
   G. With less income, employees cut business production and were laid off.
   H. Businesses began cutting production and laying off employees with less income.
   J. With less income, businesses began cutting production and laying off employees.

5. A. NO CHANGE
   B. was
   C. are
   D. were to have been

6. Which of the following expressions best fits in with the tone of the article?

   F. NO CHANGE
   G. lose their minds.
   H. go flat broke.
   J. go out of business.

GO ON TO THE NEXT PAGE.

[3]

The Crash did not cause the Depression, but was instead a symptom of deep and widespread problems. Prosperity had returned to most of the Western world in the 1920s, but it had a shaky foundation. Much of the wealth was merely paper wealth. 7 After 1929 the United States could no longer lend money to Europe, and

its economy also fell <u>apart? Millions</u> of
                        8
workers in the industrialized nations of Europe lost their jobs, while European farmers suffered from the steep decline in prices for <u>they're</u> goods.
                          9

[4]

Measures taken to combat the Great Depression varied <u>in many ways</u> from country to country, but in
         10
general they involved government intervention of some sort. Recovery was well under way by the late 1930s. In many <u>country's,</u> however, recovery was due
                    11
in large part to increased military spending. As preparations for war mounted, Europe and America's unemployed found <u>jobs in</u> factories, farms, and the
                 12
armed forces. But for millions, the relief was only

7. What information, if any, would be most useful to support this statement?
   A. An example that demonstrates "paper wealth"
   B. A definition of wealth
   C. A discussion of different types of wealth
   D. No other information is necessary.

8. F. NO CHANGE
   G. apart, millions
   H. apart. Millions
   J. apart! Millions

9. A. NO CHANGE
   B. their
   C. its
   D. there

10. F. NO CHANGE
    G. differently
    H. changes
    J. OMIT the phrase.

11. A. NO CHANGE
    B. countrys,
    C. countries,
    D. countries,

12. F. NO CHANGE
    G. jobs, in
    H. jobs. In
    J. jobs; in

GO ON TO THE NEXT PAGE.

temporary <u>for a short time</u> as the miseries of an economic
13
crisis were replaced by the horrors of total war.

13. **A.** NO CHANGE
    B. for a little while
    C. for a brief period
    D. OMIT this phrase.

Questions 14 and 15 ask about the entire passage.

14. The author of this passage uses shorter, action-oriented sentences in the opening paragraph of this essay:

    F. so she can move on to the more important information about the Great Depression.
    G. because this shows her to be a good writer.
    H. to demonstrate the excitement of the time and the quickness with which the rise and fall of the stock market took place.
    J. to indicate that stock-buying is a dangerous and risky proposition.

15. Which of the following is the most logical order for the paragraphs in this article?

    A. 1, 2, 3, 4
    B. 2, 3, 1, 4
    C. 4, 3, 2, 1
    D. 1, 3, 2, 4

PASSAGE II

[1]

Because of their steadily increasing rate of change,

<u>many thoughtful individuals recognized that the coming</u>
16
<u>years would hold even more change.</u> The Industrial
16

16. **F.** NO CHANGE
    G. many individuals thoughtfully recognized that the coming years would hold even more change.
    H. recognizing thoughtful individuals, the coming years would hold even more change.
    J. the coming years were recognized by thoughtful individuals as holding even more changes.

Revolution was <u>beginning, those</u> affected by it could detect
17

17. **A.** NO CHANGE
    B. beginning, and those
    C. beginning those
    D. beginning, yet those

GO ON TO THE NEXT PAGE.

change <u>in the course of their own lifetimes.</u>
18

18. F. NO CHANGE
G. (place after "it")
H. (place after "detect")
J. OMIT the phrase entirely.

[2]

Until modern <u>times. The</u> rate of change in the way
19
humans live was so slow as to make the process

unnoticeable in the course of any one <u>person's</u> lifetime.
20

19. A. NO CHANGE
B. times, the
C. times; the
D. times—the

20. F. NO CHANGE
G. persons
H. person
J. persons"

<u>In the face of that illusion,</u> it was therefore the illusion of
21

21. A. NO CHANGE
B. (place after "therefore")
C. (place after "view")
D. (place after "when," but separate clause from "when" with a comma)

mankind that change did not <u>take place when</u> a change
22
had clearly taken place, the response was to view it as

something that should not have taken place, as something

that represented a degeneration from the <u>"good old days."</u>
23

22. F. NO CHANGE
G. place, when
H. place. When
J. place? When

23. Which of the following options best explains why the author puts "good old days" in quotation marks?

A. To show these words are directly quoted from someone he knows personally
B. To show that the "good old days" are better than the present time
C. To indicate that he is attributing a commonly used, though possibly inaccurate, cliché to many people
D. To emphasize these words to the reader

[3]

Some people grew to understand that not only was

change taking place, but that it would continue to take

place after their deaths, <u>for the first time.</u> It meant there
24
would come to be changes still greater than a person had

24. F. NO CHANGE
G. (place before "some")
H. (place after "only")
J. (place after "place")

GO ON TO THE NEXT PAGE.

lived to <u>see. Changes</u> that he would never see. This
                25
gave rise to a new curiosity—perhaps the first really new

curiosity developed in historic <u>times, that</u> of wondering
                                          26
what life on Earth would be like after one was no longer

<u>alive. The</u> literary response to that new curiosity was what
   27
we now call "science fiction."

25. A. NO CHANGE
    B. see, changes
    C. see; changes
    D. see! Changes

26. F. NO CHANGE
    G. times—that
    H. times that
    J. times . . . that

27. A. NO CHANGE
    B. alive, the
    C. alive? The
    D. alive! The

Questions 28 to 30 ask about the entire passage.

28. What information would best supplement this paragraph?

F. A definition of science-fiction writing
G. Examples of how "curiosity killed the cat"
H. A list of changes that have occurred over the past century
J. A list of science-fiction authors

29. The writer of this passage is assigned to write an article to explain why and how science-fiction writing was created. Does the writer succeed?

A. No, because the writer doesn't mention science fiction until the last sentence of the passage.
B. No, because most of the essay is on change, not on science fiction.
C. No, because the writer gives no examples of science fiction.
D. Yes, because the article describes the conditions that brought about the curiosity that led to science fiction writing.

30. Which of the following sequences of paragraphs will make the essay most logical?

F. NO CHANGE
G. 3, 2, 1
H. 2, 1, 3
J. 2, 3, 1

GO ON TO THE NEXT PAGE.

PASSAGE III

[1]

The people of ancient <u>Israel the Hebrews,</u> never
      31
built a large empire. But their religious and moral ideas

changed the world. The Hebrews were the first

people to believe in one God. This belief is called

monotheism. <u>It gradually replaced *polytheism.*</u>
              32
Hebrew teachings about justice and the principles of

right and wrong, combined with their belief in

monotheism, gave rise to <u>Judaism it</u> became one of
                          33

the major religions of the world. <u>Eventually,</u> Jewish
                                  34
teachings influenced the development of two other

major religions, Christianity and Islam.

31. A. NO CHANGE
   B. Israel. The Hebrews
   C. Israel, the Hebrews
   D. Israel: the Hebrews

32. What, if any, information would best support this statement?

   F. Definition of polytheism
   G. A list of polytheistic cultures
   H. A list of monotheistic cultures
   J. Nothing should be added.

33. A. NO CHANGE
   B. Judaism! It
   C. Judaism, it
   D. Judaism. It

34. F. NO CHANGE
   G. Yet
   H. Therefore
   J. However

[2]

Much of the history of the Hebrews is written in the

Old Testament of the Bible. The <u>Hebrews'</u> were
                                35

originally <u>at first</u> tribes of wandering herders from
          36
Mesopotamia. They were brought to Israel, also

called Canaan, by Abraham. During a time of famine,

some Hebrews moved to Egypt, where they were made

<u>slaves. After</u> a long period of captivity, the Hebrews were
37

35. A. NO CHANGE
   B. Hebrew's
   C. Hebrews
   D. Hebrew

36. F. NO CHANGE
   G. at one time
   H. the first
   J. OMIT the phrase entirely.

37. A. NO CHANGE
   B. slaves after
   C. slaves? After
   D. slaves, after

GO ON TO THE NEXT PAGE.

freed and led back to Israel by Moses. <u>Needing a code of</u>
                                              38
<u>moral standards, God came to Moses on Mount Sinai and</u>
                          38
<u>gave him the Ten Commandments to give to the Hebrews.</u>
                          38

38. F. NO CHANGE
    G. Needing a code of moral standards, Moses was given the Ten Commandments to give to the Hebrews from God.
    H. Needing a code of moral standards, Moses took the Ten Commandments from God to give to the Hebrews.
    J. Needing a code of moral standards, the Hebrews followed the Ten Commandments, which God had given them through Moses.

[3]

From about 1200 to 600 B.C., the Hebrews <u>develop</u>
                                            39
an advanced civilization. Around 1025 B.C., the tribes

united under Saul, their first king. Saul led the fight

against the Philistines, a neighboring people, <u>who wanted</u>
                                                  40
control of Israel. He was followed on the throne by David.

The great king built the city of Jerusalem and made it

his capital.

39. A. NO CHANGE
    B. will develop
    C. develops
    D. developed

40. F. NO CHANGE
    G. that wanted
    H. whom wanted
    J. which wanted

[4]

The Hebrew Kingdom reached its peak of strength

and wealth under David's son, Solomon. During his rule,

from about 975 B.C. to 935 B.C., Solomon made alliances

with other kings, sents ships to trade in distant lands,

<u>and Jerusalem was made beautiful.</u> He built a great temple
                  41

41. A. NO CHANGE
    B. and Jerusalem became beautiful
    C. and beautified Jerusalem
    D. and beautifulled Jerusalem

in Jerusalem. <u>It's</u> size and beauty amazed those who saw
              42

42. F. NO CHANGE
    G. Their
    H. They're
    J. Its

GO ON TO THE NEXT PAGE.

it. The Temple of Solomon became the center of Jewish

religious life. 43

43. Based on the language in the paragraph, which of the following sentences best explains what the author means when she claims that "The Temple of Solomon became the center of Jewish religious life"?

   A. The temple was located at the center of the city of Jerusalem.
   B. The Temple of Solomon was in the middle of the religious community.
   C. The temple was the focus of the Jewish religion.
   D. The religious activity of Jews revolved around the events and services that took place at the Temple of Solomon.

[5]

[1] After Solomon's death, his kingdom split into

two parts. Civil wars weakened the Hebrew
  44

kingdoms. [2] Israel did not become an independent

nation again until A.D. 1948. [3] Many different people

conquered the Jews. [4] In time (63 B.C.), Israel became

part of the Roman Empire. [5] To punish the Jews for

their constant rebellions, the Romans destroyed Jerusalem

and scattered many of the Jews around the world

(about A.D. 135). 45

44. F. NO CHANGE
   G. two various parts
   H. two separate parts
   J. two different parts

45. What is the most logical order for the sentences in the paragraph?

   A. 1, 2, 3, 4, 5
   B. 1, 5, 2, 3, 4
   C. 1, 3, 4, 5, 2
   D. 4, 5, 1, 2, 3

GO ON TO THE NEXT PAGE.

PASSAGE IV

At the end of this passage, there is a question about the organization of these paragraphs.

[1]

Sample a typical days headlines: "War Breaks Out in
the Middle East." "Child Killed in Gang Shooting."
"Bribery Scandal Rocks City Hall." "Stock Market Falls."

46. F. NO CHANGE
G. days'
H. day's
J. day

[2]

Once in a while, a note of hope creeps in: "Doctors
Conquer Fatal Illness." "Neighbors Aid Homeless
Family." "Hero Risks Life to Rescue Fire Victim."

47. A. NO CHANGE
B. while. A
C. while: a
D. while . . . a

[3]

The word *psychology* comes from the Greek *psyche,*

which means "soul," and *logos,* which has come to mean

"logic" or "science" in practice, however, this "science of

the soul" is defined as a modern definition, *the study of*

human behavior.

48. F. NO CHANGE
G. "science," in practice
H. "science!" In practice
J. "science." In practice

49. A. NO CHANGE
B. the definition,
C. a definition
D. OMIT the entire phrase.

[4]

People, apparently, are capable of great cruelty.

And great compassion. If so, you might wonder why

50. F. NO CHANGE
G. And also of great compassion.
H. They are also capable of great compassion.
J. And their great compassion.

GO ON TO THE NEXT PAGE.

humanity so often chooses violence over <u>caring. After all,</u>
51

poets and artists have created great art <u>and we are reminded</u>
52
of the heights to which our species can aspire. A play by

Shakespeare or a painting by Rembrandt speaks to the

human potential within everyone. <u>Shakespeare and</u>

<u>Rembrandt, however, don't tell us *how* to achieve inner</u>
53
<u>peace. That's the task the psychologist has taken on.</u>
53

[5]

Psychologists use the scientific method to collect

data about <u>behavior. Using</u> the insights gained through
54

<u>checking stuff out</u> and experiment, they answer some of
55
life's most important questions: Why do people act as they

do? Can behavior be predicted or changed? Can people's

lives be made happier and more productive? What can be

done to help people who have lost touch with reality?

51. **A.** NO CHANGE
    B. caring?
    C. caring!
    D. caring:

52. **F.** NO CHANGE
    G. that reminds us
    H. who reminds us
    J. we were reminded

53. Which of the following choices best explains why the author has chosen to italicize the word *"how"*?

    A. To show his anger that the art will not give us the answers that we as humans seek
    B. To reveal that artists like Shakespeare and Rembrandt are unable to reach inner peace themselves; therefore they don't know how to show others
    C. To emphasize that artists like Shakespeare and Rembrandt can demonstrate inner peace, but they cannot tell someone how to achieve it as a psychologist tries to do
    D. To imply that art is insignificant

54. **F.** NO CHANGE
    G. behavior using
    H. behavior, using
    J. behavior, but using

55. **A.** NO CHANGE
    B. checking information out
    C. observing stuff
    D. observation

GO ON TO THE NEXT PAGE.

[6]

[1] If people were simple creatures like dogs or horses, the answers to these questions would be relatively easy. [2] Human beings are <u>very uniquely</u> gifted with the
56
power of reason and language and the ability to create a complex culture. [3] Psychologists, therefore, have their work cut out for them. [4] The study of behavior yields few easy answers. [5] But our lives are not controlled by the same instincts and drives that dominate other forms of animal life. 57

56. **F.** NO CHANGE
    G. strongly uniquely
    H. most uniquely
    J. uniquely

57. What is the best, most logical order for the sentences in this paragraph?

    A. 1, 2, 3, 4, 5
    B. 5, 4, 3, 2, 1
    C. 1, 5, 4, 3, 2
    D. 1, 5, 2, 3, 4

Questions 58 to 60 ask about the entire passage.

---

58. Of the following choices, which best describes the author's intended audience for this passage?

    F. Medical doctors
    G. People who are unfamiliar with the field of psychology
    H. People who are currently undergoing psychiatric treatment
    J. Young women

59. The reason that best explains why the author begins this passage by quoting negative and positive headlines is:

    A. to show he is abreast of current events.
    B. to demonstrate the wide range of human behavior.
    C. to engage the reader's emotions.
    D. to paint a picture of modern society.

GO ON TO THE NEXT PAGE.

60. What is the most logical order for the paragraphs in this passage?

    F. 1, 2, 3, 4, 5, 6
    G. 6, 5, 4, 3, 2, 1
    H. 1, 3, 4, 2, 5, 6
    J. 1, 2, 4, 3, 5, 6

PASSAGE V

[1]

Ever since I was a small <u>young</u> girl in school, I've
       61
been aware of what the school textbooks say about Indians.

I am <u>a</u> Indian and, naturally, am interested in what the
 62
school teaches about natives of this land.

[2]

One day in the grammar school I attended, I read that

a delicacy of American Indian people was dried <u>fish. Which,</u>
                           63

according to the textbook, tasted <u>"like an old shoe, or was</u>
                            64
<u>like chewing on dried leather."</u> To this day I can
     64
remember my utter dismay at reading these words. We

called this wind-dried fish <u>"sleetschus."</u> and to us, it was
                  65
our favorite delicacy and, indeed, did not taste like shoe

leather. It took many hours of long and hard work to cure

the fish in just this particular fashion. Early fur traders and

61. A. NO CHANGE
    B. little
    C. child
    D. OMIT the word entirely.

62. F. NO CHANGE
    G. an
    H. the
    J. A

63. A. NO CHANGE
    B. fish! Which
    C. Fish. Which
    D. fish, which

64. Which of the following options best explains why the author puts these words in quotation marks?

    F. This quotation is taken directly from the textbook.
    G. To emphasize the importance of these words
    H. To show that these words are false
    J. To indicate that she has spoken these words out loud

65. A. NO CHANGE
    B. sleetchus"
    C. sleetschus,
    D. sleetschus

GO ON TO THE NEXT PAGE.

other non-Indians must have agreed, for they often used this food for subsistence as they traveled around isolated areas.

[3]

[1] My father was the youngest son of one of the last chiefs of the Nooksack Indian Tribe of Whatcom County in the state of Washington. [2] I brought the textbook home to show it to my father, leader of my tribe at that time. [3] On this particular day, he told me in his wise and humble manner that the outside world did not always understand <u>Indian's</u> people, and that I should
66

not let it hinder me from learning the <u>well</u> parts of
67

education. 68 , 69

66. **F.** NO CHANGE
    G. Indians
    H. Indians'
    J. Indian

67. **A.** NO CHANGE
    B. well,
    C. good
    D. goodest

68. What would be the most logical arrangement of the sentences in this paragraph?

    F. 1, 2, 3
    G. 3, 2, 1
    H. 2, 1, 3
    J. 3, 2, 1

69. Based on the information given in this paragraph, the author's feelings about her father are:

    A. hostile and angry.
    B. respectful and proud.
    C. embarrassed.
    D. indifferent.

[4]

Since those early years I have learned we were much better off with our own delicacies, which did not rot our

GO ON TO THE NEXT PAGE.

teeth and bring about the various dietary problems that

plague Indian people in modern <u>times, I</u> was about eight
                                     70

years old when this incident happened, and it <u>does</u> much to
                                                 71
sharpen my desire to pinpoint terminology in books used

to describe American Indian people, books which are,

most often, not very <u>complimentary?</u>
                         72

70. F. NO CHANGE
    G. times I
    H. times . . . I
    J. times. I

71. A. NO CHANGE
    B. had done
    C. done
    D. did

72. F. NO CHANGE
    G. complimentary.
    H. complimentary,
    J. complimentary!

Questions 73 to 75 ask about the entire passage.

---

73. What is the most appropriate order for the paragraphs in this essay?

    A. 1, 2, 3, 4
    B. 1, 4, 3, 2
    C. 4, 3, 2, 1
    D. 1, 2, 4, 3

74. Based on the language in this passage, which of the following choices seems to best describe the author's reason for recounting this episode from her childhood?

    F. To describe the tastiness of sleetschus to those people who have never tried it
    G. To criticize the modern dietary habits of Indians
    H. To comment on the negative way many people in mainstream America describe Native Americans and their culture
    J. To pay tribute to her tribe

75. The audience the writer of this essay seems to be targeting is:

    A. people living in mainstream American culture.
    B. members of her own tribe.
    C. historians who are examining the behavior of Native Americans.
    D. researchers who are studying the dietary habits of Native Americans.

END OF TEST 1

Model Reading ACT II

40 Questions — 35 Minutes

INSTRUCTIONS: There are four passages on this test with ten items about each passage. Choose the best answer for each item based on the passage. Then fill in the appropriate circle on the answer sheet. Check pages 320 and 330–333 for answers and explanations.

PASSAGE I

PROSE FICTION: This passage is from "One Throw" edited by W.C. Heinz.

I checked into a hotel called the Olympia, which is right on the main street and the only hotel in the town. After lunch I was hanging around the lobby, and I got to talking to the guy at the desk. I asked him if this
5 wasn't the town where that kid Maneri played ball.

"That's right," the guy said. "He's a pretty good ballplayer."

He was leaning on the desk, talking to me and looking across the hotel lobby. He nodded his head.
10 "This is a funny thing," he said. "Here he comes now."

The kid had come through the door from the street. He had on a light gray sport shirt and slacks.

"I'm sorry, Pete," the guy at the desk said, "but no mail today."
15 "That's all right, Nick," the kid said.

"Excuse me," I said, "but you're Pete Maneri?"

"Pete's a good ballplayer," the guy said.

"Not very," the kid said.

"Don't take his word for it, Mr. Franklin."
20 That's the way I got talking with the kid.

"What do you do, Mr. Franklin?" he said.

"I sell hardware," I said. "I can think of some things I'd like better. I played some ball once myself, and I was going to ask you how you like playing in this league."
25 "Well," the kid said, "I suppose it's all right. I guess I've got no kick coming."

"Oh, I don't know," I said. "I understand you're too good for this league. What are they trying to do to you? Who manages this ball club?"
30 "Al Dall," the kid said. "Maybe he's all right, but I don't get along with him. He's on my neck all the time. If I get the big hit or make the play, he never

says anything. The other night I tried to take second on a loose ball and I got caught in the run-down. He bawls
35 me out in front of everybody. There's nothing I can do."

"Oh, I don't know," I said. "This is probably a guy who knows he's got a good thing in you, and he's looking to keep you around."
40 "That's what I mean," the kid said. "When the Yankees sent me down here they said, 'Don't worry. We'll keep an eye on you.' So Dall never sends a good report on me. Nobody ever comes down to look me over. What chance is there for a guy like Eddie Brown
45 or somebody like that coming down to see me here?"

"You have to remember that Eddie Brown's the big shot," I said, "the great Yankee scout."

"Sure," the kid said. "I never even saw him, and I'll never see him in this place. I have an idea that if
50 they ever ask Dall about me, he knocks me down."

"Why don't you go after Dall?" I said. "I had trouble like that once myself, but I figured out a way to get attention."

"You did?" the kid said.
55 "I threw a couple of balls over the first baseman's head," I said. "I threw a couple of games away, and that really got the manager sore. I was lousing up his ball club and his record. So what does he do? He blows the whistle on me, and what happens? That gets the
60 brass curious, and they come to see what's wrong."

"Is that so?" the kid said. "What happened?"

"Two weeks later, I was up with Columbus. I'd try it," I said.

"I'll try it," the kid said. "Are you coming out to
65 the park tonight?"

"I wouldn't miss it," I said.

The first game wasn't much, with the home club winning something like 8 to 1. The second game was different, though.

GO ON TO THE NEXT PAGE.

70   I was trying to wish the ball down to the kid, just to see what he'd do with it, when the batter drives one on one big bounce to the kid's right.

     The kid was off for it when the ball started. He made a backhand stab and grabbed it. He was deep
75 now, and he turned in the air and fired. If it goes over the first baseman's head, it's two runs in and a panic— but it's the prettiest throw you'd want to see. It's right on a line, and the runner is out by a step, and it's the ball game.

• • •

80   I walked back to the hotel, thinking about the kid. I sat around the lobby until I saw him come in.

     "Why didn't you throw that ball away?" I said.

     "I don't know," the kid said. "I had it in my mind before he hit it, but I couldn't."

85   "You're going to be a major-league ballplayer," I said, "because you couldn't throw that ball away, and because I'm not a hardware salesman and my name's not Harry Franklin."

     "What do you mean?" the kid said.

90   "I mean," I explained to him, "that I tried to needle you into throwing that ball away because I'm Eddie Brown."

1. The narrator checks into the Olympia hotel:

  A. to spend the night in town so he could sell hardware.
  B. because he is visiting relatives.
  C. because he has been stranded in town.
  D. because he is scouting Pete Maneri for the Yankees.

2. The narrator tries to convince Pete to make a bad throw:

  F. because he is working with Al Dall to keep Pete in the minor leagues.
  G. to psych out the players on the opposing team.
  H. because he wants to see if Pete is worthy of playing in the major leagues.
  J. because he thought it would make the game more entertaining.

3. Pete is so frustrated with Al Dall because:

  A. Al is trying to throw him off the team.
  B. Al criticizes him and seems to be holding him back from the major leagues.
  C. Al Dall keeps substituting other players for Pete.
  D. Al Dall used to play for the Yankees, and Pete does not play for them.

4. Based on the information given in the story, to "throw the ball away" means:

  F. to take the baseball and put it in the trash can.
  G. to throw the ball at the batter.
  H. to purposely throw the ball poorly.
  J. to throw the ball in a different manner.

5. What is significant about the desk clerk's statement to Pete that there is "no mail today"?

  A. Pete has not received any word from the major leagues.
  B. Pete's family, embarrassed by his failure, will no longer write to him.
  C. It's a national holiday, so no mail was delivered.
  D. No one knows where Pete lives, so he never gets mail at the hotel.

6. Which of the following does NOT describe Pete Maneri?

  F. He is not fond of his manager.
  G. He will never play major league baseball.
  H. He is a good baseball player.
  J. He is frustrated because he isn't playing for the Yankees.

7. Eddie Brown is:

  A. Mr. Franklin's cousin.
  B. the desk clerk.
  C. the narrator.
  D. the team coach.

8. Pete says that he is not a very good ballplayer because:

  F. he is having a terrible season.
  G. he takes Al Dall's criticisms to heart.
  H. he got caught trying to steal second base.
  J. he is a modest and frustrated young man.

9. In the double-header played by Pete's team:

  A. they won both games.
  B. they won one game and lost one.
  C. they lost both games.
  D. the second game was called on account of rain.

10. Most likely, Al Dall treats Pete the way he does because:

  F. he is jealous of Pete's skill.
  G. he wants to keep Pete on his team.
  H. Pete is a terrible player.
  J. he wants to help Pete become a major-league player.

GO ON TO THE NEXT PAGE.

PASSAGE II

SOCIAL SCIENCE: This passage is from *Psychology: A Way to Grow* by Carl R. Green and William R. Sanford.

Humanist psychology is based on the research and influence of Abraham Maslow (1908–1970). An American psychologist, Maslow told his fellow psychologists to stop the practice of defining personality in
5 terms of their disturbed patients. Instead, he said, psychology should study healthy people.

Along with Carl Rogers, the other guiding spirit of the humanist movement, Maslow believed that all members of society should be given the chance to
10 realize their full potential as human beings. This goal is achievable, he thought, because people are basically good. His beliefs contrast with those of Freud, who seemed to define human beings as victims of their biological and psychological past. Not so, Maslow
15 claimed. If their basic needs are met, most men and women build happy, productive lives for themselves.

Maslow criticized the older schools of psychology for what he saw as their negative attitudes toward human nature. He attempted to paint a brighter, more
20 optimistic picture of emotional life. In doing so, Maslow defined five basic concepts that relate to the human personality.

1. Humanity's essential nature is made up of needs, capacities, and tendencies that are good (or nat-
25 ural) rather than harmful.

2. Full, healthy personality development comes when people develop their basic natures and fulfill their potential. People must grow from within rather than be shaped from without. Unless they do, they can
30 never reach true maturity.

3. Mental illness results when people's basic needs are not satisfied, thereby frustrating or twisting their inner nature. The role of the therapist is to restore the patient to the path of growth and self-knowledge
35 along the lines dictated by the patient's own inner nature.

4. Each person's inner nature is weak, delicate, and subtle, unlike the overpowering instincts of animals. Although a person's inner nature can grow tall
40 and strong, it begins as a tiny seed. As it grows, it can easily be stunted by cultural pressures, the failure to satisfy basic needs, or unhealthy habits. No one's basic goodness ever disappears, even though it may be submerged for a while under self-defeating behaviors.

45 5. As people mature, their potential goodness shows itself even more clearly. The *self-actualizing* person, as humanist psychologists describe the fully mature personality, stands out in any environment. Perhaps only a few people reach full self-actualization.
50 But even those who are making progress toward that level of maturity are recognized and sought after by others.

11. Maslow's theory differs from that of many other psychologists because:

   A. he bases his theories on animal behavior.
   B. he bases all of his theories on Freud's theories.
   C. he believes psychologists should base their studies on the lives of well-adjusted humans.
   D. his theories show that no one is truly mentally healthy.

12. If a child is deprived of basic needs such as food and love:

   F. he or she will have more difficulty coming to terms with his or her inner nature.
   G. his or her inner nature will not be affected.
   H. his or her inner nature will bloom.
   J. he or she will mature and fully develop.

13. According to the information in this passage:

   A. Maslow and Rogers agree with Freud's theory that a person's past dictates his or her psychological future.
   B. Maslow, unlike Rogers, believes that people can lead successful, happy lives despite their troubled pasts.
   C. Maslow believes that a person can achieve full potential despite his or her past experiences.
   D. Neither Maslow or Rogers believes that self-fulfillment is possible.

14. According to the information in the final paragraph, the term *self-actualizing* person means:

   F. one who can create oneself.
   G. a fully developed person.
   H. one who can find themselves in others.
   J. a person who is selfish.

GO ON TO THE NEXT PAGE.

15. It is NOT true that:

    A. a person's inner nature is fragile in its early stages.
    B. a person's inner nature never varies in strength.
    C. a person's inner nature can be harmed by outside influences.
    D. a person's inner nature is always basically good.

16. Carl Rogers is:

    F. the author of this article.
    G. the partner of Abraham Maslow.
    H. a pupil of Sigmund Freud.
    J. a humanist psychologist.

17. According to Maslow:

    A. people are always riddled with self-doubt.
    B. people are basically angry and violent.
    C. no matter what happens, people are always happy.
    D. people are innately good.

18. According to Maslow, mental illness will affect a person who:

    F. was deprived of basic needs during childhood.
    G. must always live alone.
    H. is innately evil.
    J. will always be depressed.

19. Maslow's outlook on human nature would be described as:

    A. pessimistic.
    B. fatalistic.
    C. positive.
    D. superficial.

20. Maslow would most likely say that a good therapist should:

    F. help patients discover their own true path to self-actualization.
    G. tell patients exactly how to live their lives.
    H. encourage people to suppress their inner desires.
    J. discourage people from exploring their needs.

GO ON TO THE NEXT PAGE.

PASSAGE III

HUMANITIES: This passage is from *Western Civilization* by Gerson Antell and Walter Harris.

In 1874 a group of French painters organized a show of their own works, which were too unusual to be accepted elsewhere. One painting, called "Impression: Sunrise," led the public to call the painters "impres-
5 sionists." (The name was meant to be an insult, but the painters adopted it proudly.)

The impressionists, trying to paint the fleeting moment just as it looked, broke a painting's surface into hundreds of seemingly disconnected strokes. Re-
10 cent scientific discoveries had revealed that all colors were made of the three primary ones. With this knowledge, the impressionists placed blobs of paint side by side and allowed the viewer's eye to "mix" them. Viewed closely, a dash of blue and another of yellow
15 appear as two separate colors. When we back off, however, we see green. This technique would not be regarded as unusual today, but viewers seeing it for the first time were shocked. In 1876 a critic wrote:

20 An exhibition has just been opened which allegedly contains paintings. I enter and my horrified eyes behold something terrible. Five or six lunatics, among them a woman, have joined together and exhibited their works. I have seen people rock with laughter
25 in front of these pictures, but my heart bled when I saw them. These would-be artists call themselves revolutionaries, "impressionists." They take a piece of canvas, color and brush, daub a few patches of color on at random,
30 dom, and sign the whole thing with their name.

Most of the impressionists were French. Claude Monet excelled at landscape. He painted several series of pictures—of haystacks, of the Rouen cathedral, of
35 water lilies—to show the effects of light at different times of day. Solid forms seem to dissolve in sun and shadow.

Edgar Degas and Auguste Renoir were more interested in the human figure. Degas is noted especially
40 for his ballet scenes. They make use of unusual compositions to communicate, in unsentimental terms, the hard work that dancing entails. Renoir's scenes of busy outdoor life are among the most joyous of all paintings.

Several Americans living in Europe also became
45 noted as impressionists. One, James Whistler, was known for both landscape and portraits. His "Arrangement in Grey and Black" is also known as "Whistler's Mother." Another American, Mary Cassatt, liked to paint mothers with their children. She was responsible
50 for introducing impressionism to America, where she persuaded her wealthy friends to begin collecting the new art.

21. A characteristic of impressionism is NOT:

   A. disconnected painting strokes.
   B. use of the primary colors.
   C. the way light changes throughout the day.
   D. extremely detailed, realistic pictures.

22. Which of the following statements best describes the critical reaction to impressionism?

   F. Critics lauded it.
   G. It was considered foolish and disturbing.
   H. It was considered the new, great art form.
   J. It was completely ignored by critics.

23. Impressionism was at its height in:

   A. the early nineteenth century.
   B. the late eighteenth century.
   C. the late nineteenth century.
   D. the early eighteenth century.

24. An artist not considered an impressionist is:

   F. Mary Cassatt.
   G. Edgar Degas.
   H. Auguste Renoir.
   J. Pablo Picasso.

25. Claude Monet painted numerous pictures of the Rouen cathedral because:

   A. he was French and very proud of French landmarks.
   B. it was about to be destroyed and he wanted to capture its image forever.
   C. he wanted to show how different it looked in the morning, the afternoon, and the evening.
   D. he lived near the cathedral and it served as his only source of inspiration.

GO ON TO THE NEXT PAGE.

26. According to this article, the impressionists used the three primary colors:

    F. by placing them next to each other, rather than mixing them, to create other colors.

    G. by mixing them together to make all the other colors.

    H. because they only liked red, yellow, and blue.

    J. individually, because they do not mix together well.

27. Impressionist paintings:

    A. were painted only by French artists.

    B. were painted only by Americans.

    C. were painted mostly in Europe, but they were painted by people of several nationalities.

    D. were painted only by Italians.

28. A subject for impressionist painting was NOT:

    F. mothers and children.

    G. landscapes.

    H. ballet dancers.

    J. medical subjects.

29. Most likely, Claude Monet's painting "Water Lilies" is:

    A. extremely detailed.

    B. perfectly realistic.

    C. painted with many separate brushstrokes.

    D. very dark and frightening.

30. The ballet scenes of Edgar Degas:

    F. show that ballet is a difficult activity.

    G. concentrate only on the beauty of dance.

    H. make dancing look easy and fluid.

    J. tend to romanticize the art of dance.

GO ON TO THE NEXT PAGE.

PASSAGE IV

NATURAL SCIENCE: This passage is from "Smart Skin" by Shawna Vogel.

If we're ever to have the future promised us by "The Jetsons," we're at the very least going to need personal robots that can serve us breakfast. But to do that those robots will have to be able to sense the dif-
5 ference between a glass of orange juice and a soft-boiled egg, and to hold each with just enough pressure to keep it from either breaking or dropping to the floor. At the moment such a fine-tuned grip is beyond the capacity of any robot in existence.

10 Robots have no innate "feel" for the objects they are handling primarily because they lack one of our most useful sense organs: skin. That isn't to say they can't get a grip on things. Industrial robots can repeatedly pick up objects like carburetors by exerting a pre-
15 programmed pressure on them. But robots capable of functioning autonomously will need a "smart skin" to sense whether they should, say, grasp a wrench more firmly or ease up their death grip on a tomato.

One of the most sophisticated approaches to this
20 goal is being developed at the University of Pisa by Italian engineer Danilo De Rossi, who has closely modeled an artificial skin on the inner and outer layers of human skin: the dermis and epidermis. His flexible, multilayered sheathing even has the same thickness as
25 human skin—roughly that of a dime.

De Rossi's artificial dermis is made of a water-swollen conducting gel sandwiched between two layers of electrodes that monitor the flow of electricity through the squishy middle. Like the all-natural human
30 version, this dermis senses the overall pressure being exerted on an object. As pressure deforms the gel, the voltage between the electrodes changes; the harder the object being pressed, the greater the deformation. By keeping tabs on how the voltage is changing, a skin-
35 clad robot could thus distinguish between a rubber ball and a rock.

For resolving the finer details of surface texture, De Rossi has created an epidermal layer of sensor-studded sheets of plastic placed between thin sheets of
40 rubber. The sensors are pinhead-size disks made of piezo-electric substances, which emit an electric charge when subjected to pressure. These disks can sense texture as fine as the bumps on a braille manuscript.

45 Other researchers have developed texture-sensitive skins, but De Rossi's has a unique advantage. Because his disks respond to pressure from any direction—including forces pulling sideways across the surface of the skin—they can also sense friction.
50 "No other sensor today can do that," says De Rossi. Most smart skins detect only pressure perpendicular to the surface and cannot feel lateral deformation. But a robot wearing De Rossi's skin could easily feel the tug from a sticky piece of tape or, conversely, sense an
55 alarming lack of friction when a greased motor bearing is slipping from its grasp.

Either of De Rossi's layers could be used separately to meet the specialized needs of industrial robots, but he envisions them as parts of an integrated
60 skin for multipurpose mechanical hands. At the moment, however, De Rossi faces a small dilemma: his two layers are incompatible. The water essential to the working of the dermis invariably short-circuits the sensitive epidermis. De Rossi will need to separate the two
65 layers, but no matter what material he chooses he will probably have to compromise among several ideals, such as extreme thinness, strength, and flexibility.

Even if he does manage to unite his layers, there will still be a number of hurdles to get over before a ro-
70 bot with artificial skin can become as adept as a human. Foremost among them is the basic question of how to coordinate all the tactile information transmitted. Robotics engineers still puzzle over how people use all the tactile messages conveyed by their hands to
75 accomplish a feat as simple as threading a nut onto the end of a bolt.

31. A scientific name for the outer layer of skin is:

    A. dermis.
    B. extradermis.
    C. intradermis.
    D. epidermis.

32. Danilo De Rossi is:

    F. a Renaissance painter.
    G. the author of this article.
    H. an Italian engineer.
    J. the name of a special robot.

33. The unique property of De Rossi's artificial skin is that:

    A. it can feel hard and soft objects.
    B. it can sense friction by responding to pressure from all angles.
    C. it can decide whether or not something is fragile.
    D. it can fit on robots of any size.

GO ON TO THE NEXT PAGE.

34. According to the author, a robot has trouble gripping different types of objects because:

F. it cannot be programmed to hold different objects.
G. it can hold only special magnetic items.
H. it has no inborn way to determine the difference between one item and another.
J. robots crush every object that they hold because they are too powerful for man-made items.

35. The best description of the situation of "smart-skinned" robots is:

A. they will be on the market in the very near future.
B. they will never exist.
C. scientists must do more research if this experiment is to succeed.
D. they have existed for years.

36. Based on De Rossi's present experiment, what will allow a robot to determine the difference between a fragile object and a durable one?

F. Special computer chips that allow computers to think about each object individually
G. The changing voltage of the electrodes in the skin
H. The amount of gel used when the robot picks up a new object
J. The water that short-circuits the system when an object is fragile

37. The main purpose of this article is:

A. to demonstrate that robots with skin will be able to grip objects of varying strengths, sizes, and frictions.
B. to show that De Rossi's theories are false.
C. to relate modern life with the science fiction cartoon "The Jetsons."
D. to prove that robots will never be able to do the jobs that most humans presently do.

38. The way "smart skin" can sense different objects will NOT be affected by:

F. flexibility.
G. strength.
H. thinness.
J. color.

39. According to the author, once "smart skin" is perfected, the next hurdle faced by scientists will be:

A. to build robots that can breathe.
B. to find a way to process all the information received by the sensitive skin.
C. to watch old episodes of "The Jetsons" for new scientific ideas.
D. to find a way to keep the smart skin on the robot without it falling off whenever the robot moves.

40. The word *tactile* is used twice in the final paragraph. Based on its context, the meaning of the word *tactile* is:

F. related to hearing.
G. related to touch.
H. related to military tactics.
J. related to sight.

END OF TEST 3

 ANSWERS

Model English ACT II

PASSAGE I	**PASSAGE II**	**PASSAGE III**	**PASSAGE IV**	**PASSAGE V**
1. B	16. J	31. C	46. H	61. D
2. F	17. B	32. F	47. A	62. G
3. C	18. F	33. D	48. J	63. D
4. J	19. B	34. F	49. D	64. F
5. B	20. F	35. C	50. H	65. A
6. J	21. D	36. J	51. A	66. J
7. A	22. H	37. A	52. G	67. C
8. H	23. C	38. J	53. C	68. H
9. B	24. G	39. D	54. F	69. B
10. J	25. B	40. F	55. D	70. J
11. D	26. G	41. C	56. J	71. D
12. F	27. A	42. J	57. D	72. G
13. D	28. F	43. D	58. G	73. A
14. H	29. D	44. F	59. C	74. H
15. A	30. H	45. C	60. J	75. A

Model Reading ACT II

PASSAGE I	**PASSAGE II**	**PASSAGE III**	**PASSAGE IV**
1. D	11. C	21. D	31. D
2. H	12. F	22. G	32. H
3. B	13. C	23. C	33. B
4. H	14. G	24. J	34. H
5. A	15. B	25. C	35. C
6. G	16. J	26. F	36. G
7. C	17. D	27. C	37. A
8. J	18. F	28. J	38. J
9. A	19. C	29. C	39. B
10. J	20. F	30. F	40. G

ACT II English Answers Explained

PASSAGE I

ANSWERS

1: B. Clearly, the name of the event is important. If the writer is writing an essay on the topic, clearly she knows what the event is called and wants her readers to know what she is writing about. She leaves the event unnamed at first to give the article dramatic effect.

2: F. Both times the author uses the word "millions," she is referring to a number of people, not an amount of money. She has specifically chosen to use this number twice for emphasis.

3: C. Since the words "The Great Depression" explain what is "much worse," a colon is needed to separate the original statement from the explanation that follows. Using a period or exclamation point here makes the words "The Great Depression" a sentence fragment.

4: J. Since the businesses were bringing in less money, they were responsible for cutting production and laying off employees. Therefore, the phrase "with less income" needs to be followed by a statement about the businesses, not one about the employees.

5: B. The subject of this sentence is the *one* in the "one out of every four employees." Therefore, the verb must be singular to agree with the singular subject.

6: J. The other expressions are of a more casual tone. The author uses a serious tone to focus on a serious subject. Using clichés does not support this tone.

7: A. Because this term is unusual, it could be confusing to the reader. A definition of the term "paper wealth" might be useful. However, "paper wealth" could also be explained by example. A definition of *wealth* would not be helpful because it has a very different meaning than *paper wealth*. A full discussion of different types of wealth would give the reader too much information, because the discussion here focuses on only one type of wealth.

8: H. The first sentence is neither a question nor a point of special emphasis. It is, however, an independent clause, as is the second sentence. Therefore, the two sentences must be separated by a period rather than a comma, which would make the sentence a comma splice.

9: B. This word should be a pronoun which refers back to the European farmers. The word "they're" is a contraction that makes no sense here. The sentence would seem to be saying that the farmers themselves are goods. The word "there" is not a pronoun at all. While "its" is a pronoun, it is a singular, ungendered pronoun which would not refer to the plural noun "farmers."

10: J. Any of the given phrases simply reiterate the meaning of *varied,* which suggests difference. Therefore, the phrase is not necessary.

11. D. In all options except D, the noun is a possessive. However, the sentence does not indicate that the country possesses anything. Instead, the word is followed by "however," rather than something that is possessed by the countries.

12: F. This sentence is fine as it is. If you put in a period or a semicolon, you would be separating a dependent clause from an independent clause. No comma is necessary here to separate "jobs" from the list that follows.

13: D. These phrases all reiterate the meaning of temporary; therefore, the phrase is not needed.

14: H. The tone of this passage is short, choppy, and exciting. The passage emphasizes how quickly and forcefully the stock market affected the lives of *millions* of people.

15: A. The article describes a progression of events starting with the stock market crash, then the Great Depression and the events that followed. Any other order would be confusing to the reader.

PASSAGE II

ANSWERS

16: J. The "coming years," rather than "thoughtful individuals," have a "steadily increasing rate of change." Because this opening adverbial clause contains the pronoun "their," the pronoun should refer to the subject of the sentence. However, in choices F and G, "thoughtful individuals" seems to be the subject of the sentence. The ordering of the phrases in choice H do not make logical sense.

17: B. As this sentence stands, it is a type of run-on known as a comma splice (two independent clauses joined together by only a comma). Choice C, where no punctuation is indicated, is also a run-on sentence. While choice D offers a grammatically correct option (two independent clauses connected by a comma and a coordinating conjunction), it implies that *despite* the Industrial Revolution, change occurred. However, the nature of any revolution, especially the Industrial Revolution, indicates disruption and change. Since choice B indicates that change occurred as a result of the Industrial Revolution, it provides the best option.

18: F. This clause makes best logical sense when it is left in its current position within the sentence. This clause adds relevant information to the paragraph, so it should not be deleted. By moving the clause in front of the word "it," it appears that the clause refers to the Industrial Revolution rather than change. Moving the clause after the word "detect" makes the sentence read awkwardly because it breaks up the verb and the object of the sentence.

19: B. In a sentence with an opening adverbial clause (which, in this case explains when an action takes place), the adverbial clause is generally separated from the remainder of the sentence by a comma. By placing a period after "times," the writer creates a sentence fragment. Similarly, neither semicolon nor a dash can be used to separate a dependent clause from an independent clause.

20: F. This word should be a possessive because it is describing whose lifetime the author is referring to. Adding closing quotation marks is incorrect because there are no opening quotation marks to indicate that the author is quoting a source.

21: D. By noting "in the face of that illusion" indicates that an illusion has already been mentioned. Therefore, this clause must come after the mention of the illusion in the sentence. However, this clause should come before and lead into the information that contradicts the illusion mentioned. Thus the clause fits best after "when," where it separates the illusion from its contradiction.

22: H. As this sentence currently stands, it is a run-on (or fused) sentence, where two independent clauses are joined together without proper punctuation. To separate these clauses, some form of adequate punctuation must be used; in this case, a period is the most logical option given. Though a question mark would make this sentence grammatically correct, it would be illogical because the first half of the sentence is not a question. A comma would not solve the problem of the run-on sentence; instead, the run-on would become an equally problematic comma splice.

23: C. The "good old days" is a cliché because it has been used by many people over time. By putting quotation marks around these words, the author attributes this cliché to generations of people, not to one person in particular. The language of this paragraph does not indicate that the author genuinely believes that these old days were better than the present time, nor does he place any special emphasis on these words, which are not the focus of the paragraph.

24: G. This adverbial clause is referring to how some people had just begun to realize that change would continue. By placing this clause after "only" or "place," the clause seems to indicate that change was actually taking place for the first time, which is clearly false. By placing the clause after "deaths," it seems as though change would only really begin to take place after some people's deaths.

25: B. A comma is needed to separate this clause from the remainder of the sentence. All of the other options listed make the final dependent clause of this sentence a sentence fragment.

26: G. Here, the writer has set off a nonessential clause from the rest of the sentences by an opening dash. In order for the sentence to remain grammatically correct, the nonessential clause must also end with a dash. Therefore, nothing but a dash would be suitable in this location.

27: A. In this option the period serves to break up two independent clauses. Choice B is a comma splice. While choices C and D are grammatically correct, they are not logically correct because this sentence is not a question, nor does it need any special emphasis.

28. F. This paragraph ends by referring to the broad category of science fiction. To someone very familiar with the genre, the meaning of this term would be obvious. However, this term could be clarified for most people by the addition of a definition. While examples of changes that have occurred and lists of science fiction authors would be interesting, they would not help the readers grasp the concept of the genre of science fiction. Choice G is designed to throw the reader off with a cliché that has nothing to do with the information conveyed by the writer.

29: D. Though the article doesn't mention science fiction until the end, the author describes the conditions that led up to the creation of science fiction. The essay builds the historical precedent before it introduces the main subject.

30: H. The second paragraph listed introduces the concept of change in modern society, and therefore it should come first in the passage. While Paragraphs 1 and 3 both expand upon this notion of change, Paragraph 1 directly builds upon the information presented in Paragraph 2, explaining how the rate of change was increasing. Paragraph 3 builds upon the ideas in the previous two paragraphs, demonstrating how this increasing change brought about science fiction writing.

PASSAGE III

ANSWERS

31: C. The phrase "the Hebrews" is nonessential and does not significantly affect the meaning of the sentence; rather, it simply adds a bit of extra information. Nonessential clauses should be set off from the sentence by commas.

32: F. Though the reader might be able to infer the meaning of polytheism based on the given definition of monotheism, the addition of this definition would clarify both terms. Though the lists of cultures with similar beliefs would be interesting, it would not help clarify the definition of either polytheism or monotheism.

33: D. As this sentence stands, it is a run-on. Adding a comma, as in choice C, makes the sentence into a comma splice. To break the run-on into two sentences, end punctuation is necessary. Since there is no special emphasis on the first part of this sentence, an exclamation point would be inappropriate; therefore, a simple period is the best solution.

34: F. Choices G and J imply that a contradiction to what has already been stated will follow. However, the sentence does not contradict the prior sentence. Choice H implies a cause-and-effect relationship, though in this case the effect is stated before the cause. "Eventually" indicates that Judaism "became" a major religion over time, as it is stated in the prior sentence.

35: C. Since the passage refers to the people of Israel as "the Hebrews," this reference should also be plural. This cancels out choices B and D. Choice A is also incorrect because it is a possessive, yet the sentence does not indicate any possession by the Hebrews.

36: J. This phrase should be omitted because the phrase included in the paragraph and all of the other choices listed simply repeat the idea that is conveyed by the word "originally."

37: A. These are two perfectly logical sentences. When the period is removed entirely, the sentence forms a run-on. When a comma is substituted, the sentence becomes a comma splice. Since the first sentence is not a question, a question mark would not be appropriate punctuation either.

38: J. The phrase "Needing a code of moral standards" modifies the Hebrews, not God (who creates the moral standards) or Moses. Therefore, "the Hebrews" should follow directly after the modifier.

39: D. Because this sentence describes events that took place in the past, a verb in the past tense must be used.

40: F. Since this sentence is referring to the Philistines, a group of people, rather than a thing, the word *who* should be used. *Whom* is inappropriate because the pronoun serves as the subject of the clause, rather than the object.

41: C. This sentence indicates that Solomon achieved many things during his rule. The first two examples are described using the past tense. Choices A and B show a shift into the passive voice, altering the parallel construction of the sentence. Choice D is incorrect because "beautifulled" is not a real verb.

42: J. Because this sentence is discussing the size and beauty of one temple, the pronoun describing the temple must be singular. Since the singular possessive pronoun does not have an apostrophe, "its" (J) is the correct choice.

43: D. The term "center" in this sentence does not refer to the physical positioning of the Temple of Solomon; therefore, choices A and B are incorrect. Choice C indicates that the temple itself was the main concern of the religion. Choice D indicates that the Temple of Solomon is a symbol that represents the activities that take place within the physical structure of the temple.

44: F. The insertion of any of the given words between *two* and *parts* is redundant because these words reiterate the idea that the kingdom split into parts. Clearly, these parts must be separate and different, otherwise they would not be parts.

45: C. With the sentences in this order, the paragraph shows the logical progression of how Israel and the Hebrews were defeated by outside forces in the past. The final sentence explains that in 1948, Israel once again became an independent country.

PASSAGE IV

ANSWERS

46: H. Because this sentence refers to the headlines that occur on a particular day, the headlines belong to that particular day. Therefore, a possessive must be used. Since the sentence refers to one typical day, the author must use a singular possessive.

47: A. Because "Once in a while," an adverbial clause that describes when a particular action takes place, opens the sentence, it is set apart from the main clause of the sentence by a comma. A period or a colon would make the adverbial clause a sentence fragment. Ellipses are generally used to indicate missing words, which does not seem to be the case here.

48: J. As it stands, this sentence is a run-on because it contains two independent clauses not connected by a conjunction such as *and* or *but.* By adding a comma, the sentence becomes a comma splice, another common form of a run-on sentence. Though an exclamation point could be used to break up these two independent clauses, no special emphasis is needed on the first independent clause; therefore, a period is the best choice for punctuation.

49: D. Obviously, a word is defined by a definition. Using the word twice is redundant. The sentence is more direct when the phrase is simply left out.

50: H. Choices F, G, and J are all sentence fragments that do not contain a subject or a verb. Only choice H is an independent clause and a complete sentence.

51: A. This sentence contains an indirect question, which tells what has been asked but does not directly quote the speaker's words. Because this sentence is an indirect question, it does not take a question mark. The exclamation point would indicate an unneeded emphasis on this sentence. Since no definition or list follows the punctuation here, a colon is also inappropriate punctuation.

52: G. Choices F and J show a shift in sentence construction from the active voice to the passive voice. In order to remain in the active voice, we must be the object of the art's reminding. Choice H is illogical because *who* cannot refer to art, which is an inanimate object rather than a person.

53: C. The author emphasizes *"how"* to demonstrate that psychologists have a special function. Unlike artists, psychologists are the ones who can actually tell you ways that you might be able to achieve inner peace. The *how* in the first sentence stresses that artists cannot do this, while psychologists can.

54: F. Choice G turns these two independent clauses into one long run-on sentence. Choice H turns them into a sentence with a comma splice. Choice J connects the two ideas with a conjunction, but the conjunction *but* implies that a contradiction will follow. Since the remainder of the sentence does not contradict the first part of the sentence, choice J is also inappropriate.

55: D. While all of these answers convey the same meaning, the expressions used are too casual for a formal essay on a scientific procedure. *Checking out* is a slang expression. And the use of the word "stuff" is too casual and general to have any meaning. The word "observation" is formal and names part of the scientific process.

56: J. The word "unique" means "one of a kind." Because this word has an absolute meaning, it cannot be modified by other adjectives, or in the case of the adverb "uniquely," by other adverbs. Therefore, all of the other choices must be dismissed.

57: D. In the opening sentence of this passage, the author compares humans to horses and dogs. Sentence 5 follows up on this idea, noting that humans have different instincts than animals. Sentence 2 then focuses more specifically on what makes humans unique. Therefore, Sentence 5 should be inserted between Sentences 1 and 2.

58: G. Both medical doctors and psychiatric patients would most likely have a more in-depth knowledge of the field of psychology and its methods. Though this passage may be intended for young women as well as young men, there is nothing in the language that indicates the passage was directed at young women specifically. Since the explanations here are very basic, the passage is clearly written for someone with little or no knowledge of psychology.

59: C. This author attempts to capture the reader's attention by giving headlines which might engage the reader's emotions.

60: J. Paragraph 1 and Paragraph 2 belong at the beginning of the passage. That narrows the answer choices to F and J. The current Paragraph 4 follows logically the current Paragraph 2. So the first three paragraphs should be 1, 2, 4. **J** is the correct answer.

61: D. The words "little," "young," and "child" are redundant, repeating the concepts indicated by the words "small" and "girl." Since none of these choices offer new meaning to the sentence, this word can simply be omitted.

62: G. Because the word "Indian" begins with a vowel, the proper article is "an." Since she is not referring to herself as the only Indian, "the" is incorrect.

63: D. In choices A, B, and C, the sentence beginning with "which" is a sentence fragment. The sentence has a verb ("tasted"), but no subject. The word "which" is a pronoun that refers to the subject but does not replace it.

64: F. The words just prior to this statement indicate that they are "according to the textbook." Direct quotations must always be put in quotation marks.

65: A. Because there is an opening quotation mark, there must be a closing quotation mark as well; this rules out choices C and D. Choice B does not contain the comma necessary to lead into the coordinating conjunction and second independent clause in this compound sentence.

66. J. "Indian" is an adjective describing the word "people," not a possessive showing ownership of the people. Choice G is incorrect because when the name of a culture is used as an adjective, it should not be plural.

67: C. Since the word "well" means "in a good manner" or refers to a state of feeling, it is not an appropriate choice to describe parts of education. "Goodest" is an incorrect superlative; a correct choice would be *best*. Of the choices listed, only "good" is an appropriate adjective here.

68: H. In order for there to be a smooth transition between paragraphs, this paragraph should begin by referring to the story in the textbook mentioned in the last paragraph. Additionally, the description of the father's lineage makes more sense following his connection to the textbook story and the author's reference to him as the leader of her tribe. Therefore, the first and second sentences should be in reverse order.

69: B. The author describes her father's prestigious lineage and position within the tribe. She also describes him with the adjectives "wise" and "humble," which are both good and noble characteristics. Clearly, she has great respect for her father. There are no indications that she is hostile toward or embarrassed by her father, and, based on the tone of this paragraph, she is not indifferent to him.

70: J. As it stands, this long sentence is a comma splice in which two complete sentences are joined only by a comma. This is a form of run-on sentence. Choice G is also a run-on sentence. The use of ellipses in choice H would indicate that words have been left out of this sentence, which does not seem to be the case. Therefore, the use of a period to break up the two sentences is the best option listed.

71: D. In order for the construction of this sentence to remain parallel, the verb tenses must remain the same throughout the sentence. The second verb must be in past tense to remain parallel to the verb "was" in the previous clause. Therefore, the past tense of *to do (did)* is the appropriate choice.

72: G. This sentence is a simple statement, not a question or a point for unusual emphasis. End punctuation is needed, and the period is the best choice.

73: A. The essay begins with the author looking back on an experience that occurred when she was eight years old, tells the story in chronological order, then returns to the present to explain why she has told this story. The paragraphs in any other order would disrupt the natural flow of the story.

74: H. Though this essay focuses on a criticism of a particular type of food considered a delicacy by Native Americans, the subject of the essay really isn't about food. Rather, the subject of food is just one example of the "not very complimentary" way that mainstream prejudicial portrayal is unfair to Native Americans.

75: A. This essay describes the deep-seated prejudices of mainstream American culture—prejudices that most people in her own tribe would have experienced themselves. Both historians and researchers would most likely not need the very general information about Native Americans presented in this essay. However, many Americans would not recognize these prejudices in themselves. This essay awakens Americans to the negative picture of Native Americans that is portrayed in schools, textbooks, and elsewhere.

ACT II Reading Answers Explained

PASSAGE I

ANSWERS

1: D. At the end of the story, the narrator reveals that he is actually a major-league baseball scout. Because he asks about Maneri when he arrives in town, it can be inferred that he has come to watch Maneri play.

2: H. When Pete cannot explain why he didn't make a bad throw, the narrator responds, "You couldn't throw that ball away . . . you're going to be a major-league ballplayer someday." The narrator implies that a truly great player could never throw the ball away; Pete's decision shows that he has what it takes to be a professional.

3: B. Pete believes that Al is purposely trying to hold him back from advancing to the major leagues. Additionally, he is frustrated by Al's criticism of him in front of his teammates. As a result, he is angry, but tries to keep his anger in check.

4: H. When the narrator tells Pete that he once "threw the ball away," he explains that he threw the ball over the first baseman's head. In other words, he purposely missed the first baseman to cause problems for his coach.

5: A. Pete is waiting desperately to hear from the Yankee management that he will be moved up to the major leagues. He hopes to get a letter from them, but clearly, he no longer expects to hear from them.

6: G. The story implies that Pete will play major-league baseball because he is a talented young man. As a scout, Eddie Brown will most likely now recommend that the Yankees bring him up to the major league.

7: C. The narrator assumes the name Mr. Franklin, an alias that allows him to test Pete without being recognized. However, at the end of the tale, the narrator admits that he is actually Eddie Brown, the famous Yankee scout.

8: J. Through the details given about Pete in the story, he is an excellent ballplayer who is being held back from the major leagues. He clearly is frustrated by this. Moreover, his dialog shows him to be a likable and modest young man.

9: A. The narrator tells us that the home team (which we know to be Pete's, since the scout comes to this town where "that kid Maneri played ball") won the first game. Because of Pete's skill and integrity, he makes the final out of the second game to make sure his team won.

10: J. Dall, a former Yankee player, obviously maintains contact with the Yankees. His criticism helps to inspire Pete and to improve Pete's performance. Because Pete is frustrated by playing for a minor-league team, he focuses his hostilities on Dall, who is actually working on his behalf.

PASSAGE II

11: C. The author notes (lines 5–6) that Maslow's humanist psychology is based on information discovered from healthy patients rather than disturbed patients.

12: F. According to Maslow's theory, when children are deprived of their basic needs, their inner selves are frustrated. A therapist can help a person restore this frustrated inner harmony.

13: C. The author notes (line 12) that Maslow disagrees with the basic tenets of Freud's theories which indicate that a person is ruled by his or her past psychological experiences.

14: G. The author defines a *self-actualizing* person as a fully mature personality; in other words, one who has fully developed.

15: B. A person's inner nature can grow stronger or weaker depending on outside influences and other factors, according to the information in lines 40–42. Therefore, a person's inner nature is not constant.

16: J. Carl Rogers is described as the "other guiding spirit of the humanist movement" (lines 7–8). Though he and Maslow held similar ideas about human nature, there is nothing in the article to indicate that they were partners.

17: D. In lines 11–12 and 42–43, the author reiterates Maslow's concept that people are basically good at heart.

18: F. Maslow believes that every disturbed adult has unmet childhood needs. According to Maslow, adult depression would indicate that the person was deprived of some basic needs in childhood.

19: C. The author describes Maslow's outlook as optimistic, or positive (lines 19–20).

20: F. The author notes that a good therapist will help to restore a patient to the path of self-knowledge (lines 33–34), leading to eventual self-actualization.

PASSAGE III

✔ANSWERS

21: D. Impressionism, by its very name, indicates that these paintings only give impressions of objects, rather than realistic detailed views. Characteristics A and B are discussed in lines 12–16, while characteristic C is discussed in lines 35–36.

22: G. In the long quotation, lines 19–31, a critic ridicules impressionism and impressionists for their style. The author points out that the name impressionism is meant to be an insult (line 5), while the critic quoted claims the works were laughable and his "heart bled" when he saw them.

23: C. The first show of impressionist works took place in 1874, relatively close to the end of the nineteenth century.

24: J. Pablo Picasso, known for his cubist paintings and eccentric personality, worked in the twentieth century.

25: C. Lines 33–36 explain that Monet's object in painting a series of pictures was to show how the effects of light made an object look at different times of day. The Rouen cathedral was one of many objects he painted in this manner.

26: F. In lines 14–16, the author describes the technique in which impressionist painters placed the primary colors side by side to create the visual look of other colors (to the human eye from a distance) rather than actually blending the colors together. This was based on the fact that all colors are derived from a mixture of red, blue, and yellow.

27: C. The author lists Frenchmen, including Claude Monet, Edgar Degas, and Auguste Renoir, as well as the expatriate Americans (Americans living in Europe) James Whistler and Mary Cassatt.

28: J: The only one of these items not mentioned in the article is J, medical subjects.

29: C. Based on the information in this passage, only answer C is listed as a characteristic of impressionist painting. Since Monet is an impressionist, his works most likely share these characteristics.

30: F. Degas used interesting compositions to demonstrate that dancing is a difficult physical activity, rather than a sentimental, easy act.

31: D. In lines 22–23, the author points out that the inventor has modeled his artificial skin on the "inner and outer layers of human skin: the dermis and epidermis." Logically, the sentence is set up to indicate that the first words in each pair are connected; in other words, the inner layer of skin is the dermis, and the outer layer is the epidermis.

32: H. According to the article, De Rossi, an Italian engineer, has created a type of "smart skin" (lines 21–22). Though this skin still is not fully effective, De Rossi's experiments may lead to exciting developments in new robots.

33. B. The author notes that the advantage of De Rossi's artificial skin is that it can sense friction (line 49).

34: H. Robots can hold on to a variety of different objects, but they cannot sense the differences among objects that need to be held with firm grips, soft grips, or other grips. The author indicates this in the first two paragraphs.

35: C. The article indicates that De Rossi has many problems with his current model of "smart skin." However, the article implies that these problems will most likely be worked out through continued experimentation. At this point, though, the article does not indicate that solutions to these problems will be discovered in the near future.

36: G. According to the information in line 31, pressure will deform the gel that is encapsulated between two layers of electrodes. As the pressure changes, so will the voltage between these electrodes. This will send a message to the robot that the object requires a specific type of grip.

37: A. The purpose of this article is to discuss how the development of "smart skin" can affect and improve the grips of robots.

38: J. The author lists certain important factors, not including color, that adversely affect De Rossi's attempts to fix the problems with his "soft skin" (line 67). These other factors could negate the potential effectiveness of "smart skin."

39: B According to the final paragraph of this article, once the scientists are able to collect data, they must figure out how to coordinate all of the information they have received.

40: G. The author refers to "tactile information" and "tactile messages" that are conveyed by the hands of robots with "smart skin" and by humans. Tactile information allows the robot to adjust its grip.

Chapter 17

MODEL ENGLISH AND READING ACT III
With Answers Explained

This Model English and Reading ACT III is just like a real ACT. Take this test after you take Model English and Reading ACT II. If you plan to take the optional ACT Writing Test, you should also complete ACT Writing Test III on page 421.

Take this model test under simulated test conditions. Allow 45 minutes to answer the 75 English items and 35 minutes to answer the 40 Reading items. Use a pencil to mark the answer sheet, and answer the questions in the Test 1 (English) and Test 3 (Reading) sections.

Use the answer key on page 360 to mark the answer sheet. Review the answer explanations on pages 361-373.

The test scoring charts on pages 374 and 376 show you how to convert the number correct to ACT scale scores. Other charts on pages 380 and 384 show you how to find the Usage/Mechanics and Rhetorical Skills and Social Studies/Sciences and Arts/Literature subscores.

DO NOT leave any answers blank. There is no penalty for guessing on the ACT. Remember that the test is yours. You may mark up, write on, or draw on the test.

When you are ready, note the time and turn the page and begin.

ANSWER SHEET

The ACT answer sheet looks something like this one. Use a No. 2 pencil to completely fill the circle corresponding to the correct answer.
If you erase, erase completely; incomplete erasures may be read as answers.

TEST 1—English

1 Ⓐ Ⓑ Ⓒ Ⓓ	11 Ⓐ Ⓑ Ⓒ Ⓓ	21 Ⓐ Ⓑ Ⓒ Ⓓ	31 Ⓐ Ⓑ Ⓒ Ⓓ	41 Ⓐ Ⓑ Ⓒ Ⓓ	51 Ⓐ Ⓑ Ⓒ Ⓓ	61 Ⓐ Ⓑ Ⓒ Ⓓ	71 Ⓐ Ⓑ Ⓒ Ⓓ
2 Ⓕ Ⓖ Ⓗ Ⓙ	12 Ⓕ Ⓖ Ⓗ Ⓙ	22 Ⓕ Ⓖ Ⓗ Ⓙ	32 Ⓕ Ⓖ Ⓗ Ⓙ	42 Ⓕ Ⓖ Ⓗ Ⓙ	52 Ⓕ Ⓖ Ⓗ Ⓙ	62 Ⓕ Ⓖ Ⓗ Ⓙ	72 Ⓕ Ⓖ Ⓗ Ⓙ
3 Ⓐ Ⓑ Ⓒ Ⓓ	13 Ⓐ Ⓑ Ⓒ Ⓓ	23 Ⓐ Ⓑ Ⓒ Ⓓ	33 Ⓐ Ⓑ Ⓒ Ⓓ	43 Ⓐ Ⓑ Ⓒ Ⓓ	53 Ⓐ Ⓑ Ⓒ Ⓓ	63 Ⓐ Ⓑ Ⓒ Ⓓ	73 Ⓐ Ⓑ Ⓒ Ⓓ
4 Ⓕ Ⓖ Ⓗ Ⓙ	14 Ⓕ Ⓖ Ⓗ Ⓙ	24 Ⓕ Ⓖ Ⓗ Ⓙ	34 Ⓕ Ⓖ Ⓗ Ⓙ	44 Ⓕ Ⓖ Ⓗ Ⓙ	54 Ⓕ Ⓖ Ⓗ Ⓙ	64 Ⓕ Ⓖ Ⓗ Ⓙ	74 Ⓕ Ⓖ Ⓗ Ⓙ
5 Ⓐ Ⓑ Ⓒ Ⓓ	15 Ⓐ Ⓑ Ⓒ Ⓓ	25 Ⓐ Ⓑ Ⓒ Ⓓ	35 Ⓐ Ⓑ Ⓒ Ⓓ	45 Ⓐ Ⓑ Ⓒ Ⓓ	55 Ⓐ Ⓑ Ⓒ Ⓓ	65 Ⓐ Ⓑ Ⓒ Ⓓ	75 Ⓐ Ⓑ Ⓒ Ⓓ
6 Ⓕ Ⓖ Ⓗ Ⓙ	16 Ⓕ Ⓖ Ⓗ Ⓙ	26 Ⓕ Ⓖ Ⓗ Ⓙ	36 Ⓕ Ⓖ Ⓗ Ⓙ	46 Ⓕ Ⓖ Ⓗ Ⓙ	56 Ⓕ Ⓖ Ⓗ Ⓙ	66 Ⓕ Ⓖ Ⓗ Ⓙ	
7 Ⓐ Ⓑ Ⓒ Ⓓ	17 Ⓐ Ⓑ Ⓒ Ⓓ	27 Ⓐ Ⓑ Ⓒ Ⓓ	37 Ⓐ Ⓑ Ⓒ Ⓓ	47 Ⓐ Ⓑ Ⓒ Ⓓ	57 Ⓐ Ⓑ Ⓒ Ⓓ	67 Ⓐ Ⓑ Ⓒ Ⓓ	
8 Ⓕ Ⓖ Ⓗ Ⓙ	18 Ⓕ Ⓖ Ⓗ Ⓙ	28 Ⓕ Ⓖ Ⓗ Ⓙ	38 Ⓕ Ⓖ Ⓗ Ⓙ	48 Ⓕ Ⓖ Ⓗ Ⓙ	58 Ⓕ Ⓖ Ⓗ Ⓙ	68 Ⓕ Ⓖ Ⓗ Ⓙ	
9 Ⓐ Ⓑ Ⓒ Ⓓ	19 Ⓐ Ⓑ Ⓒ Ⓓ	29 Ⓐ Ⓑ Ⓒ Ⓓ	39 Ⓐ Ⓑ Ⓒ Ⓓ	49 Ⓐ Ⓑ Ⓒ Ⓓ	59 Ⓐ Ⓑ Ⓒ Ⓓ	69 Ⓐ Ⓑ Ⓒ Ⓓ	
10 Ⓕ Ⓖ Ⓗ Ⓙ	20 Ⓕ Ⓖ Ⓗ Ⓙ	30 Ⓕ Ⓖ Ⓗ Ⓙ	40 Ⓕ Ⓖ Ⓗ Ⓙ	50 Ⓕ Ⓖ Ⓗ Ⓙ	60 Ⓕ Ⓖ Ⓗ Ⓙ	70 Ⓕ Ⓖ Ⓗ Ⓙ	

TEST 2—Mathematics

1 Ⓐ Ⓑ Ⓒ Ⓓ Ⓔ	9 Ⓐ Ⓑ Ⓒ Ⓓ Ⓔ	17 Ⓐ Ⓑ Ⓒ Ⓓ Ⓔ	25 Ⓐ Ⓑ Ⓒ Ⓓ Ⓔ	33 Ⓐ Ⓑ Ⓒ Ⓓ Ⓔ	41 Ⓐ Ⓑ Ⓒ Ⓓ Ⓔ	49 Ⓐ Ⓑ Ⓒ Ⓓ Ⓔ	57 Ⓐ Ⓑ Ⓒ Ⓓ Ⓔ
2 Ⓕ Ⓖ Ⓗ Ⓙ Ⓚ	10 Ⓕ Ⓖ Ⓗ Ⓙ Ⓚ	18 Ⓕ Ⓖ Ⓗ Ⓙ Ⓚ	26 Ⓕ Ⓖ Ⓗ Ⓙ Ⓚ	34 Ⓕ Ⓖ Ⓗ Ⓙ Ⓚ	42 Ⓕ Ⓖ Ⓗ Ⓙ Ⓚ	50 Ⓕ Ⓖ Ⓗ Ⓙ Ⓚ	58 Ⓕ Ⓖ Ⓗ Ⓙ Ⓚ
3 Ⓐ Ⓑ Ⓒ Ⓓ Ⓔ	11 Ⓐ Ⓑ Ⓒ Ⓓ Ⓔ	19 Ⓐ Ⓑ Ⓒ Ⓓ Ⓔ	27 Ⓐ Ⓑ Ⓒ Ⓓ Ⓔ	35 Ⓐ Ⓑ Ⓒ Ⓓ Ⓔ	43 Ⓐ Ⓑ Ⓒ Ⓓ Ⓔ	51 Ⓐ Ⓑ Ⓒ Ⓓ Ⓔ	59 Ⓐ Ⓑ Ⓒ Ⓓ Ⓔ
4 Ⓕ Ⓖ Ⓗ Ⓙ Ⓚ	12 Ⓕ Ⓖ Ⓗ Ⓙ Ⓚ	20 Ⓕ Ⓖ Ⓗ Ⓙ Ⓚ	28 Ⓕ Ⓖ Ⓗ Ⓙ Ⓚ	36 Ⓕ Ⓖ Ⓗ Ⓙ Ⓚ	44 Ⓕ Ⓖ Ⓗ Ⓙ Ⓚ	52 Ⓕ Ⓖ Ⓗ Ⓙ Ⓚ	60 Ⓕ Ⓖ Ⓗ Ⓙ Ⓚ
5 Ⓐ Ⓑ Ⓒ Ⓓ Ⓔ	13 Ⓐ Ⓑ Ⓒ Ⓓ Ⓔ	21 Ⓐ Ⓑ Ⓒ Ⓓ Ⓔ	29 Ⓐ Ⓑ Ⓒ Ⓓ Ⓔ	37 Ⓐ Ⓑ Ⓒ Ⓓ Ⓔ	45 Ⓐ Ⓑ Ⓒ Ⓓ Ⓔ	53 Ⓐ Ⓑ Ⓒ Ⓓ Ⓔ	
6 Ⓕ Ⓖ Ⓗ Ⓙ Ⓚ	14 Ⓕ Ⓖ Ⓗ Ⓙ Ⓚ	22 Ⓕ Ⓖ Ⓗ Ⓙ Ⓚ	30 Ⓕ Ⓖ Ⓗ Ⓙ Ⓚ	38 Ⓕ Ⓖ Ⓗ Ⓙ Ⓚ	46 Ⓕ Ⓖ Ⓗ Ⓙ Ⓚ	54 Ⓕ Ⓖ Ⓗ Ⓙ Ⓚ	
7 Ⓐ Ⓑ Ⓒ Ⓓ Ⓔ	15 Ⓐ Ⓑ Ⓒ Ⓓ Ⓔ	23 Ⓐ Ⓑ Ⓒ Ⓓ Ⓔ	31 Ⓐ Ⓑ Ⓒ Ⓓ Ⓔ	39 Ⓐ Ⓑ Ⓒ Ⓓ Ⓔ	47 Ⓐ Ⓑ Ⓒ Ⓓ Ⓔ	55 Ⓐ Ⓑ Ⓒ Ⓓ Ⓔ	
8 Ⓕ Ⓖ Ⓗ Ⓙ Ⓚ	16 Ⓕ Ⓖ Ⓗ Ⓙ Ⓚ	24 Ⓕ Ⓖ Ⓗ Ⓙ Ⓚ	32 Ⓕ Ⓖ Ⓗ Ⓙ Ⓚ	40 Ⓕ Ⓖ Ⓗ Ⓙ Ⓚ	48 Ⓕ Ⓖ Ⓗ Ⓙ Ⓚ	56 Ⓕ Ⓖ Ⓗ Ⓙ Ⓚ	

TEST 3—Reading

1 Ⓐ Ⓑ Ⓒ Ⓓ	6 Ⓐ Ⓑ Ⓒ Ⓓ	11 Ⓐ Ⓑ Ⓒ Ⓓ	16 Ⓐ Ⓑ Ⓒ Ⓓ	21 Ⓐ Ⓑ Ⓒ Ⓓ	26 Ⓐ Ⓑ Ⓒ Ⓓ	31 Ⓐ Ⓑ Ⓒ Ⓓ	36 Ⓐ Ⓑ Ⓒ Ⓓ
2 Ⓕ Ⓖ Ⓗ Ⓙ	7 Ⓕ Ⓖ Ⓗ Ⓙ	12 Ⓕ Ⓖ Ⓗ Ⓙ	17 Ⓕ Ⓖ Ⓗ Ⓙ	22 Ⓕ Ⓖ Ⓗ Ⓙ	27 Ⓕ Ⓖ Ⓗ Ⓙ	32 Ⓕ Ⓖ Ⓗ Ⓙ	37 Ⓕ Ⓖ Ⓗ Ⓙ
3 Ⓐ Ⓑ Ⓒ Ⓓ	8 Ⓐ Ⓑ Ⓒ Ⓓ	13 Ⓐ Ⓑ Ⓒ Ⓓ	18 Ⓐ Ⓑ Ⓒ Ⓓ	23 Ⓐ Ⓑ Ⓒ Ⓓ	28 Ⓐ Ⓑ Ⓒ Ⓓ	33 Ⓐ Ⓑ Ⓒ Ⓓ	38 Ⓐ Ⓑ Ⓒ Ⓓ
4 Ⓕ Ⓖ Ⓗ Ⓙ	9 Ⓕ Ⓖ Ⓗ Ⓙ	14 Ⓕ Ⓖ Ⓗ Ⓙ	19 Ⓕ Ⓖ Ⓗ Ⓙ	24 Ⓕ Ⓖ Ⓗ Ⓙ	29 Ⓕ Ⓖ Ⓗ Ⓙ	34 Ⓕ Ⓖ Ⓗ Ⓙ	39 Ⓕ Ⓖ Ⓗ Ⓙ
5 Ⓐ Ⓑ Ⓒ Ⓓ	10 Ⓐ Ⓑ Ⓒ Ⓓ	15 Ⓐ Ⓑ Ⓒ Ⓓ	20 Ⓐ Ⓑ Ⓒ Ⓓ	25 Ⓐ Ⓑ Ⓒ Ⓓ	30 Ⓐ Ⓑ Ⓒ Ⓓ	35 Ⓐ Ⓑ Ⓒ Ⓓ	40 Ⓐ Ⓑ Ⓒ Ⓓ

TEST 4—Science Reasoning

1 Ⓐ Ⓑ Ⓒ Ⓓ	6 Ⓐ Ⓑ Ⓒ Ⓓ	11 Ⓐ Ⓑ Ⓒ Ⓓ	16 Ⓐ Ⓑ Ⓒ Ⓓ	21 Ⓐ Ⓑ Ⓒ Ⓓ	26 Ⓐ Ⓑ Ⓒ Ⓓ	31 Ⓐ Ⓑ Ⓒ Ⓓ	36 Ⓐ Ⓑ Ⓒ Ⓓ
2 Ⓕ Ⓖ Ⓗ Ⓙ	7 Ⓕ Ⓖ Ⓗ Ⓙ	12 Ⓕ Ⓖ Ⓗ Ⓙ	17 Ⓕ Ⓖ Ⓗ Ⓙ	22 Ⓕ Ⓖ Ⓗ Ⓙ	27 Ⓕ Ⓖ Ⓗ Ⓙ	32 Ⓕ Ⓖ Ⓗ Ⓙ	37 Ⓕ Ⓖ Ⓗ Ⓙ
3 Ⓐ Ⓑ Ⓒ Ⓓ	8 Ⓐ Ⓑ Ⓒ Ⓓ	13 Ⓐ Ⓑ Ⓒ Ⓓ	18 Ⓐ Ⓑ Ⓒ Ⓓ	23 Ⓐ Ⓑ Ⓒ Ⓓ	28 Ⓐ Ⓑ Ⓒ Ⓓ	33 Ⓐ Ⓑ Ⓒ Ⓓ	38 Ⓐ Ⓑ Ⓒ Ⓓ
4 Ⓕ Ⓖ Ⓗ Ⓙ	9 Ⓕ Ⓖ Ⓗ Ⓙ	14 Ⓕ Ⓖ Ⓗ Ⓙ	19 Ⓕ Ⓖ Ⓗ Ⓙ	24 Ⓕ Ⓖ Ⓗ Ⓙ	29 Ⓕ Ⓖ Ⓗ Ⓙ	34 Ⓕ Ⓖ Ⓗ Ⓙ	39 Ⓕ Ⓖ Ⓗ Ⓙ
5 Ⓐ Ⓑ Ⓒ Ⓓ	10 Ⓐ Ⓑ Ⓒ Ⓓ	15 Ⓐ Ⓑ Ⓒ Ⓓ	20 Ⓐ Ⓑ Ⓒ Ⓓ	25 Ⓐ Ⓑ Ⓒ Ⓓ	30 Ⓐ Ⓑ Ⓒ Ⓓ	35 Ⓐ Ⓑ Ⓒ Ⓓ	40 Ⓐ Ⓑ Ⓒ Ⓓ

Model English ACT III

75 Questions – 45 Minutes

INSTRUCTIONS: Certain words or phrases in the following five passages are underlined and numbered. There is a corresponding item for each underlined portion. Each item offers three suggestions for changing the underlined portion to conform to standard written English, or to make it understandable or consistent with the rest of the passage. If the underlined portion is not improved by one of the three suggested changes, mark NO CHANGE. Some items are about the entire passage, and the numbers for these items come at the end of the passage.

Choose the best answer for each question based on the passage. Then fill in the appropriate circle on the answer sheet.

Check pages 360–368 for answers and explanations.

PASSAGE I

[1]

Nothing is more <u>frustrating, than</u> hunting down that
1

elusive "any" key. After all, <u>the screen says,</u> "Press any
2

key to continue." So where is it?

1. **A.** NO CHANGE
   B. frustrating than
   C. frustrating than,
   D. , frustrating, than

2. **F.** NO CHANGE
   G. the characters on the screen prompt you to
   H. the words on the monitor read
   J. the computer shouts at you to

GO ON TO THE NEXT PAGE.

[2]

Any key refers to, <u>in a way,</u> any key on your
3

keyboard. But let's <u>be specific when</u> it says to press the
4

"any" key, press the spacebar. If you can't find the

spacebar, or you think it's the place where you order

drinks on the Starship Enterprise, <u>try pressing the Enter Key.</u>
5

Enter Key = Any Key.

[3]

You can press almost any key on the keyboard

for the "any" key. The problem is that some keys

<u>don't respond; are ill suited</u> to be "any" keys. These
6

<u>include</u> the Shift Keys, CapsLock, Pause, the 5 key on the
7

numeric keypad, and other "dead" keys. You can pound

away on them all you like, and the <u>program had never</u>
8

continue.

[4]

[1] So why do they say "Press any key" instead of

saying "Press spacebar to continue"? [2] I guess <u>it's</u>
9

because they want to make things easy for you by giving

3. A. NO CHANGE
B. in a sense,
C. symbolically,
D. literally,

4. F. NO CHANGE
G. be specific when,
H. be specific: when
J. be specific, when

5. A. NO CHANGE
B. (Place after *spacebar*)
C. (Place after *place*)
D. (Place after *drinks*)

6. F. NO CHANGE
G. don't respond. Are ill suited
H. don't respond and are ill suited
J. don't respond, are ill suited

7. A. NO CHANGE
B. including
C. includes
D. is including

8. F. NO CHANGE
G. program will never
H. program is never
J. program are never

9. A. NO CHANGE
B. its'
C. its
D. i'ts

GO ON TO THE NEXT PAGE.

you the whole keyboard to choose from. 10

[3] <u>And</u> if that's really the case, why not just break down
 11
and say, "Slap your keyboard a few times with your open

palms to <u>continue. . ."</u> 13
 12

10. For the sake of coherence, what is the proper placement of Sentence 2?

    F. NO CHANGE
    G. before Sentence 1
    H. after Sentence 3
    J. at the end of Paragraph 3

11. **A.** NO CHANGE
    B. Nevertheless,
    C. In spite of this,
    D. In the meantime,

12. **F.** NO CHANGE
    G. to continue. . . !"
    H. to continue. . . "?
    J. to continue. . . ?"

13. Given the tone of the piece, a closing sentence could read:

    A. However, that would be silly and not accomplish what you are trying to do.
    B. Of course, if you did that, the "dead keys" might mess you up.
    C. On a computer, "any key" is not the specific key, but really means what it says -- any key.
    D. If you don't realize what "any" key means, you should probably give up on learning computers.

Questions 14 and 15 ask about the entire passage.

14. The author has been asked to submit an article on computer use to a conservative business magazine. Will this passage be suitable?

    F. Yes, because it describes computers and how they function
    G. Yes, because the article is easy to understand
    H. No, because the article is too informal for a business magazine
    J. No, because it doesn't talk enough about computer use

15. A good title for this piece would be:

    A. "Stay out of the Spacebar."
    B. "Any Key. Calling Any Key."
    C. "How to Use a Computer."
    D. "Watch Out for Death Traps."

GO ON TO THE NEXT PAGE.

PASSAGE II

Pounds and Pence and Guineas

[1]

"Guineas, shillings, half-pence. You know what they

are?" Mr. Dombey asks <u>their</u> little son Paul.
               16

<u>Paul Dickens tells us,</u> knew,
      17

<u>since</u> the average reader of today is not always likely to
18
be so knowledgeable.

[2]

In the 1800s, British money <u>was</u> calculated in units
                   19

of pounds, shillings, and pence. 20 These were the units

of value—like the American mill, cent, and dollar—in

---

16. F. NO CHANGE
   G. her
   H. our
   J. his

17. A. NO CHANGE
   B. Paul, Dickens tells us
   C. Paul, Dickens tells us,
   D. Paul Dickens tells us

18. F. NO CHANGE
   G. but
   H. unless
   J. so

19. A. NO CHANGE
   B. will be
   C. would be
   D. were

20. The writer considers adding the following sentence after the first sentence in Paragraph 2

   Today, however, British money is calculated slightly differently.

   The most logical reason for NOT including this sentence is that:

   F. it does not flow logically from the sentence before it.
   G. it changes the focus from the past to the present, and then switches abruptly back to the past without explaining the new changes.
   H. it seems to say today's calculations are slightly better than the old, which is not what the author wishes to imply.
   J. it suggests that the student knows what the new calculations are.

GO ON TO THE NEXT PAGE.

which all transactions were reckoned, <u>regardless of</u>
<u>whether</u> the value was represented by a bookkeeping
                21
entry, by coin, by banknotes, or by notations written on a

check. The actual physical <u>instruments</u> of currency were
                                    22
paper banknotes and gold, silver, copper and bronze coins
like the sixpence, the crown, the sovereign, the shilling
piece, and the penny. Thus, for example, the physical units
called pennies<u> and created by an equivalent number of</u>
                                    23
<u>pence used to measure the value.</u> (The guinea, uniquely,
        23
was a unit of physical currency that became an

abstract measure of value <u>as well; that is,</u> long after the
                                    24
actual guinea coin itself stopped being minted in the early
1800s, prices for luxury items like good horses and
expensive clothes continued to be quoted in guineas
as if they were some independent unit of value like the
pound.) 25

[3]

[1] Sovereigns and half sovereigns were gold;
crowns, half crowns, florins, shillings, sixpences, and
threepences were silver; <u>pence ha'pence and farthings</u>
                                            26

---

21. Which best represents the idea that it doesn't matter
    how the value was represented?
    A. NO CHANGE
    B. even if
    C. depending on whether
    D. except for when

22. F. NO CHANGE
    G. conditions
    H. values
    J. leverages

23. A. NO CHANGE
    B. were used to measure the value and created by an
       equivalent number of pence.
    C. were used to measure the value created by an
       equivalent number of pence.
    D. created by an equivalent number of pence used to
       measure the value.

24. F. NO CHANGE
    G. as well that is,
    H. as well: that is
    J. as well, that is

25. This sentence is in parentheses because it:
    A. is unrelated to the other information in the para-
       graph.
    B. provides additional information through an example.
    C. is not a full sentence.
    D. is a run-on sentence.

26. F. NO CHANGE
    G. pence, ha'pence, and farthings
    H. pence ha'pence, and farthings
    J. pence ha'pence and, farthings,

GO ON TO THE NEXT PAGE.

were copper until 1860, after which they were bronze. 27

[2] The coins were issued by the Royal Mint, but the

banknotes got <u>its name</u> from the fact that they were not
28
issued by a government agency but by a bank, in fact—

after the mid-1800s—only by *the* bank—the Bank of

England. 29

27. A good introductory sentence to this paragraph would be:

   A. Guineas and shillings were different values of coins.
   B. The different coins were minted in different mediums to help people tell them apart.
   C. The units of value of the coins were all different.
   D. Guineas, today, are no longer even abstract measurements.

28. F. NO CHANGE
   G. it's name
   H. their name
   J. their names

29. The author wants to add this sentence to Paragraph 3:

   Until then banks all over the country issued their own banknotes (or promises to pay), which circulated more or less like money.

   Where should it go?

   A. Before Sentence 1
   B. After Sentence 1
   C. After Sentence 2
   D. As a parenthetical expression between Sentences 1 and 2

Question 30 asks about the preceding passage as a whole.

---

30. A good title for this essay would be:

   F. "How Money Has Changed."
   G. "American vs. British Currency in the 19th Century."
   H. "Pounds, Shillings and Guineas—English Money in the 19th Century."
   J. "Money Doesn't Grow on Trees."

GO ON TO THE NEXT PAGE.

PASSAGE III

Just Desserts

[1]

New York restaurateur Warner LeRoy once said, "A restaurant is a fantasy—a kind of living fantasy in which diners are the most important members of the <u>cast."</u>
31

31. A. NO CHANGE
    B. cast".
    C. cast?"
    D. cast"!

He might have added, "and dessert is <u>the more important</u>
                             32

32. F. NO CHANGE
    G. the better important
    H. the most important
    J. the best important

prop on the stage," <u>unless</u> nothing is closer to fantasy than
              33
dessert.

33. A. NO CHANGE
    B. however
    C. since
    D. as a result

[2]

You can try to make a case for chocolate as a major food <u>group (I've tried for years),</u> or for getting your
         34
Recommended Dietary Allowance of calcium by eating gobs of whipped cream, but it's a no-go. The only reason for dessert is <u>pleasure; pure and simple.</u> And that pleasure
             35

34. F. NO CHANGE
    G. group I've tried for years,
    H. group, I've tried for years
    J. group; I've tried for years,

35. A. NO CHANGE
    B. pleasure. Pure and simple.
    C. pleasure, pure and simple.
    D. pleasure, pure, and simple.

doubles when dessert is <u>beautiful</u> presented in a restaurant.
             36

36. F. NO CHANGE
    G. beautifuler
    H. beauty
    J. beautifully

GO ON TO THE NEXT PAGE.

[3]

[1] The evening depends upon this last impression.

[2] All the chefs who handle the savory portion of a restaurant meal will <u>surely protest,</u> but anyone with a
                            37
serious sweet tooth believes that appetizers and main

courses are merely the <u>stage directions</u> for dessert.
                           38

[3] We save room for it and expect it to deliver. 39

37. **A.** NO CHANGE
    B. sure
    C. suren't
    D. sureful

38. **F.** NO CHANGE
    G. entrance
    H. props
    J. setup

39. Which is the best order of sentences in Paragraph 3?

    A. NO CHANGE
    B. 1, 3, 2
    C. 2, 3, 1
    D. 3, 1, 2

[4]

Pastry chefs impress us first by serving up drama—spun-sugar cages, gravity-defying pastry towers, and cocoa-speckled plates make all of us smile like little kids at the circus. But while the look is often architectural, the foundation is always <u>the same; rich flavor.</u>
                            40

40. **F.** NO CHANGE
    G. the same: rich flavor.
    H. the same rich flavor.
    J. the same, rich, flavor.

[5]

[1] If there's a trend today, it's toward even more taste. [2] America's top pastry chefs are working to extract as much flavor as they can from every ingredient. [3] Chocolate is bitter as well as sweet; nuts are toasted

GO ON TO THE NEXT PAGE.

for intensity; cream is infused with not-so-subtle flavors,
41
often with herbs and unusual spices; and fruit purees,

sauces and syrups are so concentrated that they often taste

fruitier than the fruit itself. [4] Sure, chefs fuss over

presentation—everyone knows we eat with our eyes

first—but it's taste that captures their imaginations and

galvanizes their creativity. 43
42

41. A. NO CHANGE
  B. not-so-subtle flavors; often
  C. not-so-subtle flavors: often
  D. not so subtle, flavors, often

42. F. NO CHANGE
  G. destroys
  H. manifests
  J. liquidates

43. The author wants to insert the following parenthetical comment in Paragraph 5:

  (Of course, the chefs make sure the flavors enhance one another, rather than overpowering other ingredients or the entire dish.)

  It should go:

  A. after Sentence 1.
  B. after Sentence 3.
  C. after Sentence 4.
  D. before Sentence 1.

Questions 44 and 45 ask about the preceding passage as a whole.

---

44. Suppose the author had been asked to write an article that focused on the effect the health craze was having on diners. Would this essay have fulfilled that?

  F. Yes, because the essay focuses on the fact that diners are still eating desserts even today.
  G. Yes, because the essay focuses on the varied ingredients included in the desserts the chefs are creating.
  H. No, because the essay does not make a connection between the health craze and eating dessert.
  J. No, because the essay focuses on the failure of diners to stop eating desserts.

45. The writer wants to add the following sentence to the essay.

No matter how simple the main courses, the desserts are always elegant and inspired creations.

The sentence most logically fits in

A. Paragraph 1.
B. Paragraph 4.
C. Paragraph 5.
D. Paragraph 2.

PASSAGE IV

Best Friends

[1]

[1] Finding and working is one of the primary

initiations of the shaman <u>with an animal helper</u>. [2] In
                                                    46

worldwide folk-story the younger son or daughter who <u>are</u>
                                                          47
sent out into the wide world without goods or friends

invariably meets with an animal or series of <u>animals</u>
                                                  48

which help and <u>enable</u> them. [3] Many Celtic saints
                  49

<u>with animals</u> are associated: St. Gobhnat of Ballyvourny
  50
in County Cork is led to her monastic foundation by nine

white deer, and her enclosure is guarded by bees, while

46. F. NO CHANGE
 G. (Placed before *finding* with capitalization corrected)
 H. (Placed after *working*)
 J. (Placed after *initiations*)

47. A. NO CHANGE
 B. were
 C. is
 D. aren't

48. F. NO CHANGE
 G. animales
 H. animals'
 J. animal's

49. Which word bests portrays the idea that the animals lend the people strength?

 A. NO CHANGE
 B. entrap
 C. empower
 D. entreat

50. F. NO CHANGE
 G. Place after *Celtic.*
 H. Place after the colon, before *St. Gobhnat.*
 J. Place after *associated,* before the colon.

GO ON TO THE NEXT PAGE.

St. Kevin of County Wicklow offers it's hand as nest for
51
a blackbird and learns patience while the eggs hatch.

[4] These stories have little to do with "kindness to

animals." 52 53

51. **A.** NO CHANGE
   B. their
   C. its
   D. his

52. The author wishes to add the following sentence to
    Paragraph 1.

    Rather, they concern a total understanding of and
    attunement to the animal teachers of the natural
    world.

    Where would it best fit?

    F. Before Sentence 1
    G. As part of Sentence 2, added on at the end, with a
       comma separating *them* from *rather*
    H. At the end of the last sentence, with a semicolon
       after *animals* and before *rather*
    J. Between Sentences 2 and 3

53. The main idea of Paragraph 1 is best stated as:

    A. animals can talk and help people.
    B. in folklore, being kind to animals eventually helps
       people.
    C. in shamanic lore, being kind to animals helps
       people, but does not give them understanding of
       those animals.
    D. in shamanic folklore, people often gain an under-
       standing of the animal world through animal teach-
       ers, rather than just learning the lesson to be kind
       to animals.

[2]

The notion that animals can teach humans is

profoundly present in shamanic work. The animal helpers
54
whom we meet in the inner-worlds are wiser in the ways

of the otherworld than we, and we discover they can be

trusted to help her in ways unknown to us. The animals
55
we meet in the world about us teach us the simple and

54. The word *profoundly* is used here to mean:

    F. eerily.
    G. uneasily.
    H. shallowly.
    J. intensely.

55. **A.** NO CHANGE
   B. his
   C. our
   D. us

GO ON TO THE NEXT PAGE.

manifest truths about life and relationship to <u>life-forms,</u>
                                                    56
<u>which</u> are extraordinarily therapeutic for human beings

who have forgotten their place in the universe. The

memory of the animals helps us remember our <u>paradisal</u>
                                                 57
<u>interconnection.</u>
    57

[3]

The destiny of human beings is often regulated by or

connected with helping animals, which may be seen as

properly totemic to a person or tribe. [**58**]

56. F. NO CHANGE
    G. life-forms; which
    H. life-forms: which
    J. life-forms. Which

57. Which phrase best expresses the idea that we are part of heaven?

    A. NO CHANGE
    B. heretical connection
    C. edenic separation
    D. earthly spirit

58. This sentence should:

    F. be part of Paragraph 1 because it talks about helping animals.
    G. be part of Paragraph 2 because it discusses connections.
    H. remain as the start of Paragraph 3 because it begins a new idea: the regulation of our destiny.
    J. be placed as the opening paragraph before Paragraph 1 because it talks about destiny.

Questions 59 and 60 ask about the preceding passage as a whole.

---

59. The author wants to add the following sentences:

> In one story, a boy gains his name (The Hound of Culainn) after fighting the smith's hound. As compensation for killing the dog, he then becomes the smith's watchdog. It is then his duty never to eat meat. Similarly, it is another man's duty never to hunt wild boar. In the end, both men die because they violate their duties—eating meat and hunting boar.

It would best fit:

    A. in Paragraph 1 because it gives examples of men meeting with animals.
    B. in Paragraph 3 because it gives examples of how human destinies are regulated by animals.
    C. in Paragraph 2 because the animals teach the men their duties.
    D. as an introductory paragraph because they provide initial examples of animals in stories about men.

GO ON TO THE NEXT PAGE.

60. The overall theme of this essay seems to suggest that:

    F. many people learn through stories that the animal kingdom can help them understand the world better.

    G. many people learn to be kind to animals through shaman stories.

    H. many people learn not to hunt boar through shaman stories.

    J. if you fail at your duty, you will die.

PASSAGE V

[1]

Standing in a circle of adult students in a <u>bright</u> lit
             61
classroom, Christine Youngblood signals a classmate with

a wink and a smile. What might appear to be <u>sultry</u> body
                         62
language is an American Sign Language continuing-

education class.

61. A. NO CHANGE
    B. brighter
    C. brightly
    D. brightest

62. What word best conveys the idea of flirtatious and inviting?

    F. NO CHANGE
    G. surly
    H. elated
    J. melodic

[2]

As students perfect the <u>wink. One</u> of many facial
                63
expressions that accompany signing, instructor Myrna

Orleck-Aiello <u>offers</u> gestures of encouragement. The
          64

classroom <u>are</u> silent except for some laughter while the
      65

63. A. NO CHANGE
    B. wink; one
    C. wink, one
    D. wink one

64. F. NO CHANGE
    G. offer
    H. offered
    J. were offering

65. A. NO CHANGE
    B. were
    C. were being
    D. is

GO ON TO THE NEXT PAGE.

students struggle through <u>one's</u> beginning phrases.
66

Orleck-Aiello, like all sign-language instructors at the

University, is deaf, and there is no oral communication

even on the first day <u>of class?</u>
67

[3]

In any language, experts have concluded, the <u>faster</u>
68

<u>and best</u> way to learn is through total immersion. Though

beginning sign-language students find it tough at first not

to vocalize their questions, they grow used to gesturing

and raising their eyebrows at one another as pleas for

help. **69**

[4]

The dozen <u>pupil</u> here range from a new high school
70

graduate to a grandmother. <u>There</u> reasons for learning sign
71

language also are diverse. One woman is preparing for

66. F. NO CHANGE
G. their
H. her
J. its

67. A. NO CHANGE
B. of class
C. of class,
D. of class.

68. F. NO CHANGE
G. faster and better
H. fastest and better
J. fastest and best

69. Which of the following sentences would best fit in Paragraph 3?

A. However, they find speaking and asking questions much easier.
B. Since they must either communicate or be shut out from the conversation, they find it easier to learn than to protest.
C. They need help because they find it very difficult to learn this way.
D. Sign language is not like any other language.

70. F. NO CHANGE
G. pupiles
H. pupils
J. pupil's

71. A. NO CHANGE
B. They're
C. Their
D. Her

GO ON TO THE NEXT PAGE.

law school and <u>has chosen</u> this intensive two-week class
72
to broaden her potential client base. Another woman and

her husband speak <u>singular</u> languages in public to keep
73
people nearby from understanding their conversations.

<u>"But</u> a lot of people already know French and Spanish,"
74
she laments. "I'm trying to get him to learn sign language

with me, so we can keep our secrets to ourselves."

72. F. NO CHANGE
G. had chosen
H. has choosed
J. choosed

73. Which word best conveys the idea of many languages?

A. NO CHANGE
B. various
C. generous
D. melded

74. F. NO CHANGE
G. As a result,
H. Therefore,
J. So

Question 75 asks about the preceding passage as a whole.

75. The author has been asked to add a sentence stating that learning sign language is similar to learning French or Spanish. In which paragraph should it go?

A. Paragraph 4
B. Paragraph 2
C. Paragraph 3
D. Paragraph 1

END OF TEST 1

Model English and Reading ACT III   351

Model Reading ACT III

40 Questions – 35 Minutes

INSTRUCTIONS: There are four passages on this test with ten items about each passage. Choose the best answer for each item based on the passage. Then fill in the appropriate circle on the answer sheet. Check pages 360 and 369–373 for answers and explanations.

PASSAGE I

PROSE FICTION: This passage is from "The Three Swimmers and the Educated Grocer" by William Saroyan.

One day in April I set out for Thompson Ditch with my cousin Mourad and a pal of his named Joe Bettencourt, a Portuguese who loved nothing more than to be free and out-of-doors.

5 It was a bright Saturday morning. We had two baloney sandwiches each, and ten cents between the three of us. We decided to walk to the ditch so that we would get there around noon, when the day would be warm. We walked along the railroad tracks to Calwa.
10 Along the state highway to Malaga. And then east through the vineyard to the ditch. When we said Thompson Ditch, we meant a specific place. It was an intersection of country roads, with a wooden bridge and a headgate. The swimming was south of the
15 bridge. West of the ditch was a big fenced-in pasture, with cows and horses grazing in it. East of the ditch was the country road. The road and the ditch traveled together many miles. The flow was south, and the next bridge was two miles away. In the summertime a day
20 of swimming was incomplete until a boy had gone downstream to the other bridge, rested a moment in the pasture land, and then came back up, against the stream, which was a good workout.

By the time we got to Thompson Ditch the bright-
25 ness of morning had changed to a gloom that was un-mistakably wintry; in fact, the beginning of a storm. The water was roaring, the sky was gray, growing black, the air was cold and unfriendly, and the land-scape seemed lonely and desolate.

30 Joe Bettencourt said, I came all this way to swim and rain or no rain I'm going to swim.

So am I.

You wait, my cousin Mourad said. Me and Joe, we'll see how it is. If it's all right, you can come in.
35 Can you really swim?

Aw shut up, I said.

This is what I always said when it seemed to me that somebody had unwittingly insulted me.

Well, Joe Bettencourt said, *can you*?
40 Sure I can swim.

If you ask *him,* my cousin Mourad said, he can do anything. Better than anybody in the world.

Neither of them knew how uncertain I was as to whether or not I could swim well enough to negotiate
45 a dive and a swim across the body of cold roaring wa-ter. If the truth were known, when I saw the dark water roaring I was scared, challenged, and insulted.

Aw shut up, I said to the water.

I brought out my lunch and bit into one of my
50 sandwiches. My cousin Mourad whacked my hand and almost knocked the sandwich into the water.

We eat after we swim, he said. Do you want to have cramps?

I had plumb forgotten. It was because I was so
55 challenged and scared.

One sandwich won't give me cramps.

It'll taste better after we swim, Joe said.

He was a very kind boy. He knew I was scared and he knew I was bluffing. I knew *he* was scared, but
60 I knew he was figuring everything out a little more wisely than I was.

Let's see, he said, We'll swim across, rest, swim back, get dressed, eat, and unless the storm passes, start for home. Otherwise we'll swim some more.

65 This storm isn't going to pass, my cousin Mourad said. If we're going to swim, we're going to have to do it in a hurry.

By this time Joe was taking off his clothes. My cousin Mourad was taking off his, and I was taking off 70 mine. We stood together naked on the bank of the ditch looking at the unfriendly water. It certainly didn't invite a dive, but there was no other honorable way to enter a body of water. If you tried to walk in, you were just naturally not a swimmer. If you jumped in feet first 75 it wasn't exactly a disgrace, it was just bad style. On the other hand, the water was utterly without charm, altogether unfriendly, uninviting, and sinister. The swiftness of the water made the distance to the opposite bank seem greater than it was.

80 Without a word Joe dived in. Without a word my cousin Mourad dived in. The second or two between the splashes seemed like long days dreamed in a winter dream because I was not only scared but very cold. With a bookful of unspoken words on my troubled 85 mind, I dived in.

The next thing a knew—and it wasn't more than three seconds later—I was listening to Joe yelling, my cousin Mourad yelling, and myself yelling. What had happened was that we had all dived into mud up to our 90 elbows, had gotten free only with great effort, and had come up worried about what had happened to the other two. We were all standing in the cold roaring water, up to our knees in soft mud.

The dives had been standing dives. If they had 95 been running dives we should have stuck in the mud up to our ankles, head first, and remained there until summer, or later.

This scared us a little on one hand and on the other hand made us feel very lucky to be alive.

1. According to the passage the author said "Aw shut up" when:

   A. he was afraid.   C. he was insulted.
   B. he was criticized.   D. he was challenged.

2. The author says that the two people with him:

   F. had no idea how uncertain about swimming he was.
   G. loved nothing more than to be out-of-doors.
   H. said that he could not swim well.
   J. watched while he ate his sandwich after he had gone swimming.

3. We can tell from the passage that the swimming took place:

   A. south of the other bridge.
   B. downstream from the wooden bridge.
   C. downstream from the other bridge.
   D. north of the wooden bridge.

4. According to the passage the boys dove into the water rather than enter some other way:

   F. because the water was cold.
   G. because the water was fast-moving.
   H. because it was bad style.
   J. because it was honorable.

5. According to the passage, after the boys dove into the water they were:

   A. standing up to their knees in mud.
   B. standing up to their ankles in mud.
   C. head first in mud.
   D. running in mud.

6. In the story the country road:

   F. often had cows and horses grazing on it.
   G. and the ditch traveled together for many miles.
   H. was along the railroad tracks to Calwa.
   J. was a good workout when you traveled up the road.

7. When the characters in the story reached the ditch, the weather was:

   A. bright.   C. springlike.
   B. warm.   D. wintry.

8. Mourad said that the author:

   F. could not swim.
   G. was scared, challenged, and insulted.
   H. thought the author could do anything.
   J. should not eat the sandwich before swimming.

9. According to the passage, it was bad style:

   A. to admit that you could not really swim.
   B. to do a standing dive.
   C. to do a feet-first dive.
   D. to admit when you are scared.

10. Joe's advice about swimming was to:

   F. swim back and forth a few times and then get dressed and eat.
   G. swim across and back only once unless the storm passes.
   H. make sure it was all right to go swimming before the main character went swimming.
   J. swim quickly, as the storm wasn't going to pass.

GO ON TO THE NEXT PAGE.

PASSAGE II

SOCIAL SCIENCE: This passage is from "Freeze Frame: Calais Remembered" by Gordon Marsden.

Calais Falls to Edward III and His English Army

The surrender of the French Channel port of Calais to the besieging English king Edward III not only was a key element in the English successes in the
5 early stages of the Hundred Years' War but its fall and the progress of what had been an eleven-month siege illumine the complex temperament that underpinned the conduct of war by medieval chivalry.

Edward had claimed the throne of France through
10 his mother Isabella after the direct line of her Capetian brothers had died out, leaving the native claimant as Philip of Valois (who became Philip VI). His motives for the claim have been variously ascribed by historians....

15 Whatever the case, the energy with which Edward conducted his campaign in France from 1340 onwards cannot be doubted. He reaped a rich reward with his famous victory at the battle of Crecy in August 1346, where the firepower of English archers wrought havoc
20 on the heavily armored but ponderous noble cavalry of the French. His success there left him free to besiege Calais which, lying as it does at the narrowest crossing point to England across the Channel, was a vital strategic objective to secure supplies and safe passage for
25 the conduct of the invasion.

The town's defenses reflected this significance: a double wall with towers and ditches, supplied by sea by Philip's forces. The town's governor, Jean de Vienne, was resourceful and ruthlessly practical in
30 making the best of his resources, turning out of the town noncombatant men, women, and children at the start of the siege to save food, an occasion on which Edward showed chivalrous generosity by feeding them and allowing them to pass through the lines.

35 The siege tied down Edward's resources of men and material over the winter of 1346-47; his army had to be victualed by the Flemish in a wooden town he erected outside the walls to protect his troops, and via raids on the surrounding countryside. The defenders in Calais re-
40 sisted doggedly, despite dwindling supplies. The appeal of the Governor to Philip VI "we have nothing left to subsist on, unless we eat each other" finally moved Philip to action. He raised an army in late spring 1347....

Philip's attempts at relief were half-hearted: his
45 last on July 27th, 1347, was followed by inconclusive parleying between the French forces and English heralds led by Henry Grossmont, Duke of Lancaster. When these broke down, Philip declined to take the risk of battle: on August 1st, his army retreated and
50 Calais was left to its fate.

Jean de Vienne parleyed with Edward's heralds for honorable terms of surrender. He had reason to be worried: the laws of war by no means guaranteed that surrender would be followed by the defendants pre-
55 serving life and limb, and persistent resistance such as Edward might well have regarded the eleven-month siege might be met by condign punishment.

Edward initially rejected the Governor's request for his men and the remaining citizens to leave un-
60 harmed, but (according to the chronicler Froissart) he softened to the extent of restricting his potential vengeance to the governor and six of Calais's leading citizens. But even they were spared when Edward's pregnant wife interceded on their behalf.

65 Calais became an English possession. Its population was expelled and the town, resettled with English merchants and an impressive garrison, became both a strategic stronghold and a symbol of English resolution in France. After the final debacles of English power a
70 century later, it alone remained the sole foothold in France after 1453, remaining an English possession until it fell to the French in the reign of Mary Tudor as a by-product of her husband Philip II's war with the French, the symbolic blow to national pride which al-
75 legedly led the Tudor queen to sigh, "When I am dead, they will find the word 'Calais' engraved upon my heart."

11. According to the passage, Edward's motive for claiming the throne:

  A. was to overthrow Philip of Valois.
  B. has been listed as different things by different historians.
  C. was through his mother, Isabella.
  D. makes us doubt his energy in campaigning in France.

12. According to the passage, what did Edward gain through his success at Crecy?

  F. The ability to cross the Channel at Calais
  G. Rich rewards of English firepower
  H. The freedom to attack Calais
  J. The assistance of France's noble cavalry

GO ON TO THE NEXT PAGE.

13. In the first paragraph, what does the author set up as the thesis for his essay?

    A. Calais's surrender was a key element in the English successes during the Hundred Years' War.
    B. King Edward III forced Calais to surrender during the Hundred Years' War.
    C. Medieval chivalry made it possible for Edward to be victorious at Calais.
    D. The fall of Calais in an almost yearlong siege shows the complexity of the conduct of war under medieval chivalry.

14. The author states that Calais was important because:

    F. Calais was a strategic crossing point from England.
    G. in this battle, Edward could finally defeat Philip and claim the throne for good.
    H. the governor of Calais was resourceful and ruthless.
    J. Edward showed his chivalry in the battle by giving the town's women and children food and safe passage.

15. The author implies in this passage that Philip:

    A. was a brave soldier who fought Edward for the throne.
    B. was apathetic toward the throne and not interested in fighting.
    C. worked for the surrender of Calais.
    D. rejected the governor's request not to harm his men.

16. The author includes the note about Edward feeding the townspeople and sparing the men following his wife's plea for them to show:

    F. that Edward had power over people's lives and deaths.
    G. that while he was a tough commander, Edward was also benevolent and chivalrous.
    H. that the people of Calais should have surrendered earlier.
    J. that Edward was a better ruler than Jean de Vienne was.

17. According to the passage, what happened to Calais?

    A. It returned to the French after the debacles of English power a century later.
    B. It was resettled with English merchants until 1453.
    C. It became one of England's strongholds in France, and the only English-owned town after 1453 until Mary Tudor's time.
    D. It was engraved on Mary's heart.

18. The author mentions Jean de Vienne's worry about surrender because:

    F. he had to inform the reader that the laws of surrender were different then and could not guarantee safety.
    G. he wanted to show that surrender guaranteed freedom from death or torture.
    H. he wanted to show that Edward was set on vengeance at Calais.
    J. he wanted to portray Jean de Vienne as a coward.

19. Are the details of the surrender of Calais and Edward's sparing of the burghers treated as fact in the passage?

    A. Yes, because it states that the scene was a famous one.
    B. Yes, because it portrays Edward's change of heart.
    C. No, because it does not state specifically why Edward softened.
    D. No, because it notes that these things happened "according to Froissart."

20. According to the author:

    I. Calais was lost, in part, because Philip refused to fight.
    II. Philip's forces were supplying Calais by sea.
    III. Philip surrendered to Edward at Calais with Jean de Vienne.

    F. I only
    G. I and III only
    H. II and III only
    J. I and II only

GO ON TO THE NEXT PAGE.

PASSAGE III

HUMANITIES: This passage is from *Madwoman in the Attic* by Sandra Gilbert and Susan Gubar.

Frankenstein (1818) and *Wuthering Heights* (1847) are not usually seen as related works, except in-
sofar as both are famous nineteenth-century literary puzzles, with Mary Shelley's plaintive speculation
5   about where she got so "hideous an idea" (for the mon-ster in Frankenstein), finding its counterpart in the position of Heathcliff's creator as a sort of mystery woman of literature. Still, if both Emily Brontë and Shelley wrote enigmatic, curiously unprecedented
10   novels, their works are puzzling in different ways: Shelley's is an enigmatic fantasy of metaphysical horror, Brontë's an enigmatic Romantic, and "mascu-line," text in which the fates of subordinate female characters seem entirely dependent upon the actions of
15   ostensibly male heroes or anti-heroes...

Despite these dissimilarities, however, *Franken-stein* and *Wuthering Heights* are alike in a number of crucial ways. For one thing, both works are enigmatic, puzzling, even in some sense generically problemati-
20   cal. Moreover, in each case the mystery of the novel is associated with what seem to be its metaphysical intentions, intentions around which much critical controversy has collected. For these two "popular" novels—one a thriller, the other a romance—have
25   convinced many readers that their charismatic surfaces conceal (far more than they reveal) complex ontologi-cal depths, elaborate structures of allusion, fierce though shadowy moral ambitions. And this point in particular is demonstrated by a simpler characteristic
30   both works have in common. Both make use of what in connection with *Frankenstein* we have called an evi-dentiary narrative technique, a Romantic storytelling method that emphasizes the ironic disjunctions be-tween different perspectives on the same events as well
35   as the ironic tensions that inhere in the relationship between surface drama and concealed authorial inten-tion. In fact, in its use of such a technique, *Wuthering Heights* might be a deliberate copy of *Frankenstein*. Not only do the stories of both novels emerge through
40   concentric circles of narration, both works contain significant digressions. Catherine Earnshaw's diary, Isabella's letter, Zillah's narrative, and Heathcliff's confidences to Nelly function in *Wuthering Heights* much as Alphonse Frankenstein's letter, Justine's nar-
45   rative, and Safie's history do in *Frankenstein*.

Their common concern with evidence, especially with written evidence, suggests another way in which *Wuthering Heights* and *Frankenstein* are alike: more than most novels, both are consciously literary works,
50   at times almost obsessively concerned with books and with reading as not only a symbolic but a dramatic—plot-forwarding—activity. Can this be because, like Shelley, Brontë was something of a literary heiress? The idea is an odd one to consider because the four
55   Brontë children, scribbling in Yorkshire's remote West Riding, seem as trapped on the periphery of nine-teenth-century literary culture as Mary Shelley was embedded in its...center. Nevertheless, peripheral though they were, the Brontës had literary parents just
60   as Mary Shelley did.

21. According to the passage, how are *Frankenstein* and *Wuthering Heights* different?

   A. *Frankenstein* is puzzling while *Wuthering Heights* is not.
   B. *Frankenstein* is a nineteenth-century work while *Wuthering Heights* is written in the eighteenth century.
   C. *Frankenstein* is a horror thriller while *Wuthering Heights* is a romance.
   D. *Frankenstein* is a masculine text while *Wuthering Heights* is a feminine text.

22. As used throughout this passage, the word *enigmatic* means:

   F. mysterious.
   G. transparent.
   H. crystalline.
   J. lucid.

23. When speaking of Brontë's work as a "masculine" text, the author implies:

   A. that a male author actually wrote the work.
   B. that this is positive because men are the heroes.
   C. that this is negative because women are subordi-nated to both the heroes and anti-heroes just be-cause those characters are male.
   D. that Heathcliff's creator was a mystery woman.

GO ON TO THE NEXT PAGE.

24. In the first paragraph, the author sets up the idea that:

- **F.** Shelley and Brontë were unrelated writers.
- **G.** *Frankenstein* and *Wuthering Heights* are completely different books: a thriller and a romance.
- **H.** Shelley's work is better because it is unprecedented.
- **J.** while the two works are both puzzling, they are puzzling in different ways.

25. The author says that despite their differences, the two works are similar because:

- **I.** they are both nineteenth-century puzzles.
- **II.** they are both consciously literary works.
- **III.** they are both evidentiary novels.

- **A.** None of the above
- **B.** I and II only
- **C.** I and III only
- **D.** All of the above

26. According to the passage, what is used as evidence in the two works?

- **F.** Clues revealed through concentric circles
- **G.** Similar perspectives on different episodes
- **H.** Digressions through letters and other forms of communication
- **J.** Isabella's narrative and Justine's diary

27. What reason does the author give for the two books being highly literary?

- **A.** Both writers were embedded in the center of literary culture.
- **B.** Both writers had literary parents.
- **C.** Both writers use reading solely as a symbolic activity.
- **D.** Both books are obsessed with plot.

28. Overall, this passage seems to be setting up the idea that

- **F.** while books and authors may appear to be dissimilar, they may in fact hide underlying similarities that should be examined.
- **G.** most books should be studied for what they are and not compared to other works.
- **H.** *Frankenstein* and *Wuthering Heights* were two nineteenth-century books written by women.
- **J.** most writers with literary parents will have similarities in their works.

29. According to the passage, many readers over the years have been convinced:

- **A.** that the novels are merely "popular" reading.
- **B.** the surfaces of the novels reveal complex depths and elaborate structures within them.
- **C.** complex depths and structures are concealed beneath the charismatic surfaces of the novels.
- **D.** that while the novels appear problematical, they are really simple to understand.

30. In the passage, the author implies:

- **F.** that *Wuthering Heights* is a copy of *Frankenstein*.
- **G.** that *Frankenstein* is a copy of *Wuthering Heights*.
- **H.** that *Frankenstein* is modeled on *Wuthering Heights*.
- **J.** that when she wrote *Wuthering Heights*, Brontë might have copied the technique Shelley used in writing *Frankenstein*.

GO ON TO THE NEXT PAGE.

NATURE SCIENCE: This passage is from "Freak Frogs" by Kurt Kleiner.

The breakdown products formed when the sun's ultraviolet rays act on common pesticides could be to blame for a wave of deformed frogs and other amphibians turning up across North America.

5 John Bantle, a researcher at Oklahoma State University in Stillwater, has discovered that exposing methoprene, a pesticide used against mosquitoes, to sunshine produces chemicals that can trigger the abnormalities seen in the wild. Methoprene mimics an insect hormone, and is sprayed on mosquito breeding 10 pools to prevent the larvae from developing into adults.

North America's malformed amphibians have been a focus of attention for two years, ever since schoolchildren in Minnesota who were studying wetlands found a high number of frogs with missing or 15 extra legs. Similar reports have since come in from all over the U.S. and Canada.

The cause was unclear, but researchers saw possible culprits as chemicals released into the environment, an increase in UV radiation because of the thinning 20 ozone layer, or natural triggers such as parasites.

Bantle's research suggests that an interaction between the first two factors could be the key. By itself, methoprene seems to have little effect on developing amphibians, and so can't explain the deformities. But 25 Bantle has exposed frog spawn to cismethoprenic acid and transmethoprenic acid, two methoprene breakdown products formed on exposure to UV. He found they caused malformations within 96 hours at 100 30 times the rate of methoprene itself.

Other chemicals may behave similarly. Ed Little of the US Geological Survey in Columbia, Missouri, has found that under UV light the common insecticide carbonyl breaks down into a much more toxic sub-35 stance that seems to harm tadpoles.

These findings fit with the observations of Martin Ouellet of McGill University in Montreal, who has found that frogs in ponds exposed to pesticides are much more likely to show deformities than those in 40 ponds that are not.

However, the leading proponent of the idea that the malformations are natural also has evidence to back that theory. Stanley Sessions, a developmental

45 biologist at Hartwick College in Oneonta, New York, believes the deformities are triggered by fluke parasites that burrow into tadpoles and form small hard cysts.

Sessions has previously inserted plastic beads the same size as the cysts into tadpoles and found that they grew malformed legs. Now he has succeeded in infect-50 ing tadpoles with the parasites in the lab. The experiments are still in progress, but one frog has already developed an extra leg.

But other researchers remain unconvinced. "He's on his way to showing parasites can cause deformi-55 ties," says Bantle, "but it's still a long shot whether that's what's happening in the wild." And Robert McKinnell of the University of Minnesota in Minneapolis has found that many frogs with deformed legs also have internal abnormalities, such as guts that 60 appear to be unable to digest food—defects that are unlikely to be caused by the local actions of parasites.

31. The author states that deformities in amphibians could be caused by:

A. common pesticides.
B. pesticides reacting to the sun.
C. either pesticides reacting to the sun or parasites attacking the animals.
D. parasites and pesticides.

32. What is methoprene?

F. An insect hormone used in Minnesota
G. Transmethoprenic acid
H. Plastic beads inserted into tadpoles
J. A mosquito pesticide that mimics an insect hormone

33. What happens when methoprene is exposed to the sun?

A. It prevents mosquito larvae from developing into adults.
B. Within four days it causes malformations at 100 times the rate of methoprene alone.
C. It causes hard cysts to form in frogs.
D. It causes missing legs in students from Minnesota.

GO ON TO THE NEXT PAGE.

34. Other than pesticides, what theory do some scientists have for the cause of the deformities?

    F. People dropping hard plastic beads in tadpoles

    G. Parasites that burrow into tadpoles to form hard cysts

    H. UV rays acting on cismethoprenic and transmethoprenic acids

    J. Carbonyl breaking down into toxic substances

35. What proof does Sessions offer for his theory?

    A. The frogs in Minneapolis have internal abnormalities.

    B. Several frogs infected with the parasite are now missing legs.

    C. Tadpoles with beads inserted grew malformed legs, and one tadpole infected with the parasite grew an extra leg.

    D. Frogs in ponds with pesticides are more likely to show deformities than those in ponds without pesticides.

36. According to the passage, Ed Little's and Martin Ouellet's findings:

    F. support the idea that the deformities are caused by nature.

    G. support the idea that pesticides are causing the deformities.

    H. refute the idea that pesticides are causing the deformities.

    J. support the idea that the thinning ozone layer is increasing UV rays.

37. What does the passage mention that might refute the parasite theory?

    A. The plastic beads cause larger cysts than the parasites.

    B. The tadpoles infected by the parasites have not developed extra legs.

    C. The internal abnormalities are unlikely to have been caused by parasites.

    D. Carbonyl seems to be a more toxic substance than methoprene.

38. What does the author seem to be saying about the cause, overall?

    F. The cause appears to be connected to a reaction between pesticides and the sun, but other possibilities cannot be ruled out.

    G. The cause is definitely connected to a reaction between pesticides and the sun, and not by parasites.

    H. The deformities are caused by methoprene reacting to the sun's UV rays.

    J. The deformities are caused by the thinning of the ozone layer.

39. What purpose does the author seem to have in writing this article?

    A. To inform people to look out for deformed frogs across the country

    B. To show readers the amount of research that goes into determining the scientific cause for something

    C. To inform readers that pesticides may be causing deformities so that they can regulate their use of those pesticides

    D. To warn people about the dangers of the thinning ozone

40. The quote in the last paragraph is inserted to show:

    F. that while the research may indicate a connection, it has not yet proved that parasites cause the deformities.

    G. that researchers pay attention to what other scientists are doing.

    H. that John Bantle agrees with Sessions that parasites cause deformities.

    J. that Sessions' research on parasites is wrong and does not show a connection between parasites and deformities.

END OF TEST 3

 ANSWERS

Model English ACT III

PASSAGE I	**PASSAGE II**	**PASSAGE III**	**PASSAGE IV**	**PASSAGE V**
1. B	16. J	31. A	46. H	61. C
2. F	17. C	32. H	47. C	62. F
3. D	18. G	33. C	48. F	63. C
4. H	19. A	34. F	49. C	64. F
5. A	20. G	35. C	50. J	65. D
6. H	21. A	36. J	51. D	66. G
7. A	22. F	37. A	52. H	67. D
8. G	23. C	38. J	53. D	68. J
9. A	24. F	39. C	54. J	69. B
10. F	25. B	40. G	55. D	70. H
11. A	26. G	41. A	56. F	71. C
12. H	27. B	42. F	57. A	72. F
13. B	28. J	43. B	58. H	73. B
14. H	29. C	44. H	59. B	74. F
15. B	30. H	45. B	60. F	75. C

Model Reading ACT III

PASSAGE I	**PASSAGE II**	**PASSAGE III**	**PASSAGE IV**
1. C	11. B	21. C	31. A
2. F	12. H	22. F	32. J
3. B	13. D	23. C	33. B
4. J	14. F	24. J	34. G
5. A	15. B	25. D	35. C
6. G	16. G	26. H	36. G
7. D	17. C	27. B	37. C
8. H	18. F	28. F	38. F
9. C	19. D	29. C	39. C
10. G	20. J	30. J	40. F

ACT III English Answers Explained

PASSAGE I

ANSWERS

1: **B.** The entire sentence is one complete thought, and parts do not need to be separated by commas.

2: **F.** No change is necessary. Also, the tone of "the screen says" fits in with the rest of the passage better than any of the other possibilities. Choices G and H are too straightforward for the passage, and choice J is overly dramatic.

3: **D.** The term "any key" actually means you can push any one of the keys on the keyboard. Therefore, the term "literally" is correct. It is not "in a sense" or "in a way." Rather, it means the same as "in every way."

4: **H.** The first part of the sentence shows the author is going to be specific. The colon separates that complete thought from the second, specific, thought. Therefore, choice H is correct. Putting a comma after the word "when" does not make sense because the phrase "let's be specific when" is not complete. Since both parts of the sentence are complete, the comma in choice J creates a comma splice.

5: **A.** The logical placement for the underlined phrase is its current position. In all of the other choices, the phrase breaks up the sentence in a way that makes the sentence illogical and hard to follow.

6: **H.** The words following the semicolon, "are ill-suited. . . ," is a phrase because it contains no noun. Therefore, choices F and G are incorrect. Choice J is incorrect because it makes the sentence a comma splice. Choice H is correct because it coordinates the sentence parts with the conjunction "and."

7: **A.** No change is necessary because the noun "these" and the verb "include" are both plural. Choices C and D are incorrect because they include singular forms of the verb. The verb in choice B does not make sense.

8: **G.** The sentence refers to what will happen if you pound on the keys, so the verb must be in future tense. Choice G has the future tense.

9: **A.** The word "it's" is spelled correctly here to mean *it is.* The word "its" with no apostrophe means *belonging to it,* which is incorrect here.

10: **F.** The sentence makes the most sense where it is. Sentence 3 logically follows Sentence 2, and Sentence 2 logically follows Sentence 1.

11: **A.** This sentence is a continuation of the first thought. The word "and" coordinates these thoughts. The words "Nevertheless" and "In spite of" subordinate the second thought. It is permissible to begin a sentence with "And."

12: F. The sentence is a question, so only choice H is appropriate.

13: B. Choice A is too serious and condescending for the passage. Choice C is too straightforward, while choice D is too condescending. Choice B captures the tone of the piece.

14: H. While the article does describe how computers function and it is easy to understand, the tone is not formal enough for a conservative magazine. Therefore, choice H is appropriate. We do not know how much the article is supposed to say about computer use; this could be enough. Therefore, choice J is incorrect.

15: B. Choice A is an incorrect reference to a remark in the piece, as is choice D. Choice C is too formal for this piece. Since the passage concerns the "any key" and the title is appropriately informal, choice B is correct.

PASSAGE II

 ANSWERS

16: J. The pronoun refers to the noun, "Mr. Dombey." Therefore, the correct answer is J — "his" son.

17: C. The phrase "Dickens tells us" is separated from the main phrase, which reads "Paul knew." A and D are incorrect because it is not "Paul Dickens" telling us.

18: G. According to the sentence, Paul knew about guineas and shillings, but readers today may not. Therefore, the correct answer is G. The word "since" implies that Paul knew because today's reader did not. The word "so" implies that today's reader does not know because Paul did. The word "unless" means that Paul knew except when today's reader did not know.

19: A. The paragraph is about the past, the 1800s, so the correct verb tense is past. This narrows the choices to A and D. However, money is singular, so the correct choice must be A, "was," rather than D, "were."

20: G. This sentence does flow logically from the first sentence. The sentence does not judge which calculation is better, nor does it state that the reader would know the new calculation. In light of this, Choices H and J cannot be correct. The first sentence shifts to the present, and the third sentence shifts back to the past, as stated in G.

21: A. Whether someone paid by bill, coin, check, or on account, the same monetary values (pounds, shillings, and pence) were used. Of the answers, the phrase that best expresses this idea is "regardless of whether the value was represented."

22: F. *Instruments* means the actual items used for currency. The values of each type of currency are not discussed in this passage, so H is incorrect. The word *conditions* is used to mean the atmosphere of the era under which currency was able to be produced. The word *leverages* means the importance attached to each type of currency that gave it more value than another did.

23: C. Since pennies are used to measure the value of something, either choice B or choice C is most logical. Choice A makes no sense because there is no verb in the first part of the sentence which is required by the linking word *and.* In other words, the sentence would have to read that pennies were made of something AND created by an equivalent number of pence.

24: F. The sentence as it stands is correct. It consists of two independent clauses that can be separated by a semicolon. Choices G and J create a run-on sentence. Since the second sentence can stand alone and is not a list, choice H is incorrect.

25: B. We have already established that the sentence is correct. Therefore, choices C and D are incorrect. Parentheses are used to provide additional information. Choice B is the only answer possible.

26: G. In a list of more than three items, items must be separated by commas. Therefore, choice G is correct.

27: B. Since the following paragraph does not discuss guineas, choices A and D can be ruled out. The paragraph does not discuss how much they were worth, so choice C is incorrect. The sentence does discuss the different materials the coins were made from, so choice B makes the most sense.

28: J. The noun *banknotes* is plural, so the pronoun must also be plural. This leaves H and J as possible choices. Choice J is the only correct choice because each banknote has a different name so "names" must also be plural.

29: C. The sentence adds to the information in Sentence 2. It makes sense to put it after Sentence 2 .

30: H. The essay does not discuss the changes in money, so choice F is incorrect. The sentence does not compare British money to American, except in a small aside, so choice G is incorrect. Choice J is irrelevant to the topic discussed. Choice H makes sense—the 1800s would be the 19th century, and the discussion is about English money.

ANSWERS

31: A. Punctuation must be placed inside the quotation marks, so the possible choices are A and C. However, the opening sentence is not a question, so choice C is ruled out.

32: H. Since dessert is not being compared to a singular prop or subject, *better* and *more* cannot be used. The correct superlative with *important* is *most,* so choice H is correct.

33: C. Desserts are the most fantastic items, and the word *since* shows their contribution to the concept of a restaurant as a fantasy. The words *unless* and *however* lead to incorrect conclusions.

34: F. The sentence is correct as it stands with the aside in parentheses. Choice G makes a run-on sentence, as does choice H. Choice J makes the second part of the sentence a fragment, which cannot be separated by a semicolon.

35: C. The sentence is incorrect because a semicolon can separate only two independent clauses, and "pure and simple" is not an independent clause. The same is true for choice B; "pure and simple" cannot stand alone as a sentence. Choice D must be ruled out because the three items—*pleasure, pure, simple*—are not part of a list and should not be separated by commas.

36: J. The correct adverbial form is *beautifully.*

37: A. The correct adverbial form of *sure* is *surely,* as used in the sentence.

38: J. Stage directions order the movement of a play, which is clearly not what the author is trying to imply here. Nor are main courses and appetizers the props or the entrance. In fact, dessert has already been called the most important prop, so choice H is doubly incorrect. However, appetizers and main courses are the *setup* for dessert.

39: C. Sentence 1 must follow Sentences 2 and 3 because otherwise the word *this* has no reference. What last impression does the evening depend upon? For the same reason, Sentence 3 must follow Sentence 2 because otherwise the word *it* has no referent. What do we save room for and expect to deliver? Therefore, the best order is 2, 3, 1.

40: G. *Rich flavor* defines *same,* so a colon is used.

41: A. The sentence is correct as it is. The phrase "often with herbs and un-usual spices" modifies *not-so-subtle flavors*. Therefore, it should be set apart by a comma or parentheses. It cannot be separated by a semicolon.

42: F. The sentence is correct as it is. The word *galvanize* coveys the same idea as *excite* or *arouse*. The taste does not destroy creativity, or beau-tiful creations would have no taste. The verb *manifest* means to *make evident*. Taste does not make creativity evident, instead it inspires creativity. Finally, *liquidate* means to convert assets into cash or deter-mine liabilities. Therefore, this verb makes no sense in the sentence.

43: B. The parenthetical aside provides additional information about Sentence 3. Therefore, it follows Sentence 3.

44: H. The essay does not discuss health in any form—only taste. Choice F is incorrect because no connection is made between dessert and the health of the diners. Choice G is also incorrect because the healthiness of the ingredients is not discussed. Choice J is incorrect because the essay does not say that not eating dessert is either good or bad.

45: B. Paragraph 4 discusses the creation of the desserts, and discusses taste inspiring creativity.

ANSWERS

46: H. The underlined part is misplaced. The phrase "with an animal helper" is supposed to explain what a shaman is working with.

47: C. The verb must agree with the subject. The sentence reads "son *or* daughter." So the verb must be singular—*is,* not *are.* The sentence could read, "the younger son is sent out *or* the younger daughter is sent out. . . ."

48: F. The sentence is correct as written. *Animal* is made plural by adding *s.*

49: C. The word *enable* is a synonym for *help,* so using *enable* is redun-dant. The animals don't entrap the shaman, or they would not be help-ing. The animals also don't *entreat* them; the word entreat means *to beg* or *plead,* and the animals are aiding the humans, not begging them to do something. Therefore, the best word is *empower,* meaning *to give power to.*

50: J. The underlined portion of the sentence is misplaced. It should follow the verb.

51: D. The pronoun must agree with the noun. Here, Kevin (a man) extends *his* hand.

52: H. For the pronoun "they" to make sense, "they" must come after a description of "they." Therefore, choice F cannot be correct. If placed after Sentence 2, the pronoun is still vague—does it refer to the humans or the animals? Therefore, placing it after Sentence 3 makes the most sense.

53: D. The paragraph does not focus on animals talking, so choice A is incorrect. Choice B is in direct opposition to the final sentence, which states that the stories have little to do with being kind to animals. Choice C opposes the sentence added to the paragraph, which states that the people gain a total understanding of the animal world. Therefore, choice D is best.

54: J. The idea in the first sentence is that animals teaching humans is common in these works. Therefore, the first three choices do not make much sense. However, choice J conveys the right idea.

55: D. The pronoun must agree with the noun. In this case, the noun *we* needs to have the pronoun *us*.

56: F. The sentence is correct as written. The second part of the sentence, starting with *which,* is a dependent clause and cannot be separated by a period or semicolon. Choice H is incorrect because the second part is not a list relating to the first part of the sentence.

57: A. The sentence correctly implies that we are part of heaven. Choice C is not correct because it refers to us as separated from heaven. Choice D connects us to the earth, rather than heaven. Choice B connects us to the heretical—the opposite of being connected to heaven and religion.

58: H. Each paragraph should contain one main idea. In Paragraph 3, it is about how animals regulate the destiny of humans. This sentence introduces this main idea, and so it should be the first sentence in Paragraph 3.

59: B. In Paragraph 1, the examples are very general, and refer to a person meeting with an animal. In Paragraph 2, the examples are more specific, but refer to the animals that are associated with different people. Neither paragraph mentions duties or destiny. Therefore, the best place for this example is in Paragraph 3 as an explanation of how a person's destiny is connected with the animals.

60: F. Choices H and J refer solely to limited lessons a person might learn from Paragraph 3. Choice G refers to an incorrect lesson that may be learned from the opening paragraph. Choice F, however, refers to a general lesson provided by the entire essay.

ANSWERS

61: C. The correct adverbial form of *bright* is *brightly,* which modifies the adjective, *lit.*

62: F. The word *surly* means *arrogant* or *sullen, in a bad mood.* The word *elated* means *extremely happy.* The word *melodic* means *musical.* Therefore, the best word is the one used in the sentence, *sultry.* It means *hot with passion* or *exciting desire,* which is something a flirtatious or inviting person would want to do.

63: C. The phrase "as students perfect the wink" is not an independent clause and therefore cannot be separated by either a period or a semi-colon. Therefore, choices A and B are incorrect. However, "as students perfect the wink" is a dependent clause, which must be separated from the independent clause by a comma.

64: F. The verb must be singular and present tense because the passage is written in the present and the noun "instructor Myrna Orleck-Aiello" is singular. Therefore, *offers* is correct. The word *offer* is present plural. The word *offered* is past tense. The verb *were offering* is both past and plural.

65: D. The noun, *classroom,* is singular, so the verb must also be the singular *is.*

66: G. The pronoun must agree with the noun. Here, *students* is plural, so the pronoun must be the plural *their.*

67: D. The sentence states a fact—that Orleck-Aiello is deaf. The correct punctuation is a period.

68: J. The two adjectives must both be in the comparative form, or in the superlative form. In this sentence, more than two things are being compared (not one form of study to another, but one form of study over ALL others), so both must be in superlative form. The correct forms are in choice J.

69: B. Paragraph 3 describes why total immersion is the best way to learn. Choices A and C would seem to refute this idea. Choice D is not correct because it states that sign language is unlike other languages, meaning that while total immersion is best for most languages, it is not best for sign language.

70: H. The adjective *dozen* takes the plural noun *pupils.*

71: C. The word *their* in this sentence is a pronoun, referring to the pupils. *There* indicates a place, as in *over there. They're* is a contraction meaning *they are. His* is the singular form of the pronoun, but since *pupils* is plural, it takes a plural pronoun.

72: F. The correct form of the verb here is the present participle. Therefore, the verb should be *has,* not *had.* The correct form of the verb *choose* is *chosen.*

73: B. The word *singular* implies *one language.* The word *generous* means *abundant.* The word *melded* means two or more things joined together to form one. Therefore, *various* is the best choice.

74: F. The other three choices all imply that a lot of people know French or Spanish because the woman and her husband speak different languages in public. This is not the case, however. Instead, it is because many people speak French or Spanish that the couple is trying to learn a different language.

75: C. Paragraph 3 discusses how the best way to learn sign language is through total immersion, just as it is in any other language. This would be the best place to compare sign language to other languages, like French or Spanish, in order to reinforce that idea.

ACT III Reading Answers Explained

 ANSWERS

1: C. In the story the author says, "This [Aw shut up] is what I always said when it seemed to me that somebody had unwittingly insulted me."

2: F. The author writes that "Neither of them knew how uncertain I was as to whether or not I could swim well enough. . . ." Choice G is true only for Joe. Choice H is incorrect because while he was questioned about his ability to swim, his friends never said he could not swim well enough.

3: B. In the second paragraph we learn that ". . . with a wooden bridge and a headgate. The swimming was south of the bridge," obviously referring to the wooden bridge. The story also mentions that the flow was south from the wooden bridge, meaning that south was downstream.

4: J. The author writes, "It [the water] certainly didn't invite a dive, but there was no other honorable way to enter a body of water."

5: A. At the end of the story we learn that after diving into the water the boys ". . . were all standing in the cold roaring water, up to our knees in soft mud." Choice C describes how the boys might have ended up had the dives been standing dives.

6: G. In the second paragraph we learn that, "The road and the ditch traveled together many miles." The other choices are images described in the second paragraph, but unrelated to this item.

7: D. According to the third paragraph, by the time the boys got to the ditch the weather was "unmistakably wintry."

8: J. Choices F, G, and H describe thoughts the other boys had about the author, or thoughts the author had about himself. Only choice H is something that Mourad said to the author.

9: C. We learn near the end of the passage, "If you jumped in feet first it wasn't exactly a disgrace, it was just bad style."

10: G. Only choice G accurately reflects Joe's advice about swimming, which was, "We'll swim across, rest, swim back, get dressed, eat, and, unless the storm passes, start for home. Otherwise we'll swim some more."

11: B. In lines 12–14, the author states that Edward's motives for claiming the throne "have been variously ascribed by historians."

12: H. In line 21, the author states that Edward's success in the battle of Crecy "left him free to besiege Calais."

13: D. While A and B are both mentioned in the first paragraph, they are secondary to the main point—the complexity of the conduct of war under medieval chivalry. This can be seen through the organization of the sentence as "not only" did A and B occur, "but" the main point is the complexity of war.

14: F. The author states in lines 21–24 that Edward "was free to attack Calais, which, lying as it does at the narrowest crossing point to England, was a vital strategic objective."

15: B. The author states that Philip's defense was "half-hearted" (line 44). Philip then retreated rather than risk battle.

16: G. The idea that Edward had power of life and death could be made without the note about sparing the men. Even if the men had surrendered earlier, the stakes would have been the same. Also, Jean de Vienne has been shown to be a good ruler because he tried to save the lives of his citizens. However, because Edward spares the men, it shows he is not simply ruthless.

17: C. The last paragraph shows that it was still settled by Englishmen after 1453, a century later, so choices A and B are incorrect. The word "Calais" was not inscribed on Mary Tudor's heart, but she allegedly said it was to show how important the city was to her.

18: F. Jean de Vienne's worry about surrender would not have been necessary if either G or J were correct. Also, while Edward may have wanted vengeance, he did not take it to the full extent. However, Jean de Vienne could not have known what Edward wanted, but he knew that under those laws the men were in trouble.

19: D. Since the author puts in that these details were "according to Froissant" (line 60), they cannot be taken as fact.

20: J. Lines 27–28 state that Philip was supplying Calais by sea and lines 49–50 state that once Philip retreated, Calais was left to its own fate. Therefore, I and II are both correct. However, Philip retreated and, therefore, did not surrender at Calais, so choice III is incorrect.

ANSWERS

21: C. The first sentence states that both are puzzling and, since both are written in the 1800s, both are nineteenth-century works. The last sentence of the first paragraph says that *Wuthering Heights,* Brontë's work, is a "masculine" text. It also states that Shelley's work is a thriller and Brontë's is a romance.

22: F. The word *enigmatic* means *relating to an enigma (a riddle); mysterious.*

23: C. The author states that Brontë's work is "masculine" because "the fates of subordinate female characters seem entirely dependent upon the actions of ostensibly male heroes or anti-heroes" (lines 12–15). In other words, in a "masculine" work, the males control the action, no matter whether they are good or bad.

24: J. The author states that Brontë's and Shelley's works were unrelated, but does not mention whether the authors were related or not. She also states that both are unprecedented works, not just Shelley's. Although she does say they are different types of books—a thriller and romance— the important part to the author is that both are puzzling in different ways, since this is what she focuses on for the rest of the essay.

25: D. From the first paragraph, we know that both are nineteenth-century novels which are puzzling, so choice I is correct. The author states (lines 48–49) that "more than most novels, both are consciously literary works," so II is correct. In lines 30–32, the author states that "Both make use of what in connection with Frankenstein we have called an evidentiary narrative technique," so III is correct.

26: H. The clues are not revealed through concentric circles, but the story itself is. These stories are told through different narratives on the same episode, rather than one narration of different episodes (as is usual in a story). Choice J is incorrect because it is Isabella's *letter* and Justine's *narrative.* Each digression is through a different type of narration— letters, diaries, narratives, etc.

27: B. The author wonders if both books are conscious literary novels be- cause, "like Shelley, Brontë was something of a literary heiress" (lines 52–53)—born to literary parents.

28: F. While H is true, it is only the starting point for the passage. Obvi- ously the authors don't feel one should not compare books, because they are comparing these two authors. Also, while they discuss the fact that both had literary parents, they think this may be a reason for the lit- erary nature of the works, not for underlying similarities. The main point, set up in the first paragraph, is that while these works have been seen as unrelated, or dissimilar, they actually have similarities such as narrative digressions, puzzles, and a literary nature.

29: C. The two "popular" novels have convinced readers that the surfaces conceal the complex depths, rather than reveal them, according to lines 26–27. Although they appear simple, they are, in actuality, very complex.

30: J. G and H cannot be correct because *Frankenstein* was written *before Wuthering Heights.* In Paragraph 2, the author states that *Wuthering Heights* might be a copy of *Frankenstein,* in terms of the technique of evidentiary writing, not as a whole novel.

PASSAGE IV

 *ANSWERS*

31: A. The author states that common pesticides acted on by the sun's rays or parasites could cause the deformities.

32: J. The author defines methoprene as a mosquito pesticide that "mimics an insect hormone."

33: B. In line 8, the author describes Bantle's research on the interaction of methoprene with the sun. Lines 29–30 say that within 96 hours, methoprene, when exposed to the sun, causes malformations at 100 times the rate of methoprene alone.

34: G. The plastic beads are not the cause of the malformations, but were used by one scientist to mimic the actions of a parasite burrowing into the tadpole.

35: C. Sessions' experiment features the implanted beads. Choice A has nothing to do with his theory, while choice B misstates the facts stated in the article. Sessions would not offer choice D, which does not support his theory.

36: G. Ed Little's finding that pesticides in reaction with UV rays harm tadpoles is used to support the main theory of the essay (lines 31–35). Martin Ouellet's findings support Little's findings (lines 36–40). Therefore, choice G is correct.

37: C. Robert McKinnell's study of the internal abnormalities (lines 56–61) states is used to refute Sessions' theory about parasites. Although Bantle admits that Sessions has a potential theory, McKinnell's evidence shows that parasites are unlikely to have caused the internal abnormalities found in frogs.

38: F. The author admits that there may be other theories, like that of Sessions, but his overall emphasis is on the strong possible link between pesticides and UV rays.

39: C. While the first two choices may be part of the author's intentions, the primary point is that if pesticides are causing these deformations, we should be careful not to harm more frogs. The ozone is only mentioned in the article as a reason for increased UV rays—which are harmful only in reaction with the pesticides.

40: F. Choices H and J are incorrect because what Bantle says is that although Sessions may be on to something, he hasn't proved it yet. In other words, Sessions' research is not wrong (choice J), but neither can Bantle agree solely with Sessions (choice H) because he still has a lot more work to do. Although researchers are shown to pay attention to other researchers, this quote is intended to show that "other researchers remain unconvinced," as the lead-in tells us.

Chapter 18

SCORING THE TESTS

This chapter shows you how to find the ACT scale scores and subscores.

The **raw score** on the English Test is the number correct. Use the chart below to convert the raw score for each English Test to a scale score. Charts on following pages show you how to find the English subscores.

Scale scores are the scores reported to colleges. Because different ACTs have different difficulty levels, the same raw score does not always convert to the same scale score. The scale scores here are approximations and are given only to familiarize you with the process of converting raw scores to scale scores. The scale scores for these tests will almost certainly be different from the scale scores on the ACT you take.

Scoring the English Tests

Use the chart below to convert the raw score for each English Test to a scale score. Charts on following pages show you how to find the English subscores.

The highest possible raw score is 75; the lowest is 0. The highest possible scale score is 36; the lowest is 1. In the chart below, a raw score of 75 yields a scale score of 36. A raw score of 0 yields a scale score of 1.

English Scale Scores

Raw score	Scale score	Raw score	Scale score	Raw score	Scale score	Raw score	Scale score
75	36	56	24	37	16	18	10
74	35	55	23	36	16	17	9
73	34	54	23	35	15	16	9
72	—	53	22	34	15	15	9
71	33	52	22	33	15	14	8
70	32	51	21	32	15	13	8
69	32	50	21	31	14	12	7
68	31	49	20	30	14	11	7
67	30	48	20	29	13	10	6
66	29	47	20	28	13	9	6
65	28	46	19	27	13	8	5
64	28	45	19	26	12	7	5
63	27	44	18	25	12	6	4
62	27	43	18	24	12	5	4
61	26	42	18	23	11	4	4
60	26	41	17	22	11	3	3
59	25	40	17	21	11	2	2
58	25	39	17	20	10	1	1
57	24	38	16	19	10	0	1

Convert your raw scores to scale scores:

Diagnostic English ACT

Raw score _____

Scale score _____

Model English ACT I

Raw score _62_

Scale score _27_

Model English ACT II

Raw score _____

Scale score _____

Model English ACT III

Raw score _____

Scale score _____

What Does Your Score Mean?

The chart below shows the approximate percent of students who receive a particular scale score or below. The percent of students at or below a score shows the percentile rank of that score.

Use the chart this way. Find your English scale score in the chart. Then find the percentage of students who scored at or below that score. Say your English scale score was 18. In the chart, 18 matches 40%. This means that about 40% of the students will get a score of 18 or lower, and that 60% of the students will get a score above 18.

English Test—Percent of Students At or Below a Scale Score

Scale score	At or below	Scale score	At or below	Scale score	At or below	Scale score	At or below
36	99%	27	92%	18	40%	9	1%
35	99%	26	89%	17	33%	8	1%
34	99%	25	84%	16	27%	7	1%
33	99%	24	78%	15	21%	6	1%
32	99%	23	72%	14	15%	5	1%
31	99%	22	66%	13	11%	4	1%
30	98%	21	60%	12	7%	3	1%
29	97%	20	53%	11	4%	2	1%
28	94%	19	47%	10	1%	1	1%

Scoring the Reading Tests

The highest possible raw score is 40; the lowest is 0. The highest possible scale score is 36; the lowest is 1. In the chart below, a raw score of 40 yields a scale score of 36. A raw score of 0 yields a scale score of 1.

Reading Scale Scores

Raw score	Scale score	Raw score	Scale score	Raw score	Scale score	Raw score	Scale score
40	36	29	25	19	16	9	7
39	35	28	24	18	15	8	6
38	34	27	23	17	14	7	5
37	33	26	22	16	14	6	4
36	32	25	21	15	13	5	4
35	31	24	20	14	12	4	3
34	30	23	19	13	11	3	2
33	29	22	18	12	10	2	2
32	28	21	18	11	9	1	1
31	27	20	17	10	8	0	1
30	26						

Convert your raw scores to scale scores:

Diagnostic Reading ACT

Raw score _____

Scale score _____

Model Reading ACT I

Raw score _____

Scale score _____

Model Reading ACT II

Raw score _____

Scale score _____

Model Reading ACT III

Raw score _____

Scale score _____

What Does Your Score Mean?

The chart below shows the approximate percent of students who receive a particular scale score or below. The percent of students at or below a score shows the percentile rank of that score.

Use the chart this way. Find your Reading scale score in the chart. Then find the percentage of students who scored at or below that score. Say your Reading scale score was 18. In the chart 18 matches 40%. This means that about 40% of the students will get a score of 18 or lower, and that 60% of the students will get a score above 18.

Reading Test—Percent of Students At or Below a Scale Score

Scale score	At or below	Scale score	At or below	Scale score	At or below	Scale score	At or below
36	99%	27	92%	18	40%	9	1%
35	99%	26	89%	17	33%	8	1%
34	99%	25	84%	16	27%	7	1%
33	99%	24	78%	15	21%	6	1%
32	99%	23	72%	14	15%	5	1%
31	99%	22	66%	13	11%	4	1%
30	98%	21	60%	12	7%	3	1%
29	97%	20	53%	11	4%	2	1%
28	94%	19	47%	10	1%	1	1%

DIAGNOSTIC ACT
English Scoring Key
Check the box of each correct answer.

Item	Answer	Usage/ Mechanics	Rhetorical Skills	Item	Answer	Usage/ Mechanics	Rhetorical Skills	Item	Answer	Usage/ Mechanics	Rhetorical Skills
1	D	☐		26	G	☐		51	A	☐	
2	G	☐		27	D	☐		52	J		☐
3	A		☐	28	H		☐	53	B	☐	
4	F	☐		29	B		☐	54	G		☐
5	B	☐		30	J		☐	55	D	☐	
6	H	☐		31	D	☐		56	H	☐	
7	D	☐		32	H		☐	57	A		☐
8	J		☐	33	B	☐		58	J		☐
9	B	☐		34	H		☐	59	D		☐
10	H	☐		35	D		☐	60	F		☐
11	B		☐	36	J	☐		61	C	☐	
12	G		☐	37	B	☐		62	F	☐	
13	D	☐		38	F		☐	63	B		☐
14	G		☐	39	D		☐	64	J		☐
15	C		☐	40	H	☐		65	C	☐	
16	G	☐		41	C	☐		66	H	☐	
17	A		☐	42	F	☐		67	C	☐	
18	J	☐		43	B		☐	68	J		☐
19	D	☐		44	G		☐	69	B	☐	
20	H	☐		45	A		☐	70	F	☐	
21	C		☐	46	F	☐		71	A	☐	
22	J		☐	47	C		☐	72	H	☐	
23	A	☐		48	J	☐		73	D		☐
24	G	☐		49	B		☐	74	J		☐
25	C	☐		50	G		☐	75	A		☐

Number Correct:

Usage/Mechanics _____

Rhetorical Skills _____

Total _____

MODEL ACT I
English Scoring Key
Check the box of each correct answer.

Item	Answer	Usage/ Mechanics	Rhetorical Skills	Item	Answer	Usage/ Mechanics	Rhetorical Skills	Item	Answer	Usage/ Mechanics	Rhetorical Skills
1	C		☐	26	J	☐		51	C		☐
2	F	☐		27	C	☐		52	J	☐	
3	B	☐		28	H	☐		53	B	☐	
4	H	☐		29	B		☐	54	F	☐	
5	A		☐	30	J		☐	55	D	☐	
6	G		☐	31	B	☐		56	G		☐
7	B	☐		32	J		☐	57	B	☐	
8	J	☐		33	C	☐		58	J		☐
9	D	☐		34	G	☐		59	A		☐
10	F		☐	35	C	☐		60	H		☐
11	A	☐		36	H	☐		61	C	☐	
12	H		☐	37	D	☐		62	J	☐	
13	D	☐		38	H	☐		63	C	☐	
14	G	☐		39	D		☐	64	F		☐
15	C		☐	40	H	☐		65	D		☐
16	G	☐		41	D		☐	66	F	☐	
17	D	☐		42	G	☐		67	B	☐	
18	H		☐	43	C		☐	68	J		☐
19	A	☐		44	F		☐	69	A		☐
20	G	☐		45	D		☐	70	H		☐
21	D		☐	46	F	☐		71	B	☐	
22	F	☐		47	C	☐		72	H	☐	
23	A		☐	48	J		☐	73	C		☐
24	H		☐	49	C		☐	74	F		☐
25	A		☐	50	J		☐	75	B		☐

Number Correct:

Usage/Mechanics   _____

Rhetorical Skills   _____

  Total   _____

MODEL ACT II
English Scoring Key
Check the box of each correct answer.

Item	Answer	Usage/ Mechanics	Rhetorical Skills	Item	Answer	Usage/ Mechanics	Rhetorical Skills	Item	Answer	Usage/ Mechanics	Rhetorical Skills
1	B		☐	26	G	☐		51	A	☐	
2	F		☐	27	A	☐		52	G	☐	
3	C	☐		28	F		☐	53	C		☐
4	J		☐	29	D		☐	54	F	☐	
5	B	☐		30	H		☐	55	D	☐	
6	J		☐	31	C	☐		56	J		☐
7	A		☐	32	F		☐	57	D		☐
8	H	☐		33	D	☐		58	G		☐
9	B	☐		34	F	☐		59	C		☐
10	J		☐	35	C	☐		60	J		☐
11	D	☐		36	J		☐	61	D	☐	
12	F	☐		37	A	☐		62	G	☐	
13	D		☐	38	J		☐	63	D	☐	
14	H		☐	39	D	☐		64	F		☐
15	A		☐	40	F	☐		65	A	☐	
16	J		☐	41	C	☐		66	J	☐	
17	B	☐		42	J	☐		67	C	☐	
18	F		☐	43	D		☐	68	H		☐
19	B	☐		44	F		☐	69	B		☐
20	F	☐		45	C		☐	70	J	☐	
21	D		☐	46	H	☐		71	D	☐	
22	H	☐		47	A	☐		72	G	☐	
23	C		☐	48	J	☐		73	A		☐
24	G		☐	49	D	☐		74	H		☐
25	B	☐		50	H	☐		75	A		☐

Number Correct:

Usage/Mechanics _____

Rhetorical Skills _____

Total _____

MODEL ACT III
English Scoring Key
Check the box of each correct answer.

Item	Answer	Usage/Mechanics	Rhetorical Skills	Item	Answer	Usage/Mechanics	Rhetorical Skills	Item	Answer	Usage/Mechanics	Rhetorical Skills
1	B	☐		26	G	☐		51	D	☐	
2	F		☐	27	B		☐	52	H		☐
3	D		☐	28	J	☐		53	D		☐
4	H	☐		29	C		☐	54	J		☐
5	A		☐	30	H		☐	55	D	☐	
6	H	☐		31	A	☐		56	F	☐	
7	A	☐		32	H	☐		57	A		☐
8	G	☐		33	C	☐		58	H		☐
9	A	☐		34	F	☐		59	B		☐
10	F		☐	35	C	☐		60	F		☐
11	A		☐	36	J	☐		61	C	☐	
12	H	☐		37	A	☐		62	F		☐
13	B		☐	38	J	☐		63	C	☐	
14	H		☐	39	C		☐	64	F	☐	
15	B		☐	40	G	☐		65	D	☐	
16	J	☐		41	A	☐		66	G	☐	
17	C	☐		42	F	☐		67	D	☐	
18	G	☐		43	B		☐	68	J	☐	
19	A	☐		44	H		☐	69	B		☐
20	G		☐	45	B		☐	70	H	☐	
21	A		☐	46	H		☐	71	C	☐	
22	F		☐	47	C	☐		72	F	☐	
23	C		☐	48	F	☐		73	B		☐
24	F	☐		49	C		☐	74	F		☐
25	B		☐	50	J		☐	75	C		☐

Number Correct:

Usage/Mechanics _____

Rhetorical Skills _____

  Total _____

DIAGNOSTIC ACT
Reading Scoring Key
Check the box of each correct answer.

Item	Answer	Social Studies	Arts/ Literature	Item	Answer	Social Studies	Arts/ Literature	Item	Answer	Social Studies	Arts/ Literature
1	C		☐	15	B	☐		28	G		☐
2	H		☐	16	F	☐		29	A		☐
3	A		☐	17	C	☐		30	G		☐
4	J		☐	18	J	☐		31	D	☐	
5	B		☐	19	B	☐		32	E	☐	
6	G		☐	20	G	☐		33	C	☐	
7	A		☐	21	D		☐	34	H	☐	
8	G		☐	22	F		☐	35	B	☐	
9	B		☐	23	D		☐	36	J	☐	
10	H		☐	24	H		☐	37	C	☐	
11	C	☐		25	D		☐	38	F	☐	
12	J	☐		26	J		☐	39	B	☐	
13	C	☐		27	A		☐	40	J	☐	
14	H	☐									

Number Correct:

Social Studies/Sciences _____

Arts/Literature _____

Total _____

MODEL ACT I
Reading Scoring Key
Check the box of each correct answer.

Item	Answer	Social Studies	Arts/ Literature	Item	Answer	Social Studies	Arts/ Literature	Item	Answer	Social Studies	Arts/ Literature
1	B		☐	15	A	☐		28	G		☐
2	H		☐	16	G	☐		29	C		☐
3	B		☐	17	D	☐		30	G		☐
4	F		☐	18	G	☐		31	D	☐	
5	D		☐	19	B	☐		32	H	☐	
6	J		☐	20	F	☐		33	A	☐	
7	C		☐	21	A		☐	34	H	☐	
8	J		☐	22	J		☐	35	B	☐	
9	C		☐	23	A		☐	36	J	☐	
10	F		☐	24	J		☐	37	B	☐	
11	D	☐		25	B		☐	38	J	☐	
12	H	☐		26	H		☐	39	D	☐	
13	C	☐		27	D		☐	40	H	☐	
14	F	☐									

Number Correct:

Social Studies/Sciences _____

Arts/Literature _____

   Total _____

382   Model English and Reading Tests

MODEL ACT II
Reading Scoring Key
Check the box of each correct answer.

Item	Answer	Social Studies	Arts/ Literature	Item	Answer	Social Studies	Arts/ Literature	Item	Answer	Social Studies	Arts/ Literature
1	D		☐	15	B	☐		28	J		☐
2	H		☐	16	J	☐		29	C		☐
3	B		☐	17	D	☐		30	F		☐
4	H		☐	18	F	☐		31	D	☐	
5	A		☐	19	C	☐		32	H	☐	
6	G		☐	20	F	☐		33	B	☐	
7	C		☐	21	D		☐	34	C	☐	
8	J		☐	22	G		☐	35	C	☐	
9	A		☐	23	C		☐	36	G	☐	
10	J		☐	24	J		☐	37	A	☐	
11	C	☐		25	C		☐	38	J	☐	
12	F	☐		26	F		☐	39	B	☐	
13	C	☐		27	C		☐	40	G	☐	
14	G	☐									

<u>Number Correct:</u>

Social Studies/Sciences _____

Arts/Literature _____

    Total _____

MODEL ACT III
Reading Scoring Key
Check the box of each correct answer.

Item	Answer	Social Studies	Arts/Literature	Item	Answer	Social Studies	Arts/Literature	Item	Answer	Social Studies	Arts/Literature
1	C	☐		15	B		☐	28	F	☐	
2	F	☐		16	G		☐	29	C	☐	
3	B	☐		17	C		☐	30	J	☐	
4	J	☐		18	F		☐	31	A		☐
5	A	☐		19	D		☐	32	J		☐
6	G	☐		20	J		☐	33	B		☐
7	D	☐		21	C	☐		34	G		☐
8	H	☐		22	F	☐		35	C		☐
9	C	☐		23	C	☐		36	G		☐
10	G	☐		24	J	☐		37	C		☐
11	B		☐	25	D	☐		38	F		☐
12	H		☐	26	H	☐		39	C		☐
13	D		☐	27	B	☐		40	F		☐
14	F		☐								

<u>Number Correct:</u>

Social Studies/Sciences   _____

Arts/Literature   _____

   Total   _____

The ACT Writing Test

Chapter 19

INTRODUCTION

The ACT Writing Test gives you thirty minutes to write a persuasive essay in response to a prompt. The prompt will ask you to convince someone or some group about something. For example, you may write an essay about how a college should use grant funds, or whether a school should have a dress code.

Two readers evaluate your essay and assign a score from 1 to 6. ACT trains its readers to score holistically by showing them many examples of essays. Holistic scoring means a reader's evaluation is based on his or her informed impression of your writing. The readers do not go into detailed analysis. If readers' scores differ by more than 1 point, a third reader also evaluates the essay.

ACT does not require the Writing Test; however, some colleges and scholarship programs do. Find out whether the test is recommended or required by any of the colleges or programs to which you're applying. You can visit *What Colleges Have Decided about the Writing Test* on the ACT Web site (*www.act.org*) for a list of institutions that have announced their policies regarding the Writing Test. You should contact admissions offices and scholarship agencies directly for the most up-to-date and reliable information.

The Inside Story of the ACT Writing Test

Testing companies such as ACT were criticized because college-admissions tests were all multiple-choice. Colleges wanted more. In particular, colleges wanted evaluated samples of student writing. In response, the folks at ACT created this test. Creating a writing test has special challenges. A multiple-choice item has exactly four or five possible answers and only one correct answer. The test can be quickly scored by computer. But an essay prompt leads to widely varying responses, and each essay must be scored individually.

ACT had to limit the complexity of the essays to make them easier to score. That is why you have only thirty minutes to write your essay. In one state, English teachers found that a student needed at least forty minutes to write a complete essay. However, giving students forty minutes allows them to create longer essays that take longer to score. So thirty minutes is what you have, and we will show you how to take best advantage of that time.

About 1,700,000 ACTs are administered each year, with some students taking the test more than once. At least two readers look at every essay. If every test-taker completes the Writing Test, there is a minimum of 3,200,000 essay readings. That equals about 270,000 hours if it takes approximately five minutes to read each essay. ACT promises to make test scores available quickly. The pressure is on, and you can be sure that readers won't spend much time on any one essay.

A reader doesn't have to be an English teacher. The minimum requirement to be a reader is a four-year college degree, with a preference for people who have experience teaching and scoring student essays. ACT shows these readers how to score essays in response to each prompt, and readers have to demonstrate that they can do this reliably before they get the job.

ACT reproduces your essay and sends it to the readers over the Internet. The readers score your essay on a computer, and they work as quickly as they can. A third reader scores your essay only if the original scores differ by more than one point. If one reader gives a 4, but another reader gives a 3 or a 5, that is fine with ACT. In other words, precision is not the priority.

One reader may be a recent college graduate, working on a laptop computer with a wireless modem while lounging on the beach in North Carolina. Another reader may be an experienced English teacher working at home in Illinois on a desktop computer with a broadband connection. The reader may be wherever there is Internet access.

Keep these readers in mind as you write your essay. They work very quickly. They will not read your essay in detail. It's the impression your essay makes that matters. Reading essays can be tedious. Give the readers what they are looking for. Make it easy for them to give your essay a high score.

Beginnings

You will start with a diagnostic test. Then you will use model essays and feedback from your teacher to understand what you need to do to improve your writing. Then, following a brief review of writing skills, you'll learn a step-by-step strategy for writing a persuasive essay. Once you're acquainted with the process, you'll write and evaluate your first practice essay in a structured format. You'll then have the chance to sharpen your skills by writing and evaluating two more practice essays.

ACT readers think about five essential questions as they rate your essay.

1. How well do you explain your position on the issue?

2. Do you maintain your focus on the issue throughout the essay?

3. Do you organize your ideas logically?

4. How thoroughly do you support your position with evidence, details, and examples?

5. Do you use language appropriately, in a way that does not distract from or interfere with a reader's understanding?

Notice that grammar is not mentioned specifically. Errors that distract a reader or interfere with a reader's understanding will lower your score. However, grammar is not the reader's primary focus.

ACT does not specify how long an essay should be. But it's worth noting in the following table that essays scored in the lower half contain fewer than 300 words, while essays scored in the upper half usually contain 400 words or more. It's not just more words but, rather, the extra detail in these higher-rated essays that makes them longer. You will probably have to write a minimum of 400 words to earn a score of 4 or higher. You will probably have to write an essay of about 450 words or more to earn a score of 5 or 6.

This table shows what distinguishes an essay rated in the upper half from an essay rated in the lower half. Notice that the first item on the list is your ability to clearly communicate your position on an issue.

ACT RATING COMPARISON

Upper Half	Lower Half
You clearly express your point of view on the issue.	You may not include a clear point of view.
You support generalizations with specific examples and details.	Your development of ideas is insufficient, overly general, or repetitious.
You maintain a clear focus on the prompt throughout the essay.	Your focus strays from the issue and/or the topic of the prompt.
Your essay features a clear and logical organization with effective transitions between paragraphs.	Your essay features either a simple, but acceptable organization, or no organization at all.
Your essay demonstrates an appropriate use of language.	Your essay can be generally understood.
While your essay may contain some distracting errors, the errors do not interfere with a reader's understanding.	Your essay contains distracting errors that may interfere with a reader's understanding.

Do not just start writing when you see the essay prompt. Use the first few minutes to understand the prompt and to sketch a brief outline. You will have about twenty-five minutes to write about 450 words. That is about eighteen words a minute. You can do that. Leave a few minutes at the end to correct errors.

Chapter 20

DIAGNOSTIC ACT WRITING TEST

Let's try an essay. This is the best way to find out how much work you have to do. After you write, look over the model essays that follow and review your essay with your teacher to determine whether it falls in the upper half or in the lower half of the rating scale. We will take things from there.

Read the prompt, sketch a brief outline below, and then write your essay on the lined pages that follow. Start now—you have exactly thirty minutes.

DIAGNOSTIC PROMPT

Some parents asked the Town Council to impose a curfew that requires students under the age of 18 to be off the streets by 10:00 P.M. in order to reduce disciplinary problems and to help ensure children's safety. Other parents do not favor a curfew. They believe that imposing a curfew will not necessarily ensure children's safety and it should be up to parents to decide what time their kids should be off the streets. In your opinion, should the Town Council impose a curfew for students under the age of 18?

Take a position on the issue outlined in the prompt. You may choose one of the two points of view expressed above, or you may present your own point of view on the issue. Be sure to support your position with specific reasons and details.

Model Essays

Here are two model essays. The first essay would receive a score in the lower half of the rating scale, and the second essay would receive a score in the upper half. Review each model essay and consider the questions that follow.

Model Essay 1   Lower Half (211 words)

> Some parents asked the Town Council to impose a curfew that requires students under the age of 18 to be off the streets by 10:00 PM in order to reduce disciplinary problems and to help ensure children's safety. Other parents do not favor a curfew. They believe that imposing a curfew will not necessarily ensure children's safety and it should be up to parents to decide what time their kids should be off the streets. In your opinion, should the Town Council impose a curfew for students under the age of 18? It is my opinion that the Town Council should vote for a curfew.
>
> First off, if parents know there is a time a child should be home they will find the child if they are not. And second a child is probably going to be at a friends house if they are not on the streets and not home. They can always go there. Finally, a child is a child even if that person is in high school and they are their parents responsibility. The parents have a right to know where they are and that they are not on the street with drugs. Other they could end with a big drug problem.
>
> The Town Council should vote for a curfew to have everyone who is under 18 off of the streets after 10:00 PM.

Consider the five questions for Model Essay 1.

1. How well is the position explained?

   The position is fairly well explained, but almost the entire first paragraph is taken directly from the prompt.

2. Is the focus maintained throughout the essay?

   The focus is not consistent throughout the essay; it switches from one point of view to another.

3. Are the ideas logically organized?

The strongest part of this essay is organization. There is a point of view and three associated ideas, but there are no clear transitions and no logical connections between paragraphs.

4. How thoroughly is the position supported with evidence, details, and examples?

This is the essay's main weakness. There is almost no support for any of the ideas developed in the essay.

5. Is language used appropriately, in a way that does not distract from or interfere with a reader's understanding?

The errors do distract the reader, but they do not interfere with the reader's understanding.

Model Essay 2   Upper Half (475 words)

The question of whether there should be a curfew for students under the age of 18 has been an issue over the years at many towns throughout America. People who support a curfew say it will help keep students off the streets and out of trouble. People who oppose a curfew think being off the streets will not keep students out of trouble, or think parents should decide how late their children are out. My view is the Town Council should vote for a curfew for students on school nights.

Some parents and other citizens in a town may believe that keeping students of the streets will not stop drug use and gang violence. That is not right. The reality is that the curfew will make enough of a difference to reduce these problems so that is well worth the effort, even if it saves only one child.

In the same way some parents think that they can control their children and keep them off the streets and off the street corners on their own. This is not right either. Students will always find some way to get to the street corner without their parents knowledge and we need rules the police can enforce to prevent these kinds of activities. No one says that a curfew all by itself will stop all these problems, but a curfew will be a first step to solving the problem.

A curfew will not only clear the streets of students it will also help solve other problems as well. With school children off the streets police will be able to concentrate on other problems. I remember a story about one town where crime was reduced overall once there was a curfew in place. That is what we need in this town, children off the streets, less crime and a safe place for everyone to live.

Perhaps the most important thing of all is that a curfew teaches responsibility. Students will know that being on the street after the curfew time will lead to consequences. The consequences might be a warning, punishment by parents, or in the very worst of cases some sort of detention. Parents will be responsible as well. They will face consequences if their minor children are on the street after the curfew. Over time both students and parents will have to learn that there is a right and a wrong.

Everyone in the town will be better off with a curfew. Minor children do not have the right to be wherever they want whenever they want. That is up to their parents and up to us the members of this a larger town who care about them and want what is best for everyone. The Town Council should vote for the curfew and we should all join in together with all of them to make it work.

Consider the five questions for Model Essay 2.

1. How well is the position explained?

   The position is well explained.

2. Is the focus maintained throughout the essay?

   The focus on the specific topic of the prompt is maintained throughout the essay.

3. Are the ideas logically organized?

   The essay has a clear and logical organization, and the writer provides transitions between paragraphs.

4. How thoroughly is the position supported with evidence, details, and examples?

   The writer provides support and details for each main point in the essay.

5. Is language used appropriately, in a way that does not distract from or interfere with a reader's understanding?

   Some of the errors in the essay might distract a reader, but these errors are unlikely to interfere with a reader's understanding.

Evaluate Your Essay

Compare your essay to the model essays and decide whether it falls in the upper half or in the lower half of the rating scale. It's a very rough estimate, but this exercise will help you identify what you need to work on in order to write a top-scoring ACT essay. With your teacher, go over your strengths and weaknesses and determine the steps you should take to improve your writing.

Chapter 21

HOW TO WRITE THE ACT ESSAY

Writing Review

You will find a comprehensive review of English skills and a full range of practice activities on pages 25–175. If the evaluation of your essay reveals specific difficulties with English skills, you should review the pages that address those concerns.

Before moving on, take note of the following pointers about how to improve the quality of your writing.

Avoid the Passive Voice

Whenever possible, you should avoid writing in the passive voice. Although the passive voice is not always inappropriate, it is unlikely to enhance your short essay.

Passive Voice

Sentences constructed in the passive voice emphasize the action rather than the actor. They often take the long way around to explain something. Passive sentences usually include a form of the "to be" verb with a past participle.

Look at these examples of passive sentences. The form of the "to be" verb is underlined. "Completed" is the past participle in each sentence.

The essay <u>is</u> completed.
The essay <u>was</u> completed.
The essay <u>is being</u> completed.
The essay <u>has been</u> completed.
The essay <u>had been</u> completed.
The essay <u>will be</u> completed.
The essay is waiting <u>to be</u> completed.

Revise passive sentences into active sentences. Notice that the actor appears at the beginning of each corrected sentence, whereas it is either missing or placed toward the end of each passive sentence.

Passive (Incorrect): The essay is completed.
Active (Corrected):   I completed the essay.

Passive (Incorrect): The essay will be completed.
Active (Corrected):   I will complete the essay.

Passive (Incorrect):	The Writing Test was designed by ACT.
Active (Corrected):	ACT designed the Writing Test.
Passive (Incorrect):	The curfew was approved by the Town Council
Active (Corrected):	The Town Council approved the curfew.
Passive (Incorrect):	The curfew is opposed by some students.
Active (Corrected):	Some students oppose the curfew.

The Past Tense Is Not the Passive Voice

Sometimes the past tense is mistaken for the passive voice, and vice versa. They are not the same thing. The past tense indicates that something happened in the past. The past tense can be expressed in both active and passive voices.

Past Tense—Passive Voice (Incorrect):	The ACT was taken yesterday.
Past Tense—Active Voice (Corrected):	I took the ACT yesterday.
Past Tense—Passive Voice (Incorrect):	The test was registered for by Ryan.
Past Tense—Active Voice (Corrected):	Ryan registered for the test.

Write Effective Transitions

Include transitions in your writing to guide the reader from one idea to the next, and from one paragraph to the next. The transition words and phrases discussed below will help you write a coherent essay.

Transition Words

Cause and Effect: These transition words establish a cause-and-effect relationship:

> and so   as a result of   because   consequently   hence
> therefore   thus

Continuation: Some transitions show that the same theme is continued or explained in more detail:

> also   and   by the same token   further   in addition   in other words
> that is   then

Difference: These transition words point out differences:

> although   but   contrarily   despite   however   as opposed to
> in contrast to   not   nevertheless   to the contrary   unlike

Example: These transition words signal an explanation:

> for example   for instance   that is

Order: These transition words suggest that elements are being ordered:

> first   primarily   then   last   before   after

Similarity: These transition words point out similarities:

> alike   also   in common   similar to

Writing Strategy

You want to write an essay that presents your position on the topic and tries to persuade the reader that your position is correct. You should provide three main points or reasons that support your position. Make sure you clarify these points with specific examples and details. Then you want to summarize your position and supporting evidence in a final attempt to convince the reader. You can do all of this in five paragraphs. Here's the format.

The Five-Paragraph Essay

Paragraph 1 (75 to 85 words; 2–4 sentences)

Introduce the issue and clearly state your position.

Paragraphs 2, 3, and 4 (100 to 110 words each; 4–7 sentences each)

For each of these paragraphs, write a topic sentence that states a main point or reason in support of your position. Then provide specific details and examples that illustrate your point to the reader.

Paragraph 5 (65 to 80 words; 2–4 sentences)

Use this paragraph to summarize your argument in a final attempt to persuade the reader that your position is correct.

The Five Questions

As you write the five paragraphs, remember the five questions that ACT readers consider when scoring your essay.

1. How well do you explain your position on the issue?
To earn points here, clearly state your position in the first paragraph.

2. Do you maintain your focus on the issue throughout the essay?
To earn points here, avoid straying from your position, unless you choose to explain why an opposing position is inappropriate. In other words, resist the urge to digress.

3. Do you organize your ideas logically?
To earn points here, provide transitions between paragraphs, making sure that the second through the fifth paragraphs relate clearly to your first paragraph. Develop your ideas in a logical way.

4. How thoroughly do you support your position with evidence, details, and examples?
To earn points here, provide explanations and specific details to support the main point of each paragraph.

5. Do you use language appropriately, in a way that does not distract from or interfere with a reader's understanding?
To earn these points, write clear sentences, avoid the passive voice, use appropriate vocabulary, and leave yourself time to correct grammatical errors, particularly those that might interfere with the reader's understanding.

ACT 6-Point Rating Scale

Readers award points based on this 6-point scale. In practice, readers categorize an essay as upper third, middle third, or lower third. Then they decide whether the essay is in the upper part or the lower part of that third.

ACT 6-Point Rubric

UPPER THIRD   Competent Writer

6: Outstanding. This essay takes a clear position on the issue in the prompt and provides complete, clear, and convincing support for the position. The essay is well organized, and it features a logical development and effective transitions. Sentences are clear and well written. The superior command of language and vocabulary in the essay help convince the reader of the essay's position. The few errors of grammar, usage, and punctuation in the essay do not distract the reader and do not interfere with the reader's understanding.

5: Advanced. This essay takes a clear position on the issue in the prompt and provides some convincing support for the position. The essay is organized, and it features some transitions. Sentences are usually clear and well written. Sound command of language and vocabulary help convince the reader of the essay's argument. The few errors of grammar, usage, and punctuation usually do not distract the reader and do not interfere with the reader's understanding.

MIDDLE THIRD   Developing Writer

4: Acceptable. This essay takes a position on the issue in the prompt and provides some support for the position. The essay is usually organized. Sentences are usually clear and well written. Acceptable command of language and vocabulary may help convince the reader of the essay's position. Although the few errors of grammar, usage, and punctuation do not interfere with the reader's understanding, they may distract the reader.

3: Marginal. This essay takes a position on the issue in the prompt and provides very little support for the position. The essay usually has some organization, but it may be difficult to follow. Uncertain command of language and limited vocabulary do not help to convince the reader of the essay's position. Frequent errors of grammar, usage, and punctuation may distract the reader and interfere with the reader's understanding.

LOWER THIRD Emerging Writer

2: Poor. This essay is marked by significant errors. The essay may take a position on the issue in the prompt but provides almost no support for the position. The essay is unorganized and difficult to read. Sentences are often unclear and poorly written. The essay features poor command of language and vocabulary. Frequent errors of grammar, usage, and punctuation distract the reader and interfere with the reader's understanding.

1: Unacceptable. This essay is marked by significant errors. The essay may take no position on the issue in the prompt or provide no support for the position. The essay is unorganized and difficult to read. Sentences are unclear and poorly written. The essay features poor command of language and vocabulary. Frequent errors of grammar, usage, and punctuation interfere with the reader's understanding.

Steps for Writing the Essay

Follow these steps to write a top-scoring essay.

PLAN

Use the first few minutes to plan your essay.

1. Understand the prompt and determine your position. (1 minute)

Stop! Don't start writing immediately. You'll end up writing yourself into a corner. Instead, take a moment to consider the prompt, making sure you understand what it's asking. Then write a sentence that states your position on the issue presented in the prompt. This statement will be the keynote of your entire essay.

2. Write a brief outline. (3 minutes)

Under your position statement, write three sentences, each expressing a different point in support of your position. Then write a summarizing sentence to begin your conclusion. These five sentences will become the topic sentences of your essay.

WRITE

Use this time to write well.

3. Write your essay. (24 minutes)

Paragraph 1

Restate your position in the first paragraph.

Paragraphs 2–4

For each of the body paragraphs, start by rewriting the topic sentence that you devised in your outline. Then provide specific examples and other supporting details to reinforce that statement.

Paragraph 5

Rewrite your summarizing sentence to begin your concluding paragraph. Complete the essay by writing one final sentence to convince the reader of your position.

CORRECT

Readers know that the essay is a first draft, and they expect to see corrections.

4. Proofread and edit. (2 minutes)

Take the last few minutes to look over your essay and to correct any obvious errors.

Chapter 22

ACT DEVELOPMENTAL WRITING TEST I

This section will take you step by step through the process of writing an essay. Complete each step in order. Let's start with the prompt.

PROMPT 1

School administrators frequently recommend that school boards adopt a strict attendance policy for high school seniors. This policy requires high school seniors to limit their absences in the last month of school in order to be eligible for participation in the graduation ceremonies. Some school board members support the policy because they believe it encourages seniors to attend school regularly and to act appropriately at the graduation exercises. Other school board members do not support the policy because they think it interferes with parents' prerogatives and with students' opportunity to visit colleges. In your view, should school boards adopt a strict attendance policy for high school seniors?

In your essay, state your position on the issue. Your essay may address either of the points of view above, or you may present your own point of view on the issue. Remember to support your position with reasons and examples.

1. **Understand the prompt and write your position. (1 minute)**

   The issue is whether or not strict attendance should be a requirement for graduation participation. We can argue for the strict attendance policy, or we can argue against it. Or we can take another point of view altogether. I don't know about you, but I'm going to stick with one of the two points of view in the prompt.

   Personally, I'm in favor of the strict attendance policy.

   My position statement: <u>School boards should adopt a strict attendance policy as a requirement for graduation participation.</u>

   What's your position on this issue? Don't just use mine. Write your own position statement below.

   Your position statement: _____

   _____

   _____

   Remember to include your position statement in the first paragraph. Let's move on to the outline.

2. Write a brief outline. (3 minutes)

I'm going to use this time to think and plan. You should too. Once we start to write, we need to concentrate on writing well. Here are draft topic sentences for the five paragraphs that I'll write. They don't have to be perfect. I can rewrite them when I get to the essay.

My Outline

I rewrite my position statement.

School boards should adopt a strict attendance policy as a requirement for graduation participation.

I write three important points that support my position statement.

1. *Rules lead to appropriate behavior.*

2. *Students who've been absent from school often disrupt graduation ceremonies.*

3. *We must respect the rights of all students and all families.*

I write a statement that will begin my summary paragraph.

We must defend standards that benefit the entire school community.

Your Outline

Now, you write your own outline. Write one sentence for each of the five paragraphs.

_____

_____

_____

_____

_____

_____

_____

_____

_____

_____

_____

_____

_____

We've done our planning and thinking. It's time to write the essay.

3. Write a five-paragraph essay. (24 minutes)

The first paragraph states your position. The second, third and fourth paragraphs present points or reasons, along with explanations and details, that support your position. The fifth paragraph summarizes your position and makes one last attempt to convince the reader.

Write your essay in the space provided.

4. Proofread and edit. (2 minutes)

Leave two minutes to go over your essay and make any necessary changes and corrections. After you've finished, review the three model essays on pages 408–410.

_____

_____

_____

_____

_____

_____

_____

_____

_____

_____

_____

Model Essays

Model Essay 1   **Lower Third (121 words)**

> *I am a high school senior who knows people who cut school a lot. This essay says that I think it is a good idea to have strict school attendance policy as a requirement to participate in the graduation ceremonies.*
>
> *Our last graduation was a mess. Students were running around yelling and they interrupted things. Almost every problem was caused by those kids who were absent from school a lot. Students at the graduation should not be running around drunk or drugging and other things like that. I do not want my parents to see that kind of stuff. The people on the school board should be busy and do something before there is more problem and the police have to come.*

Model Essay 2   **Middle Third (320 words)**

> *Even though I am a high school student I am in favor of a strict school attendance policy as a requirement to participate in the graduation ceremonies.*
>
> *Our last graduation was a mess. Students were running around yelling and they interrupted things. That showed what can happen when high school seniors cut school and their parents just give them notes. How about students that forge their parents names on the office signature card and just write notes for themselves. A simple attendance policy will help solve a lot of problems.*
>
> *I think students who are absent from school a lot are more likely to disrupt graduation ceremonies than those who have regular attendance. Students who are frequently absent often do not have as solid a connection to the school as other students. In previous years it has been the truant students who have interrupted speakers and embarrassed their classmate and the school. When this happens we realize that we should have a strict attendance policy.*

Each student family should be able to enjoy the graduation. These people should not have to put up with a lot of problems that were caused by a few students who think they can do whatever they want because their parents do not have any rules at home.

Students at the graduation should not be drunk or using drugs because that causes more problems. My parents should know that I am there because I followed the rules and that everyone there followed the rules.

I hope then when I graduate and some day I am on the school board that I know how to make rules that will help the graduation be better. But I hope I do not have to wait until that day to see the school board have rules that say a student must be in school or they will not be able to go to the graduation with their parents.

Model Essay 3   Upper Third (436 words)

It is very common for a board of education for the best high schools to adopt a strict attendance policy. Many students and some parents may not like the idea but it is a good one. My position is that schools boards should adopt a strict school attendance policy as a requirement to participate in the graduation ceremonies.

Rules lead to appropriate behavior. It is the very basis of our society that everyone must follow reasonable rules that are in the common good. Experience has taught us that without an attendance policy, without rules to follow, high school seniors will cut school and convince their parents to give them notes excusing them from school. It is an open secret that many students forged their parents names on the office signature card and these students will just write notes for themselves. A simple attendance policy will help solve a lot of problems.

Our school administrators say students who are absent from school a lot are more likely to disrupt graduation ceremonies than those who are attending school. Since college admissions decisions have already been made, there is no reason for a high school senior to visit a college on a school day during June. The students who are frequently absent often do not have as solid a connection to the school as other students. In previous years it has been the truant students who have interrupted speakers and embarrassed their classmate and the school. When this happens we realize that we should have a strict attendance policy. But by then it is too late.

It is more important to respect the rights of a majority of the students and their parents than it is to respect the rights of students who want to skip school. The many should not have to sacrifice for the comfort of the few. I know that when my parents come to my graduation I don't want anyone interrupting anything. I want my parents to know that I am there because I followed the rules and that everyone there followed the rules. All of the student's families should be able to enjoy the ceremony.

The school board should take a stand now for standards. Students belong in school when school is in session, not at the mall or somewhere else. Attending graduation is a right and it is not a privilege. Students who do not show respect for the school and themselves should not be there. The board should implement this policy immediately and have an atmosphere that will encourage everyone to follow the rules and to want to be at the graduation.

Evaluate Your Essay

Work with your teacher to evaluate your essay. Remember that readers base their evaluation on an informed impression of your essay. They don't read the essay in detail. With this in mind, let's look at the similarities and differences among these three essays.

How are the essays similar?

Each essay takes a clear position on the issue.

Each essay is essentially free of significant grammatical and usage errors, although errors are more noticeable in the lowest-rated essay.

How are the essays different?

There is a single obvious difference. The higher-rated essays have more words. That means the higher-rated essays provide more evidence to back up the main points and reasons that support the position. The highest-rated essays provide at least three main points or reasons in support of the position and strengthen each of these points with examples and specific details. These essays feature smooth transitions between ideas, good sentence structure, parallel form, and a diverse vocabulary.

Rewrite Your Essay

If your essay is not in the upper third, you should write it again. Even if your essay falls within the upper third, it wouldn't hurt to rewrite it. The exercise of revision is one of the best ways to improve your writing skills. Do the extra practice now to get the score you want on the ACT.

Use the following guidelines:

Respond to the same prompt.

Take 30 minutes to rewrite your essay.

Use the lessons you learned from writing and evaluating the first essay.

Incorporate your teacher's suggestions.

Prompt 1

School administrators frequently recommend that school boards adopt a strict attendance policy for high school seniors. This policy requires high school seniors to limit their absences in the last month of school in order to be eligible for participation in the graduation ceremonies. Some school board members support the policy because they believe it encourages seniors to attend school regularly and to act appropriately at the graduation exercises. Other school board members do not support the policy because they think it interferes with parents' prerogatives and with students' opportunity to visit colleges. In your view, should school boards adopt a strict attendance policy for high school seniors?

In your essay, state your position on the issue. Your essay may address either of the points of view above, or you may present your own point of view on the issue. Remember to support your position with reasons and examples.

1. Understand the prompt and write your position. (1 minute)

Your position statement: _____

_____

_____

2. Write a brief outline. (3 minutes)

Your outline:

_____

_____

_____

_____

_____

_____

_____

_____

_____

_____

_____

_____

_____

_____

3. Write your essay. (24 minutes)

4. Proofread and edit. (2 minutes)

_____

_____

_____

_____

_____

_____

_____

_____

_____

_____

_____

_____

_____

Chapter 23

ACT WRITING TEST II

In response to the prompt below, write an essay just like the one you will write for the ACT. That is, write an essay that will make the best impression on a reader. Clearly state your position on the issue. Include three main points or reasons in support of your position and back up each point or reason with details and examples. Compose a summary paragraph. All in all, be sure to write at least 450 useful words.

Use the model essays on pages 418–420 as you work with your teacher to evaluate your essay. The essays are rated as lower third, middle third, and upper third.

Write a persuasive essay for Prompt 2. You have exactly thirty minutes.

PROMPT 2

A high school plans to construct a parking lot close to the campus. It will be used for either faculty parking or student parking. Those in favor of a faculty lot claim that faculty members often get to school earlier than students and that seniority entitles them to convenient parking. Those in favor of a student parking lot believe that students deserve to use the lot since their tuition will be paying for its construction. In your view, should the parking lot be designated for faculty or student use?

In your essay, state your position on the issue. Your essay may address either of the positions above, or you may present your own point of view on the issue. Remember to support your position with reasons and examples.

Review the three model essays and their evaluations after you write your essay.

_____

_____

_____

_____

_____

_____

_____

_____

Model Essays

I am grateful to Jonathan Moore for permission to use these student essays and evaluative comments. Mr. Moore teaches junior-level and A.P. English as well as creative writing at Shepherd High School in Shepherd, Montana. He is also a trainer for both the Montana holistic scoring system and the 6 + 1 Trait Writing model.

PROMPT 2

A high school plans to construct a parking lot close to the campus. It will be used for either faculty parking or student parking. Those in favor of a faculty lot claim that faculty members often get to school earlier than students and that seniority entitles them to convenient parking. Those in favor of a student parking lot believe that students deserve to use the lot since their tuition will be paying for its construction. In your view, should the parking lot be designated for faculty or student use?

In your essay, state your position on the issue. Your essay may address either of the positions above, or you may present your own point of view on the issue. Remember to support your position with reasons and examples.

Model Essay 1   Lower Third (78 words)

> Currently our high school is building a parking lot. This lot is being bilt next to our school. Right now their is a lot of noise due to the tractors and trucks, coming and going. This is a distraction for students. This is why I think students should park in the new lot. Teachers aren't bothered as much by the noise. The students are under more stress which will be helped by not having to walk as far.

Model Essay 1 Evaluation

The paper represents an emerging writer. Its score would fall at the low end of the scale. Although the essay starts slightly off topic, the writer does take a position on the issue (that the new lot should be reserved for students since they suffer from stress) but fails to develop that idea. In addition, the writer provides no evidence to support the claim that teachers are less stressed than students. The organization of the response is unclear, lacking paragraph division. While the essay demonstrates a basic command of language, a few errors in spelling and punctuation are apparent. Sentence structure is simple and lacks variety.

Model Essay 2

> The proposed high school parking lot is a subject of much discussion. Some say the faculty should park in the new lot. Some say students should park in the new lot. All we know for sure is that both can't park there. I believe the new lot should be used for the faculty.
>
> First and fore most is most teachers are way older than the students. They would have more trouble walking a big distance.
>
> Second, students have more energy, especially after school, and need to burn of that energy before driving home or going into school.
>
> Last, I've seen teachers carry boxes of work to and from their car. At most students only have a school bag and gym bag.
>
> That's why teachers should park in the new parking lot.

Model Essay 2 Evaluation

The paper represents the work of a developing writer. It would score in the low middle of the scale. The writer provides several points in support of a position, but the ideas remain undeveloped.

The essay is sufficiently organized so that the introduction relates to points in each paragraph. However, the writer makes no apparent effort to link ideas, leaving the reader to make the necessary connections.

Although each of the main points has merit, the first and second points represent the same idea (that teachers' seniority should be respected).

Language and grammar are functional but simplistic. While sentence structure is generally repetitive, there is some evidence of advanced syntax.

Model Essay 3

> One of the landmark occasions of any teen's life is the acquisition of a driver's license. Cars symbolize a teenagers freedom and spirit. Conversely, cars are merely a functional tool to adults. This issue relates to the ongoing debate in our high school. At issue is who should park in the newly constructed lot; a lot that is mere feet from the front door. I believe the new lot should be for student use due to the following issues: economics, self-esteem, and logistics.
>
> First the issue of economics must be examined. Teachers while not highly paid, make anywhere from fifteen to twenty times more

than students. Economic solvency means teachers can afford nicer cars and the maintenance costs required for parking in older, smaller lots. Students, on the other hand, cannot always afford to pay for door dings from those who park too closer or tires shredded by potholes. The economic advantage afforded to teachers means they need not park in the newer, bigger lot, that privilege should be for the students.

The second reason students should be parking in the new lot is status and self-esteem. To a high school student, a nice car is a status symbol. Students spend time and what money they have making their vehicles look nice. When they succeed, they raise their social status and therefore their self-esteem. Low self-esteem is a problem that plagues high schools. While the new lot will not solve the issue completely, it will help some students. Teachers, the greatest advocates for students, must give up the new lot to help students feel better about themselves.

The third and final reason students should, indeed must be allowed to park in the new lot is simple logistics. When I arrive at school, the current faculty lot is full. In fact, I don't know if I have ever beaten a teacher to school. In that situation I am not alone. The teachers arrive early enough that they need not rush to their classrooms. Teachers are even required to arrive early, as much as twenty minutes before students. Yet students are often late due to lack of preparedness. A new lot will motivate students to be early in order to be in the prime spots. Early arriving students will cut down on tardies. In this case, as with the previously stated scenarios the greatest benefit is for students to park in the new lot.

Many people will argue that teachers are older or that they have more items to carry to the school, therefore they need closer spaces. But examining the situation rationally will lead anyone to see how the greatest benefit is for students to park in the new lot.

In conclusion there can only be one outcome for the current debate: students must park in the new lot.

Model Essay 3 Evaluation

The paper demonstrates solid writing and thinking ability. It would score near the top of the scale.

The essay has a strong thesis that provides the focal point of the paper. The thesis statement is preceded by an engaging introduction that captures the reader's attention. The essay stays on topic, and most ideas are well developed. One apparent weakness is the writer's assumption that the new lot would have larger parking spaces and no potholes.

While there isn't much variety in sentence structure, the essay demonstrates a sound command of language and vocabulary.

Chapter 24

ACT WRITING TEST III

In response to the following prompt, write an essay just like the one you will write for the ACT. That is, write an essay that will make the best impression on the reader. Clearly state your position on the issue. Include three main points or reasons in support of your position and back up each position or reason with details and examples. Compose a summary paragraph. All in all, be sure to write at least 450 useful words.

Use the model essays on pages 424–427 as you work with your teacher to evaluate your essay. The essays are rated as lower third, middle third, and upper third.

Write a persuasive essay for Prompt 3. You have exactly thirty minutes.

PROMPT 3

A neighborhood association is trying to decide how to use an improvement grant. There is enough money to fund only one of two projects. The first project is upgrading underground water and sewer pipes, which will vastly improve water quality and sanitation. The second project is beautifying neighborhood streets and buildings, which will increase property values. Write a letter to the neighborhood association in which you argue for one of the projects, explaining how your choice will improve the neighborhood.

In your letter, state your position on the issue. Your letter may address either of the proposals above, or you may present your own point of view on the issue. Remember to support your position with reasons and examples.

Review the three model essays and evaluations after you write your essay.

_____

_____

_____

_____

_____

_____

_____

_____

_____

Model Essays

I am grateful to Robyn Wingo for permission to use these student essays and evaluative comments. Ms. Wingo is Director of the Educational Opportunity Program at the University of Montana–Western and a participant in the Montana holistic scoring system. She also has fourteen years of experience teaching secondary-school English.

Prompt 3

A neighborhood association is trying to decide how to use an improvement grant. There is enough money to fund only one of two projects. The first project is upgrading underground water and sewer pipes, which will vastly improve water quality and sanitation. The second project is beautifying neighborhood streets and buildings, which will increase property values. Write a letter to the neighborhood association in which you argue for one of the projects, explaining how your choice will improve the neighborhood.

In your letter, state your position on the issue. Your letter may address either of the proposals above, or you may present your own point of view on the issue. Remember to support your position with reasons and examples.

Model Essay 1   Lower Third (117 words)

> To whom it may concern,
>
>   I hear you have some extra money to buy more beautiful streets and buildings or new water pipes. Everyone knows the neighborhood looks real run down. If this is your choice I hope you know you need alot of money. We need the trash picked up and grass planted. Trees would help too. Some of the stores and houses look bad and need fixing. New water and sewer pipes are needed for better water quality and sanitation so we don't all get sick, like in Mexico when they tell you don't drink the water. But everybody drinks bottle water anyway. So you should take my advice and make the neighborhood more beautiful.

Model Essay 1 Evaluation

This response scores in the lower third of the scale.

The writer doesn't commit to a definite position until the last sentence. The few points made in the letter stand alone, without supporting details or examples. Organizational structure lacks paragraph divisions and transitions, making the ideas difficult to follow. The letter format is also incomplete, since the writer did not include a closing salutation. Although the letter is comprehensible, there are numerous errors in vocabulary, usage, and sentence structure.

Model Essay 2

> *Dear neighborhood association,*
>
> *I am writing to tell you that you should use your improvement grant to beautify the neighborhood streets and building fronts. We have water and sewer pipes already, but we don't have a beautiful neighborhood!*
>
> *What this neighborhood needs are sidewalks! We need a place for people to walk and ride their bikes without getting run over by the cars and making the drivers nervous!*
>
> *Also what this neighborhood needs are flowers! The neighborhood would be more beautiful with colorful flowers, some shrubbery and trees, and bark chips around all the new plants. Better landscaping will give everything more curb appeal, and people would enjoy walking through the landscape on the new sidewalks.*
>
> *We need paint too! Lots of the buildings and houses have peeling paint and faded paint. Also, some of the colors are tacky and clashing. We need to hire somebody to paint everything in nice colors that don't clash with the next door neighbor, like someone on my street who painted their house pink even though they say it's really just light brick. If everything was fixed up and looked nice, I think people would try harder to keep their yards cleaned up too.*
>
> *There would be better moral if you could look around and like what you see. Especially now that its getting to be springtime, you want to go outside and enjoy the environment. Therefore the choice for more beautiful streets and buildings is the best decision for improving the neighborhood.*
>
> *Sincerely,*
>
> *Your neighbor*

Model Essay 2 Evaluation

This response scores in the middle third of the scale.

The writer takes a clear position and supports it throughout the letter. Ideas are organized logically, and paragraph structure is appropriate. Examples are evident. Although there are some errors in sentence structure, word choice, and punctuation (such as the overuse of exclamation points), they do not distract the reader. The writer demonstrates a good command of language, usage, and vocabulary.

Dear Neighborhood Association,

I am writing to let you know that the members of the neighborhood would prefer to see your improvement grant money used for the beautification project, rather than improved water and sewers. Beautifying the streets and building fronts would be a more noticeable use of the funds and increase property values.

The streets need the most immediate improvement. There are pot holes everywhere, especially on the side streets. It would be nice if curbs and grass could be added to the roadsides, so you could actually tell where the street edge is. Sidewalks would give pedestrians a great place to walk. If there are enough funds, I think a bike lane would be a very safe thing to have on the main streets. Another good safety feature would be to have "walk/don't walk" signs on the corners where the traffic lights are located. All of these improvements to the streets would enable people to get around town more safely and easily. Everyone in the neighborhood would appreciate this!

Improved fronts on all the buildings and houses would be another reason for the neighborhood to be appreciative to the association. I know the neighborhood association can't really control what the private property looks like for the business and home owners, but I think you can have people improve them in a fair way. You could let people write in to explain how they want to improve their store fronts and front yards, and distribute the money based on what each person wants to do. But, that would only improve some buildings. The ones that are the most run down are probably owned by people who don't care, so they wouldn't try to improve them anyway. The best way to improve the private property would be to have everyone do something. The worst ones could be given a list of repairs that need to be made, with a deadline to do it, and the association would pay for it. Places that already look nice could be given another tree to plant. That way, everyone would get something, and all the property would be improved. The entire neighborhood would be more beautiful, and everyone will have helped.

Beautifying the streets and building fronts will make everyone proud to live here, and proud of what the neighborhood association was able to get done. I know new water and sewer pipes are needed. However, I don't think this is the responsibility of the neighborhood association. Our water bill is paid to the city, so this is the city's responsibility. After the city earns more money from our neighborhood when our property taxes go up because of the added value the beautiful streets and buildings will bring, we will all have to sign a petition for the city to upgrade the water and sewer pipes!

Looking forward to a more beautiful neighborhood,

A concerned citizen

Model Essay 3 Evaluation

This response scores in the upper third of the scale.

The writer takes a strong position, maintains it throughout the letter, and refutes the opposing view. The letter is well organized, with appropriate transitions between ideas. Examples provide logical support for the ideas presented. The letter demonstrates excellent command of writing conventions, apparent in the variety of sentence structure, fluent word choice, and grammatical clarity.

Keep Writing

Practice writing persuasive essays until you score consistently in the upper third of the scale. With your teacher's help, you can learn to produce top-scoring responses.

Section VI

College Admission

Chapter 25   Getting Into College   431

Chapter 25

GETTING INTO COLLEGE

So—You're Thinking of Going to College

The only reason to take the ACT is to get into college. If you're reading this book, you are probably among the 50 to 60 percent of American high school graduates who will go on to higher education.

Attending college is usually a good idea. You will be an educated person, practically a requirement for success in the 21st century. As a college graduate, you will find more and better job opportunities than if you had no college degree.

The average college graduate earns about 60 percent more a year than a person without a college degree, and this earnings gap will widen in the years ahead. An increasing percentage of the jobs available will require a college education as well as technical training and expertise. An undergraduate degree is required if you want to attend professional or graduate school.

This chapter summarizes the steps to follow for college admission, and gives tips on how to pay for college once you're there. At the end of the chapter is a list of resources you can go to for more help. The chapter does not offer suggestions about which high school courses or extracurricular activities will help you get accepted by a college. It goes without saying, though, that the strength of your high school program, your grades, your class rank, teachers' recommendations, and your ACT scores along with your extracurricular activities are important factors in college admission.

Remember, too, that there are about 20,000 public and private high schools in the United States. That means that there will be 20,000 valedictorians and 20,000 salutatorians seeking admission to college in the fall. You do not have to go to a competitive college to have a successful career.

Besides the factors listed here, there are lots of social reasons for choosing to apply to a particular college. Perhaps one of your parents went to the college. Or perhaps some of your friends are going there. Choosing a college for social reasons is not always the wrong approach. However, choosing a college solely on the basis of social considerations frequently leads to problems.

Follow these steps even if you think you already know the college or colleges you want to apply to. You may be surprised at the exciting and interesting choices that emerge.

STEP I. Determine the type of degree you should pursue.

(Complete by October of your junior year.)

As a high school graduate, you may pursue a two-year associate's degree or a four-year bachelor's degree. Graduate and professional degrees require a bachelor's degree, and many colleges offer programs which combine undergraduate and graduate degrees.

What are your career aspirations?

The type of college degree you will pursue will depend on your interests and the career you plan for yourself. You don't have to know exactly what you want to be, but you should have some general idea before you attend college. The United States Department of Education provides the table below in their publication "Preparing Your Child for College" to help you decide which type of degree to pursue.

COLLEGE DEGREES AND CAREERS

ASSOCIATE'S DEGREE (Two years)	BACHELOR'S DEGREE (Four years)	GRADUATE AND PROFESSIONAL DEGREE (Bachelor's Degree Required)
Surveyor	Teacher	Lawyer
Registered nurse	Accountant	Physician
Dental hygienist	FBI agent	Architect
Medical laboratory technician	Engineer	University professor
Computer technician	Visual artist	Economist
Commercial artist	Journalist	Psychologist
Hotel/restaurant manager	Diplomat	Sociologist
Funeral director	Computer systems analyst	Dentist
Drafter	Insurance agent	Veterinarian
Engineering technician	Pharmacist	Public policy analyst
Automotive mechanic	Dietitian	Geologist
Administrative assistant	Writer	Paleontologist
Cardiovascular technician	Editor	Zoologist
Medical records technician	Graphic designer	Management consultant
Surgical technologist	Social worker	Rabbi
Water and wastewater treatment plant operator	Recreational therapist	Priest
Heating, air conditioning, and refrigeration technician	Public relations specialist	Minister
	Research assistant	Chiropractor
	Investment banker	Biologist
	Medical illustrator	

List below the careers you might be interested in and the degree you will need for each career type.

CAREER	TYPE OF DEGREE
1. _____	_____
2. _____	_____
3. _____	_____

Step II. Determine whether you should apply to a two-year or a four-year college.

(Complete by October of your junior year.)

Regardless of your career choice, you can begin your college career at either a two-year or a four-year college. While most students pursuing a bachelor's degree start at a four-year college, there are good reasons for first attending a two-year college. You may decide to apply to both two-year and four-year colleges.

The two-year college may offer a low-cost alternative for your freshman and sophomore years. It may be easier to gain admission to a four-year college after attending a two-year college. In fact, many public colleges have special admission arrangements for students who have attended public two-year colleges in their state.

The descriptions of two-year and four-year colleges given below may help you choose the type or types of colleges you will apply to.

Two-Year Colleges. These colleges may offer associate's degrees (A.A., A.S., and A.A.S) based on two years of college work. Some two-year colleges offer programs of two years or shorter that lead directly to a career or job. These colleges fall into three categories:

Community colleges are usually public two-year institutions with commuter students from nearby communities and offer a full range of academic and technical courses. Most programs at these colleges lead to an associate's degree.

Junior colleges are usually private two-year institutions with dormitories and usually offer a full range of academic and technical courses. Most programs at these colleges lead to an associate's degree.

Technical colleges may be either public or private and emphasize training in technical fields and careers. Many programs at technical colleges do not lead to an associate's degree.

Four-Year Colleges. These colleges offer bachelor's degrees based on four years of college work. While the emphasis at most four-year colleges is academic, four-year schools also offer programs which lead to careers in technical and other fields.

A university is a four-year school that also grants graduate and professional degrees. Universities may offer programs which lead to both an undergraduate and a graduate degree.

Colleges and universities may be best thought of by the competitive nature of the admissions process. Some colleges and universities are extremely competitive, admitting less than 20 percent of the students who apply. Other colleges and universities have very liberal admissions policies and reject almost no one who has applied for admission. Most schools fall between these two extremes, with varying degrees of admission selectivity.

List below the types of college you are interested in attending:

1. _____

2. _____

STEP III. Determine the characteristics of the college you would like to attend.

(Complete by November of your junior year.)

You may want to attend college in a particular state or part of the country. Or you may want to attend a college of a particular size.

Write your preliminary choices for the characteristics of the college you would like to attend next to each category below. You can always change your mind.

Field(s) of study:

Include the major fields of study or the careers you are interested in or write *undecided.*

_____

_____

_____

State or states in which you would attend college:

Write the name of every state in which you would attend college or write "all" if you would attend college anywhere in the United States.

_____   _____   _____   _____

_____   _____   _____   _____

_____   _____   _____   _____

Approximate size of the student body:

Circle one of the choices below.

Under 500	500–2,500	2,500–7,500
7,500–15,000	Above 15,000	No preference

Type of school:

Circle two-year, four-year, or both. Circle private, public, or no preference. If you want to attend a college with a religious affiliation, then write the name of the affiliation in the space provided.

Two-year	Four-year	Both
Public	Private	No preference

Religious affiliation? _____

Disabilities:

Circle below whether you will need to have services for a physical or learning disability at the college of your choice.

Physical disability   Learning disability

STEP IV. List the colleges that meet your criteria.

(Complete by November of your junior year.)

The best way to get a list of colleges that meet your requirements is to use one of the free-search services on the Internet. If you, your friends, or your high school are online, you're all set. If not, I strongly recommend that you find a way to get online to complete the college search process. Many public libraries now provide access to the Internet.

Surf the Net for a List of Colleges. The College Board (www.collegeboard.com) and the ACT (www.ACT.org) have sophisticated college-search tools.

Internet resources are constantly being added and updated. You should check at the site of search programs such as Google and Yahoo to find new sites which will give you information about getting into college.

CollegeEdge (www.CollegeEdge.com). Use this Internet address to access CollegeEdge. Click on Undergraduate (Going to College?). Then click on Explore Colleges. Next, click on CollegeEdge College Search. Complete the online registration form. When you complete the form, you'll go directly to the college search page. Next time you sign on, use your User ID and your password.

At the search page, select your college preferences. If you have no preferences, just leave a category blank. Click on the information about the colleges on your list. You can print out all the information as well. You may be able to visit a college's Web site, send an e-mail, and even apply online. You can submit as many searches as you want.

Other Ways to Draw Up a List of Colleges. Your guidance counselor may have a computer program that enables you to search for colleges by certain criteria. There are also CD-ROMs for computers that permit you to make a complete college search. School and public libraries may provide access to college information, both through computers and in publications.

STEP V. Gather information about colleges on your list.

(Complete by March of your junior year.)

Look over the list of colleges that meet your criteria. Sit down with your parents, teachers, and high school counselor to see if they can think of any other colleges to add to the list. Remove the names of schools you absolutely will not attend. Remember you're just gathering information.

Write or call each college on your list and request complete information about the school, including its catalog. All the information you get from the college is advertising. This information points out strong points and does not mention weaknesses. But college advertising will provide you with useful general information about a school.

Read about colleges in guide books that give students' or others' opinions about the school. In general, avoid books which merely reprint the information provided by the college. You will find a wide array of college guide books in the guidance counselor's office and in bookstores. Make sure you are looking at the most recent versions of the books.

Attend college fairs. Colleges send representatives to college fairs throughout the country. You can talk to a representative and pick up literature and applications at these fairs. Your counselor will have information about college fairs in your area.

Talk to people who are attending the college. Your guidance counselor may be able to provide you with names of students who are currently attending a college. Don't hesitate to call the college admissions office and ask for the names of students to talk to. They probably have a list of people they refer to potential students. But don't hesitate to call the students and ask them to just tell you the truth. And if it's a dorm number, you can just talk to the first person who answers the phone.

You can also call directly into an academic department and ask to talk to a faculty member. Do not hesitate to ask the faculty member questions about her or his department.

Some colleges also distribute videotapes about their schools. The videotapes are available directly through the school, and some are available free in video rental stores.

STEP VI. Create a final list of five to fifteen schools. Visit each school.

(Complete by October of your senior year.)

Use all the information you have gathered to narrow your list of schools. There is no rule for the number of schools that should be on the list. Your counselor and parents can help you with this list.

You have to visit the schools you're thinking of attending! It is better to visit a college in session. This will give you a chance to attend classes, talk with students, and stay in the dorm. But it is okay to make your first visit during the summer between your junior and senior years. If you eventually decide you may apply to that school, you should visit again in the fall of your senior year.

Your visit to the school will probably include your first formal visit with an admissions counselor. If you are visiting a competitive school or a school that is somewhat of a reach for you, the interview can be an important factor. Your guidance counselor and teachers can help you prepare for this type of interview.

Remember that the admissions office at every college is a sales office. Different offices use different approaches, but their primary job is to attract as many applicants as possible. So it is important for you to get away from the office for a portion of your visit.

Take the official tour. You also want to talk with individual students and faculty. Make arrangements to meet personally with the chair or one of the faculty of the department you're most interested in. Be sure that the courses you need to graduate are offered frequently enough to finish in four years.

Meet individually with students who attend the school. Find out what it is really like to be at the school. If possible, spend the night in a dorm room and sit in on some classes. If your parents are with you, they can tour the school themselves while you're getting the inside scoop.

STEP VII. Apply to three to eight schools.

(Complete before the admission deadline.)

Narrow your list of schools again to three to eight choices. Talk to your parents and guidance counselor as you make up this final list. Get several copies of each application. Request letters of recommendation from teachers and others. Do not hesitate to get advice from your guidance counselor and teachers as you carefully complete each application. Whenever possible, type your essays and other information on a word processor so that you can use them over again.

If there is one school you want to go to above all others, apply to that school for early admission. If you are accepted by a college for early admission, the understanding is that you will attend that college. You are supposed to apply to only one school for early admission; if the colleges find out that you have applied to more than one, they may void your applications. If you are not accepted for early admission, your application is placed in the regular applicant pool. Check with the colleges for early admission deadlines.

STEP VIII. Accept an admissions offer.

(By the college's deadline.)

In the spring of your senior year you'll receive your acceptance notices from the colleges you applied to. Don't forget to accept one of the offers of admission and send in a deposit.

You're on your way!

Paying for College

The cost of college has increased at a faster rate than most other costs. Estimated average costs of attending two- and four-year public and private colleges are shown below. About 75 percent of all college students attend public institutions; about two-thirds attend a four-year college.

Actual tuition and fees can range from under $1,000 to over $30,000 annually and may depend on whether or not you are a resident of a particular state or county. Average room, board, and expenses for two-year public college students are lower because many of these students live at home and commute to school.

Average Estimated Recent College Costs
(Information gathered from several sources)

COLLEGE TYPE	TUITION AND FEES	ROOM, BOARD, AND EXPENSES	TOTAL
Public two-year	$ 2,500	$ 5,500	$ 8,000
Public four-year	5,000	8,500	14,500
Private two-year	9,000	7,000	16,000
Private four-year	22,000	10,000	32,000

Costs

The amount you pay for college depends on the tuition, fees, and other expenses at the school you attend. You can control your college costs by attending a less expensive school. In recent years, many of the less expensive state colleges have emerged as highly ranked schools. Many students begin their college careers at two-year schools to control costs.

But every college costs something, and someone has to pay for it. There are four ways that college costs can be paid for:

You or your parents pay.
You get a scholarship or grant.
You get a loan.
You work while attending college (including work-study at the college).

Financial Aid

Scholarships and grants are the preferred form of financial aid because they do not have to be repaid. Loans do have to be repaid, although portions of some loans can be forgiven if you enter particular forms of national service or certain professions. Work-study may be a good option if there are not better-paid jobs available off campus, and work-study may permit you to work with college faculty in your chosen field.

About half the students who attend college receive some form of financial aid. A total of over $100 billion in financial aid will be available each year you attend college. Some financial aid is need-based, which means you qualify for financial aid if your financial circumstances make it difficult for you to pay for college. Other financial aid is based on merit, which means that a college wants to support you because of your academic or athletic performance or ability.

There are many different sources of financial aid, and it is important to apply for each one you might qualify for. Sources of financial aid change constantly; you should meet with your counselor in your junior year and discuss the types of aid you might qualify for. Look over as many books and online sources of information as you can get your hands on to find all the sources of financial aid you qualify for. Contact the colleges you are interested in to find out about any special scholarships they may have. There may be local sources of college financial aid.

Your state may have special financial aid programs. See the list of sources for each state on pages 445–450

See page 41 for a list of books and online sources of information about financial aid. You will also find a glossary of admissions and financial aid terms on pages 443–444.

Apply

You have to apply to receive financial aid. It will not happen automatically. File the Free Application for Federal Student Aid (FAFSA) by January of your senior year. The forms are available by December through your high school or library. Information from this form is used by all colleges to determine your financial aid eligibility.

Call 1-800-4FED-AID for a student guide to federal financial aid and copies of the FAFSA if you can't get them through your high school or library. Copies of the FAFSA are available online at (www.fafsa.ed.gov).

Remember also to file the other financial aid forms required by a college or by private sources of financial aid.

Satisfactory Educational Progress

To be eligible for federal financial aid, and some state and other financial aid programs, you must make satisfactory educational progress. Each school has its own standards that usually include the number of credits you have completed and your grade point average (GPA). Be sure you know your college's requirements so that you do not accidentally lose financial aid eligibility.

Selective Service Registration

Male citizens of the United States and certain eligible noncitizens who are at least eighteen years of age and were born in 1960 or later must register with Selective Service to receive federal financial aid. This requirement applies to all those not currently on active duty in the armed forces.

Books About Sources of Money to Pay for College

The books listed below will help you identify sources of financial aid and identify schools which offer an excellent education at a lower cost. Use the most recent edition of each book.

College Aid Resources for Education, The Scholarship Resource Network

How to Go to College Almost for Free, Harper Collins

Meeting College Costs: A Guide for Parents, The College Board

Paying for College Without Going Broke, The Princeton Review

The Scholarship Handbook, The College Board

U.S. News and World Report publishes a college guide each year which includes information about college costs and about the best buys in college education.

Online Financial Aid Resources

There are many resources online for information about financial aid. Be aware that many of these sources charge a fee for their services. The two sources listed below were probably the best resources available as this book went to press.

Internet resources are constantly being added and updated. You should check at the site of online search programs such as Google and Yahoo to find new sites which will give you information about paying for college.

The United States Office of Postsecondary Education (www.ed.gov/offices/listope). You will be able to see or download the *Student Guide for Federal Financial Aid* and the *Free Application for Federal Student Aid.* Other information about federal and state financial aid is also available at this site.

The College Board (www.collegeboard.com). The College Board's mission is to connect high school students with colleges. The College Board has more direct contacts with colleges than any other organization. Click on "For Students" and then on "Pay for College" to access scholarship information. Other links provide additional information.

College and Financial Aid Glossary

This glossary of terms adapted from the Department of Education publication "Preparing Your Child for College" may come in handy as you get ready to go to college.

A.A.: associate of arts; a degree that can be earned at most two-year colleges.

A.A.S.: associate of applied science; a degree that can be earned at some two-year colleges.

B.A., B.S.: bachelor of arts, bachelor of science; degrees earned at four-year colleges, depending on the kinds of courses offered at the particular college.

Default rate: the percentage of students who took out federal student loans to help pay their college expenses but did not repay them properly.

Expected family contribution (EFC): an amount determined by a formula specified by law that indicates how much of a family's financial resources should be available to pay for school. Factors such as taxable and nontaxable income, assets (such as savings and checking accounts), and benefits (for example, unemployment or Social Security) are all considered in this calculation. The EFC is used in determining eligibility for federal need-based aid.

Fees: charges that cover costs not associated with the student's course load, such as costs of some athletic activities, clubs, and special events.

Financial Aid: money available from various sources to help students pay for college.

Financial aid package: the total amount of financial aid a student receives. Federal and nonfederal aid such as grants, loans, or work-study are combined to help meet the student's need. Using available resources to give each student the best possible package of aid is one of the major responsibilities of a school's financial aid administrator.

Financial need: In the context of student financial aid, financial need is equal to the cost of education (estimated costs for college attendance and basic living expenses) minus the expected family contribution (the amount a student's family is expected to pay, which varies according to the family's financial resources).

General Educational Development (GED) diploma: the certificate students receive if they have passed a high school equivalency test. Students who do not have a high school diploma but who have a GED will qualify for federal student aid.

Grant: a sum of money given to a student for the purposes of paying at least part of the cost of college. A grant does not have to be repaid.

Loan: a type of financial aid that is available to students and the parents of students. An education loan must be repaid. In many cases, however, payments do not begin until the student finishes school.

Merit-based financial aid: aid given to students who meet requirements not related to financial needs. Most merit-based aid is awarded on the basis of academic performance or potential and is given in the form of scholarships or grants.

Need-based financial aid: aid given to students in need of assistance based on their income and assets and their families' income and assets, as well as some other factors.

Open admissions: most or all students who apply to a school are admitted. At some colleges, anyone who has a high school diploma or a GED can enroll. At other schools, it means that anyone over eighteen can enroll. Open admissions, therefore, can mean slightly different things at different schools.

Pell grants: federal need-based grants, which have been given to just under 4 million students. The maximum Pell grant has been $4,050 annually.

Perkins loans: a federal financial aid program that consists of low-interest loans for undergraduate and graduate students with exceptional financial need. Loans are awarded by the school.

PLUS loans: federal loans that allow parents to borrow money for their children's college education.

Postsecondary: after high school; refers to all programs for high school graduates, including programs at two- and four-year colleges and vocational and technical schools.

Proprietary: describes postsecondary schools that are private and are legally permitted to make a profit. Most proprietary schools offer technical and vocational courses.

PSAT/NMSQT: Preliminary Scholastic Aptitude Test/National Merit Scholarship Qualifying Test; a practice test that helps students prepare for the SAT I Reasoning Test. The PSAT is usually administered to tenth- or eleventh-grade students. Although colleges do not see a student's PSAT/NMSQT score, a student who does very well on this test and who meets many other academic performance criteria may qualify for the National Merit Scholarship program.

ROTC: Reserve Officers Training Corps; a scholarship program wherein the military covers part of the cost of tuition, fees, and textbooks, and also provides a monthly allowance. Scholarship recipients participate in summer training while in college and fulfill a service commitment after college.

SAT I: This test measures a student's mathematical and verbal reasoning abilities. Colleges accept this test or the ACT. Most students take the SAT I or the ACT during their junior or senior year of high school.

SAT II Subject Test: offered in many areas of study, including English, mathematics, many sciences, history, and foreign languages. Many colleges use ACT subtest scores in place of SAT II test scores.

Scholarship: a sum of money given to a student for the purpose of paying at least part of the cost of college. Scholarships may be awarded to students based on their academic achievements or on many other factors.

SEOG (Supplemental Educational Opportunity Grant): a federal award that helps undergraduates with exceptional financial need, awarded by the school. A SEOG does not have to be paid back.

Stafford loans: student loans offered by the federal government. There are two types of Stafford loans—need-based and nonneed based. Under the Stafford loan programs, students can borrow money to attend school and the federal government will guarantee the loan in case of default. The combined loan limits have been $2,625 for the first year, $3,500 for the second year, and $5,500 for the third or subsequent years.

Transcript: a list of all courses a student has taken with the grades earned in each course. A college will often require a high school transcript when the student applies for admission.

Tuition: money that colleges charge for classroom and other instruction and the use of some facilities such as libraries. Tuition can range from a few hundred dollars per year to more than $35,000. A few colleges do not charge any tuition.

William D. Ford federal direct loans: Under this new program, students may obtain loans directly from their college or university with funds provided by the U.S. Department of Education instead of a bank or other lender.

Work-study programs: Offered by many colleges, they allow students to work part-time during the school year as part of their financial aid package. The jobs are usually on campus and the money earned is used to pay for tuition or other college charges.

Financial Aid and College Information for Each State

Listed below are sources of financial aid and college information in each state. You should contact the sources listed for your state and for each state in which you might attend school. This information was current at press time. To find other current sources of financial aid information, search online using the keywords of your state name followed by "Financial Aid" (i.e.: Alabama Financial Aid).

Alabama

Alabama Commission on Higher Education
Suite 205
3465 Norman Bridge Road
Montgomery, Alabama 36105-2310
(334) 281-1998

Alabama State Department of Education
Gordon Persons Office Building
50 North Ripley Street
Montgomery, Alabama 36130-3901
(205) 242-8082

Alaska

Alaska Commission on Postsecondary Education
3030 Vintage Boulevard
Juneau, Alaska 99801-7109
(907) 465-2967

Alaska State Department of Education
Goldbelt Place
801 West 10th Street, Suite 200
Juneau, Alaska 99801-1894
(907) 465-8715

Arizona

Arizona Commission for Postsecondary Education
2020 North Central Ave., Suite 275
Phoenix, Arizona 85004-4503
(602) 229-2531

Arizona State Department of Education
1535 West Jefferson
Phoenix, Arizona 85007
(602) 542-2147

Arkansas

Arkansas Department of Higher Education
114 East Capitol
Little Rock, Arkansas 72201-3818
(501) 324-9300

Arkansas Department of Education
4 State Capitol Mall, Room 304A
Little Rock, Arkansas 72201-1071
(501) 682-4474

California

California Student Aid Commission
Mail to:
P.O. Box 419026
Rancho Cordova, CA 95741-9026
Address:
California Student Aid Commission
3300 Zinfandel Drive
Rancho Cordova, CA 95670
Customer Service Department: (916) 526-7590

California Department of Education
721 Capitol Mall
Sacramento, California 95814
(916) 657-2451

Colorado

Colorado Commission on Higher Education
Colorado Heritage Center
1300 Broadway, 2nd Floor
Denver, Colorado 80203
(303) 866-2723

State Department of Education
201 East Colfax Avenue
Denver, Colorado 80203-1705
(303) 866-6779

Connecticut

Connecticut Department of Higher Education
61 Woodland Street
Hartford, Connecticut 06105-2326
(860) 947-1855

Connecticut Department of Education
165 Capitol Avenue
P.O. Box 2219
Hartford, Connecticut 06106-1630

Delaware

Delaware Higher Education Commission
Carvel State Office Building, Fourth Floor
820 North French Street
Wilmington, Delaware 19801
(302) 577-3240

State Department of Public Instruction
Townsend Building #279
Federal and Lockerman Streets
P.O. Box 1402
Dover, Delaware 19903-1402
(302) 739-4583

District of Columbia

Office of Postsecondary Education,
2100 Martin Luther King, Jr., Avenue, SE
Suite 401
Washington, DC 20020
(202) 727-3685

District of Columbia Public Schools
Division of Student Services
4501 Lee Street, N.E.
Washington, DC 20019
(202) 724-4934

D.C. Tuition Assistance Grant Program
Web Address: www.tuitiongrant.dc.gov

Florida

Florida Department of Education
Office of Student Financial Assistance
1344 Florida Education Center
325 West Gaines Street
Tallahassee, Florida 32399-0400
(904) 487-0649
Web address: www.floridastudentfinancialaid.org

Georgia

Georgia Student Finance Commission
State Loans and Grants Division
Suite 245
2082 East Exchange Place
Tucker, Georgia 30084
(404) 414-3000

Georgia State Department of Education
2054 Twin Towers East, 205 Butler Street
Atlanta, Georgia 30334-5040
(404) 656-5812

Hawaii

Hawaii State Postsecondary Education
Commission
2444 Dole Street, Room 202
Honolulu, Hawaii 96822-2394
(808) 956-8213

Hawaii Department of Education
2530 10th Avenue, Room A12
Honolulu, Hawaii 96816
(808) 733-9103

Idaho

Idaho Board of Education
P.O. Box 83720
Boise, Idaho 83720-0037
(208) 334-2270

Idaho State Department of Education
650 West State Street
Boise, Idaho 83720
(208) 334-2113

Illinois

Illinois Student Assistance Commission
1755 Lake Cook Road
Deerfield, Illinois 60015-5209
(708) 948-8500
Web address: www.collegezone.com

Indiana

Indiana State Student Assistance Commission of
Indiana
Suite 500, 150 West Market Street
Indianapolis, Indiana 46204-2811
(317) 232-2350

Indiana Department of Education
Room 229—State House
Center for Schools Improvement
and Performance
Indianapolis, Indiana 46204-2798
(317) 232-2305

Iowa

Iowa College Student Aid Commission
914 Grand Avenue, Suite 201
Des Moines, Iowa 50309-2824
(800) 383-4222
Web address: www.iowacollegeaid.org

Kansas

Kansas Board of Regents
700 S.W. Harrison, Suite 1410
Topeka, Kansas 66603-3760
(913) 296-3517

Kansas State Department of Education
Kansas State Education Building
120 East Tenth Street
Topeka, Kansas 66612-1103
(913) 296-4876

Kentucky

Kentucky Higher Education Assistance Authority
Suite 102, 1050 U.S. 127 South
Frankfort, Kentucky 40601-4323
(800) 928-8926

Kentucky State Department of Education
500 Mero Street
1919 Capital Plaza Tower
Frankfort, Kentucky 40601
(502) 564-3421

Louisiana

Louisiana Student Financial Assistance Commission
Office of Student Financial Assistance
P.O. Box 91202
Baton Rouge, Louisiana 70821-9202
(800) 259-5626
Web address: www.osfa.state.la.us

Louisiana State Department of Education
P.O. Box 94064
626 North 4th Street, 12th Floor
Baton Rouge, Louisiana 70804-9064
(504) 342-2098

Maine

Finance Authority of Maine
P.O. Box 949
Augusta, Maine 04333-0949
(207) 287-3263

Maine Department of Education
23 State House Station
Augusta, ME 04333-0023
Voice: (207) 287-5800

Maryland

Maryland Higher Education Commission
Jeffrey Building, 16 Francis Street
Annapolis, Maryland 21401-1781
(410) 974-2971

Maryland State Department of Education
200 West Baltimore Street
Baltimore, Maryland 21201-2595
(410) 767-0480

Massachusetts

Massachusetts Board of Higher Education
330 Stuart Street
Boston, Massachusetts 02116
(617) 727-9420

Massachusetts Higher Education Information
Center
666 Boylston St.
Boston, Massachusetts 20116
(617) 536-0200 x4719

Michigan

Michigan Higher Education Assistance Authority
Office of Scholarships and Grants
P.O. Box 30462
Lansing, Michigan 48909-7962
(517) 373-3394
Web address: www.michigan.gov/mistudentaid

Michigan Department of Education
608 West Allegan Street
Hannah Building
Lansing, Michigan 48909
(517) 373-3324

Minnesota

Minnesota Higher Education Services Office
Suite 400, Capitol Square Bldg.
550 Cedar Street
St. Paul, Minnesota 55101-2292
(800) 657-3866

Department of Children, Families and Learning
712 Capitol Square Building
550 Cedar Street
St. Paul, Minnesota 55101
(612) 296-6104

Mississippi

Mississippi Postsecondary Education
Financial Assistance Board
3825 Ridgewood Road
Jackson, Mississippi 39211-6453
(601) 982-6663

Mississippi State Department of Education
P.O. Box 771
Jackson, Mississippi 39205-0771
(601) 359-3768

Missouri

Missouri Coordinating Board for Higher
Education
3515 Amazonas Drive
Jefferson City, Missouri 65109-5717
(314) 751-2361

Missouri State Department of Elementary and
Secondary Education
P.O. Box 480
205 Jefferson Street, Sixth Floor
Jefferson City, Missouri 65102-0480
(314) 751-2931

Montana

Montana University System
2500 Broadway
Helena, Montana 59620-3103
(406) 444-6570

Montana State Office of Public Instruction
State Capitol, Room 106
Helena, Montana 59620
(406) 444-4422

Nebraska
Coordinating Commission for Postsecondary
Education
P.O. Box 95005
Lincoln, Nebraska 68509-5005
(402) 471-2847
Nebraska Department of Education
P.O. Box 94987
301 Centennial Mall South
Lincoln, Nebraska 68509-4987
(402) 471-2784

Nevada
Nevada Department of Education
400 West King Street
Capitol Complex
Carson City, Nevada 89710
(702) 687-5915

New Hampshire
New Hampshire Postsecondary Education
Commission
2 Industrial Park Drive
Concord, New Hampshire 03301-8512
(603) 271-2555
New Hampshire State Department of Education
State Office Park South
101 Pleasant Street
Concord, New Hampshire 03301
(603) 271-2632

New Jersey
New Jersey Office of Student Financial Assistance
4 Quakerbridge Plaza, CN 540
Trenton, New Jersey 08625
(800) 792-8670
New Jersey State Department of Education
225 West State Street
Trenton, New Jersey 08625-0500
(609) 984-6409

New Mexico
New Mexico Commission on Higher Education
1068 Cerrillos Road
Santa Fe, New Mexico 87501-4925
(505) 827-7383

New York
New York State Higher Education Services
Corporation
One Commerce Plaza
Albany, New York 12255
(518) 474-5642
New York State Education Department
111 Education Building
Washington Avenue
Albany, New York 12234
(518) 474-5705

North Carolina
North Carolina State Education Assistance
Authority
P.O. Box 2688
Chapel Hill, North Carolina 27515-2688
(919) 821-4771
North Carolina State Department of Public
Instruction
Education Building
Division of Teacher Education
116 West Edenton Street
Raleigh, North Carolina 27603-1712
(919) 733-0701

North Dakota
North Dakota University System
North Dakota Student Financial Assistance
Program
600 East Boulevard Avenue
Bismarck, North Dakota 58505-0230
(701) 224-4114
State Department of Public Instruction
State Capitol Building, 11th Floor
600 East Boulevard Avenue
Bismarck, North Dakota 58505-0164
(701) 224-2271

Ohio
Ohio Board of Regents
P.O. Box 182452
309 South Fourth Street
Columbus, Ohio 43218-2452
1-888-833-1133
Web Address: www.regents.state.oh.us/sgs
Ohio State Department of Education
65 South Front Street, Room 1005
Columbus, Ohio 43266-0308
(614) 466-2761

Oklahoma

Oklahoma State Regents for Higher Education
P.O. Box 3000
Oklahoma City, OK 73101-3000
(405) 858-4300
1-800-247-0420

Oklahoma State Department of Education
Oliver Hodge Memorial Education Building
2500 North Lincoln Boulevard
Oklahoma City, Oklahoma 73105-4599
(405) 521-4122

Oregon

Oregon Student Assistance Commission
Suite 100, 1500 Valley River Drive
Eugene, Oregon 97401-2130
(503) 687-7400

Oregon Department of Education
255 Capitol Street NE
Salem, OR 97310-0203

Pennsylvania

Mail to:
P.O. Box 8114
Harrisburg, Pennsylvania 17105-8114
(717) 720-2075

Address:
Pennsylvania Higher Education Assistance Agency
1200 North Seventh Street
Harrisburg, Pennsylvania 17102-1444
(800) 692-7435

Rhode Island

Rhode Island Higher Education Assistance
    Authority
560 Jefferson Boulevard
Warwick, Rhode Island 02886
(800) 922-9855

Rhode Island Office of Higher Education
301 Promenade Street
Providence, Rhode Island, 02908-5720
(401) 277-6560

South Carolina

South Carolina Higher Education Tuition Grants
    Commission
1310 Lady Street, Suite 811
P.O. Box 12159
Columbia, South Carolina 29201
(803) 734-1200

South Carolina State Department of Education
803-a Rutledge Building
1429 Senate Street
Columbia, South Carolina 29201
(803) 734-8364

South Dakota

Department of Education and Cultural Affairs
Office of the Secretary
700 Governors Drive
Pierre, South Dakota 57501-2291
(605) 773-3134

South Dakota Board of Regents
306 East Capitol Ave
Suite 200
Pierre, SD 57501-2545
(605) 773-3455

Tennessee

Tennessee Higher Education Commission
404 James Robertson Parkway
Suite 1900
Nashville, Tennessee 37243-0820
(615) 741-3605

State Department of Education
100 Cordell Hull Building
Nashville, Tennessee 37219-5335
(615) 741-1346 or (800) 342-1663
    (TN residents only)

Texas

Texas Higher Education Coordinating Board
P.O. Box 12788, Capitol Station
Austin, Texas 78711
(800) 242-3062
Web Address: www.collegefortexans.com

Utah

Utah State Board of Regents
 355 West North Temple
#3 Triad Center, Suite 550
Salt Lake City, Utah 84180-1205
(801) 321-7205

Utah State Office of Education
250 East 500 South
Salt Lake City, Utah 84111
(801) 538-7779

Vermont

Vermont Student Assistance Corporation
Champlain Mill
P.O. Box 2000
Winooski, Vermont 05404-2601
(800) 642-3177

Virginia

State Council of Higher Education for Virginia
James Monroe Building
101 North Fourteenth Street
Richmond, Virginia 23219
(804) 786-1690

State Department of Education
P.O. Box 2120
James Monroe Building
14th and Franklin Streets
Richmond, Virginia 23216-2120
(804) 225-2072

Washington

Washington State Higher Education Coordinating
  Board
P.O. Box 43430, 917 Lakeridge Way, S.W.
Olympia, Washington 98504-3430
(206) 753-7850

State Department of Public Instruction
Old Capitol Building, P.O. Box FG 11
Olympia, Washington, 98504-3211
(206) 753-2858

West Virginia

State Department of Education
1900 Washington Street
Building B, Room 358
Charleston, West Virginia 25305
(304) 588-2691

West Virginia State College & University Systems
1018 Kanawha Boulevard East, Suite 700
Charleston, West Virginia 25301-2827
(304) 558-4016

Wisconsin

Wisconsin Higher Educational Aids Board
P.O. Box 7885
Madison, Wisconsin 53707-7885
(608) 267-2206

Wisconsin State Department of Public Instruction
125 South Wester Street
P.O. Box 7841
Madison, Wisconsin 53707-7814
(608) 266-2364

Wyoming

Wyoming State Department of Education
Hathaway Building
2300 Capitol Avenue, 2nd Floor
Cheyenne, Wyoming 82002-0050
(307) 777-6265

Wyoming Community College Commission
2020 Carey Avenue, 8th Floor
Cheyenne, Wyoming 82002
(307) 777-7763

INDEX

REFERENCES

The author is indebted to the following sources for the use of material quoted in exemplary passages. Every effort has been made to obtain permission to use previously published materials. Any errors or omission are unintentional

Antell and Harris, *Western Civilization.* © 1983 by Amsco School Publications. Pages 154–156, 240, 264–267, 276, 297–300, 316.

Antell, Harris, and Dobkin, *Current Issues in American Democracy.* © 1994 by Amsco School Publications. Page 238.

Henry Brun, *America Today.* © 1996 by Amsco School Publications. Page 274.

Henry Brun, *Global Studies.* © 1998 by Amsco School Publications. Pages 160–162, 190, 194, 211, 259–261, 303–305.

James Cicarelli, *Economics, Macroeconomics, and Issues.* © 1978 by Houghton Mifflin. Pages 189–190, 193–194, 205.

Paul G. Cohen, *Chemistry: A Contemporary Approach.* © 1996 by Amsco School Publications. Pages 242–243.

James Fenimore Cooper, from *The Last of the Mohicans.* Pages 197, 208.

Stephen Crane, "The Open Boat." Page 197.

James Crockett, *Foliage House Plants.* © 1972 by Time-Life Books. Pages 186, 187, 192, 211.

Ralph V. Cutlip, "Stubby Makes His Letter," from *Action Stores of Yesterday and Today.* © 1971 by Amsco School Publications. Pages 187, 196, 210.

Mark Davidson, "Is Time Travel Possible?" © 1990 by the Society for the Advancement of Education. Pages 278–279.

Sandra Gilbert and Susan Gubar, *Madwoman in the Attic.* © 1979 by Yale University Press. Page 356.

Dan Gookin, from *DOS for Dummies®*, 2nd Edition. © 1993 IDG Books Worldwide, Inc. All rights reserved. Reproduced by permission of the publisher. For Dummies is a registered trademark under exclusive license to IDG Books Worldwide, Inc., from International Data Group, Inc. Pages 337–339.

Irving Gordon, *Review Text in American History.* © 1995 by Amsco School Publications. Pages 197, 206.

Irving Gordon, *World History.* © 1996 by Amsco School Publications. Page 190.

Green and Sanford, *Psychology.* © 1995 by Amsco School Publications. Pages 13, 149–151, 218, 220–221, 262–264, 306–308, 314.

Dorie Greenspan, "Pastry Chefs at Play." *Bon Appetit,* September 1997. Pages 343–345.

W. C. Heinz, "One Throw," reprinted by permission of the William Morris Agency, Inc., on behalf of the author. © 1950 renewed 1978, by W. C. Heinz. Pages 312–313.

Houston, Bee, Hatfield, and Rimm, *Invitation to Psychology.* © 1979 by Academic Press. Pages 188, 189, 193, 194, 202, 210.

Tom Huntington, "The Man Who Believed in Fairies." *Smithsonian,* September 1997. Pages 130–132.

Kurt Kleiner, "Freak Frogs." *New Scientist,* September 1997. Page 358.

Jack London, from *The Call of the Wild.* Pages 236–237.

Robert J. and Lila Lowenherz, *Americans of Dream and Deed.* © 1993 by Amsco School Publications. Pages 152–154.

Robert J. and Lila Lowenherz, *Science Fiction, Science Fact, and You.* © 1996 by Amsco School Publications. Pages 157–159, 257–259, 300–302.

Katherine Mansfield, "Her First Ball." Pages 272–273.

Gordon Marsden, "Freeze Frame: Calais Remembered." *History Today,* August 1997. Page 354.

Caitlin and John Matthews, from *The Encyclopedia of Celtic Wisdom.* © 1994 by Caitlin and John Matthews, used by permission of Element Books, Inc. Pages 346–348.

Mould, Geffner, and Lesser, *General Science.* © 1991 by Amsco School Publications. Pages 189, 194.

Patricia Osborn, *Finding America.* © 1995 by Amsco School Publications. Pages 268–269, 309–311.

Daniel Pool, *What Jane Austen Ate and Charles Dickens Knew.* © 1993 by Simon and Schuster. Pages 340–342.

Rachman and Mescon, *Business Today.* © 1979 by Random House. Page 189.

Martin Ratcliff, excerpt from "The Sky Show in October." *Astonomy,* October 1997. Reprinted by permission, copyright 2004, *Astronomy* magazine, Kalmbach Publishing Company. Pages 135–136.

William Saroyan, excerpt from "The Three Swimmers and the Educated Grocer from Yale," from *My Name is Aram.* © 1940, renewed 1968, by William Saroyan, reprinted by permission of Harcourt Brace & Company. Pages 352–353.

John Steinbeck, "Flight," from *The Long Valley.* © 1938 by Viking Press. Page 197.

Henry David Thoreau, *Walden.* Pages 189–190.

Dick Victory, from "Thrills Every Minute." *The Washingtonian,* August 1997. Reprinted with permission of *The Washingtonian.* Pages 140–141.

Shawna Vogel, "Smart Skin." © 1990 by Discover Publications. Page 318.

John T. Walsh, *Interpretation of Reading Materials in the Natural Sciences.* © 1973 by Cambridge & Coules. Pages 187, 188, 193.

Anon., "How Do You Say That. . . .?" *The Washingtonian,* August 1997. Pages 349–351.